TOWARD A NEW WORLD OUTLOOK

Asian Studies Series: 2

Also published:
Mongolian Heroes of the Twentieth Century by Urgunge Onon

TOWARD A NEW WORLD OUTLOOK

A Documentary History of Education in the
People's Republic of China, 1949-1976

Edited by
Shi Ming Hu and Eli Seifman
State University of New York at Stony Brook

AMS PRESS, INC.
New York

FIRST AMS PRESS EDITION: 1976

Library of Congress Cataloging in Publication Data
Main entry under title:
Toward a new world outlook.

  (Asian studies: 2)
  1. Education—China—History. I. Hu, Shi
Ming, 1927-   II. Seifman, Eli. III. Series:
Asian studies (New York)
LA1131.T64   370'.951   76-23977
ISBN 0-404-15401-8

TABLE OF CONTENTS

ADMINISTRATION DIVISIONS xii
CHINESE CONVERSION TABLES xii
TRANSLITERATION TABLE xiii
INTRODUCTION xv

PART ONE (1949-1952)
"Reorientation and Reorganization" 1

Documents:

1.1 "Common Program of the Chinese People's Political Consultative Conference" 9

1.2 "Speech Made by the Minister of Education, Mr. Ma Hsu-lun, at
the Conference on Higher Education on June 1, 1950" 12

1.3 "The Central Ministry of Education Announcement on Carrying
out Curriculum Reform of Higher Education in Order to Achieve
the Combination of Theory and Practice Step by Step" 16

1.4 "Cultural and Educational Work During the Past Year" 18

73303

1.5 "The Joint Announcement Made by the Central Ministry of Education and the Publishing Headquarter Concerning the Decision on the Texts to be Used in the Primary and Middle Schools for the Spring Semester, 1951" 22

1.6 "Minister of Education Ma Hsu-lun Reports on Educational Accomplishments During the Past Year" 23

1.7 "Implementation of New Educational System Promulgated" ... 30

1.8 "Government Administration Council Directive on Reform and Development of Intermediate Technical Education" 34

1.9 "Directive of Ministry of Education on 1952 Plan for Training State Construction Cadres" 37

PART TWO (1953-1957)
"Strong Russian Influence" 39

Documents:

2.1 "The Policy and Tasks of Higher Education" 49

2.2 "Summary Report on Cultural-Educational Activities of Local Organizations of China Democratic League" 52

2.3 "Ministry of Education Revises Middle School Teaching Program" 55

2.4 "Government Administration Council Directive Concerning the Reorganization and Improvement of Primary School Education" 58

2.5 "Government Administration Council Directive Concerning the Improvement and Development of Higher Education for Teacher Training" 63

2.6 "National Secondary Education Conference Closed" 66

2.7 "Central People's Government Ministry of Education Issues Directive Concerning Establishment, Development and Reorganization of Normal Schools" 69

2.8 "Rules of Conduct for Primary School Students" 72

2.9 "Rules of Conduct for Middle School Students" 73

2.10 "Decision of the Chinese Communist Party Central Committee and State Council Concerning Elimination of Illiteracy" 74

2.11 "Let All Flowers Bloom Together, Let Diverse Schools of Thought Contend" 77

2.12 "National Education in China" 80

2.13 "Problems in This Year's Educational Work That Merits Attention" 82

2.14 "Regulation Governing Certain Problems of Correspondence and Sparetime Normal School Promulgated" 84

PART THREE (1958-1959)
"The Great Leap Forward" 87

Documents:

3.1 "Two Major Reform Measures on General Education" 93

3.2 "Onward to the Goal of 'Thoroughly Red and Profoundly Expert' " 97

3.3 "Collectivization of the School Life of Children Realized in the Hsingchuang School District" 99

3.4 "Agricultural Middle Schools in Their First Year" 101

3.5 "Educational Work Achievements in 1958 and Arrangements for 1959" 105

PART FOUR (1960-1963)
"Retrenchment" 111

Documents:

4.1 "Actively Carry Out the Reform of the School System to Bring About Greater, Faster, Better, and More Economical Results in the Development of Education" 119

4.2 "Our Schooling System Must Be Reformed" 122

4.3 "Launch Mass Campaigns and Carry Out Communist Cooperation on a Large Scale in the Struggle for Reform of Curriculums
for Middle and Primary Schools" 126

4.4 "Several Problems of Pedagogic Reform for Workers'
Education" 129

4.5 "Teaching of English in Kweiyang Middle School Improved
Through Penetrating Investigation and Research" 131

4.6 "Concerning the Question of Study" 133

4.7 "On the Correct Handling of the Relations Between Teaching,
Productive Labor, and Scientific Research" 136

4.8 "Firmly Adhere to the Guiding Principle of Walking on Two
Legs, Actively Develop and Consolidate People-Operated Primary Schools" 141

4.9 "Some Suggestions Concerning the Unfolding of Research Work
in Educational Psychology" 144

4.10 "Peking Young Communist League Committee and Young
Communist League Committee of Tsinghua University Call
Separate Forums on 'Redness' and Expertness" 148

4.11 "Primary and Middle Schools in Peking and Wuhan Guide Stu-
dents to Compare the Bitterness of the Old Society With the
Sweetness of the New Society, Receive the Stimulation of Class
Education, and Sow the Seeds of Revolutionary Thought" ... 151

4.12 "Energetically Train a Force of Red and Expert Teachers" .. 153

4.13 "How Should We Educate Our Children?" 154

PART FIVE (1964-1965)
"Two-Line Party Struggle" 157

Documents:

5.1 "A Hundred Examples of Liu Shao-ch'i's Speeches Opposing
the Thought of Mao Tse-tung" 166

5.2 "Give the Students Education in the Revolutionary World View,
Starting with Class Education" 170

5.3 "Some Experiences in Implementing the Principle of 'Less But Better' in Pedagogical Work" 172

5.4 "Curricula for Half-Work (Farming) Half-Study Schools" 177

5.5 "Rural Farming-Study Primary Schools in Kirin" 179

5.6 "Problems Revealed by Two Statistical Tables" 182

5.7 "Steadfastly Promote the Part-Farming and Part-Study Education System" 184

PART SIX (1966-1969)
"The Cultural Revolution" 187

Documents:

6.1 "May 7th Directive, 1966" 201

6.2 "Decision of C.P.C. Central Committee and State Council on Reform of Entrance Examination and Enrollment in Higher Educational Institutions" 202

6.3 "Chinese Communist Party Central Committee's Notification (Draft) Concerning the Great Proletarian Cultural Revolution in Primary Schools" (February 4, 1967) 203

6.4 "Notice of the Chinese Communist Party Central Committee and the State Council Concerning [Urban] Educated Youths Working in Rural and Mountainous Areas Who Go Out to Exchange Revolutionary Experience, Make Revolution, or Call on People at Higher Levels" (February 17, 1967) 204

6.5 "Chinese Communist Party Central Committee's Opinion on the Great Proletarian Cultural Revolution in Middle Schools" (February 19, 1967) 205

6.6 "Chinese Communist Party Central Committee's Regulations (Draft) Governing the Great Proletarian Cultural Revolution Currently Under Way in Universities, Colleges and Schools" (March 7, 1967) 207

6.7 "Decision of the Military Commission of the Chinese Communist Party Central Committee Concerning the Enforcement of Military Control in Higher Military Academies and Schools" (April 19, 1967) 209

6.8 "*Jen-min Jih-pao* Editorial on Importance of Transforming Chinese Educational System" 210

6.9 "Loud Cheers for the Results of Paichiachuang Middle School in Military Training" 213

6.10 "Universities and Middle and Primary Schools Must Resume Classes While Making Revolution" 216

6.11 "The Road for Training Engineering and Technical Personnel Indicated by the Shanghai Machine Tools Plant" 218

6.12 "Shanghai Workers' Propaganda Teams Mobilize Revolutionary Teachers and Students of Institutes of Higher Learning to Gradually Carry Out Chairman Mao's Latest Directives" 225

6.13 "The Question of Prime Importance in the Revolution of Education in the Countryside Is That the Poor and Lower-Middle Peasants Control the Power in Education" 226

6.14 "Hungch'i Middle School in Penhsi, Liaoning, Forms Textbook Compiling Group" 228

6.15 "Draft Program For Primary and Middle Schools in Chinese Countryside" 230

6.16 "Some Suggestions Concerning the Running of Middle Schools by Factories" 236

6.17 "Establish a New Proletarian System of Examination and Assessment" 239

PART SEVEN (1970 to the Present)
"The Post-Cultural Revolution" 241

Documents:

7.1 "Transform Educational Position in Schools With Mao Tse-tung's Thought" 255

7.2 "Brilliant 'May 7 Directive' Is Guideline for Running Socialist Engineering College Well' 257

7.3 "Operation of Factories by Schools Helps To Push Forward Educational Revolution" 260

7.4 "Aomen Road No. 2 Primary School, Shanghai, Puts Extra-curricular Activities on the Agenda of Its Revolutionary Committee" 262

7.5 "A Middle School That Serves the Three Great Revolutionary Movements" 264

7.6 "Persevere in Letting the Poor and Lower-Middle Peasants Manage the Schools" 267

7.7 "Apply Mao Tse-tung's Thought to the Training of a Force of Teachers" 269

7.8 "Extracts From Chinese Middle School Level Science Textbook" 270

7.9 "Bring Up New Men Who Develop Morally, Intellectually and Physically" 271

7.10 "Firmly Insist on Selecting Students From Among Workers and Peasants Who Have Practical Experience" 274

7.11 "Some Experiences in Teaching English to Primary One Students" 277

7.12 "Mass Physical Training" 279

7.13 "Nursery Classes Universally Set Up in Hsihsinchuang Brigade, Ku-an *Hsien,* Hopei Province" 281

7.14 "The 'May 7' Cadre School" 283

7.15 "Establish a New System of Examination Through Practice" . 287

7.16 "Big Schools Where Education in Ideology and Political Line Is Carried Out—Criticizing Swindlers Like Liu Shao-chi for Slandering the '7 May' Cadre Schools" 289

7.17 "On Reforming Written Chinese" 291

7.18 "Why the University Enrolling System Should Be Reformed" 295

7.19 "Interviews With Middle School Graduates Recently Arrived in Hong Kong (October, 1973)" 299

7.20 "Socialist 'New Things' in Chinese Education" 305

7.21 "The Constitution of the People's Republic of China" 316

7.22 "Program (Draft) of Educational Revolution for Experimental
Primary Schools in Shanghai" 322

7.23 "Considerations on the Concept of Culture" 326

7.24 "The Great Cultural Revolution Will Shine For Ever" 330

Administrative Divisions

The People's Republic of China is divided into a number of administrative divisions; the major ones are as follows: twenty-two provinces (*shĕng*), Anhwei, Chekiang, Fukien, Heilungkiang, Honan, Hopeh, Hunan, Hupeh, Kansu, Kiangsi, Kiangsu, Kirin, Kwangtung, Kweichow, Liaoning, Shansi, Shantung, Shensi, Szechwan, Taiwan, Tsinghai, and Yunnan; five autonomous regions (*zì zhì qū*), Inner Mongolia, Kwangsi Chuang, Ningsia Hui, Sinkiang Uighur, and Tibet; three municipalities (*shì*), Peking, Shanghai, and Tientsin.

At the subprovince level, provinces and autonomous regions are divided into special districts (*zhuān qū*) or autonomous *qū* (*zì zhì qū*).

Further major subdivisions are: counties (*xiàn*), districts (*qū*) and villages (*xiāng*).

According to the Wade-Giles romanization system, the equivalents are as follows: counties (*hsien*), districts (*ch'u*) and villages (*hsiang*).

Chinese Weights, Measures and Currency

1 *mŭ*	= $^1/_{15}$ hectare or $^1/_6$ acre
1 *jīn* (catty)	= $^1/_2$ kilo or 1.1 lbs.
1 *chĭ* (Chinese foot)	= $^1/_3$ meter
1 *lĭ* (Chinese mile)	= $^1/_2$ kilometer
1 *yuan* (Chinese dollar)	= HK$ 2.50 or US$ .51

Transliteration Table

CONVENTIONAL	WADE-GILES ROMANIZATION	PINYIN ROMANIZATION
PROVINCE	SHENG	SHENG
Anhwei	An-hui	Anhui
Chekiang	Che-chiang	Zhejiang
Fukien	Fu-chien	Fujian
Heilungkiang	Hei-lung-chiang	Heilongjiang
Honan	Ho-nan	Henan
Hopeh	Ho-pei	Hebei
Hunan	Hu-nan	Hunan
Hupeh	Hu-pei	Hubei
Kansu	Kan-su	Gansu
Kiangsi	Chiang-hsi	Jiangxi
Kiangsu	Chiang-su	Jiangsu
Kirin	Chi-lin	Jilin
Kwangtung	Kuang-tung	Guangdong
Kweichow	Kuei-chou	Guizhou
Liaoning	Liao-ning	Liaoning
Shansi	Shan-hsi	Shanxi
Shantung	Shan-tung	Shandong
Shensi	Shen-hsi	Shaanxi
Szechwan	Ssu-ch'uan	Sichuan
Taiwan	T'ai-wan	Taiwan
Tsinghai	Ch'ing-hai	Qinghai
Yunnan	Yun-nan	Yunnan
AUTONOMOUS REGION	TZU-CHIH CHOU	ZIZHIQU
Inner Mongolia	Nei-meng-ku	Nei Mongol
Kwangsi Chuang	Kuang-hsi	Guangxi Zhuang
Ningsia Hui	Ning-hsia	Ningxia Hui
Sinkiang Uighur	Hsin-chiang	Xinjiang Uygur
Tibet	Hsi-tsang	Xizang
MUNICIPALITY	SHIH	SHI
Peking	Pei-ching	Beijing
Shanghai	Shang-hai	Shanghai
Tientsin	T'ien-chin	Tianjin

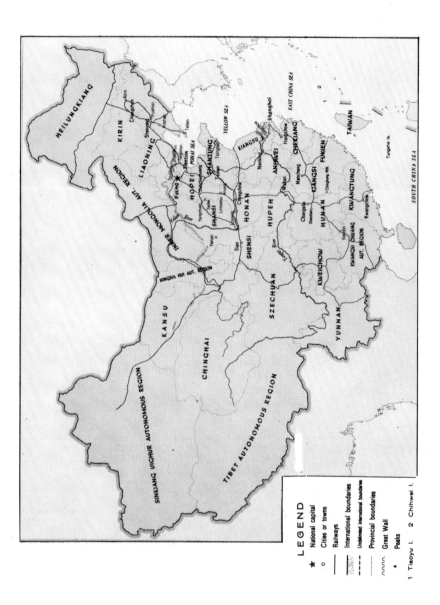

INTRODUCTION

The objectives of this volume are to identify a number of distinct periods of educational development in the history of the People's Republic of China from its creation in 1949 to the present, to analyze the distinctive features of each of these educational periods, and to offer a selection of materials from Chinese sources which document and illustrate the nature of each of these periods of educational development. The section on contemporary educational policies and practices includes transcriptions of tape recorded interviews and discussions gathered by the editors during their respective visits to the People's Republic of China in 1974 and 1975.

Political changes occur at both linear and exponential rates. Some are quite minor and take place with relatively little notice; some are simply "old wine in new bottles"; a few are of such an order of magnitude that they command world wide attention and notice. The victory of the Chinese Communist Party (CCP) and its army in 1948-1949, and the downfall of the Kuomintang (KMT), was a political change of such magnitude.[1] The new regime's commitment to building a *new* China had been clearly enunciated by its spokesman, Mao Tse-tung:

> For many years we Communists have struggled for a cultural revolution as well as for a political and economic revolution, and our aim is to build a new society and a new state for the Chinese nation. That new society and new state will have not only a new politics and a new economy but a new culture. In other words, not only do we want to change a China that is politically oppressed and economically exploited into a China that is politically free and economically prosperous, we also want to change the China which is being kept ignorant and backward under the sway of the old culture into an enlightened and progressive China under the sway of a new culture. In short, we want to build a new China. Our aim in the cultural sphere is to build a new Chinese national culture.[2]

We have attempted to trace the historical development of the educational system of the People's Republic of China and to document the distinguishing features of this educational system—the pattern of organization and administration, the different types and functions of various kinds of schools, the educational philosophy which sets forth the principles according to which the curriculum is organized and the objectives toward which the instructional process is to be directed.

There are certain "caveats" associated with studying "other" nations, societies, cultures, and peoples. We need to be especially aware of such problems as: ethnocentrism; communication (i.e. language and translation, etc.); misinformation; lack of information; sensitivity to the sensitivities of others; conflicts of attitudes, feelings, or values, etc. These problems increase in direct proportion to one's "distance" from the "other" nation, society, or culture. "Distance," as we use it here, refers not simply to its common geographical or physical sense, but, even more importantly, to the cultural or psychological sense of the term. There is the danger of rejecting out-of-hand the institutions of some "other" nations because they are in conflict with the basic political, economic, or ideological values of one's "own" society. Similarly, there is the danger of looking to the institutions of some "other" nation to provide the panacea for the deficiencies of one's "own" society.

A growing number of Americans are now beginning to have the opportunity to visit the People's Republic of China. In the field of education, some of these visitors have returned to the United States and urged wholesale adoption and institutionalization in the American school system of practices of the Chinese educational system: e.g. widespread availability of pre-school education, including provisions for full boarding or children staying at the schools during the week and returning home on weekends and holidays; "half-work half-study" schools; the practice of having secondary school graduates delay going on to higher education until they have completed a period of "productive labor"; the abolition of all examinations (which is really a misreading of current Chinese educational practice); a thorough reappraisal of the function of examinations (which is a more accurate interpretation of current policy); etc. Some other visitors return with the conviction that Chinese education is simply "brainwashing" and as such is anathema, thereby concluding that there is absolutely nothing at all the United States can learn from the Chinese educational experience.

Both of these reactions suffer from the problem of "distance"; both are simplistic responses to highly complex issues. We believe that an educational system has to be seen in the context of a particular society, not simply in terms of the current state of that society but also in the light of its historical development. Therefore, the transformation of Chinese education since 1949 must also be viewed in relation to China's very long history, which includes: its role as one of the major civilizations of the ancient world, with a continuous written tradition of nearly 4,000 years; recognition that traditional Chinese society had internalized the Confucian belief in a social pyramid in which everyone had a position, accepted that position, and willingly fulfilled the duties attached to it; an understanding that old China had developed an educational system centered around the identification and training of civil servants to be selected on the basis of highly competitive objective examinations. Acceptance of the "Confucian harmony" and its social pyramid dominated Chinese history for so many centuries that the nation was often referred to (by outside observers) as "changeless China." These are but a few of the considerations which should be kept in mind when studying the development of education in new China.

The field of education is uniquely susceptible to "fads"—enthusiastically introduced, widely heralded with extravagant claims, and then later quietly discarded. There is a tendency in the field of education to look "outward," to search elsewhere for a model to adopt or a system to emulate. This is not to say that there is nothing that can be learned from the study of other educational systems. Quite the contrary! However, there is also a need for nations to look "inward," to analyze their unique circumstances and their unique needs.

The peoples of the world are undeniably bound together as members of humankind; similarly, the nations of the world share certain common needs and problems. Yet, even on matters of common concerns, nations will develop responses or solutions which are unique reflections of a particular national experience. Institutions, like certain species of plants, are not all easily transplanted to foreign soil. Of course, some species may well find the new soil even more hospitable than their native climates; others can be sustained only through artificial means; and yet others, once removed from their native environment, take root not at all or are but short-lived.

Surveying the history of the People's Republic of China from 1949 to the present, we have attempted to identify, describe, and document seven distinct periods of educational development: Reorientation and Reorganization (1949-1952); Strong Russian Influence (1953-1957); The Great Leap Forward (1958-1959); Retrenchment (1960-1963); Two-Line Party Struggle (1964-1965); The Cultural Revolution (1966-1969); The Post-Cultural Revolution (1970 to the Present).

Each of the seven parts of this volume begins with an introductory essay which analyzes that period in terms of its unique characteristics—political emphases, educational policy, curriculum trends, etc. At this point we would like to offer a very brief overview of each of these seven periods.

I. Reorientation and Reorganization (1949-1952): The founding of the People's Republic of China in 1949 marked the beginning of a period of major reform directed toward reorienting and reorganizing Chinese education. Education had, and continues to play, a major role in the ideological conversion of the Chinese people. Educational policy was directed toward: training for national construction work and developing the ideology of serving the people; reforming the old educational system (both subject matter and teaching methods); moving toward universal education as a means of meeting the needs of "revolutionary work and national construction work." Educational reform in this period reflected the political and economic demands of the restoration of the country.

II. Strong Russian Influence (1953-1957): Although there were signs of Soviet influence during the period of 1949-1952, it was within the period of 1953-1957 that this influence reached its peak. Some of the major documents written during this period reflect this strong Soviet influence—e.g. the Constitution of the New Democratic Youth League (1953), the Constitution of the Chinese People's Republic (1954), the Constitution of the Chinese Communist Party (1956), etc. Chinese education was characterized by imitation of Soviet models—translations of Soviet textbooks (content) as well as Soviet teaching guides (pedagogy).

III. The Great Leap Forward (1958-1959): In response to the psychological thrust of slogans announcing the "Great Leap Forward" and the launching of the rural commune movement, educational policy adopted the objective of "combining education with productive labor"—for the purpose of developing education with "greater, faster, better, and more economical results." There was a call for a general speed-up of the attack on illiteracy and in the production of the "red and expert" intellectual from the working class. The half-work, half-study plan was popularized, and many new as well as different types of schools mushroomed at a fantastic rate.

IV. Retrenchment (1960-1963): Sino-Soviet tensions which had developed during the Great Leap Forward now worsened to the point of an open attack on Soviet revisionism, and in 1960 the Soviet Union withdrew its technicians from China. The unprecedented rate of educational growth during the Great Leap Forward had created problems of quality. This new period was marked by the growing attention to the quality of education as the widening gap in Sino-Soviet relations left the Chinese no other choice but to train their own scientists and technicians. Soviet-oriented subjects and teaching materials were either reduced or eliminated, and there was official encouragement of a revival of the study of English in Chinese schools.

V. Two-Line Party Struggle (1964-1965): This period was dominated by the polarization within the Central Committee of the Chinese Communist Party between the Rightists (Liu Shao-chi) and the Maoists (Mao Tse-tung)—the former advocating a hierarchal structure based upon a chain of command from the top down, the latter urging principles of cooperation and collective responsibility. Educational policy maintained both the existing full-time schools as well as furthering the development of the "half-work, half-study" schools. Special emphasis and attention was given to political education.

VI. The Cultural Revolution (1966-1969): The struggle between the Rightists and the Maoists that began in 1964 became a political revolution, calling for a thorough reform, which brought education to a complete halt. When the primary and middle schools returned to a more normal operation in 1968 there were to be major changes: the cycle of primary and secondary school had been reduced to 9 or 10 years, and the number of school subjects had been reduced (concentration was now to be on five major areas—political theory and practice, language, mathematics, military and physical training, and industrial and agricultural production). Most important of all, Maoism was incorporated in every subject in an effort to revolutionize education.

VII. The Post-Cultural Revolution (1970 to the Present): Education in the People's Republic of China is considered as part of the "superstructure"—the way people think, their values, the rules they live by, their institutions, etc.—and therefore education is recognized as playing a major role in the process of social change. The unprecedented Cultural Revolution looked to education as a vehicle for preparing a new breed of youth—as a means of remolding their world outlook. Indeed, at the end of the Cultural Revolution the state both posed and answered the fundamental question of the purpose of education; the answer being that education must serve the workers, peasants and soldiers, and be combined with productive labor. The nation has embarked on a widespread and thoroughly comprehensive movement to *apply* these principles, to carry forward what Mao Tse-tung has called the "revolution in education."

The documents selected for inclusion in this study are translations of original documents, directives, speeches, announcements, investigative reports, and assorted articles on education which have appeared in Chinese Communist publications or monitored news broadcasts. Generally, these documents can be categorized as follows: First, those available originally in English-language translation from official Chinese Communist sources: for example, New China News Agency (NCNA) English-language releases; publications of Peking's Foreign Language Press, such as the journal *Peking Review,* or the multi-volume *Selected Works of Mao Tse-tung,* etc. Second, those available originally in English-language translation from United States government agencies in Hong Kong or the National Technical Information Service of the United States Department of Commerce, etc. These include *Survey of China Mainland Press, Current Background, Translations on People's Republic of China, Daily Report: People's Republic of China,* etc. (The editors wish to express their appreciation for permission to include these translations in this collection of documents.) Third, those available originally in Chinese and translated by Shi Ming Hu for this collection. Fourth, transcriptions of tape-recorded interviews and discussions gathered by the editors during their respective visits to the People's Republic of China in 1974 and 1975.

Some documents are presented in their entirety, others have been edited to conserve space, but materials originally available in English-language translation (whether those from Peking or from U. S. government sources) are reproduced as they appeared in their original format—spelling, transliteration, phrasing, etc. We believe the benefits to be derived from the authenticity and the "tone" of these original sources will outweigh any awkwardness in the translations.

It will be obvious to the reader that there are numerous instances of apparent inconsistencies in the Roman alphabetic transliterations (some of which are extremely confusing) of the original Chinese names, places, titles, etc. Our policy has been to reproduce the transliterations employed by the original translator—i.e. as the original translator spelled them. There are, however, a number of different transliteration systems using different Roman alphabetic spellings—e.g. Wade-Giles, Yale, Pinyin, etc. This is further complicated by the fact that there are a variety of so-called Chinese dialects which have completely different sounds (e.g. Mandarin, Cantonese, Wu, Hakka, Amoy-Swatow, Foochow, etc.). For example, "Canton," "Kuang-tung," and "Kwangtung" are three different transliterations of the "sound" of the Chinese characters for "wide" and "east."[3] This brief explanation is intended to sensitize the reader to the problems of transliteration. By way of illustration, let us use *People's Daily,* the official newspaper of the Chinese Communist Party, printed in Peking; the reader is likely to encounter the following different Roman alphabetic spellings: *Jen-min Jih-pao,* or *Jen-Min Jih-Pao* (following the Wade-Giles system of romanization, used in translations originating from the U.S. government agencies in Hong Kong); *Ren-min Ri-Bao, Ren-Min Ri-Bao,* or *Renmin Ribac* (variations of spelling following the Pinyin system, the latter being the standard spelling used by English language publications of Peking's Foreign Language Press).

This volume is intended as an introduction, a conceptual organization and categorization of educational development in the People's Republic of China from 1949 to the present—that is, as a suggested periodization. By *periodization* we mean an attempt to identify and order chronological sequences, which we have designated as periods of educational development. Periodization has its limitations, and it should be recognized that while we use conventional chronological groupings of years to delimit certain educational periods (such as 1949-1952, 1953-1957, etc.) historical events rarely conform to such neat annual demarcations. It is much more likely that certain time lags occurred, that in some cases previous trends were propelled by their own momentum beyond the limits of the period and spilled over into the following period. In a geographic region as large as China, important exceptions to, or at least significant variations of, these general educational trends are to be expected.

The foregoing is not a disclaimer of the periodization but rather a reminder that while we believe the suggested conceptualization of seven educational periods is a helpful historical periodization, it is after all subject to the inherent weaknesses of the process of periodization itself.[4]

The question of "Education for whom?" (that is, whom does education serve) is an important one. We hope this book will lead to an increased awareness and understanding of educational developments in the People's Republic of China. At the same time, we hope it will be taken by the reader as an invitation to apply the question of "Education for whom?" to an examination of the educational system of his or her own society.

NOTES:

[1]Chinese Communist historians divide the chronology from the founding of the Chinese Communist Party in 1921 to the establishment of the People's Republic of China in 1949 into four periods: (1) the First Revolutionary Civil War (1921-1927); (2) the Second Revolutionary Civil War (1927-1937); (3) the War of Resistance Against Japan (1937-1945); (4) the Third Revolutionary Civil War (1945-1949). Committee for the Publication of the Selected Works of Mao

Tse-tung, Central Committee of the Communist Party of China, "Publication Note," August 25, 1951, *Selected Works of Mao Tse-tung,* I (Peking: Foreign Language Press, 1967), pp. 5-6.

[2]"On New Democracy" (January 1940), ibid., II, p. 340.

[3]For a comprehensive introduction to Chinese characters we recommend *Chinese Characters: Their Origin, Etymology, History, Classification and Signification. A Thorough Study From Chinese Documents* (New York: Paragon Book Reprint Corporation and Dover Publications, Inc., 1965), by L. Wieger. According to Wieger, Chinese philologists divide characters into two major classes: simple figures and compound letters. These two classes are further divided into six categories of characters; the first four categories are based upon the composition of characters while the last two are based upon their use: (1) imitative drafts, rough sketches representing the object; (2) indicative symbols, a figure that suggests the meaning; (3) logical aggregates, made up of two or several simpler characters—their signification resulting from the meanings of the different elements; (4) phonetic complexes, made up of two or more simple characters—one giving the meaning and the other indicating the pronunciation; (5) use of the character in a meaning more extended, derived, generalized, metaphorical, etc.; (6) use of the character in a sense which is not its own (i.e. a "false borrowing"). For readers interested in pursuing the issue of transliteration, we recommend Ireneus Laszlo Legeza's two-volume *Guide to Transliterated Chinese in the Modern Peking Dialect* (Leiden: E. J. Brill, 1968).

[4]For an analysis of the nature of periodization, we recommend George H. Nadel's article entitled "Periodization" in the *International Encyclopedia of the Social Sciences* (1968), 11, pp. 580-584.

PART ONE

Reorientation
and
Reorganization
(1949-1952)

PART ONE
Reorientation and Reorganization (1949-1952)

September 21, 1949 marked the beginning of an historic ten-day conference held in Peking, the convening of delegates who formed the Chinese People's Political Consultative Conference (CPPCC) which proclaimed the establishment of the People's Republic of China, adopted the "Common Program" as the basis of the new government, and elected Mao Tse-tung as Chairman of the Central Government and Chou En-lai as Premier of the State Council. The new regime embarked upon a dramatic program of reorientation and reorganization designed to implement the guiding principles of the newly established "people's democratic dictatorship."

Earlier in the year, on the eve of winning full control over the mainland, Mao Tse-tung in his essay, "On the People's Democratic Dictatorship," written on the occasion of the twenty-eighth anniversary of the Communist Party (July 1, 1949), had affirmed the fact that the new government would be a dictatorship of the people, with state power vested in a coalition of four classes (the working class, the peasantry, the petty bourgeoisie, and the national bourgeoisie) under the leadership of the working class. Mao carefully defined "the people's democratic dictatorship" as "democracy for the people and dictatorship over the reactionaries," and stated:

> Who are the people? At the present stage in China, they are the working class, the peasantry, the urban petty bourgeoisie and the national bourgeoisie. These classes, led by the working class and the Communist Party, unite to form their own state and elect their own government. . . . Democracy is practiced within the ranks of the people, who enjoy the right of freedom of speech, assembly, association and so on. The right to vote belongs only to the people, not to the reactionaries. The combination of these two aspects, democracy for the people and dictatorship over the reactionaries, is the people's democratic dictatorship. . . . The people's state protects the people. Only when the people have such a state can they educate and remould themselves on a country-wide scale by democratic methods and, with everyone taking part, shake off the influence of domestic and foreign reactionaries, . . . rid themselves of the bad

habits and ideas acquired in the old society, not allow themselves to be led astray by the reactionaries, and continue to advance—to advance towards a socialist and communist society.[1]

At this early stage Mao Tse-tung seemed to tolerate all members of the reactionary classes as long as they created no trouble or did not rebel. He believed that it was possible to remold reactionaries through education and re-education. Chinese educational reform was to reflect these basic political guiding principles and emphases.

Article 1 of the Common Program proclaimed the establishment of a "people's democratic dictatorship led by the working class, based on the alliance of workers and peasants, and rallying all democratic classes and all nationalities in China." Initially there was little systematic educational reform; however, the application of Marxism-Leninism was omnipresent. Articles 41 through 49 of the Common Program established the cultural and educational policy. Culture and education were to be "New Democratic, that is national, scientific and popular." The "unity of theory and practice" was identified as the touchstone for educational method, and the old educational system was to be systematically reformed, both as to subject matter and teaching practices. Educational reform was directed toward meeting the "needs of revolutionary work and national construction work." Specifically, this called for: universalization of education; strengthening of middle and higher education; stressing technical education; strengthening education of workers and cadres; and providing revolutionary political education for the intellectuals.

In 1950, Lu Ting-yi, Director of the Department of Propaganda, stated:

> The Central People's Government regards the development of education for workers and peasants and the turning out of new intelligentsia from among the workers and peasants as its foremost cultural and educational task.[2]

This was considered as an important task not only for the purpose of meeting the cultural demands of workers and peasants, but as a means of paving the way for China's future socialist reconstruction.

Toward this end, the Central People's Government drew up a plan which stated that beginning in 1950 all educational institutions, factories, and military units were to help establish three-year short-term middle schools for workers and peasants. Cadres with worker or peasant backgrounds and members of the People's Liberation Army (PLA) were given an opportunity to study three basic middle-school subjects by attending these short-term schools. The "old-time intelligentsia" were to be reformed by giving them political education, for as Lu Ting-yi stated:

> The people's cultural and educational construction of China requires a common effort on the part of the intelligentsia from all revolutionary social strata.[3]

Commenting on cultural and educational work during 1950, Kuo Mo-jo, Vice Premier and Chairman of the Committee of Cultural Affairs of the State Administration Council, singled out as the most notable accomplishment, "the marked heightening of the political and cultural level of the people through the implementation of a mass study movement on a nation-wide scale." He identified three problems which were given special attention: first, the development of the cultural and educational reconstruction of China's national minorities (besides the Han majority which accounts for approximately 96 percent of the population there are 54 national minorities); second, the readjustment of the public-private relationship in cultural and educational enterprises; third, the relief of unemployed intellectuals (teachers) and assistance to students who were deprived of schooling.

The Central Government took steps to assume responsibility for conducting a comprehensive reform of the educational system. On October 1, 1951, Premier Chou En-lai announced the Central Government's "Decision on the Reformation of the

Educational System'' which acknowledged a number of ''defects in our original educational system,'' and established a system built around the following major categories: (1) Children's Education, (2) Elementary Education, (3) Intermediate Education, (4) Higher Education, and (5) Political Schools.

Children's education consisted of the kindergarten, admitting children from 3 to 7 years of age. Elementary education was organized around elementary schools for children (a 5 year school admitting children at the age of 7) *and* elementary schools (of varying duration) for uneducated youths and grown-ups.

Intermediate education consisted of four different sub-categories of schools, each with a specific purpose and emphasis. The ''middle school,'' a 6 year school admitting students of approximately 12 years of age, was divided into two 3-year periods (junior middle school and senior middle school). The ''workers' and peasants' short course middle school'' offered a period of attendance of 3 to 4 years. The ''sparetime middle school''—like the ''middle school''—was divided into two categories (sparetime junior and sparetime senior middle schools) of 3 to 4 years attendance each. A fourth intermediate school sub-category was the ''vocational middle school,'' which was further sub-divided into ''technical schools'' (2 to 4 years) and ''normal schools'' (3 year schools for the training of elementary teachers). The task of the ''vocational middle school'' was to train individuals for the reconstruction needs of the nation, while the role of the other three middle schools was to offer students a comprehensive course of education in general culture and knowledge.

Higher education comprised universities, specialized colleges, and technical colleges, each with varying periods of attendance. Finally, there was a fifth major category, that of political schools and political training classes offering ''revolutionary political education.''

The rationale given for the new educational policy appeared in the official government newspaper *Renmin Ribao (People's Daily)*:

> A school system is the reflection of the development of production and science in a given society. . . . The school system of capitalist states is a reflection of capitalist production and serves the purpose of the monopolistic economy of the capitalist class. The school system of the socialist states, on the other hand is a reflection of the advanced methods of socialist and Communist construction. The school system of old China was an imitation of the system of capitalist states and reflected the reactionary ideology of landlords, bureaucrats, and the comprador class of semi-colonial, semi-feudal society. . . . The laboring people had no position in the culture and education of old China.[4]

The influential newspaper called for the elimination of the most serious defects in the existing school system, which it identified as follows:

> . . . the schools for worker-peasant cadres and different types of adult schools and training classes are not given their rightful place in the system; the prolongation of elementary education makes it difficult for the children of the broad laboring masses to obtain complete education; and there is no definite system of technical schools to meet the nation's needs for competent personnel to undertake national construction.[5]

Educational policy in this formative period drew most heavily upon the principles and ideas set forth by Mao Tse-tung in his seminal article, ''On New Democracy,'' which appeared in the first issue of the magazine *Chinese Culture* (January 1940).[6] New China required an educational system that would build a new revolutionary culture which was ''democratic, national, and scientific.'' A culture which was ''democratic,'' according to Mao, ''belongs to the broad masses.'' Such a democratic culture would serve the masses of workers and peasants who constituted the overwhelming majority of the population, and who in turn would then gradually come to view this culture as their very own.

A culture which was "national" was characterized as opposing imperialist oppression and upholding both the dignity and independence of the Chinese nation. Such a national culture, Mao stated, "belongs to our own nation and bears our own national characteristics." This was not a call for a prohibition against the assimilation of "foreign culture" or western culture. Indeed, Mao urged the assimilation of "whatever is useful to us today not only from the present-day socialist and new-democratic cultures but also from the earlier cultures of other nations." However, he cautioned against uncritical wholesale westernization and stated that a revolutionary national culture could "never link up with any reactionary imperialist culture of whatever nation."

A culture which was "scientific" was "opposed . . . to all feudal and superstitious ideas, it stands for seeking truth from facts, for objective truth and for the unity of theory and practice." This was not a call for a denial of China's old culture, but rather a caution that "respect for history means giving it its proper place as a science"—for in dialectical philosophy the new is always viewed as an outgrowth or development of the past. In this respect it can be said that the function of the past is to serve the present and the future.

Such were the fundamental principles which guided and shaped educational reform during this formative period. Indeed, these fundamental principles—with somewhat different stress given to each—form a common thread of ideology running through the various educational periods since 1949, and continue to dominate the educational policy of the People's Republic of China.

Thus, a new China was to have a new educational direction. Emphasis was placed on the requirement that education serve the needs of national construction. Curriculum revision was patterned after the principles set forth in the Common Program, with changes in both subject matter and teaching method reflecting a "unity of theory and practice." At all educational levels, the focal point for curriculum development was that of political studies.

The Central Ministry of Education initiated a comprehensive program of curriculum reform. At the level of higher education it issued a directive calling for the realization of the combination of theory and practice, cautioning that while striving to achieve this unity, "narrow-minded utilitarianism or empiricism that refuses theoretical learning" must be prevented. Higher education was assigned the task of training specialists needed for national construction. Courses of study and teaching methods were to be developed (and submitted for approval to the Central Ministry of Education) according to these guidelines. At the primary and secondary levels, schools had to select texts from a list promulgated by the Central Ministry. If a regional education department wished to select a text which was not on the list it had to secure approval from the Ministry beforehand. (There are several regional educational departments throughout the country. Each department controls two or more provinces, serving as an intermediate organ and linking the provincial education commission to the Central Ministry of Education.)

Curriculum reform stressed the following: (1) reinforcement of political-ideological education; (2) the importance of productive labor; (3) development of specialized technical fields needed for national construction; (4) Marxist-Leninist thought and theory; (5) uniformity and centralization. Here we would like to cite a report from Amoy University (of which S. M. Hu is an alumnus):

> After Liberation, we taught the students patriotism, love of the people, of science, of labor, and care about public property, and inculcated a mental attitude of serving the people.
> In order to train working-class intellectuals who are both red and expert, and train some to have the working-class world-view and communist morality,

teaching of political ideology follows two lines:

a. Start courses in Marxist-Leninist theory and through technical courses, carry on teaching of political ideology.

b. Conjoin social and political revolutionary movements, practice in productive labor, organized life of party and Corps and teaching about duties of the situation, with teaching about the viewpoints of dialectical materialism, class, labor, and the masses.[7]

With respect to the secondary school curriculum in these early years, C. T. Hu, the noted historian, offers us the following descriptive account:

Their curriculums usually consist of political indoctrination, Chinese language and literature, mathematics, agricultural techniques, and/or other vocational courses. Occasionally, when teachers are available, courses such as biology, chemistry, and physics are added to the curriculum. . . . To make political indoctrination interesting to the students, the Ministry of Education instructed that it should be related to the important events of the day. Formal lectures were held to a minimum and no textbook for the course was issued on the ground that events in the country had moved so rapidly that textbooks would become outdated in a relatively short time. Instead, the students were asked to study theoretical treatises of current interest such as Mao Tse-tung's speech, "On the Correct Handling of Contradictions Among the People," and related documents and editorials from the People's Daily.[8]

Liu Shih, Vice-Minister of Education, commenting on China's new educational system stated:

Schools of various types and grades throughout the whole country . . . all follow the general educational line pointed out by Mao Tse-tung to fulfill the common tasks. . . . Schools of the same grade and of the same type must work according to a uniform curriculum.[9]

There were at this time growing signs of Soviet influence. Chen Po-ta, a member of the Central Committee of the Chinese Communist Party stated:

It is very important to study Soviet science. . . . The contributions the Soviet scientists have made and their methods of work are things we must learn. . . . Generally speaking, the good things in British and American science have already been absorbed by the Soviet scientists; hence, the quickest and best way is to learn from the Soviet Union.[10]

With the assistance of Soviet educators, and the policy of studying and learning from the Soviet Union's advanced educational experiences, education in the People's Republic of China became more and more Soviet-oriented. Russian influence was to reach its peak in the next period.

NOTES:

[1]Mao Tse-tung, "On the People's Democratic Dictatorship" (June 30, 1949), *Selected Works of Mao Tse-tung,* IV (Peking. Foreign Language Press, 1969), pp. 417-418.

[2]Lu Ting-yi, "Education and Culture in New China," *People's China,* I, No. 8 (April 16, 1950), p. 5.

[3]Ibid., p. 7.

[4]*Renmin Ribao,* S. M. Hu (trans.), October 3, 1951, p. 1.

[5]Ibid., p. 1.

[6]Mao Tse-tung, "On New Democracy" (January 1940), *Selected Works of Mao Tse-tung,* II (Peking: Foreign Language Press, 1967), pp. 339-384.

[7]P'an Mou-yuan, "Educational Reforms at Amoy University" [Originally published in *Lun-T'an,* No. 5, October 1959], Joint Publications Research Service, Doc. 3179 (April 25, 1960), p. 71.

[8]Chang-tu Hu, *China: Its People, Its Society, Its Culture* (New Haven: HRAF Press, 1960), pp. 422-423.

[9]Liu Shih, "China's New Educational System," *People's China,* IV, No. 11 (December 1951), pp. 5-8.

[10]Chen Po-ta, "Speech Before the Study Group of Research Members of [the] Academia Sinica," *Chinese Communist Education: Record of the First Decade,* ed. Stewart Fraser (Nashville: Vanderbilt University Press, 1956), pp. 184-185.

1.1 "Common Program of the Chinese People's Political Consultative Conference"

PREAMBLE

The great victories of the Chinese People's war of liberation and people's revolution have ended the era of the rule of imperialism, feudalism and bureaucratic capitalism in China. From the status of the oppressed, the Chinese people has become the master of a new society and a new state, and replaced the feudal, compradore, fascist, dictatorial Kuomintang reactionary rule with the republic of the people's democratic dictatorship. The Chinese people's democratic dictatorship is the state power of the people's democratic united front of the Chinese working class, peasantry, petty bourgeoisie, national bourgeoisie and patriotic democratic elements based on the alliance of workers and peasants and led by the working class. The Chinese People's Political Consultative Conference composed of the representatives of the Communist Party of China, all democratic parties and groups, people's organization all areas, People's Liberation Army, all national minorities, overseas Chinese and patriotic democratic elements is the form of organization of the Chinese people's democratic united front. The Chinese People's PCC representing the will of the people throughout the country, proclaims the establishment of the People's Republic of China and organizes the people's own central government. The Chinese People's PCC unanimously agrees that the New Democracy, namely the people's democracy, shall be the political foundation for national construction of the People's Republic of China. The Chinese People's PCC has also worked out the following Common Program which should be observed in common by all units participating in the Chinese People's PCC, all levels of the people's government and people throughout the country.

CHAPTER I.   GENERAL PRINCIPLES

Article 1.   The People's Republic of China is a state of New Democracy, that is, people's democracy. This republic carries out the people's democratic dictatorship led by the working class, based on the alliance of workers and peasants, and rallying all democratic classes and all nationalities in China. This republic opposes imperialism, feudalism and bureaucratic capitalism and strives for the independence, democracy, peace, unification, prosperity and strength of China.

Article 2.   The Central People's Government of the People's Republic of China must undertake to wage the people's war of liberation to the very end, liberate all the territory of China and accomplish the cause of unifying China.

Article 3.   The People's Republic of China must abolish all prerogatives of imperialist countries in China, confiscate bureaucratic capital for ownership by the people's state; systematically transform the feudal and semi-feudal land ownership

---

"Common Program of the Chinese People's Political Consultative Conference ' (Passed by the PPCC on September 29, 1949), *Current Background,* No. 9 (September 21, 1950), pp. 1-3, 11-12.

system into the system of peasant land ownership; protect the public property of the state and the property of cooperatives, protect the economic interests and private property of workers, peasants, petty bourgeoisie and national bourgeoisie; develop the people's economy of New Democracy and steadily transform the country from an agricultural into an industrial country.

Article 4.   The right of the people of the People's Republic of China to elect and be elected is prescribed by law.

Article 5.   The people of the People's Republic of China shall have the freedom of thought, speech, publication, assembly, association, correspondence, person, domicile, moving from one place to another, religious belief and the freedom of holding processions and demonstrations.

Article 6.   The People's Republic of China abolishes the feudal system which holds women in bondage. Women shall enjoy equal rights with men in political, economic, cultural and educational and social life. Freedom of marriage for men and women shall be enforced.

Article 7.   The People's Republic of China must suppress all counter-revolutionary activities, severely punish all Kuomintang counter-revolutionary war criminals and other obdurate arch counter-revolutionary elements who collude with imperialism, commit treason to the fatherland and oppose the cause of people's democracy. Reactionary elements, feudal landlords, bureaucratic capitalists in general, must, according to law, also be deprived of their political rights within a necessary period after they have been disarmed and their special power abolished, but they shall at the same time be given a means of living and compelled to reform themselves through labor to become new men. If they continue their counter-revolutionary activities, they shall be severely punished.

Article 8.   It is the duty of every national of the People's Republic of China to defend the fatherland, to observe the laws, to maintain labour discipline, to protect public property, to perform public service and military service and pay taxes.

Article 9.   All nationalities in the People's Republic of China have equal rights and duties.

Article 10.   The armed forces of the People's Republic of China, that is, the People's Liberation Army, the people's public security forces and people's police, are armed forces belonging to the people. Their tasks are to defend the independence, integrity of territory and sovereignty of China and the revolutionary fruits and all legitimate rights and interests of the Chinese people. The Central People's Government of the People's Republic of China shall endeavour to consolidate and strengthen the people's armed forces to enable them to accomplish their tasks effectively.

Article 11.   The People's Republic of China unites with all peace and freedom loving countries and peoples throughout the world, first of all the Soviet Union, all people's democracies and all oppressed nations,, and stands in the camp for international peace and democracy to oppose jointly imperialist aggression and defend world lasting peace.

*

CHAPTER V.   CULTURAL AND EDUCATIONAL POLICY ·

Article 41.   The culture and education of the People's Republic of China are New Democratic, that is, national, scientific and popular. The main tasks of the cultural and educational work of the people's government shall be the raising of the cultural level of the people, training of personnel for national construction work, liquidating of feudal, compradore, fascist ideology and developing of the ideology of serving the people.

Article 42. Love for the fatherland and the people, love of labour, love of science and the taking care of public property shall be promoted as the public spirit of all citizens of the People's Republic of China.

Article 43. Efforts shall be made to develop the natural sciences to place them at the service of industrial, agricultural and national defence construction. Scientific discoveries and inventions shall be encouraged and awarded and scientific knowledge shall be popularised.

Article 44. The application of scientific historical viewpoint to the study and interpretation of history, economics, politics, culture and international affairs shall be promoted. Outstanding works of social science shall be encouraged and awarded.

Article 45. Literature and arts shall be promoted to serve the people, to heighten the political consciousness of the people, and to encourage the labour enthusiasm of the people. Outstanding works of literature and arts shall be encouraged and awarded. The people's drama and cinema shall be developed.

Article 46. The method of education of the People's Republic of China is the unity of theory and practice. The people's government shall reform the old educational system, subject matter and teaching method systematically, according to plan.

Article 47. In order to meet the widespread needs of revolutionary work and national construction work, universal education shall be carried out, middle and higher education shall be strengthened, technical education shall be stressed, the education of workers during their spare time and education of cadres who are at their posts shall be strengthened, and revolutionary political education shall be accorded to young intellectuals and old-style intellectuals in a planned and systematic manner.

Article 48. National sports shall be promoted. Public health and medical work shall be extended and attention shall be paid to safeguarding the health of mothers, infants and children.

Article 49. Freedom of reporting true news shall be safeguarded. The utilization of the press to slander, to undermine the interests of the state and the people and to provoke world war is prohibited. The people's broadcasting work and the people's publication work shall be developed and attention paid to publishing popular books and newspapers beneficial to the people. . . .

1.2 "Speech Made by the Minister of Education, Mr. Ma Hsu-lun, at the Conference of Higher Education on June 1, 1950"

I am very pleased and excited about the opening of the first Conference on Higher Education which is an important event of the new China construction. The great people's revolution won the victory and the people's regime has laid down a firm foundation. Our country will soon be on the way of constructing the "New Democracy." Because of this new national condition, we are able to call this Conference on Higher Education to discuss the work on higher education in China. Of course, we know that the liberation task is not yet finished; Taiwan and Tibet are still to be liberated, and the people of the entire nation are needed to support with all their efforts, the Liberation Army its glorious mission. Furthermore, there are still economic difficulties after the long-term war and the extensive transformation of our society. That is why we cannot renovate all national constructions at the present time. However, as soon as we extinguish the remaining power of Chiang's Kuomintang and overcome the famine as well as the economic difficulties, we shall enter the phase of nationwide construction. We will then be in great need for massive manpower to engage in economic, national-defense, and cultural constructions. This phenomenon has already appeared in the Northeast; it will soon appear throughout the nation. Hence, it is necessary to follow the Common Program of the National Political Conference, to study, to adjust and to improve our higher education.

Now, let me first give you a general picture of the existing higher education. Statistically, there are all together 227 schools of higher education in our country without counting those on Taiwan, (this number does not include the people's universities and the military-political universities.) Total students of higher education are 134,000. The breakdown of the schools in terms of their support is as follows:

138 state colleges and universities, which is 61% of the total number;
65 private colleges and universities, which is 29% of the total number;
24 missionary colleges and universities, which is 10% of the total number.

Among all the institutions of higher education, there are 65 universities (29%), 92 specialized institutes (40%) and 70 junior colleges (31%). The distribution of all institutions of higher education is very uneven; there are 85 schools in the East (37%), Shanghai alone has 43 schools (25%). According to the need of our country, the number of institutions of higher education is no doubt very low, and the quality is not high enough. Therefore, it is far from meeting the need of our national construction. As far as the environment is concerned, there are about 15% of the institutions of higher education located in the old liberated areas or the areas that have been completely reformed. These schools have educated thousands of thousands revolutionary and constructional cadres. Generally, the teaching methods and materials were practical; theory was integrated much better with practice. However, most of them are still operated in the manner of the short-term training classes; they are not yet developed into the normal operation of a college or university. The other 85% of the institutions of higher education which are in the newly liberated areas, also educated a lot of useful people in the past; many of them contributed a great deal in democratic movement, but this does not mean that these schools do not need im-

---

"The Speech Made by the Minister of Education, Mr. Ma Hsu-lun, at the Conference on Higher Education on June 1, 1950," S. M. Hu (trans.), Peking, *Renmin Ribao* [*People's Daily*], June 14, 1950, p. 1.

provement. Basically their teaching materials do not meet the need of national construction and the teaching methods are inconsistent in terms of theory and practice. There have been very few students from peasants and workers. All these are not agreeable with our national condition and needs. The shortcomings existing in the newly liberated areas are the natural result of semi-colonization of the old China, which requires long-term efforts to overcome. Since the establishment of the People's Republic of China and the People's Government, the institutions of higher education in those old liberated areas have gradually normalized and the institutions in the newly liberated areas have also had administrative and curriculum reforms, especially the offering of political education. The great success was made possible by all the teachers and students of all the institutions of higher education, and a firm foundation has been laid.

The above mentioned is the present state of our higher education. Now let's see what is the direction for our higher education under the national policy as well as cultural and educational reform; what will be the responsibilities of our higher education? I feel that Articles 41 through 47 of the Common Program have provided us with a starting point to the answers. According to the Common Program, the goal of our higher education is to employ the educational method of combining theory and practice to cultivate the advanced constructional personnel who are high in cultural standard and able to make successful achievement in scientific technology of our modern time, and have determination of serving the people with their whole heart. We should carry out the revolution of political education, destroy the thoughts of feudalism, exploiting class, and facism, and develop the concept of serving the people. Therefore, our higher education must meet the national needs in industry, agriculture, and national-defense; our higher education must employ scientific viewpoints and methods to advance research in history, economics, politics, international affairs, literature, and arts to popularize scientific and technological knowledge among the public to raise their standard in culture and sciences, and then to promote national construction. In order to fullfill the above responsibilities, the following are suggested as the directions for our higher education.

1. The first and utmost point is that our higher education must meet the need of national economics, politics, culture, and national defense. First of all, higher education must serve the economic construction which is the foundation for all the other constructions. Since the goals of our higher education is to train advanced construction power, our institutions must offer systematically the education which will combine theory and practice. Based upon this principle, specialized scientific techniques are to be taught. Without systematic education in scientific knowledge, our higher education is not adequate. The theoretical education must never fall into the old trap of "academic for academic per se" again, nor neglect the need of our people and our country. Our higher education must be based upon the principle of combining theory and practice, integrated fundamental scientific knowledge and special technical knowledge, and unite theoretical learning and actual practice to educate all-around specialists with true knowledge, analytical ability, and creativity. Therefore, we must be very careful in planning our curriculum reform. The basic principle for the curriculum reform is combining theory and practice; the classroom materials must meet the need of the national construction. On the one hand, we must correct the old concept of separation between theory and practice; on the other hand, we must prevent neglecting the long-term and overall benefits of our people, and eliminate the narrow-minded pragmatism that looks down upon the theoretical learning. The reform must have a carefully planned strategy, because the task is indeed very complicated. Without thorough preparation in thoughts and manpower, the reform will be very difficult to accomplish. We are not quite ready in these two aspects—thoughts

and manpower. We must, based upon the degree of readiness of each individual institution and department, and the cooperative efforts of all educators of higher education, obtain the common goals step by step. In this Conference, there are many professors and specialists who have planned to make a series of reform drafts which were the result of their research and discussion for several months, and offered some suggestions on proceeding curriculum reform. I hope that all of you will study carefully to amend and correct the draft. It is not for this Conference to make the final decision, but to make suggestions for each school to form its own programs. After a considerable period of time to discuss and study, each institution must make a definite plan during summer for the new school year, and submit the plan to the Central Ministry of Education for approval. The second important item is to strengthen the operation of Chinese people's universities and other new types of higher education through the cooperation of the Central Ministry of Education and the other government divisions; departments of colleges and universities must also set up special courses and training classes.

2. Our higher education must prepare and begin to open doors for peasants and workers, in order to cultivate a large group of intellectuals from peasants and workers. As we know, the fact that it is important to have scientists and technical specialists from peasants and workers as the new backbone is one of the vital responsibilities of new China's education. Under this direction, some of our institutions of higher education must immediately make preparation to set up affiliated industrial and agricultural short-term high schools as the preparatory school for higher education. In the meantime, the institutions of higher education must begin to take in industrial and agricultural cadres as well as industrial and agricultural youths; after they are admitted to the schools, they must be given extra help and attention. All educators must consider educating industrial and agricultural cadres as their glorious responsibility. They must work hard to overcome the mistake of looking down upon workers and peasants and the mistake of separating from them.

3. Our higher education must follow our national construction in order to get on the right track gradually. In the past, China was a semi-colonial feudal country; the ununified political and economic situation reflected on higher education was shown as an extremely anarchic state, with each department operating its own way. Thus, first of all, we must gradually have a united and centralized leadership. The Central Ministry of Education should take the leadership for all institutions of higher education in direction, system, planning, hiring and firing leaders of each institution, courses, teaching materials and methods. Comprehensive universities and normal universities should be directly under the control of the Central Ministry of Education; some of the independent colleges and technical institutes should also be under the Central Ministry of Education; others should be under the appropriate divisions of the government offices. Their presidents, directions, system, course offering must be decided by the Central Ministry of Education. Financing, equipment, and other administrative affairs may be under the various divisions of the government offices. The private and missionary institutions of higher education must obey the law of the People's Republic of China, and follow the educational policy of "New Democracy." Our government has responsibility to guide those private institutions to the proper track of "New Democracy" for the service of educating constructional personnel of a new China. Right now because of the immature conditions, the Central Ministry of Education has asked the Regional Education Departments to take over the leadership of higher education. As the situation requires, the Central Ministry of Education will take over the direct control of our higher education. Secondly, we must make preliminary adjustment of all the institutions of higher education (state and private) to meet the need of our national construction, under the unified direc-

tion, needs and possibilities. To the private institutions, except for those very poor ones that have to be closed down, we must support them and have them reformed; particularly we should give financial aid to those departments that have been highly successful. Lastly, we must have a careful plan to reform and train teachers of our higher education. We all know that the teachers are the key to reform and strengthen our higher education. After the liberation, most teachers have advanced themselves and participated in learning, especially in political learning. This is a very exciting phenomenon in the process of educational construction. As the old saying states, ''After learning we see the need, and after teaching we see the difficulties. Seeing the need, we are then able to reflect, and seeing the difficulties we are then able to overcome them and strengthen ourselves. Hence, teaching and learning reinforce each other.'' Our teachers of higher education have followed the old saying to make our higher education reform promising. In order to solve the quantity and quality problems of teachers of our higher education, we must make plans to strengthen the political and professional learning. For example, we may set up teaching-research guidance to raise the efficiency of research and teaching. In order to have a closed relationship between the scientific research institution and the productive departments, we must have careful plan and organization to make research institutions a place to train teachers. We also need to send experienced and knowledgeable intellectuals abroad to learn new things, particularly the experiences of the USSR and that of the Eastern European countries. After the curriculum problem is resolved, we must begin to edit new teaching materials and references. We must translate massive Soviet texts as our professional references; in the meantime, we must edit the texts. Thus, I hope that a curriculum editing committee may emerge from this Conference to lead and organize the specialist to be in charge of this difficult task.

Dear delegates and comrades, the above statements are the directions, responsibilities and some vital steps toward our higher education that I would like you to consider and discuss. Since the establishment of the People's Republic of China, our higher education has improved with the hard work of our comrades all over the country; it has been successful in building up new things and reforming the old. This proves that our higher education will have a bright future. Of course, we must not forget that we have a lot of difficulties, especially financial difficulty which makes it impossible for us to have a large scale of reform and development, even to maintain the schools in some areas. However, these are unavoidable consequences of a long-term war; they are only temporary and will disappear when our economic condition recovers. All our obstacles will be overcome under the leadership of Chairman Mao, the people's government, and the efforts made by all of our comrades.

With my best wishes to the success of the significant Conference and good health to you all.

1.3 "The Central Ministry of Education Announcement on Carrying out Curriculum Reform of Higher Educaiton in Order to Achieve the Combination of Theory and Practice Step by Step"

1. The objectives of higher education of the People's Republic of China are based upon the Common Program issued by the National Committee of the Chinese People's Political Consultative Conference on the policy of culture and education; that is, to employ the educational method of combining theory and practice to cultivate highly constructive personnel who are totally committed themselves to the concept of serving the people, with high standard in culture and in command of scientific and technological success.

2. In the recent years, the content of higher education throughout the country has been preliminarily reformed with a definite result. However, there is still a relatively large portion of the existing curriculum in higher education that is not derived from "New Democracy." In other words, that part of the curriculum is not of people and science, nor in line with the need of establishing a new China. Thus, the curriculum in higher education must, based on the 46th Article of the Common Program, be reformed step by step to realize the combination of theory and practice. On the one hand, we must get rid of the empty notion of "academic for academic per se," and to strike for the integration of national construction and practice, which is the direction of our higher education; on the other hand, we must prevent the narrow-minded utilitarianism or empiricism that refuses theoretical learning.

3. According to the Articles 11 and 47 of the Common Program, all the institutions of higher education must abolish the part of curriculum that is politically reactional, offer political courses on New Democracy and revolution for the purpose of eliminating the thought of feudalism, exploiting class, and fascism, and develop the concept of serving the people.

4. All the institutions of higher education must follow the departmental system to train specialists; the curriculum must be closely in accordance with the present and long-term national needs of economics, politics, national defense and cultural construction. Appropriate specialization should be carried out on the foundation of theoretical knowledge. Based upon the principle of conciseness, important and necessary courses are to be strengthened; the repetition and unnecessary courses as well as the contents are to be eliminated. All courses are to be related and cohesive. While eliminating repetition and unnecessary courses and contents, careful thinking must be exercised, and discussion of all concerned parties must be made. It should never be done casually. Courses offered by all the institutions of higher education must be agreeable to the practical needs of the national construction.

5. In order to strengthen the combination of practice and teaching, the institutions of higher education must have close contact with government offices and governmental enterprises. Teachers of all institutions of higher education must work with government in public matter, production, and scientific research, and organize the students to do practical work and observation which should be a vital part of teach-

---

"The Central Ministry of Education Announcement of Carrying out Curriculum Reform of Higher Education in Order to Achieve the Combination of Theory and Practice Step by Step," S. M. Hu (trans.), Peking, *Renmin Ribao* [*People's Daily*], August 3, 1950, p. 3.

ing. For the sake of educating effectively national construction personnel, all government offices and governmental enterprises must help all the colleges and universities in teaching, practice and research as if a part of their own job. To the practicing students, they have the same responsibility of leadership as that of the Central Ministry of Education.

6. In order to meet the need of educating a large number of national construction personnel, each institution should assist all the constructional divisions to set up special training courses, training schools, or the correspondence schools under the leadership of the Central Ministry of Education.

7. Each department of the institution should decide the length of the study within the range of three to five years. Each semester must consist of 17 weeks. The weekly study hours (including homework and lab.) for the students will be 44 hours, or no more than 50 hours. Extra-curriculum activities should not be over six hours.

8. The key to curriculum reform is to raise the standard of teachers and to train new teachers. Therefore, all teachers teaching at the institutions must strengthen their political learning, professional learning and research. They must organize teaching research for the major courses and make reports to the supervisory group; the teachers should help one another to improve teaching materials and methods. Research in the institution must also be strengthened step by step with careful planning; the institution should be used as the teacher training agencies. They should guide and care for teaching assistants and graduate students to encourage their enthusiasm in research, and train them into teachers of New China.

9. To use scientific methods for editing the texts for the institutions, is an important criteria to carry out curriculum reform. Thus, under the leadership of the Central Ministry of Education, a curriculum editing committee was formed; they will follow the Articles 11, 42, 43, 44, 45, 46, and 47 of the Common Program to edit and translate teaching materials and references. From now on, all the texts must be in Chinese except for the foreign languages.

10. All the institutions must follow the above guidelines together with the Draft of the First Conference on Higher Education, and their own situations to write up teaching plans and materials; then submit to the Central Ministry of Education for approval.

11. This decision was announced by the Central Ministry of Education with the approval of the Executive Yen.

1.4 "Cultural and Educational Work During the Past Year"

The concrete task of our cultural and educational work today lies chiefly in "the eradication of feudalistic, compradore, and fascist ways of thought, and the development of the ideology of serving the people," and the popularization of culture and education so as to raise the level of the cultural life of the working people, the strengthening of the coordination among cultural, educational, scientific, and public health activities with our economic reconstruction institutions, the training of large numbers of industrial and agricultural cadres together with reconstruction personnel, and the gradual and planned reformation of both the contents and the system of old cultural and educational activities. During the past year, certain initial successes have been gained through the efforts of our working comrades. The most notable of our accomplishments lies in the marked heightening of the political and cultural level of the people through the implementation of a mass study movement on a nation-wide scale. As pointed out by Chairman Mao in his "On the People's Democratic Dictatorship," this is a movement of "self-education and self-reformation by democratic means carried out on a comprehensive scale throughout the nation."

Following the liberation of various parts of China, the political study movement was promoted among the workers, peasants, and intellectuals in all localities. In various urban districts and in rural district where agrarian reform has been carried out, after-work make-up schools for employees and workers were established on a comprehensive scale and the winter study movement promoted. According to available initial figures, more than 700,000 workers of various localities have entered the after-work schools; more than 10,000,000 peasants have taken part in the winter study movement, with more than 3,000,000 of these subsequently enrolled in regular elementary schools; political courses have been universally offered in universities and middle schools; and the faculty and staff members of universities, middle schools, and elementary schools have been universally organized to take part in the study movement. Study committees have been set up in various Government organs and a study system established for all working cadres. Political training colleges and political training classes have further been established in various localities to carry out ideological reformation. Incomplete statistical figures show that, up to the first half of the present year, more than 470,000 people have studied in this kind of institutions.

With a view to promoting this work, the propaganda activities using literary and art forms, the educational activities of news broadcasting, the exhibitions on scientific and cultural subjects, the printing and sale of books and publications, as carried out by cultural and educational organs of the Government, as well as the cultural and educational activities carried out among units of the armed forces, have all been coordinated with this movement. The principal activities of our different organs can be described as follows:

In the field of educational work, we have carried out a careful and well planned reformation of the curricula of institutions of higher education, promulgated the decision on the reformation of the curricula of institutions of higher education, and opposed any inclination for the practice of dogmatism to the neglect of actualities as well as the practice of narrow-minded materialism or empiricism which tend to ne-

Kuo Mo-jo [Vice Premier and Chairman of the Committee of Cultural and Educational Affairs of the State Administration Council], "Cultural and Educational Work During the Past Year" (NCNA, Peking, September 30, 1950), *Current Background,* No. 15 (October 19, 1950), pp. 1-5.

glect theoretical studies. We are planning to have the work of reformation gradually completed within a period of three years so that our institutions of higher education will be enabled to meet the needs of national reconstruction.

In the second place, with a view to opening the doors of institutions of higher education to industrial and agricultural cadres as well as youths from among workers and peasants, we have, basing ourselves on experiences drawn from the Soviet Union and taking into consideration our prevailing conditions, established a new type of institution of higher education. Twenty-one such new institutions have been established, and 11 old institutions of higher education are in the process of being turned into institutions of a new type. These new institutions of higher education now constitute some 15 percent of the total number of institutions of higher education throughout the nation, and their enrollment figure makes up over 21 percent of the total number of college students in China.

In the field of middle schools and elementary schools, in localities where agrarian reform has been carried out, we have already surpassed, quantatively, the accomplishments of the period of reactionary rule. The composition of the students have also undergone certain changes. In the Northeast, for instance, the present number of middle school students shows an increase of more than 190 percent over the figures at the time of the enemy-puppet (Japanese) rule, and the number of elementary school students shows an increase of more than 71 percent; and the greater part of these middle school and elementary school students come from worker and peasant families. With a further view to educating industrial and agricultural cadres and youths from among workers and peasants so as to enable them to attain middle school training within a comparatively short time, we have established workers' and peasants' short-term middle schools. At the moment, 18 such short-term middle schools have been set up and 10 more are being set up (those for the armed forces not included). Recently, in the course of the Conference on the Education of Workers and Peasants convened by the Central Ministry of Education, it has been decided to establish, on a comprehensive scale, workers' and peasants' after-work schools as well as workers' and peasants' cultural make-up schools for those who will devote themselves exclusively to studies and are completely freed from production work.

In the field of scientific research, we have completed the readjustment and reorganization of the old scientific institutions. At the moment, the Chinese Academy of Sciences is made up of 15 research institutes, 1 observatory, 1 engineering laboratory, and 3 preparatory offices for special research institutes. Scientific activities are centered around physics and engineering, geology, and biology. In physics, engineering and geology, the emphasis is on coordination with industrial development and national defence, while in biology the emphasis is on agricultural development. Besides, attention is also being paid to the popularization of science. Aside from special government agencies devoted to the popularization of science, the Chinese Association for the Advancement of Science and Technology has also been established in the course of this year's National Scientific Workers' Representatives' Conference, to assist the Government in this movement.

In the field of journalism, our chief activities have been centered around the improvement of newspaper work throughout the country, the strengthening of press activities designed to serve the interests of economic reconstruction and the implementation of the criticism and self-criticism campaign through the medium of the newspaper. Thus has the improvement, supervision, and examination of the various phases of our activities been facilitated, and the newspaper's prestige among the people increased. With a view to strengthening the educational influence of the newspaper on the reading masses, newspaper reading groups and workers' and peasants' correspondents have been developed in various localities on a comprehensive scale. The management and the editorial writing of newspapers in various localities have been improved, and certain papers have entrusted the Post Office with the work of circulation, thus increasing their circulation, decreasing their overhead, and enabling the newspapers to become self-sufficient. In the field of broadcasting, there now are a total of 55 people's broadcasting stations in the country. One of these, devoted to international broadcasts, is now broadcasting to foreign listeners in 12 languages. At the moment, 24 provinces and 4 administrative offices throughout the country have either established broadcast monitoring networks or are in the process of doing so.

In the field of publishing, more than 95,000,000 copies of books, and 172 varieties of periodicals with an aggregate of more than 11,000,000 copies, have been printed within the last half year. The sales of books have also increased greatly, and now the average yearly sales of a book usually run from 5,000 to 10,000 copies while the sales of popular reading material or books to be studied by cadres generally run from 50,000 to 100,000 volumes. (Before liberation, the average yearly sales of a book only ran from 2,000 to 3,000 copies.) With a view to strengthening our publishing activities, we have decided to unify the sales activities of the New China Bookstore throughout the country, carry out a system of division of labor among state bookstores concerning publishing and sales, and establish various specialized state publication enterprises.

In the field of motion picture enterprises, our fundamental policy lies in the gradual obliteration of obnoxious imperialistic films, the strengthening of the educational influence of the people's motion pictures, and in enabling the motion picture to reach out to workers, peasants, and soldiers. During the period of the reactionaries, over 70 per cent of the motion picture market in China used to be usurped by American films. Now, the situation is fundamentally changing for the better. To take Shanghai, where American motion pictures have always predominated, as an instance, whereas formerly 75 per cent of the motion picture audience used to see American pictures, the ratio has gone down to 28.3 per cent by this June. Thus has a major victory been scored by our motion picture enterprise. With a further view to popularizing the motion picture, 1,800 motion picture projectionists have been successfully trained in preparation for the establishment of 700 motion picture projection teams in the coming year.

Besides, a considerable amount of work has also been done in the cultural artistic, and dramatic fields. In the universal reformation of artistic work, attention has in particular been centered on the reformation of the Chinese operas.

Aside from the above, special attention has also been given to the following problems:

1. The development of the cultural and educational reconstruction activities of the national minorities, so as to eradicate all remnant influences of Great Hanism handed down from the days of reactionary rule and to promote cultural exchange between the brotherly national minorities. With the above aim in view, successes have been scored by the Central People's Government in the dispatch of two CPG missions to visit various national minorities in Southwest and Northwest. With regard to the cultural and educational activities of the national minorities, we emphasize the development of educational and public health work. Certain educational institutions have already been established in Sinkiang and Lanchow, and steps have been taken for the establishment of a Nationalities College in Peking. In the field of public health, we are now planning to establish more medical establishments and increase the supply of drugs. Newspapers and broadcasts designed to serve the interests of the national minorities have also been developed.

2. The readjustment of public-private relationship in cultural and educational enterprises. In this respect, basing ourselves on the principle of giving consideration

to both public and private interests, we have, in addition to assisting private cultural enterprises in the reformation of their contents of work and in making suitable investments in their enterprises or granting them loans, also paid attention to the implementation of a proper division of labor between public and private cultural enterprises. This problem has been thoroughly discussed at the various national conferences on press, publishing, public health, motion picture, and other enterprises. Much has already been accomplished in the implementation of the measure.

3. In connection with the relief of unemployed intellectuals and the help of students deprived of schooling, the State Administration Council has promulgated the "Directive on the relief of unemployed intellectuals and the disposal of students deprived of schooling," as well as allocated a sum of money for the relief of unemployed teachers and of students deprived of schooling in various localities. As a result, the serious phenomenon of unemployment of teachers has in the main been checked in various localities during the past half year.

These are our chief cultural and educational activities for the past year, and as a result of our efforts during this year, the cultural life of our people has also undergone great changes. The people of the entire nation, in particular the workers and peasants, have heightened their consciousness of their status as masters of their country, increased their understanding of the democratic camp of peace and of the camp of aggression, and established the point of view that labor creates civilization. These accomplishments find concrete manifestation in the spirit of self-sacrifice and class love exhibited by the workers of various localities in their attempt to surmount economic difficulties and to aid the unemployed, as well as their positive and inventive spirit exhibited in production emulations and new record movements; the enthusiasm exhibited by the peasants of various localities to increase agricultural production and to pay up their share of public grain; the ardor and the efforts of the intellectuals and government personnel exhibited in their studies and their reconstruction work; the determination to support peace and to oppose American imperialistic aggression exhibited by the people of the entire nation; and the unprecedented demand for culture and education exhibited by the workers' and peasants' masses. All of the above epoch-making facts form clear proof of the fundamental change which has taken place in the cultural and educational activities of New China.

Naturally we are only at the threshold of New Democratic cultural and educational reconstruction. The tasks before us are undoubtedly heavy, but our future is bright and boundless.

1.5 "The Joint Announcement Made by the Central Ministry of Education and the Publishing Headquarter Concerning the Decision on the Texts to be Used in the Primary and Middle Schools for the Spring Semester, 1951"

The announcement which was circulated to the major regional education departments made by the Central Ministry of Education and the Publishing Headquarter on December 25, 1950 includes the following:

1. Whenever the major regional education department feels that the list of the texts for the primary schools is not suitable for its particular region in terms of practicability, it may select the texts outside of the list. However, as soon as the texts are decided on, they should be reported to the Central Ministry of Education and the Publishing Headquarter immediately; in the meantime, an announcement of this new list of the texts should be sent to all the local educational offices througout the region and have them adopt the texts uniformly.

2. Except for the Northeast, all the other major regional education departments should select middle school texts from the list promulgated by the Central Ministry of Education in accordance with their own regional conditions. As soon as the texts are selected, they should be immediately reported to the Central Ministry of Education and the Publishing Headquarter. At the same time, an announcement of the list of the selected texts should be circulated to all the districts and have all middle schools adopt the texts uniformly.

If any of the major regional education departments decide to have the texts outside of the list promulgated by the Central Ministry of Education, they should first submit the list to the Central Ministry of Education for approval.

As soon as the major regional education departments receive the list of the texts for the primary and middle schools from the Central Ministry of Education, they should call a meeting of the concerned parties which include the News Publishing Bureau of the Military and political Committee, the director of the local branch of "Xinhua," (the national publisher), and the director of the textbook distribution station, to decide the texts for the primary and middle schools of their own region. The major regional education departments should also assist the branch of "Xinhua" and the textbook distribution stations in determining the total amount of the texts to be used in their own region.

After the decision on the texts is made, the major regional education departments should notify all districts which in turn inform all the local schools to note the opinions reflected from the classroom in regard to the contents, then report to the Central Ministry of Education and the Publishing Headquarter.

"The Joint Announcement Made by the Central Ministry of Education and the Publishing Headquarter Concerning the Decision on the Texts to be Used in the Primary and Middle Schools for the Spring Semester, 1951," S. M. Hu (trans.), Peking, *Renmin Ribao*, [*People's Daily*], December 31, 1950, p. 3.

1.6 "Minister of Education Ma Hsu-lun Reports on Educational Accomplishments During the Past Year"

I. A GENERAL SUMMARY OF EDUCATIONAL WORK IN 1950

In 1950, educational work throughout the country began to be carried out in a well planned and step by step manner under the over-all leadership of the Central People's Government. Our well planned, step by step, selective, and steady policy of work has been formulated on the basis of the fundamental prevailing conditions in educational work.

By following the above-mentioned policy, we succeeded in scoring these gains in the field of national educational work in the course of 1950:

1. In clearly defining our aim and policy, the Ministry of Education convened, in December 1949, the 1st National Educational Work Conference to formulate a new national policy of education by stressing the fact that education must meet the needs of national reconstruction and that the doors of the schools must be opened to the workers and peasants, and by clearly stipulating the policy and steps for reforming old education, and the direction for developing new education. The 1st National Conference of Higher Education was convened in June 1950 to determine the true aim for the reformation of higher education. The 1st National Conference on Workers' and Peasants' Education was convened in September 1950 to determine the policy and the plan for the implementation of workers' and peasants' education at the present stage. Thus have the educational workers throughout the country been provided a clear and united aim and policy in their work, and a common direction for them to advance. For the past year the emphasis in the case of schools in new areas lay in restoration and stabilization coupled with readjustment and reformation; while in old areas, the emphasis is on consolidation and improvement as well as suitable development. According to incomplete statistics, there now are more than 395,000 elementary schools throughout the country with a total enrollment of more than 29,330,000, and more than 5,100 middle schools with a total enrollment of more than 1,570,000. New developments have taken place in such old areas as the Northeast, North China, and Shantung of East China. Whether in urban or rural districts, the numbers of offsprings of workers and peasants' students have increased greatly both in middle and in elementary schools. In the old areas, the offsprings of workers and peasants make up some 80 percent of the total number of middle school and elementary school students. At the moment, there are a total of 201 public and private institutes of higher education throughout the country with an enrollment of 128,000, an increase of some 10,000 students as compared with the figures before the summer vacation of 1950.

2. In the reformation of old education on a nation-wide scale, we have proceeded according to careful plans by avoiding the two extremes of impetuosity and rashness, and procrastination and refusal to change, so as to reform the contents of education through the reformation of curricula, reformation of teaching material, improvement of pedagogical method, change of pedagogical organization, etc. First and foremost came the development of education in revolutionary political ideology and the abolition of reactionary courses, followed by the reformation of the contents of in-

---

"Minister of Education Ma Hsu-lun Reports on Educational Accomplishments During the Past Year" [May 18, 1951], (NCNA, Peking, July 21, 1951), *Survey of China Mainland Press,* No. 142 (July 25, 1951), pp. 5-12.

struction in order to meet the needs of national reconstruction, and the curtailment of unnecessary courses and teaching material. In the field of higher education, the Decision on the Reformation of the Curricula of Institutes of Higher Education has been promulgated, and the Draft Plans for the Curricula of 54 Departments, including 9 Departments of the Colleges of Arts and of Law, 11 Departments of the Colleges of Sciences and of Engineering, 4 Departments of the College of Agriculture, and various Special Courses, have been formulated. With a view to reforming normal education throughout the country, work was first started with the Peking Normal University. In this work, initial successes have been scored in the reorganization of administrative leadership, the reorganization of the colleges and departments, and the improvement of curricula and teaching material. Initial successes have also been scored in the teaching of language, politics, geography, and history in elementary schools.

3. In the development of workers' and peasants' education, the China People's University has been set up on the basis of Soviet experiences and in conformity to actual prevailing conditions in China, for the training of superior intellectual elements among the workers and peasants. Up to now, 2,981 worker and peasant cadres and young intellectuals have been enrolled in the University's regular courses, special courses, and night courses. Throughout the past year, invaluable experiences have been gained in pedagogical system, organization and method. The 1st National Conference on Workers' and Peasants' Education formulated measures for the establishment of workers' and peasants' short course middle schools, workers' and peasants' cultural schools, and for the promotion of cultural education for activist workers and peasants. Up to the moment, 22 workers' and peasants' short course middle schools have been set up with an enrollment of 3,700 students, and 135,000 activist workers and peasants cadres have enrolled in after-work cultural schools. By the end of 1950, 1,050,000 workers and employees studied in after-work schools; 13,000,000 peasants entered winter schools during the winter of 1949; 25,000,000 peasants entered winter schools during the winter of 1950; and in 1950, 3,480,000 peasants took regular part in studying all through the year.

4. In carrying out the education in revolutionary political ideology throughout the country, the educational agencies of the entire nation have, in coordination with other related quarters, universally carried out a campaign of education in political ideology among the students and the masses. Various administrative regions have accordingly set up people's revolutionary universities in the effort to rally and to reform the intellectuals. Thus has the level of political consciousness been raised for the teachers, students, and other intellectuals of the nation, and important successes scored in wiping out the feudal, compradore, and fascist ideology, and in establishing the revolutionary point of view and developing the ideology of serving the people. In particular, as a result of the patriotic education of resisting the U. S. and aiding Korea, the pro-America, revere-America, and fear-America tendencies of certain people have been successfully eradicated and national self-respect and self-confidence greatly raised.

5. In starting to practice the principle of giving due attention both to public and private interests among educational enterprises, we have universally given positive assistance to private schools, strengthened the work of leadership, and carried out step by step reforms, so as to enable them to meet the needs of national reconstruction, as well as encouraged the establishment of private schools in urban districts and encouraged the masses to set up schools in rural districts. Thus, numerous private schools have been enabled to carry on, and the masses have been given further impetus to establish schools. In the Northeast, for example, figures covering 6 provinces and 1 municipality show that 2,858 village schools have been set up by the peas-

ants with an enrollment of 205,696. Up to this moment, there are more than 70 private institutes of higher education, 1,500 private middle schools, and numerous private elementary schools throughout the country. With the assistance of the government, many of the better ones have developed rapidly and well.

6. With a view to training up large numbers of competent people to meet the needs of national defense, economic, political-judicial, and cultural-educational reconstruction, the more that 17,500 graduates from institutes of higher education in 1950 have, for the first time, being assigned work in a planned manner. More than 80 percent of these have, in accordance with overall demand, been assigned work at various posts of reconstruction. Following the start of the resist-U. S., aid-Korea movement, 40,000 university and middle school students have been mobilized, on the basis of patriotic education, to enroll in military cadres schools.

The above are the principal accomplishments in educational work throughout the country in 1950.

II. THE POLICY AND TASK OF EDUCATIONAL WORK THROUGHOUT THE NATION IN 1951

A. The policy of educational work throughout the nation in 1951:

(1) The all-out development of the patriotic education of resisting the U.S. and aiding Korea so as to eradicate all traces of imperialistic influence, in particular American imperialistic influence, in cultural aggression against China.

(2) To keep up the thorough implementation of the policy that education is designed to serve the aim of national reconstruction, and the training of all categories of reconstruction personnel, in particular economic reconstruction personnel, in coordination with economic, national defense, political-judicial, and cultural-educational enterprises. To resolutely maintain the principle that education must serve the interests of the workers, peasants, and servicemen, that the doors of education should be kept open for workers and peasants, and to practice faithfully, in all educational enterprises, the principles of giving due consideration both to public and to private interests and both to urban districts and to rural districts.

(3) To stress the work of regulation, unification, putting to order, and consolidation in the case of all schools, in preparation for future developments.

(4) The adoption of effective steps for carrying out Chairman Mao's principle of "Health above all" to improve the students' state of health, and, on the prevailing foundation, to improve the remuneration of middle school and elementary school teachers.

B. The tasks of educational work throughout the nation in 1951:

(1) The development of the patriotic education of resisting the U.S. and aiding Korea:

  i) All levels and categories of schools should, through the subjects taught and in coordination with various after-class activities, carry out the universal implementation of the patriotic education of resisting the U.S. and aiding Korea. At the same time, the students of all levels and categories of schools should be mobilized to carry out publicity work among the masses. All efforts should be made to assist all related quarters to subject every Chinese of every corner of China to this education.

  ii) On the foundation of the above-mentioned ideological education, to complete the work of calling upon a certain part of young students to take voluntary part in national defense reconstruction.

iii) To take over and manage American-subsidized schools and educational institutes in a correct and careful manner.

(2) To establish the new academic system for the People's Republic of China by the organization of a Research Committee on the Improvement of Academic System. The opinions collected and plans formulated shall be submitted to the GAC to be re-submitted to the People's Government Council for ratification and promulgation for implementation.

(3) Higher education:

i) With a view to meeting the needs of national defense reconstruction, suitable steps should be taken gradually to strengthen and readjust the existing departments and colleges of institutes of higher education. The departments of the engineering college should be the first to be readjusted, or new departments added. This work should be started in North China and East China with the readjustment of the Department of Aeronautics, the joint establishment of political-judicial training classes with the Committee of Political and Judicial Affairs, and the regulation and strengthening of political and judicial departments of various institutes of higher education. The existing normal colleges, colleges of education, and the colleges of arts and sciences of various universities should be regulated, establishing one normal college for each administrative region, and one special normal college for each one, two, or three provinces, so as to train up teachers for junior and senior middle schools.

ii) All-out efforts should be made to strengthen the Chinese People's University, the Harbin Engineering University, and the Peking Normal University, and to extend the experiences thus gained.

iii) The enrollment of new students this summer shall be carried out in a planned and selective manner in conformity to the degree of urgency of various aspects of reconstruction. A total of 35,000 new students shall be enrolled by institutes of higher education (including universities, colleges, technical schools, and technical training classes) throughout the country. In the work of enrollment, attention should be specially given to the enrollment of intellectuals who have worked for the cause for a long time, workers and peasants cadres, and production workers.

iv) To cooperate with all related quarters for the revision and formulation of draft plans for the curricula of various departments of the college of engineering, college of agriculture, and college of sciences, and to draw up curriculum standards for other departments; to revise and formulate draft plans for the curricula of departments of colleges of political science and law; to revise and formulate draft plans for the various departments of the college of finance-economics, normal college, and medical college; and to supervise and look into the implementation of curriculum reform in institutes of higher education in a strict manner, and to rectify the tendencies of procrastination and refusal to change.

v) One hundred each of finance-economics and engineering and science teachers should be selected from various institutes of higher education to undergo advanced training separately either at the China People's University or the Harbin Engineering University. Three hundred research students shall be enrolled in order to strengthen the research activities in universities. Aside from retaining 350 graduates from among the graduates of this year to act as assistants, efforts should further be made to train up new teaching personnel.

vi) The dispatch of limited numbers of students to study abroad and to try to gain over a part of the Chinese students studying in capitalist countries.

(4) Middle school education:

i) For the positive development of intermediate technical schools and in order to put them into order, and to train up large numbers of intermediate technical personnel, a conference of technical education has been convened in June to make a study of the policy, task, scholastic system, and pedagogical plan of intermediate technical schools, and to formulate concrete measures for the regulation and development of teaching material. Steps should be taken, in conjunction with the related quarters, to put into order and consolidate more than 500 existing intermediate technical schools, and to establish new intermediate technical schools and training classes according to plans; to establish technical training classes within selected senior elementary schools; and to enable all senior elementary school graduates who have not entered junior middle schools or have not found jobs, to enter various apprentice schools, technical schools, or training classes, so as to turn them into junior and intermediate technical personnel to meet the needs of national reconstruction.

ii) In the effort to put into order and consolidate the public and private middle schools within the country, appropriate steps have already been taken in the old liberated areas. In the National Conference of Middle School Education convened in March, steps were taken to determine the policy and task of middle school education; to fix the aim of regular middle schools, their educational aims, pedagogical plan, and curriculum standards; to formulate provisional regulations governing middle schools; and to make a selection of 250 better qualified middle schools for the experimental implementation of these regulations in order to gain the necessary experiences for extending the campaign. Positive steps should be taken to guide and reform all private middle schools, as well as to encourage the establishment of private schools and to offer all possible assistance in the effort to overcome their difficulties.

iii) In the effort to keep open the doors of education for workers and peasants, special quotas for the offsprings of workers and peasants should be fixed by various localities in the enrollment of middle school students. Workers and peasants' short course middle schools should be developed to attain an enrollment of 7,800 students, while 18,000 workers and peasants' cadres are to be enrolled in workers and peasants cadres cultural schools.

iv) For the appropriate consolidation and development of normal education, a conference on normal education is to be convened to determine the policy and task of all levels of normal schools, to revise pedagogical plans and curriculum standards, to formulate provisional regulations governing normal schools, to put into order and appropriately expand existing normal schools, to increase the number of *hsien* junior normal schools, and to improve pedagogical method. With a view to strengthening the work of guiding teachers to take part in studying, short-term teachers training classes should be established to improve their professional knowledge and to raise their level of proficiency.

(5) Elementary education:

The national elementary school education conference in to be convened to decide upon the policy and task of elementary school education, to draw up pedagogical plans, to formulate the provisional regulations governing elementary schools, as well as to solve other problems connected with curricula, teaching material, the advanced training of teachers, etc. Effective methods and steps should be adopted to solve such important problems as funds, improvement of the remuneration of teachers, etc. The people's representatives' conferences of all places should be called upon to activate and assist the masses in their effort to set up new schools. The emphasis in elementary school work throughout the country lies in regulation and consolidation, with the stress on consolidation and development in old areas and on restoration in new areas. All efforts should be made to struggle for the fundamental stabilization and consolidation of elementary schools and elementary school teachers throughout the country.

(6) Social education:

i)   The National Employees and Workers After-work Education Committee should be set up to promote after-work education, to improve their quality, to consolidate the work, to increase the number of students enrolled to 1,500,000, to give particular attention to the participation of worker cadres and active elements in studying, to coordinate cultural studies with political and professional studies correctly, and to overcome the two mistaken extremes of refusing to study culture and studying only culture. A bi-monthly periodical "The Study of Culture" shall be published as supplementary reading material for employees and workers engaged in cultural studies.

ii) In the continued development of the after-work education of peasants, efforts should be made to strive for the enrollment of 30,000,000 peasants in winter schools. With the winter school as a foundation, attempts should be made to strive for the enrollment of 5,000,000 peasants in regular all-the-year-round peasants after-work schools. Care should in particular be given to the enrollment of rural cadres and the active elements for the intensive study of patriotism and culture.

iii) To struggle for the sucessful establishment of after-work cultural schools for the working cadres in various organs, to formulate regular systems of study and pedagogical plans, and to strive for the enrollment of 200,000 employees, workers, and peasants cadres in after-work schools set up by their respective organs.

iv) The Committee for Research on Linguistic Reform is to be established to make a selection of the commonly-used characters and simplified characters, and for the adoption of a phonetic system, as a preparatory step for developing the literacy movement among workers and peasants.

(7) To pay attention to and to develop the education of national minorities, to keep in close touch with the Commission of Nationalities Affairs, to gain a knowledge of the state of education among the national minorities, to guide and assist various national minorities districts in the readjustment and development of educational enterprises, to stress the implementation of patriotic education, to foster their love for fatherland, to train up intellectuals, to convene national minorities educational conferences for the formulation of relevant plans, to have the problems of funds, teachers, and textbooks solved in a gradual manner, and to assist the Commission of Nationalities Affairs to make a success of the Central National Minorities Institute together with its branches.

(8) To keep in close touch with the Commission of Overseas Chinese Affairs for the establishment of a central guiding agency to improve the education of the off-springs of overseas Chinese in an effective manner.

(9) To compile new textbooks for elementary schools and middle schools: The all-out compliation of textbooks for all levels of schools is to be carried out by following the stipulations of the new academic system in the compilation of elementary and middle school textbooks on basic political knowledge, language, history, and geography. Soviet textbooks should be consulted as reference for the revision of textbooks on mathematics, physics, chemistry, biology, and other scientific subjects. At the same time, textbooks on education, teaching material, teaching method, etc. used in normal schools, textbooks for workers and peasants' short course schools, and textbooks for workers and peasants afterwork schools should also be compiled, and professors and experts are to be organized for the translation of textbooks for institutes of higher education. A start should be made in the compilation of reference books for elementary school teachers.

(10) The Physical Culture Committee should be established to guide all schools in faithfully carrying out the policy of "Health above all," in reducing the students' amount of class work and after class activities, to promote sports activities and recreation activities, to strengthen health education, to improve environmental hygiene and medical facilities, to improve the food of students, and to promote the people's athletic and health activities, so as to improve the state of health of the people.

With a view to successfully fulfilling the above-mentioned task, it is up to us to consolidate, in a step by step manner, all levels of guiding educational administration agencies, to regulate and consolidate all provincial, municipal, *hsien,* and *chu* educational administration agencies in a rational manner, fix their personnel plans, assign the principal cadres of various educational administration agencies, and in particular to strengthen the work of survey, statistics, research, and supervision and investigation so as to master the true state of affairs, to check up on the implementation of various policies, and to determine the success of implementation, in order to make timely corrections. Experiences should be summarized and disseminated in time so as to rectify all deviations and shortcomings. The "reporting to superior organ for instructions" system together with the reward and penalty system should be strictly adopted in all aspects of educational work. The monthly "People's Education" should be improved, and instructions should be issued to all localities on the regulation and improvement of educational publications so as to enable them to play their full part, in coordination with other phases of work, in the guidance of educational enterprises.

(11) Both central and local authorities should plan for the organization of vacation-time training courses, teachers' representatives' conferences, advanced studies for teachers on active service, correspondence courses, as well as mobilizing the teachers to take part in agrarian reform and other activities of the masses, so as to improve the teachers' professional proficiency and raise their level of ideological attainment. Attention should also be given to unemployed intellectuals so as to give them the chance to take part in studies and to participate in educational work.

1.7 "Implementation of New Educational System Promulgated"

Order of the Government Administration Council of the Central People's Government:

The Decision on the Reformation of the Educational System, as ratified by the 97th Meeting of the Government Administration Council of the Central People's Government, is hereby promulgated for implementation.

Premier   Chou En-lai
Oct. 1, 1951

The text of the Decision follows:

There are numerous defects in our original educational system (that is the system of different grades and categories of schools): the principle ones being, the lack of a proper place in the educational system for worker and peasant cadres schools, various make-up schools, and various training classes; the division of the 6 years of elementary school education into 2 3-year groups of senior elementary school and junior elementary school, thus making it difficult for the children of the broad working masses to go through a complete course of elementary schooling; and the lack of a system of technical school education, thus failing to meet the nation's demand for reconstructional personnel. All these should be immediately rectified. Though at the present moment, it is still difficult to unify the educational system throughout the nation, it is nevertheless both necessary and possible for us to determine the respective correct positions in the educational system of existing schools and new schools, change all irrational year limits and systems, and link up schools of different grades, so as to assist in raising the cultural level of the broad working masses, giving advanced training to worker and peasant cadres, and furthering the reconstruction work of the nation. Our new educational system is stipulated as follows:

(1) Children's Education

The kindergarten (*Yü Erh Yuan*) is the educational organization for the education of the children. Children of from 3 years to 7 years of age shall be admitted into kindergartens to assure them of healthy mental and physical development in their pre-elementary school days.

Kindergartens shall first be set up in cities where the conditions are ripe, and gradually extended to other localities.

(2) Elementary Education

By elementary education is meant both elementary education for children and elementary education for adults. Elementary schools for the education of children are designed to offer them a comprehensive educational foundation. Workers' and peasants' short course elementary schools, sparetime elementary schools and literacy schools (winter schools and literacy classes) are designed for the elementary education of uneducated youths and adults.

A. Elementary School

The elementary school education of 5 years is a straight course without the division into senior elementary school and junior elementary school. The age

---

"Implementation of New Educational System Promulgated" (NCNA, Peking, October 1, 1951), *Survey of China Mainland Press*, No. 192 (October 11, 1951), pp. 13-16.

of admission is 7. Elementary school graduates shall be admitted into middle schools together with various varieties of intermediate schools through passing an examination.

Make-up classes or vocational training classes may be set up in elementary schools to give appropriate education to elementary school graduates unable to continue their schooling. Graduates from these classes may be admitted into various appropriate classes in middle schools by passing an examination.

B. Elementary Schools for Youths and Grown-ups

1. Workers' and peasants' short course elementary schools of 2 to 3 years' period, shall offer worker and peasant cadres and other uneducated laboring people an education commensurate with elementary school education. After graduation, they may be admitted into workers' and peasants' short course middle schools or other varieties of intermediate schools by passing an examination.

2. Sparetime elementary schools, designed to offer workers, peasants, and various laboring people a sparetime education commensurate with elementary school education, do not have a fixed period of attendance. Their graduates, those who have completed the stipulated number of courses, may be admitted into sparetime middle schools or other varieties of middle schools by passing an examination.

3. Literacy schools (winter schools and literacy classes), designed to wipe out illiteracy, have no fixed time limit of attendance.

(3) Intermediate Education

Various categories of intermediate schools, that is, middle schools, workers' and peasants' short course middle schools, sparetime middle schools, and vocational middle schools, are devoted to the implementation of intermediate education. Middle schools, workers' and peasants' short course middle schools, and sparetime middle schools are designed to offer the student with a comprehensive course of education in general culture and knowledge; while vocational middle schools are devoted to the implementation of intermediate vocational education in conformity to the reconstruction needs of the nation.

A. Middle School

The middle school, with a period of attendance of 6 years, is divided into the two 3-year periods of senior middle school and junior middle school, which may also be set up independently. The teaching matter should observe the spirit of continuity but can at the same time also have appropriate division.

The junior middle school is designed to admit elementary school graduates or candidates with equivalent qualifications of around 12 years of age. Graduates of the junior middle school may be admitted into the senior middle school or equivalent vocational schools by passing an examination.

The senior middle school is designed to admit junior middle school graduates or candidates of equivalent qualifications of around 15 years of age. Graduates of senior middle schools may be admitted into various institutions of higher education by passing an examination.

Graduates of both junior and senior middle schools who do not contemplate continuing their schooling shall be given work by the government.

B. Workers' and Peasants' Short Course Middle School

Workers' and peasants' short course middle school, with a period of attendance of 3 to 4 years, shall offer an education equivalent to middle school education to worker and peasant cadres and production workers with elementary education who have taken part in the revolutionary struggle or in production work for a minimum length of time. Graduates may be admitted into various institutions of higher education by passing an examination.

C. Sparetime Middle School

Sparetime middle schools are divided into the two categories of junior and senior ones, which may be set up independently, with the time limit of attendance fixed at 3 to 4 years for each. They offer sparetime education equivalent to that of a junior or senior middle school to graduates of sparetime elementary or junior middle schools. The age of admittance may vary with different cases.

Graduates of sparetime junior middle schools may be admitted into senior middle schools, sparetime senior middle schools, or equivalent vocational middle schools; while graduates of sparetime senior middle schools may be admitted into various institutions of higher education after passing an examination.

D. Vocational Middle School

1. Technical schools (industrial, agricultural, communications, transportation, etc.):

Technical schools with a period of attendance of 2 to 4 years shall admit junior middle school graduates or candidates of corresponding qualifications. There is no over-all fixed age limit for admittance.

Junior technical schools with a period of attendance of 2 to 4 years shall admit elementary school graduates or candidates of corresponding qualifications. There is no over-all fixed age limit for admittance.

Graduates from junior technical schools and technical schools should serve in various production agencies. After a stipulated length of service, they may be variously admitted into technical schools, senior middle schools, or various institutions of higher education by passing an examination.

Short course technical training classes or make-up technical training classes may be established within various technical schools.

2. Normal schools with a period of attendance of 3 years shall admit junior middle school graduates or candidates of corresponding qualifications. There is no over-all fixed age limit of admittance.

Junior normal schools with a period of attendance of 3 to 4 years shall admit elementary school graduates or candidates of corresponding qualifications. There is no over-all fixed age of admittance.

Short course normal training classes with a period of attendance of 1 year may be established within normal schools or junior middle schools to admit elementary school graduates or candidates with corresponding qualifications; and elementary school teachers' refresher classes may be set up for the training of active elementary school teachers.

The period of attendance and the qualifications for admittance of the children's education normal school correspond to those of the normal school. Children's education normal courses may be set up within normal schools and junior normal schools.

Graduates from junior normal schools, normal schools, and children's education normal schools should serve in elementary schools or kindergartens. After a stipulated length of service they may be variously admitted into normal schools, senior middle schools, normal colleges, or other institutions of higher education by passing an examination.

3. The period of attendance and the qualifications for admittance, etc. of pharmacological schools and other intermediate vocational schools (trade, banking, cooperatives, fine arts, etc.) should conform to those stipulated for technical schools.

(4) Higher Education

Various institutions of higher education, that is, universities, specialized colleges, and technical colleges, are devoted to the implementation of higher education. Institutions of higher education are designed to offer students a high level of specialized education on an over-all foundation of general culture and knowledge, so as to train up for the nation reconstructional personnel with a high level of specialized knowledge.

Universities and specialized colleges with a period of attendance of 3 to 5 years (4 years in the case of the normal college), shall admit graduates from senior middle schools or candidates of corresponding qualifications. There is no over-all fixed age limit of admittance.

Technical colleges with a period of attendance of 2 to 3 years shall admit graduates from middle schools or candidates of corresponding qualifications. There is no over-all fixed age limit of admittance.

Special training courses, with a period of attendance of 1 to 2 years, may be set up within various institutions of higher education to admit graduates of senior middle schools or corresponding schools or other candidates of corresponding qualifications. There is no over-all fixed age limit of admittance.

Research departments, with a period of attendance of 2 years, may be set up in universities and specialized colleges to admit graduates from universities and specialized colleges or candidates with corresponding qualifications. Thus shall teachers for institutions of higher education and scientific research personnel be trained up in conjunction with the Academy of Sciences and other research agencies.

Preparatory classes or make-up classes may be set up in various institutions of higher education in order to help worker and peasant cadres, nationalities students, and overseas Chinese students. Work for graduates from institutions of higher education shall be allocated by the government.

(5) Various grades of political schools and political training classes are designed to offer young intellectual elements and old style intellectual elements revolutionary political education. The grading of the schools, period of attendance, and qualifications for admittance shall be separately stipulated.

Aside from the above-mentioned categories of schools, various levels of people's governments, with a view to meeting the needs for universal political study and professional study, may set up various categories and grades of make-up schools and correspondence schools. All levels of people's governments should set up special schools for the deaf, dumb, and blind, for the education of physically handicapped children, youths, and grown-ups.

It behooves the Ministry of Education to base itself upon this Decision and to take into consideration the actual prevailing conditions in various localities, in particular the conditions in various nationalities regions, to formulate plans for the implementation of this educational system and to formulate regulations for different categories of schools, which shall be submitted to the Government Administration Council for approval and implementation.

1.8 "Government Administration Council Directive on Reform and Development of Intermediate Technical Education"

Directive of Government Administration Council on reform and development of intermediate technical education:

Our state is in active preparation for large-scale economic construction. To foster technical personnel is the necessary condition for national economic construction while to train and foster large numbers of intermediate and junior technical personnel is, in particular, an urgent task at present. According to preliminary estimate, within the coming 5 to 6 years, around 500,000 intermediate and junior technical personnel will be needed for national economic construction. Our existing intermediate technical schools cannot by far meet these requirements both in quantity and in quality. On this account, the people's governments of all levels should lead the relevant departments to actively reform and develop intermediate technical education, thereby to solve the question of intermediate and junior technical cadres urgently required for state economic construction.

The "Decision on Reform of School System" promulgated by this Council on October 1, 1951 has clearly defined the position intermediate technical schools occupy in the school system, set forth as their task the fostering of intermediate and junior technical personnel in the sphere of industry, agriculture, communications and transportation, divided them according to grade into technical schools (equivalent to the grade of senior middle schools) and primary technical schools (equivalent to the grade of junior middle schools), and stipulated their school years and conditions for enrollment. Apart from implementing this Decision, the people's governments of all levels should, on the basis of the policies enumerated below, reform and develop intermediate technical education in a planned and systematic manner:

(1) With a view to satisfying the urgent demand of the state for technical cadres at present and to fulfilling in time the task of fostering large numbers of technical cadres for the state, the program for reforming and developing intermediate technical education at the present stage must be jointly carried out by relevant government departments as well as principal factories, mines, and farms under the direction and help of the education departments of people's governments and under a unified plan. In carrying out the educational policy, they must grasp the special feature of revolutionary construction during the early stage and adopt revolutionary methods. Apart from reforming and developing regular technical schools, they should, on the basis of practical needs, open short-course technical training classes of all types or add spare time technical classes in factories, mines, farms and various technical schools with a view to enabling regular, short-course and spare-time technical schools and training

---

"Government Administration Council Directive on Reform and Development of Intermediate Technical Education" [March 31, 1952], (NCNA, Peking, April 8, 1952), *Survey of China Mainland Press,* No. 313 (April 9, 1952), pp. 10-12.

classes to gain a proper and coordinated development. Premises and equipment for technical schools should be simple and utilitarian, personnel should be simplified and expenses economized where possible, courses and teaching materials should be adopted with attention paid to simplification and concentration and pedagogical method should be made practical as far as possible in order to fulfill the task of speedily fostering large numbers of technical cadres while maintaining the necessary level of intermediate technical education.

(2) Intermediate technical schools of all types and grades should, on the basis of concrete needs of various business departments, clearly lay down their policy and task and step by step realize specialization and simplification, and strive to unite study with application so that all their trained personnel will meet the needs of the business departments. Besides giving technical training to the students, intermediate technical schools should enforce political education as well as education on basic culture and scientific knowledge. Therefore, the courses of intermediate technical schools should comprise ordinary courses, technical courses and practice, thereby to correct and prevent the deviation of studying only technique to the neglect of political and cultural studies. The subjects of ordinary courses as well as the ratio of ordinary courses and technical courses should be determined according to the nature of the school, the students' standard and the length of school years. The schools must establish close connections with relevant factories, mines and farms, attach importance to experiments and practice about the same number of hours as lectures in technical classes. All existing intermediate technical schools should, according to the above principle, make appropriate adjustment of courses and improvement of pedagogical contents and methods, thereby to meet the needs of national construction.

(3) Intermediate technical schools of all types and grades should be guided jointly by the educational departments of the various grades of people's governments and relevant business departments under a unified policy. Questions relating to educational policy, system, pedagogical plan for ordinary courses in technical schools, national plan for school establishment and enrollment as well as questions relating to educational principles should be subject to decision by the Ministry of Education of the Central People's Government (except technical schools in the military system), and all local educational departments should lead the local technical schools to carry out the decisions of the Ministry of Education of the Central People's Government. Matters relating to establishment, change, and suspension of intermediate technical schools, curriculum, enrollment, business courses, experiments and practice, defrayal of expenses, appointment of personnel, distribution of graduates as well as other ordinary administrative affairs should, in principle, be directly decided by relevant business departments. All intermediate technical schools established hereafter should act in accordance with the above principle; all existing intermediate technical schools (including private institutions), which are under the leadership of the educational departments, should, in accordance with the above principle, readjust their leadership relations in a systematic manner and, pending the change in leadership relations, should adopt provisional measures to strengthen the connections between the business departments and technical schools. For the purpose of strengthening leadership over intermediate technical schools, the Ministry of Education of the Central Government as well as the educational departments of administrative regions and provinces should, in conjunction with personnel designated by relevant business departments of the same level, organize committees for intermediate technical education charged with the responsibility for studying and solving all important problems concerning intermediate technical education. The organizational rules for various grades of committees of intermediate technical education shall be separately provided. The relevant business departments of the Central Government, administrative regions and provinces (municipalities), should strengthen or add organs for manage-

ment of technical education if they have relatively more educational affairs to attend to; if their educational affairs are relatively few, they should also appoint special personnel to take charge of this technical educational work.

(4) Intermediate technical schools of all types and grades should take in a planned manner industrial workers with enough cultural standard, cadres who have joined the revolution for many years and model peasants into the schools to train them into technical cadres for state production-construction, offering them all kinds of facilities and necessary preferential treatment. All organs, bodies, factories, mines and farms should take the view of long-term interests of state construction and seriously recommend such personnel to study in intermediate technical schools.

(5) The Ministry of Education of the Central People's Government and the relevant business departments should proceed with the compliation of teaching materials for ordinary courses and technical courses in intermediate technical schools. The educational departments should be mainly responsible for compiling teaching materials for ordinary courses while the relevant business departments should be mainly responsible for compiling teaching materials for technical courses, but the educational departments and business departments should maintain liaison in this work. The business departments should mobilize a certain number of technical personnel in factories, mines and farms to teach in intermediate technical schools. Those personnel who concurrently act as teachers should be given remuneration according to regulations of the schools.

(6) Operational funds for intermediate technical schools should be defrayed by different grades according to the 3-level financial system. The relevant business departments of the Central Government, administrative regions, and provinces (municipalities) should take the funds for technical education as part of their construction funds and enter them into their budgets.

(7) In distributing the graduates of intermediate technical schools, the needs of local business departments should be met first as far as possible and necessary adjustment shall be made by the Central Government when necessary.

(8) The existing private intermediate technical schools and private technical make-up schools in various areas can play a certain role in fostering technical personnel: the people's governments of all levels as well as concerned business departments under their jurisdiction should encourage the establishment of such schools and should strengthen leadership over them in order to enable them to serve national construction in an effectual manner. Appropriate subsidies should be granted to those private schools with good record but really encountering financial difficulties.

(9) This Directive also applies to medical and other intermediate specialized schools (trade, banking, cooperatives, art) set forth in section 3 of ''d'' in items 3 of this Council's ''Decision of Reform of School System''.

(10) The Ministry of Education of the Central People's Government, should, in accordance with this Directive, draw up national enrollment plan for intermediate technical schools in conjunction with relevant business departments and report them to this Council for ratification and enforcement.

Premier   Chou En-lai

March 31, 1952.

1.9 "Directive of Ministry of Education on 1952 Plan for Training State Construction Cadres"

With the growing development of state construction work, the fostering of large numbers of senior and middle-level technicians becomes an urgent political task. On this account, all grades of educational administrations must lead their subordinate schools to strive to realize the 1952 plan for fostering state construction cadres. Now that summer vacation is approaching, this Ministry hereby issues the following directive on enrollment of students, construction of school buildings and distribution of teachers in various grades of schools in order to ensure success in the various phases of work:

1. Strict enforcement of centralized enrollment of students by colleges and intermediate schools is the key to the realization of this year's plan for fostering state construction cadres. On account of the fact that graduates from senior middle and junior middle schools are small in number this year while the enrollment in senior middle schools and junior middle schools is relatively large, failure to enforce centralized enrollment would lead to indiscriminate enrollment of students and might possibly make it difficult for higher normal schools and intermediate normal schools to fulfill their enrollment targets. To prevent such chaotic conditions, all districts must organize centralized enrollment committees this year (also to be participated in by all schools led by enterprises in various districts) for centralized distribution of students according to state plan for training of cadres in order to realize the plan for fostering cadres in a planned and systematic manner. In order to ensure colleges, particularly higher and intermediate normal schools, fulfillment of their enrollment targets by enrolling a certain number of senior and junior middle school graduates, all middle schools, besides conducting beforehand regular education on patriotism to the students, must also strengthen guidance of students' ideas with regard to higher education and mobilize and organize some students to enroll in normal schools as well as mobilize the students, in response to the call of fatherland, to enthusiastically go to the posts at which they are most needed by the state, and enable the students to understand that only this is most glorious and is the concrete expression of genuine patriotism. In distributing students, contact should be maintained with relevant quarters of other districts in order to ensure smooth progress of the enrollment work (For details, see the enrollment plans drawn up by this Ministry).

2. Concerning construction of school buildings, we must adopt the policy of principally utilizing existing school buildings to add more classes and secondarily providing construction of new buildings. The 3-anti and 5-anti campaigns have upset most of the building and repair organizations and as there are insufficient building funds and moreover time is very pressing now, if we do not adopt the policy of mainly utilizing available buildings to add classes, if we do not make full use of existing school premises (for instance, to add junior middle school classes, technical classes and teachers' training classes in primary schools with better conditions, to add senior middle school classes in junior middle schools, to add middle teachers' training classes in junior normal schools, to introduce two-shift system in cities, to utilize temples, public houses and houses confiscated during land reform in the countryside) and if we do not try to solve the problem by diverse methods, then we will find it very

"Directive of Ministry of Education on 1952 Plan for Training State Construction Cadres" [July 17, 1952], (NCNA, Peking, July 20, 1952), *Survey of China Mainland Press,* No. 379 (July 22, 1952), pp. 9-10.

difficult to solve the problem of school premises in time.

3. In order to fulfill this year's plan for training of cadres, it is necessary to adopt the following measures to solve the shortage of teachers:

a) Energetic adoption of the measure of employing local talents and promoting teachers to solve the shortage of school teachers, e.g. promotion of higher primary school teachers to be junior middle school teachers, of junior middle school teachers to be senior middle school teachers, of promoting elementary normal school teachers to be normal school teachers etc.

b) In distributing graduates of senior middle schools and normal schools during the summer vacation this year, all districts should select elite graduates according to quota to retain in the schools to be teachers on probation and political instructors.

c) Middle school staff members with senior middle school or college cultural level may be appointed as teachers.

d) Appropriately increase teachers' teaching hours, merge classes in the case of certain courses and reduce teachers' extracurricular task as far as possible in order to get more time for teaching.

e) Enlist unemployed intellectuals to serve as teachers after short training (nation-wide plan to be separately notified).

In short, the administrative departments of education of all levels should, according to needs of state construction, urge their subordinate schools to bring into full play the potentialities of manpower and resources through the application of revolutionary spirit and method, manifestation of creative spirit, detailed planning, and use of less money for more purpose, in order to realize the state plan for training of cadres.

In order to ensure organized progress of work, it is necessary to establish a strict system of seeking instructions and making report, under which all districts should report from time to time to this Ministry on progress of work and any difficulties encountered so that assistance may be rendered for their solution.

PART TWO

Strong
Russian
Influence
(1953-1957)

PART TWO
Strong Russian Influence (1953-1957)

Following the period of reorientation and reorganization, the new People's Republic of China formulated more ambitious programs of national construction and moved toward the centralization of power under the control of the Chinese Communist Party. Important political machinery was created to guide the centralization process; especially noteworthy in this respect were the Constitution of the New Democratic Youth League of China (1953), the Constitution of the People's Republic of China (1954), and the Constitution of the Communist Party of China (1956).

The Constitution of the New Democratic Youth League (adopted June, 1953) established the following general principles:

> The New Democratic Youth League of China is a mass organization of progressive youths, led by the Communist Party of China and is also the lieutenant and reserve force of the Party.
> The League shall assist the Party to educate youth in the spirit of communism. . . . They will follow the direction pointed out by our great leader, Chairman Mao Tse-tung, for the gradual realization of national industrialization and the gradual transition to socialism. . . . The Youth League, faithful to the principle of internationalism, will undertake to unite all democratic youths of the world and consolidate the Soviet-led democratic and socialist camp to safeguard world peace.[1]

Accoring to the Preamble of the Constitution of the People's Republic of China (adopted September, 1954):

> This Constitution consolidates the gains of the Chinese people's revolution and the new victories won in the political and economic fields since the founding of the People's Republic of China; and, moreover, it reflects the basic needs of the state in the period of transition, as well as the common desire of the broad masses of the people to build a socialist society.[2]

The 106 articles in four chapters which followed the preamble were a continuation and development of the Common Program of 1949. Specific mention was made of China's "indestructible friendship with the great Union of Soviet Socialist Republics"; it has been noted that much of the 1954 Constitution was copied directly from the Soviet Constitution of 1936 using different terminology. Winberg Chai offers the following illustration:

> For instance, the People's Republic of China is described as "a people's democratic state led by the working class and based on the alliance of workers and peasants" (Article 1), whereas, according to the Soviet Constitution, the "Union of Soviet Republics is a socialist state of workers and peasants" (Article 1). And again, the so-called "people's democratic dictatorship" in the preamble of the Chinese Communist Constitution is just another version of the Soviet Russian "proletarian dictatorship."[3]

The Constitution of the Communist Party of China (adopted September, 1956) affirms the movement toward centralization of power and control:

> The Party is formed on the principle of democratic centralism.
> Democratic centralism means centralism on the basis of democracy and democracy under centralized guidance. . . .
> Party decisions must be carried out unconditionally. Individual Party members shall obey the Party organization, the minority shall obey the majority, the lower Party organizations shall obey higher ones, and all constituent Party organizations throughout the country shall obey the National Party Congress and the Central Committee.[4]

Perhaps the highlight of Russian influence was China's adoption of its Soviet-inspired First Five Year Plan (1953-1957), which called for tremendous industrial and agricultural growth and served to further centralize the direction of the affairs of the nation under the leadership of the Party.

The Central Government announced that for 1953 educational work should follow the major policy of "readjustment and consolidation, development of the important points, qualitative improvement, and steady advance." One of the Ministry of Education's major self-criticisms was that educational efforts during the initial years suffered from a lack of planning, uniformity, and leadership—especially in the field of higher education. In 1953, the Ministry of Higher Education was established to assume responsibility for leadership in the field, and to overcome earlier tendencies toward a "prevailing deviation of bureaucratism."

Ma Hsu-lun, the first Minister of Higher Education, served as the spokesman for this new leadership and specified the direction for higher education. Ideological reform of teachers—which had indeed been a major emphasis—was to be continued and extended to those higher institutions which previously had not been subjected to ideological political reform. In September of 1951, Chou En-lai had outlined a program to reform the thinking of intellectuals and teachers—"thought reform"—by subjecting them to the dialectic struggle of "severe criticism and self-criticism," which C. T. Hu describes as "a method of mental coercion."[5] Efforts were made to select and train new teachers to meet the shortage of teaching personnel. There was to be a major readjustment to meet the critical need for training national construction personnel—especially in the field of engineering. Workers and peasant's short-course middle schools were to be "attached" to institutions of higher education, making them preparatory classes of a sort, with the objective being to increase the proportion of students of peasant and worker origin attending institutions of higher education. To improve the quality of pedagogy and teaching materials, Ma Hsu-lun called for a systematic study of the Soviet experiences in educational construction.

Extensive plans were made for translating Russian pedagogical outlines and curriculum materials. All this was to be carried out with the assistance of Soviet experts.

The major objective of national construction work in 1953 was economic development, especially industrial development (heavy industries). Educational construction work therefore focused on the improvement of technical education. During the period of reorientation and reorganization the China Democratic League (one of the "representative bodies" participating in the CPPCC of 1949, which later came under the control of the Communist Party) had directed its energies to the task of "national cultural-educational construction." The League now turned its attention to the training of "technically-qualified competent construction personnel." League members were urged to put technical activities under political direction (called the "union of politics with technical activities") and directed to study and learn from the Soviet Union.

Similarly, again using the now-familiar call to learn from the advanced educational experiences of the Soviet Union, the Ministry of Education issued a program for revising the middle-school teaching program. Readjustments were made regarding specific courses to be taught at various levels, and the number of teaching hours devoted to each course.

Elementary education had experienced a very rapid development during the preceeding two years. The quality of the existing teachers as well as the available school plants and equipment were not adequate to meet this new demand, especially in the urban areas. In November of 1953 the Central Government issued a directive for the organization and improvement of primary school education. The major effort at improvement was focused on schools in the cities in order to accommodate the needs of industrial national construction. The government would continue to operate schools but the base of operation was to be broadened to encourage the development of other non-government-operated schools (i.e. schools operated by industrial and mining enterprises, privately operated schools, locally operated schools, etc.). Given the needs of the nation, primary school students were to be made to understand that upon graduation most of them would have to take part in "labor production" rather than continue on to secondary education. Accordingly, efforts were made to "cultivate . . . the ideology and sentiment of love of labor."

Higher normal institutions for the training of secondary teachers had proven to be insufficient in quantity and quality to meet the demands of secondary education. To remedy this situation, the Central Government issued a directive concerning the improvement and development of higher education for teacher training. While the directive contained the theme of learning from the Soviet Union, it did caution that pedagogical reform should not merely copy the Soviet models without seriously considering how they relate to the "reality of China."

Normal schools were reorganized to meet the existing shortage of elementary school teachers and the growing demand for more and better-qualified primary school teachers. The major emphasis of this reorganization was to assure that the supply of normal-school graduates balanced with the regional needs of the nation. Thus, some new normal schools were to be established, certain existing ones were to be enlarged while others were directed to suspend enrollment, and other patterns of teacher training were encouraged—e.g. short-course teacher training and rotation training.

The decision had been made in 1949 to open the door of higher education to the workers and peasants. Education had become a "State Enterprise," a powerful weapon with which the State could educate the people and remold society. The major principle of socialist construction was to be continued, but the educational emphasis was to shift from that of remolding to one of progress and development. Both senior primary and junior middle-school graduates would increasingly be called upon to participate in industrial and agricultural production, rather than going on to continue their studies in a higher-level school.

The following selection from an editorial which appeared in *People's Daily* illustrates the nature of the relationship between education and productivity:

> The duty of New China's education is to raise the people's labor productivity. . . . All graduates . . . should positively engage in labor production and become politically-alert and educationally-trained builders of socialist society.
>
> The aim of our primary schools is to elevate the cultural level of the broad masses of our country enabling the workers, peasants, and other laborers to achieve a certain standard of political consciousness and cultural education so that they will have still higher enthusiasm and still better technique in socialist construction and become production experts in industry and agriculture. . . .[6]

Vice-Minister of Education Tung Shun-ts'ai summed it up as follows:

> The individual must bow to the interests of the country, and whatever lofty ideas an individual may have must be linked with the great ideal of Socialist and Communist construction.[7]

During this period the Ministry of Education promulgated a set of "Rules of Conduct" for primary-school students and another (though similar) for middle-school students, which identified "the basic principles of discipline, of study and of daily conduct." School officials (regional education departments, administrative officials, etc.) were charged with implementation of these rules, considered as a vehicle for: carrying on Communist morality, raising the political consciousness of the students, developing the spirit of collectivism, and cultivating both good character and good habits in students.

Teachers were to explain the meaning and purpose of the rules to their students, who were to be led to develop self-conscious observance of the rules. The principle of "positive education" was stressed. Teachers were urged to educate students by "inspiration and persuasion"; punishment was to be used only as a last resort. The various student organizations (Young Pioneers, NDYL, Students' Associations, etc.) were to foster observance of the rules and supervise student behavior. By maintaining close contact with parents of students, the school sought to acquaint parents with the rules and enlist their cooperation in helping to secure observance by students. Serious violators of the rules of conduct (whether primary- or middle-school students) were to be expelled from school.

China's First Five Year Plan (1953-1957) acknowledged the nation's backwardness and the problem of illiteracy. Widespread illiteracy was not simply a problem of general cultural education but an important obstacle to the attainment of economic growth through the application of technology to industry and agriculture. Thus, elimination of illiteracy among the masses of workers and peasants became a task of great strategic significance. The Central People's Government launched a movement to eliminate illiteracy within five to seven years—establishing priorities according to an individual's function (cadre, factory workers, etc.), residency (city, countryside, national minority region), and age (under 50, above the age of 50). Specific guidelines were established for the massive literacy campaign; the various provinces, municipalities and autonomous regions were required to submit their plans for implementing these guidelines to the State Council of the Central People's Government.

During this period China took the first steps toward reforming its written language. In 1940 Mao Tse-tung had stated that:

> . . . written Chinese must be reformed . . . and our spoken language brought closer to that of the people, for the people . . . are the inexhaustible source of

our revolutionary culture.[8]

The Committee for Reforming the Chinese Written Language published an outline for simplifying printed Chinese characters (the graphic symbol used in recording language). Simplification of characters, it was hoped, would enable the masses to learn the language more easily, thereby reducing illiteracy and facilitating popular education. A more widespread national written language reform was being planned and the introduction of an alphabetical romanization of Chinese characters was also being considered as a possible step in the language reform movement.

This period was also noted for the "Hundred Flowers Campaign," which took its name from the Party slogan: "Let a hundred flowers blossom and a hundred schools of thought contend." In May, 1956, Lu Ting-yi, then chief of the Propaganda Department of the Central Committee of the Chinese Communist Party, in a speech addressed to a gathering of Chinese intellectuals (scientists, doctors, writers, artists, etc.) enunciated the policy of "letting all flowers bloom together and all schools contend in airing their views."[9] Thus the Party officially advocated "freedom of thinking in literature, art, and scientific research; freedom of debate; freedom of creative work; freedom to criticize; freedom to express one's opinion, and freedom to maintain one's opinion and to reserve one's opinion."[10] So encouraged, many intellectuals accepted the invitation to participate in the "blooming and contending"—freely airing their views, performing creative works, and criticizing Party policies. However, there are limits to criticism, even in Marxism. Mao Tse-tung's February 27, 1957 speech, "On the Correct Handling of Contradictions Among the People," identified six specific criteria which could be applied to "determine what is right and what is wrong in our actions"—and clearly stated that the most important criteria were "the socialist path and the leadership of the Party."[11] Many intellectuals were subsequently attacked as revisionists or right opportunists for spreading "wrong ideas."

The goals of the First Five Year Plan could not be implemented without the aid of the Soviet Union. A steady stream of Soviet technicians, trainers, and advisors poured into China during this period. Chinese leaders openly praised developments in the Soviet Union and encouraged the people to learn from the Soviet Union. For example, Lu Ting-yi, then Chief of the Propaganda Department of the Central Committee of the Chinese Communist Party, made the following statement in a speech to a gathering of distinguished Chinese intellectuals:

> Learn from the Soviet Union! This is a correct slogan. We have already learned something, and in the future there are many things we should learn. The Soviet Union is the first Socialist state in the world and the leader of the world camp of peace and democracy. The rapidity of the development of its industry is the quickest. It has rich experience in Socialist construction, and many major departments of science have reached or exceeded the most advanced capitalist countries. Such a country and such a people are of course worthy for us to learn from. It would be a fundamental mistake if we did not learn from the Soviet Union.[12]

Unquestionably this period marked the "high tide" of Chinese borrowing and learning from the educational experiences of the Soviet Union.

Soviet influence on curriculum development in the People's Republic of China is captured in the following reflections of Chao Tzien:

> Since 1953, the Chinese People's Republic had asked the Soviet Union to send specialists to help in reforms. Within five years, there were approximately seven to eight hundred specialists arriving in the Chinese People's Republic to teach in higher institutions. They offered about nine hundred courses,

and edited close to seven hundred kinds of teaching materials. Although advisors, they had the actual controlling power over the entire curriculum. The Chinese People's Republic established thirty-seven training classes in which Soviet experts trained Chinese professors. . . . "Consultant groups of teaching and research" (the structure of each consultant group was based upon the Soviet system) were organized to select and prepare the actual teaching materials. All the teaching materials had to be approved by the consultant group.

As for curriculum, whatever the Soviet schools had, which the Chinese schools did not have, was added; whatever the Soviet schools did not have, which the Chinese schools had, was eliminated. . . . English, which heretofore had been the leading foreign language, was replaced by the study of the Russian language. [13]

Consequently, thousands of Soviet teaching guides and textbooks were translated and put into use in Chinese schools at all levels; Soviet materials and teaching methods were strongly recommended and their adoption urged, as illustrated by the following item which appeared in *Renmin Jiaoyu (People's Education)* in 1953:

Besides translating scores of course outlines used in the Soviet pedagogical institutes to serve as reference, it is still necessary to vigorously organize our resources to systematically translate Soviet teaching materials and, using Soviet teaching materials as our blueprint, step by step revise our own teaching materials in order to combine them with the actual conditions in China. [14]

Another interesting report of Soviet influence on curriculum appeared in *Kuangming Daily* of May 30, 1955:

. . . since 1953 when the Soviet Union promoted what was called Comprehensive Technical Education (which meant "to carry out thoroughly the basic policy of education to serve productive construction"), the People's Republic of China has followed suit. Therefore, in the curricula of middle and primary schools, natural sciences such as physics, chemistry, mathematics, physiology, etc. were classified as the basic subjects; language and literature, history and geography, general political knowledge, etc. were classified as social sciences; literature and arts were closely connected to Comprehensive Technical subjects. [15]

Many other examples can be found in the various summary reports on Chinese education during this period. For instance, numerous issues of *Renmin Jiaoyu (People's Education)* described how Soviet advisors played a leading role in educational conferences, how Soviet educators were invited to travel to many large cities to conduct meetings on pedagogical problems, and how Soviet experts helped to inspect Chinese schools and made suggestions for curriculum revision and improvement of educational practices. Delegations of Chinese primary and secondary school teachers were sent to Russia to observe Soviet practices in general education, polytechnic education, and teacher education. Upon their return to the People's Republic, they traveled extensively throughout the nation conveying their observations to other Chinese teachers. In addition, they made reports on their visits, and these reports were then compiled as study materials for teachers. [16]

Soviet influence on elementary and secondary teaching materials, especially textbooks, is illustrated in the following report prepared by the Union Research Institute of Hong Kong:

Beginning in 1953, all middle schools in the country adopted new teaching texts for science courses. These followed Soviet texts but with due consideration to actual conditions in China. Among the six newly prepared teaching texts, those on language study and history for primary schools will be experimentally adopted at selected key-points beginning in the next school year (1955-1956). The six new teaching texts mentioned include the following:

Han (Chinese) language, literature, and Chinese history, for junior middle school, world history for senior middle school, and language study (Book I) and history for primary school.

In the meantime, the textbooks on physics, chemistry, and algebra now used in senior middle schools were originally copied from Soviet textbooks. . . .

The textbook on geography now used in junior middle schools was re-written from the natural geography textbook prepared by the Soviet writers, Balikov and Borodin . . . .

In the textbook on language study, Book I, used in primary schools, there are two lengthy chapters which were originally translated from the textbook used in the first year class in Soviet primary schools. These chapters are Chapter XXX entitled "Big Carrot," and Chapter XXXIX entitled "Obey Mother's Word."

Outside of these instances, it may be mentioned that the language textbooks used in primary schools are replete with translated materials from Soviet texts.[17]

Education during the period from 1953 to 1957 was characterized by the call to learn from the advanced experiences of the Soviet Union. This was to be the high tide of Soviet influence on the People's Republic of China. However, tides ebb and flow. As Sino-Soviet conflicts increased, the relationship between the two nations deteriorated; Chinese education was soon to reflect the shift in China's national policy.

NOTES:

[1]"The Constitution of the New Democratic Youth League of China" (Passed at the 2nd All-China Congress of the NDYL), *Current Background,* No. 258 (September 10, 1953), p. 1.

[2]Winberg Chai (ed.), *Essential Works of Chinese Communism* (New York: Bantam Books, 1969), p. 271.

[3]Ibid., p. 269.

[4]Ibid., pp. 302-303.

[5]Chang-tu Hu, *China: Its People, Its Society, Its Culture* (New Haven: HRAF Press, 1960), p. 184.

[6]*Renmin Ribao,* S. M. Hu (trans.), May 25, 1954, p. 1.

[7]"National Secondary Education Conference Closed," NCNA, Peking (February 1, 1954), *Survey of China Mainland Press,* No. 747 (February 13-15, 1954), p. 29.

[8]Mao Tse-tung, "On New Democracy" (January 1940), *Selected Works of Mao Tse-tung,* II (Peking: Foreign Language Press, 1967), p. 382.

[9]Lu Ting-yi, *Let a Hundred Flowers Blossom, Let a Hundred Schools of Thought Contend* (Peking: Foreign Language Press, 1956), p. 2.

[10]Ibid.

[11]Mao Tse-tung, *On the Correct Handling of Contradictions Among the People* (Peking : Foreign Language Press, 1967), pp. 155-156.

[12]Lu Ting-yi, "Let All Flowers Bloom Together, Let Diverse Schools of Thought Contend" [May 1956], *Current Background,* No. 406 (August 15, 1956), p. 17.

[13]Chao Tzien, "Twenty Years of Communist Education," [Hong Kong] *Min Bao,* S. M. Hu (trans.), September 26, 1969, p. 3.

[14]Ch'in Hsuan-shan, "Normal Education in the Past Three Years," S. M. Hu (trans.), *Renmin Jiaoyu (People's Education),* (January 5, 1953), p. 23.

[15]*Kwangming Daily,* S. M. Hu (trans.), May 30, 1955.

[16]Theodore Hsi-en Chen, *Teacher Training in Communist China* (Washington, D.C.: Office of Education, 1965), p. 25.

[17]Chao Chung and Yang I-fan, *Students in Mainland China* (Hong Kong: The Union Research Institute, 1956), p. 55.

2.1 "The Policy and Tasks of Higher Education"

Comrades:

The Ministry of Higher Education has been set up for more than one month. . . . As decisions have in the main been arrived at with regard to the policy and tasks of educational work in 1953 and the principal points of our program for educational construction in 1953, I would now like to avail myself of the present occasion to transmit to you the necessary information for joint study, discussion and implementation. . . .

Following the start of large-scale, long-termed, and planned national construction in 1953, education must first be made to serve national industrialization to enable it to serve economic construction. Plans for cultural-educational construction should thus be formulated on the foundation of national economic development, the livelihood of the people, national financial resources, the availability of teachers, and other conditions. That is to say, these plans should be strictly based on "needs" and "possibilities." Following 2 recent months of hard work, the Central Government has in the main decided on the adoption of a plan for educational construction in 1953. . . .

Hereby I shall try to give a resume of the policy, tasks, important points of development, important points of our plan of work, and the important problems in the implementation of this plan, for national educational construction in 1953.

The program of national construction for 1953 has been carried out side by side with increased efforts designed to resist America and aid Korea. By taking into consideration the necessity to "fight as we build," the various degrees of serious deviations found in educational work, and the current needs of national construction and the prevailing conditions, it has been decided by the Central Government that educational construction in 1953 should be follow the policy of "readjustment and consolidation, development of the important points, qualitative improvement, and steady advance." In concrete work we should emphasize the strengthening of ideological political education, and carry out the study of advanced Soviet experiences and pedagogical reform by positive but appropriate measures in order to improve the quality of pedagogical work. I am of the opinion that this is pre-eminently the correct policy. On the basis of this over-all policy of work and these tasks, we must redouble our efforts to carry out the following aspects of work:

(1) Keep up the ideological reform of teachers in institutions of higher education. Ideological reform should be carried out in schools not subjected to ideological reform the previous year. On the basis of the preliminary stage of ideological reform, teachers should further make a systematic study of Marxism-Leninism and the thoughts of Mao Tse-tung. Numerous schools have been organized to study various documents of the 19th Congress of the Communist Party of the Soviet Union(B), Stalin's *Economic Problems of Socialism in the U.S.S.R.*, Stalin's *On Marxism and*

"The Policy and Tasks of Higher Education" (Address by Minister of Higher Education Ma Hsu-lun before discussion forum of university authorities of North China), Peking, *Jen Min Chiao Yu (People's Education)*, April 1953, *Survey of China Mainland Press*, No. 576 (May 22, 1953), pp. 23-27.

Problems of Philology, Mao Tse-tung's *On Practice, On Contradiction,* and other treatises. In coordination with the study of dialectical materialism, and historical materialism, further studies should be made of the above-mentioned treatises so to raise the ideological level of all teachers. In technical activities, all sorts of organizational forms and methods should be employed to strengthen the study program of active teachers and the work of teaching and research groups in schools. It should be further pointed out that, ideological reform and theoretical studies are not incompatible with the technical aspect of pedagogy and it is only by injecting ideological reform and theoretical studies into pedagogical activities that our ideological level will be raised and pedagogical activities turned into a success. It is accordingly wrong for certain people to consider pedagogical reform as simply "a change into the Soviet teaching material and teaching method."

(2) For the present, and in some years to come, the greatest difficulty in the development of higher education still lies in the lack of teaching personnel. What is then the solution? Aside from the attempt to rally, reform, and improve existing teaching personnel, efforts should be exerted for the selection and training of new teachers. For the present year, the Central Government shall be requested to permit the retention of larger numbers of university graduates in universities as assistants and graduate students so as to made into a new force among university teachers.

(3) Positive efforts must be exerted for the completion of the reform of senior and secondary education in specialized majors (first of all the engineering specialized majors), so that we will the better be able to shoulder the task of training national construction personnel. Within the present year, we shall basically complete the work of the readjustment of colleges and departments in institutions of higher education, the establishment of specialized majors in senior engineering schools, the experimental selective establishment of higher correspondent schools and night universities, and the readjustment and regulation of intermediate technical schools (principally intermediate engineering technical schools), so as to base our development on a solid foundation.

(4) Planned measures shall be adopted to carry out the decision on attaching workers and peasants short-course schools to institutions of higher education in the effort to turn them into preparatory classes for institutions of higher education, to carry out different pedagogical plans for different subjects, and whenever possible to admit production workers and labor models, so to increase the proportion of students of peasant and worker origin in our institutions of higher education. At the moment, many workers and peasants short-course schools attached to institutions of higher education are poorly managed. Of the many reasons, inadequate emphasis and inadequate strength on the part of the leadership authorities of institutions of higher education is an important factor. It is hoped that more attention will be paid to these aspects.

(5) The systematic study of advance Soviet experiences in educational construction. In this respect, though varying degrees of success have been scored by different schools, yet as a result of the lack of preparation, certain defects, as stated above, have also been found. We are now exerting all possible efforts to resolve the problems of pedagogical plan and teaching material. Pedagogical plans and outlines on various specialized majors which have been translated, are now being revised through our concerted efforts and with the assistance of Soviet experts, on the basis of the actual prevailing conditions, so as the better to meet the actual needs of institutions of higher education. Now, our strength is concentrated for the selective and planned translation of Soviet teaching material. For the present year, it is planned to translate some 200 kinds of teaching material within the engineering and

scientific fields and on some other subjects, so as to create the necessary conditions for the thorough implementation of pedagogical reform. The scope of the translation work should be extended whenever there are more original texts available, or when better translation and printing facilities are available.

Here, I shall give a resume of the important points of our program of higher educational enterprises for the present year.

Educational construction should be designed to complement economic construction; the focal point of economic construction lies in industrial construction; and the focal point of industrial construction lies in the heavy industries. It can thus be seen that the training of senior and intermediate industrial, mining and communications personnel should be elevated to a position of top priority in our higher education and intermediate technical education. In the second place, it is necessary to carry out the selective training of teachers in order to meet the needs of selective development. It is also necessary to train up health personnel to take care of the state of health of the ever-increasing numbers of cadres. Development must be selective since we shall not be able to accomplish anything should we try to do everything all at once. The rate of development should be determined by taking into consideration the basic prevailing conditions. In order to be assured of success, we must avoid the mistake of, being preoccupied with our needs without paying attention to the possibilities, and stressing quantity to the neglect of quality. In order to meet the over-all needs of educational enterprise for this year, it is necessary to differentiate between the urgent and the less urgent and to keep an eye on quality. This is not to say that no attention will be given to the less important schools and subjects, or that there is no need to make a success of them. To do so would again be mistaken. We must make our strength felt in all directions and try in all respects to fulfill our program. The following figures have to do with the development of institutions of higher education within the present year:

In 1953, the development of institutions of higher education throughout the nation is scheduled to register an increase of 8.9 percent by enrolling 70,000 new students in the following ratios: 30,000 new students of engineering, or 42.86 percent of the total number of new students; 18,300 new students for senior normal schools, or 26.14 percent of the total; 7,200 health students, or 10.29 percent of the total; 4,500 students of the natural sciences, or 6.43 percent of the total; 3,200 new students of agriculture and forestry, or 4.57 percent of the total; 3,000 new students of the humanities, or 4.28 percent of the total; 300 new students of the fine arts, or 0.42 percent of the total; 2,000 new students of finance and economy, or 2.86 percent of the total; 700 new students of politics and law, or 1 percent of the total; and 800 new students of physical culture, or 1.14 percent of the total. . . .

Comrades: we are entirely new to the task of proceeding from the plan-less to the planned and to working according to plans, and from blind development to proportionate development according to actual needs and existing conditions. For this it is necessary to go through a great change, or rather a fundamental change. That is to say, we must overcome the tendencies of blind development and willfulness, to abide strictly by our plans; and we must check the inclination to do things as we like and to do things as much or as little as we like. It is imperative to overcome self-center-ism so as to uphold and strengthen the over-all viewpoint. Should any one quarter, in being preoccupied with their sectional interests, try to act according to their wish, then the entire plan would be destroyed. We must also oppose the one-sided preoccupation with quantity to the neglect of quality. Above all, we must practice economy in the use of our human and material resources and try by all means to unleash our hidden strength in order to give full play to our capacity for work. All efforts should be exerted for the improvement of leadership, in the Ministry of Higher

Educations as well as in all universities and colleges, so as to be able to carry out faithfully the instructions of Chairman Mao on the rectification of bureaucratism and the all-out improvement of leadership method and leadership style of work. It is necessary to strengthen the work of survey and research, and to carry out penetrative investigation of work. Strict systems of submission of reports and requesting for approval should be enforced for the thorough consummation of our plans. It behooves the responsible personnel of all schools to examine pedagogical work regularly and in a planned manner, and to establish regular systems of work so as to eliminate precipitateness and confusion. In the attempt to improve effectively both our teaching contents and teaching method, increase teaching efficiency and improve the quality of teaching, and further consolidate unity between the teachers and the students, it is necessary to promote, regularly and under proper guidance, the practice of criticism and self-criticism between the teachers and the students, and to spread all kinds of advanced pedagogical experiences in the schools.

Comrades: in order to make a success of higher education, it behooves the Ministry of Higher Education to assume the responsibility of leadership, and it is for all the teachers and students of institutions of higher education to acquire the correct understanding, shoulder their responsibilities, and keep in step to work in unison. Only thus shall we be enabled to fulfill the glorious task entrusted us by the nation.

2.2 "Summary Report on Cultural-Educational Activities of Local Organizations of China Democratic League"

In March 1953, a conference for the discussion of the cultural-educational activities of the local organizations of the China Democratic League was convened by the China Democratic League Headquarters. The following is a summary of the report on these discussions.

I. A BASIC UNDERSTANDING OF THE CHINA DEMOCRATIC LEAGUE'S PARTICIPATION IN NATIONAL CULTURAL-EDUCATIONAL ACTIVITIES

(1) It is stipulated in the "Directive on the important points of activities in 1953" as issued by the Standing Committee of the Central Committee of the China Democratic League, that, with a view to carrying out positively the 3 major tasks of the nation in 1953, it behooves the China Democratic League to adopt the working policy of "facing culture and education." That is to say, under the leadership of the Communist Party of China, it behooves the China Democratic League to adopt as their central task the participation in the cultural-educational work of the nation. In the bigger cities provided with institutions of higher education, attention should in particular be paid to higher education construction work. . . .

"Summary Report on Cultural-Educational Activities of Local Organizations of China Democratic League," Peking, *Kuang Ming Jih Pao,* April 9, 1953, *Survey of China Mainland Press,* No. 560 (April 29, 1953), pp. 24-31.

II. THE UNION OF POLITICS WITH TECHNICAL ACTIVITIES

(1) When taking part in national cultural-educational construction (for the present mainly the pedagogical reform of institutions of higher education), it behooves the China Democratic League to mobilize League members and the masses rallied around the League to bring about a close union between politics and technical activities. Technical activities should thus be put under political direction; that is the standpoint, viewpoint and methods of Marxism-Leninism should be used to direct the technical activities and pedagogical activities; and at the same time to realize the political aim and fulfill the political mission of training national construction personnel and educating the younger generation, by means of technical activities and pedagogical activities. . . .

(2) On the problem of uniting politics with technical activities, 2 mistaken tendencies can be found within the China Democratic League: the mistaken tendency of indulging in empty talks about politics and working at technical activities in isolation, completely alienated from the technical activities and the realities; and the mistaken simple technical viewpoint which overlooks politics. As far as the League organization is concerned, the main deviation lies in the estrangement from the realities. This deviation is completely incompatible to the new era of the start of large-scale planned construction in China. It consequently is imperative to surmount the deviation of estrangement from the technical activities and from the realities, and thus to achieve a close coordination between the League's work on political ideology and its technical activities. This is the inevitable path for the thorough implementation of the work of the League. . . .

(3) While taking part in national cultural-educational construction and trying to make a success of technical activities, it is up to the more advanced members of the League to assist those who are not so advanced, and for the technically more proficient to assist those who are less proficient. All such individualistic ways of thinking as, "reluctance to be bothered," "reluctance to give," "individual perfection," and arrogance and pride, should be overcome. It behooves League members to set themselves up as models in work as well as in study in order to lead the rallied masses to progress. All the good experiences acquired by League members in work and study should be faithfully publicized and imparted to the masses outside of the League. Conferences for the exchange of pedagogical experiences and similar activities should also be undertaken by the League for joint participation by League members and the masses. At the same time, it is the duty of League members to employ suitable means to assist other League members and the masses in the solution of problems encountered in trying to make a success of pedagogical activities. In a work, it behooves the organization of the League and all League members to keep in close touch with the masses, assist the masses, and to unite and educate the masses rallied around the League, in the concerted effort to advance.

III. ON THE PROBLEM OF STUDYING AND LEARNING FROM THE SOVIET UNION

(1) Participation in cultural-educational construction is inseparable from studying and learning from the Soviet Union. As pointed out by Chairman Mao at the 4th Session of the National Committee of the China People's Political Consultative Conference, "we shall not only study and learn from the theories of Marx, Engels, Lenin, and Stalin, but we shall also study and learn from the advanced scientific technique of the Soviet Union." It is because that the Soviet Union is the first country in the world to have victoriously completed Socialist construction in its progress towards Communism, under the guidance of Marxism-Leninism. Inasmuch as the masses are

enabled to give full play to their creativeness and positive spirit as a result of the superiority of the Socialist system of society; and inasmuch as under this system, everything is for the good of the masses, it naturally follows that the scientific technique of the Soviet Union is the most advanced in the world and is all inclusive. Why shouldn't we study and learn from England and America? It is because that at the present moment, the political, social, and economic systems of England and America imperialism are in an extreme state of degeneracy, and their scientific technique is being daily left further behind.

To study and learn from the Soviet Union is a deciding factor in our glorious national construction. Chairman Mao thus declared, ''We have to carry out our glorious national construction; the work is difficult and we are inexperienced; consequently we must make a faithful study of and learn from the advanced experiences of the Soviet Union.'' As far as the cultural-educational circles are concerned, the study of the Soviet Union is a further development and a concrete manifestation of ideological reform of the intelligentsia. In our study of the Soviet Union, it is important to realize that the path of the Soviet Union at the present moment is precisely the path to be taken by the Chinese people, and that the Soviet Union's present is exactly our future. Only thus can we make a successful study of the Soviet Union. . . .

(2) As directed by Chairman Mao, in our attempt to study and learn from the Soviet Union, we must be both conscientious and faithful. By studying conscientiously, we mean to study with both feet planted solidly on the ground, to study both the spirit and the substance of the advanced experiences of the Soviet Union, and to avoid both formalism and dogmatism. By studying faithfully, we mean to study with resolute courage, facing the realities and the truth. It is like learning to swim, we must plunge into the water with the greatest of determination.

Only 3 to 4 months after the start of the readjustment of colleges and departments, quite a number of university teachers (some originally possessed of some knowledge of Marxism-Leninism, some with a very slight knowledge, and some without any contact with it) exhibited a conscientious attitude and adopted and correct method of study in the current study of the Soviet Union. They made a faithful study of Soviet science and pedagogical system and method; made a conscientious study of the spirit and substance of Soviet science and pedagogy, and learned to apply the Marxist-Leninist standpoint, viewpoint, and method to pedagogical activities; and to carry out pedagogical activities in a spirit of collectivism. By making the plunge and keeping up their efforts, they inevitably made rapid progress and attained definite success. However, taken as a whole, such people are rare for the present. It is accordingly imperative for the League to call upon everybody to emulate their superior examples, and to publicize their experiences.

(3) As a political party, how should the China Democratic League act to impel the movement for studying and learning from the Soviet Union? In the first place, regular discussions should be made of problems connected with the study of the Soviet Union in the basic organizational units of the League, and all League members should be mobilized to take the lead and set themselves up as examples. It is up to League members to take an active part in the study of the Russian Language and other such activities. In the second place, in the course of studying, all those who exhibit the wrong stand and employ the wrong method should be subjected to constructive criticism with intent to convince. All criticisms should be based on facts so that all those who are skeptical and conservative minded shall be convinced of the superiority and the advanced nature of Soviet science through their own experiences and the experiences of others. In the third place, in cooperation with the Communist Party, the Youth League, and the administrative authorities, regular investigations should be carried out to find out the effectiveness and the accuracy of the study of the

Soviet Union carried out in our pedagogical activities. Proposals of a constructive nature shall thus be made on the basis of these investigations. In the fourth place, typical experiences in the study of Soviet scientific technique should be regularly published in League publications, so that all those who did well in the study of the Soviet Union shall be publicly commended and mistaken views and attitudes criticized. In the fifth place, educational lectures or discussion forums on Soviet scientific technique should be staged in connection with various phases of technical activities.

In a word, the current central task of the China Democratic League lies in the mobilization of all League members and the masses rallied about the League so as to make a study of and learn from the Soviet Union, and in thus doing to create a new high tide in the universal attempt to study and learn from the Soviet Union.

2.3 "Ministry of Education Revises Middle School Teaching Program"

In order to meet the State requirement for training construction personnel, the Ministry of Education of the Central People's Government has completed revision of the draft middle school teaching program after a careful study and with reference to the Soviet advanced experience, and has issued the revised draft program to all middle schools throughout the country to be put on trial as from August. In the revised draft program, comparatively rational readjustments of the 1951 draft program have been made as regards the provision of courses and the number of teaching hours.

(1) In regard to mathematics, Analytical Geometry, a subject which belongs to the sphere of higher education, has been cancelled, and the number of teaching hours for Arithmetic, Algebra, Geometry and Trigonometry has been increased.

(2) In respect of biology, in junior middle schools the teaching of Human Anatomical Physiology (originally called Physiological Hygiene) has been postponed to the first year in senior middle schools, that of the Foundations of Darwinism has been postponed to the second year in senior middle schools; Botany and Zoology have both been made one and a half year courses (the number of teaching hours has been slightly increased), and a course on General Knowledge of Hygiene has been added to the first year curriculum in junior middle schools.

(3) The teaching of chemistry has been postponed to the third year in junior middle schools and the number of teaching hours has also been slightly decreased on the basis of actual conditions.

(4) In order to avoid repetition in the teaching of history, the courses of Chinese History and World History in junior middle schools have been changed to those of Ancient Chinese History and Ancient World History, while the history courses in senior middle schools will remain Modern World History and Modern Chinese History so that the students' knowledge of ancient and modern history may attain a rational proportion.

"Ministry of Education Revises Middle School Teaching Program" (NCNA-English [distributed in an English-language news release by NCNA], Peking, July 5, 1953), *Survey of China Mainland Press,* No. 629 (August 12, 1953), pp. 25-28.

(5) With regard to political science, Policy on Current Events, a very difficult course to teach, has been cancelled and instead a report on current events will be delivered at every weekly meeting. At the same time, the number of teaching hours for General Knowledge of the Chinese Revolution and the Common Program has been increased.

Apart from these changes, the number of teaching hours for Language, Physics and Geography, has been slightly changed. After the readjustment of the courses, the curricula for various classes have become lighter than before.

In order to avoid confusion in teaching during the trial period, the Ministry of Education of the Central People's Government has enacted the "Readjustment Measures for Trying the Revised Draft Middle School Teaching Program from August 1953 to July 1954," in which the courses that must be readjusted in the first year of trial, and their readjustment measures have been clearly prescribed.

The full text of the *Readjustment Measures* is as follows:

In order that the revised program will not give rise to confusion in teaching in the course of its first year's trial, the Readjustment Measures for Trying the Revised Draft Middle School Teaching Program from August 1953 to July 1954 are hereby provided in accordance with the past conditions of establishing curricula for the various classes in middle schools and with the present supply of text books. Within this year, the provision of curricula for various classes in middle schools will be carried out according to the revised program, with the exception of the following readjustments:

I.   *First year in junior middle schools.*

1. General knowledge of Hygiene shall not be offered for the time being.

2. In regard to History, Ancient Chinese History shall be taught.

II. *Second year in junior middle schools.*

1. During the first term the number of teaching hours for Botany shall be changed to two hours a week. The teaching of Zoology shall not commence until the second term even in schools where Botany has been taught in the first year.

2. In regard to History, Ancient Chinese History shall be taught in the first term, and Ancient World History in the second term.

3. Regarding Geography, the Geography of China shall be taught.

4. For General Knowledge of the Chinese Revolution, the "General Political Knowledge Reader," Vol. 1 (published by the People's Press), will be used as teaching material for the time being.

III. *Third year in junior middle schools.*

1. If Chemistry has been taught in the second year, no further instruction in this subject will be given. If Zoology has been taught in the second year, no further instruction shall be given, and instead Human Anatomical Physiology will be taught. But the latter will not be offered if Physiological Hygiene has been taught in the second year. If the courses of Chemistry and Physiological Hygiene have not been completed, they will be continued, and the number of teaching hours per week will be decided upon by various schools on the basis of their actual conditions, provided that they are less than the number of hours stipulated in this program. The hours thus saved may be added to the teaching hours for Geometry and Physics.

2. In regard to History, Foreign History will be taught.

3. In respect of Geography, World Geography will be taught.

4. For General Knowledge of the Chinese Revolution, "General Political Knowledge Reader" (published by the People's Press) or "Teaching Materials for Elementary General Political Knowledge" (published by the Youth's Press) will be used as textbooks.

IV. *First year in senior middle schools.*

1. If Physiological Hygiene has been taught in junior middle schools, Human Anatomical Physiology will not be offered. The Foundations of Darwinism, which should be taught in the second year in senior middle schools, will be taught in advance in the first year, and the number of teaching hours will still be two hours a week.

V. *Second year in senior middle schools.*

1. The number of teaching hours for Physics will be three hours per week.

2. If the Foundations of Darwinism have been taught in the first year, no further instruction will be given.

3. In regard to History, Contemporary History of the Soviet Union will be taught in the first term, and modern Chinese History in the second term.

4. Regarding Geography, Economic Geography of China will be taught.

5. If Map Drawing has not been taught in the first year, it may be offered with "Senior Middle School Textbook on Map Drawing," Vols. I and II, as textbooks for the first and the second term respectively.

VI. *Third year in senior middle schools.*

1. If Trigonometry has been taught in the first year, no further instruction will be given.

2. A total of five teaching hours a week will be given to Algebra and Geometry, and the distribution of hours between the two will be decided upon by various schools in accordance with their actual conditions.

3. The number of teaching hours for Physics will be five hours per week.

4. Regarding History, Modern World History will be taught in the first term with reference to "Condensed Teaching Material for Senior Middle School Modern World History, Vols. I and II, For Self Study" in the August number of "People's Education," and Contemporary History of the Soviet Union will be taught in the second term.

5. Geography will be added to the curriculum. Economic Geography of China will be taught two hours a week.

6. If Map Drawing has not been taught in the second year, it may be offered with "Senior Middle School Textbook on Map Drawing," Vols. I and II, as textbooks for the first and the second term respectively.

2.4 "Government Administration Council Directive Concerning the Reorganization and Improvement of Primary School Education"

In the course of the past four years, the primary school education of the country has been restored to a scale which surpasses the pre-liberation days. Students in primary schools now number over 55,000,000 which represents an increase of 155 percent compared with the number of primary school students of old China in the peak year (1946). Preliminary reform has also been carried out in respect of the contents of primary school education and the pedagogical method. Because most of the primary school teachers have taken part in various social reform movements and political studies, their political awakening has been further enhanced. They have contributed their great efforts to the education of the rising generation, and many of them have become the pre-eminent teachers of the people. The preliminary foundation for making the future primary school education a success has thus been set. It should be pointed out, however, that the present primary school education work is beset with numerous serious problems. On the one hand, the quality of the existing teachers is low and the school premises and equipment are poor. Because of the rapid development in the last two years, no adequate consideration has been given to solving the problems of teachers and school premises. As a result, the schools are in a chaotic state and the quality of teaching is rather poor. On the other hand, because the political awakening and the economic life of the masses have both risen, their demand for culture is daily on the increase. The schools presently available are therefore insufficient to admit all the children of the masses and the problem is especially acute in the industrial and mining districts and the big cities. All these difficulties are inevitable in the course of victorious development and we are quite capable of solving them step by step. It should be understood, however, that this state of affair will take a prolonged period of time and a good deal of efforts to rectify. To accommodate the principal problems known to be existing in the present primary school education, the following directive is hereby issued:

1) Primary school education constitutes the foundation of the whole educational construction. It has the task to educate the rising generation and to make healthy citizens of them for new China. Basing on the possibility of the present educational construction and the practical cultural demand of the masses, primary school education should in the course of the next several years carry out keynote development in a planned manner on the foundation of reorganization and consolidation.

Because of the industrialization of the country and the rapid growth of urban population, the ratio of increase in the number of schools is generally speaking lower in the cities than the villages in the past several years. Consequently, public schools should be adequately developed in the industrial and mining districts and the cities, especially the large cities. Because of the general shortage of teachers and school premises at the moment, the various places must adopt positive measures to keep the children who reach school age and the graduates of junior primary schools suitably provided with schooling facilities in accordance with the concrete conditions of their places. These measures should include the reorganization of classes, the increase of number of students taken in, the adoption of the two-session system, the opening of evening schools, helping the industrial and mining enterprises as well as the organs and organizations to run their schools, helping the private schools, allowing the

---

"Government Administration Council Directive Concerning the Reorganization and Improvement of Primary School Education" [November 26, 1953], (NCNA, Peking, December 14, 1953), *Survey of China Mainland Press,* No. 726 (January 13, 1954), pp. 19-24.

masses and the industrialists and merchants to continue operating their schools, and other practicable methods.

In the rural villages, in order to suitably solve the question of schooling for the children of the peasants, the principle of voluntariness and need should be based upon to promote the operation of primary schools (including full-scale primary schools) by the people, so that the masses may fully manifest their positive desire to operate schools. The people's governments of the various places must appreciate their importance and work to intensify guidance towards helping the solution of the problems of teachers and teaching materials. In the case of public schools in rural villages, with the exception of the school-short national minority areas and old revolutionary bases where more schools should be adequately built, all the other districts should concentrate on reorganization and elevation without attempting further development.

2) Because of the unbalanced development of our economy, the development of primary school education is also off balance. We should base on the dissimilar conditions to carry out primary school education with different forms and demands, since it is impractical to demand uniformity for all the primary schools in the country. Hereafter, emphasis should be given to the successful operation of the primary schools in the cities and the industrial and mining districts as well as the full-scale and central primary schools in the villages. In the rural villages, apart from centrally operating the regular primary schools, steps may also be taken to operate dispersed and non-regular primary schools like half-day classes, morning schools, evening schools, etc.

3) Primary school education is the fundamental education for the people. In a considerably prolonged period to come, most of the primary school students will have to take part in labor production after their graduation, and only part of them can find a place in a higher school. In their ordinary education therefore, the schools should not make one-sided emphasis on how the students should plan for further study in a higher school after graduation. Rather, they should emphasize the need of planning for labor production upon graduation. This is necessary to cultivate the students with the ideology and sentiment of love of labor, to make them become accustomed to labor and to overcome their present tendency to belittle physical labor. At the same time, this reasoning must be clearly explained to the masses. From now on, the people's governments of all levels and all the primary school teachers should carry out this publicity and educational work among the masses and the primary school students.

4) The overwhelming central task of a school is to teach. This is also the principal task for the school principals and teachers, while the principal task for the students is to learn. In order to rectify the biased tendency of the teachers and students in indulging in too many social and non-pedagogical activities, to overcome the prevailing confusion in the schools, to carry out pedagogical work successfully, to elevate the pedagogical result and to improve the health of the teachers and students, the following measures are specially provided:

a) Primary school work and study should be centrally led and arranged by the educational administrations. Other units and organizations must have no direct part in the arrangement of school work so that the carrying out of school work plan would not be obstructed.

b) The time devoted by a teacher to social activities inside and outside the school must not exceed 12 hours a month while the school is open. In the case of summer and winter vacations, the time spent in social activities must not exceed one-sixth of the whole vacation (the time consumed in make-up study during the vacation should be included). During the school session, the time devoted by a student to social activities inside and outside the school must not exceed one and a half hours per week.

c) The primary school teachers must not be required to change their job at random so that they may settle down in their work to get acquainted with the conditions of the children and to raise their pedagogical attainment.

d) The classrooms and offices of a school must not be lent out at random while the school is open. In the eve t that such lending is necessary, this should be done only when the classes are not in session to ensure that the teaching of the teachers and the study of the students are in no way obstructed.

e) The non-pedagogical organizations of a school should be simplified appropriately, and the number of meetings and the number of posts concurrently taken up by the teachers should be reduced.

f) The schools of all places should coordinate the conditions of their places with the pedagogical plan stipulated by the CPG Ministry of Education to formulate their curricula and teaching program and to base on same to set up systems governing attendance, leave, and verification of attainment. Apart from the holidays stipulated by the government, the schools must not suspend classes or declare holidays indiscriminately, and the teachers must not absent themselves from classes at will. During the busy farm season, the rural primary schools may declare holidays at their discretion or allow the older children to absent themselves from classes to enable them to help their families in production.

g) The pedagogical method must be improved upon. This calls for the practice of serious lesson-preparing and teaching and the promotion of intuitional teaching by the teachers. The teachers should lead the students to collect and make by themselves specimens and simple models.

h) The method of painstaking persuasion should be relied upon in implementing the teaching and management of the primary school students. Such vulgar methods as corporal punishment and "struggle" must be prohibited, but the adoption of an indifferent attitude must also be opposed. Disciplinary education should be strengthened so that the students may be cultivated to acquire the habit of consciously obeying discipline. The good habit of making the teachers love the students and the students respect the teachers to bring the students and teachers into fraternal unity should also be promoted.

i) The schools should strengthen their sports and athletic as well as their ex-curricular cultural and recreational activities and see to it that the teachers and students are suitably rested after school and on Sundays. This is essential if the health of the teachers and students is to be maintained and the sound development of the students in body and mind is to be ensured.

5) The elevation of the quality of the primary school teachers is a determining factor for the successful operation of primary school education. Hereafter, the teachers must be led and organized to carry out their studies in a planned manner to elevate their political, cultural and business level. Teachers who are graduates of junior normal schools and above should pay special attention to study politics and business, while the primary concern for those teachers with a lower standard is to study the lessons of the junior normal school with the object of bringing himself up to the level of a junior normal school graduate. There are three methods which can be used to organize these teachers to take up the study of the lessons of a junior normal school. The first is to transfer the teachers with senior primary school standard to a junior normal school. The second method is to operate a teacher training class and give the teachers with junior middle school standard (first and second year) from one

to two years of training. The third method is to set up afterwork schools and correspondence schools for the teachers to advance their studies and have the teachers organized to take up studies as they work. The work to elevate the quality of the teachers is a prolonged and regular task which cannot be speedily accomplished with too high demands set all at once. Attention should also be paid to coordinate the work with the practical conditions to prevent it from becoming formalistic.

The ranks of the primary school teachers should be suitably reorganized. Positive steps should be taken to help those who have too low a cultural level and are actually incapable of taking up teaching work to further their studies or to change their occupation. Those who are fit to return home to take up production work should be mobilized to take that direction. Those who are old and infirm and are unable to carry on with their work, and those with serious contagious diseases which constitute a menace to the health of the children should be suitably disposed of according to the concrete conditions. In the case of teachers who are required to seek further study or to change their occupation, apart from granting the necessary travelling allowance, they should all be paid one month's salary as subsistence allowance. In the case of those who are required to return home to take part in production, apart from the necessary travelling allowance, they should be paid two months' salary as subsistence allowance. In reorganizing the ranks of the teachers, great care must be exercised to avoid the occurrence of chaos. All the teachers who are retrenched must be disposed of in a positive and responsible manner. Before their final disposition is made, they must be paid their original salary and must in no case be left uncared for.

6) There are at present quite a large number of over-age students in the rural villages. This is a good phenomenon which reflects the cultural demand of the laboring people after the victory of the revolution. The People's Government should take care of them. Consequently, these over-age students must be allowed to remain in school to continue their study, and positive measures must be taken to have them successfully taught. In no case must we adopt the irresponsible and negligent attitude which seeks the expulsion of these students. In order to have these over-age students better organized in study, in places where there is a large number of over-age students and an adequate supply of teachers, rapid course classes may be organized to accommodate them, or alternatively, independent rapid course primary schools may be operated to serve the purpose. In places where there are rapid course classes, rapid course schools and satisfactorily operated regular people's schools, no children should in future be admitted if they exceed the age of 12 full years in the case of junior primary school and the age of 16 full years in the case of senior primary school. The same principle should apply to children who seek to enter a higher grade in these schools. In places where there are no rapid course classes, rapid course schools and regular people's schools, care should be taken to have the over-age students suitably accommodated. To ensure the sound development of children in body and mind, children who have not reached the school age should in future be strictly barred from entering these schools.

7) It has been found from the conditions of enforcement that in view of inadequate preparation made in the matter of teachers and teaching materials, it is unsuitable to press for the continued enforcement of the system of a five-year straight course for primary school. Consequently, as from the current school year, the enforcement of this system should be temporarily suspended. The primary school should continue to adopt the system of four years for junior primary school and two years for senior primary school.

8) Practical concern must be shown toward the political and material treatment for the primary school teachers. Cadres of all levels and the masses of the people should

recognize that the primary school teachers have the responsibility to foster the rising generation and that a glorious and ardous task is on their shoulders. They should be respected so that their zeal to serve the people may be intensified. Any action to discriminate against and cast away the primary school teachers is a mistake and should be corrected. Generally speaking, the salaries for the primary school teachers should be maintained at their present level, but in the case of teachers who have a large family to support and are therefore in a specially difficult position because their salaries constitute their sole means of income, a suitable subsidy should be granted them. On the completion of the primary school reorganization work, steps may be taken to determine their grades according to the professional ability of the teachers and their years of service. In the case of the few whose salaries are too low, suitable readjustment may be made with due consideration given to the local conditions and the budgetary appropriation of the next fiscal year.

9) Concerning the management of appropriations for primary school education, as from January 1, 1954, the various places should include them in the various budgets according to the relations of their schools with the administrative leadership. In the case of public schools in cities, the expenditure incurred in connection with school equipment and the repair and construction of school premises should be borne by the budgetary expenditure of their respective municipal or *hsien* governments. In the case of public schools in villages, the expenditure incurred in connection with the repair and construction of school premises and the purchase of additional equipment should be borne by the *hsien* people's governments. When sufficient funds are not available for the purpose, the masses may be asked to donate on a voluntary basis the amount required for the purchase of materials, or alternatively the method of requiring the masses to donate labor and material may be adopted. In the case of *hsien* which have reserved land to meet emergency requirements in the course of land reform, part of the land should be allotted for use as school land to make up the expenditure incurred by the primary schools.

10) The reorganization and improvement of primary school education is an arduous and delicate work. The various provincial and municipal people's governments should attach great importance to it and strengthen their leadership over the work. First, they should investigate, study and grasp the conditions. Such basic figures as the number of primary schools, the number of classes and the number of students, teachers and employees must be clearly investigated. The concrete conditions of the various places should then be based on to carry out keypoint experiments. With experience thus acquired, plans can then be drawn up for systematic and careful enforcement. This work should be basically completed in the first half of 1954.

11) In order to strengthen the leadership over primary school education, the various places must pay attention to strengthen the leadership of the educational administrations of the *hsien* level and below. In the course of the next year or two, vigorous steps should be taken in a planned manner to replenish and strengthen the educational administrations of the *hsien* level with cadres who are comparatively strong in the political and professional sphere. The educational establishments should be positively helped to set up systematic and regular work. The allocation of too much work to them should be avoided. They should be urged to study diligently their own business so that they may get familiar with the things they are unfamiliar with and acquire a knowledge of what they do not know. The cadres of the educational administrations of the *hsien* and *chu* level must not be transferred at random. This is necessary to keep them acquainted with their business and to ensure that the leadership work of people's education is satisfactorily carried out.

Dated December 11, 1953   Premier Minister   Chou En-lai

2.5 "Government Administration Council Directive Concerning the Improvement and Development of Higher Education for Teacher Training"

Our country has entered into the period of planned economic construction. According to the general line and general task of the state during the transition period and the basic tasks of the first five-year construction plan, the basic tasks of our educational enterprise call for the vigorous fostering of construction personnel and the gradual elevation of the cultural level of the people. Higher education for teacher training holds the key to the successful development of secondary education which has much to do with the fostering of construction personnel for the nation and the elevation of the cultural level of the people. The quantity and quality of the higher normal institutions have therefore a direct bearing on secondary education and the fostering of the rising generation of new China. They have also an indirect bearing on the development and elevation of higher education, and hence the fulfillment of the plans for fostering construction cadres and for national construction. During the past four years, the speedy rehabilitation of our higher normal institutions have met with great development. There are now 31 higher normal institutions with students more than double those of old China at the peak year (1946). During the past four years, over 20,000 graduates have been made available to keep the secondary schools partially supplied with teachers. At the same time, the higher normal institutions have carried out a series of reforms like the ideological remolding of teachers, college reorganization and pedagogical reform, with considerable success. At the present moment, however, the higher normal institutions are far insufficient in quantity or quality to meet the demand of the secondary schools. Consequently, the development and elevation of higher education for teacher training to meet the needs of national construction is a task of utmost importance in the present educational construction. For this purpose, the following directive is issued:

1) Hereafter, the work of higher education for teacher training should adopt the policy of vigorous development on a well planned and prepared basis based on reorganizing and consolidating the present higher education for teacher training in accordance with the needs and possibilities. It should be affirmed that in order to meet the needs of national construction, higher education for teacher training must hereafter be vigorously developed with simultaneous attention given to reorganization and consolidation to enhance its quality. In a number of years to come, the development of higher education for teacher training will primarily rest with the expansion of the existing schools, with the construction of new schools in a well prepared manner ranked next in importance. It is wrong to entertain the conservative thought which neglects the construction needs of the nation and makes no attempt to manifest the potentials, to create conditions, to overcome difficulties and to seek vigorous development. It is also wrong to indulge in blind and adventurist progress and the tendency to over-stress quantity and to neglect quality based purely on subjective desire with no consideration shown to the possible conditions.

2) In order to keep the supply and demand of teachers for middle schools on balance, we must continue to operate the four-year regular collegiate course, the two-year special course and normal institutes with two-year course in accordance

---

"Government Administration Council Directive Concerning the Improvement and Development of Higher Education for Teacher Training" [November 26, 1953], (NCNA, Peking, December 14, 1953), *Survey of China Mainland Press,* No 726 (January 13, 1954), pp. 16-19.

with the present system governing higher normal institutions. Apart from this, a number of provisional transitional measures must be adopted on the principle that the specified quality is upheld. These include the graduation of regular collegiate course students one year in advance, the selection of part of the special course graduates to serve as teachers in senior middle schools, and the arrangement to provide selected teachers from junior middle and primary schools with short-term training to foster them as teachers for senior and junior middle schools. The various places should base on the needs and possibilities of their places to formulate concrete plans and submit them to the CPG Ministry of Education for approval and enforcement.

3) The comprehensive universities have the task to foster part of the teachers for secondary schools. Concrete measures studied and formulated jointly by the Ministry of Higher Education, the Ministry of Education and the Ministry of Personnel should be submitted to the CPG Committee of Cultural and Educational Affairs for approval and enforcement. The institutes of physical culture and the institutes of fine arts have also the task to foster a specified number of physical instructors and music and fine art teachers for the secondary schools. This should be studied and formulated jointly by the GAC Commission of Physical Culture, the Ministry of Culture, the Ministry of Higher Education, the Ministry of Education and the Ministry of Personnel and their decision should be submitted to the GAC Committee of Cultural and Educational Affairs for approval and enforcement. Apart from this, in the course of retrenchment carried out by the CPG and the local organs and organizations, the CPG Ministry of Personnel and the personnel organizations of all levels should undertake to pick out a number of personnel with suitable qualifications and arrange for their transfer to take up teaching work in the middle schools. This is one of the methods we can use to make up the shortage of teachers presently experienced by the middle schools, and the people's governments of all levels should pay attention to make a success of the work.

The problem of teachers for higher normal institutions holds the key to the successful development of higher education for teacher training. The various higher normal institutions must seriously enforce the policy of uniting and remolding the intellectual elements. They should also strengthen their leadership over the political and theoretical study of the teachers to elevate the political and business level of the existing teachers. There exists right now the phenomenon of disunity between the old and new teachers. This must be vigorously corrected. The old and new teachers should respect each other and learn from each other to absorb what they lack. They should unite to make the education work a success. In order to cope with the future development of higher education for teacher training, all the higher normal institutions with the necessary conditions should plan for the vigorous development of new teachers. Basing on the future need for development of higher education for teacher training, the Ministry of Education should formulate concrete plans for fostering post-graduate students and assistants for enforcement by the higher normal institutions to solve the problem of teachers for higher normal institutions. Apart from this, the comprehensive universities and other institutions of higher education as well as the institutions and organizations for scientific research should undertake to foster part of the teachers for higher normal institutions. The Ministry of Higher Education, the Academia Sinica, the Ministry of Education and the Ministry of Personnel should jointly study and define the concrete measures and submit them to the GAC Committee of Cultural and Educational Affairs for approval and enforcement.

4) In order to elevate the quality of higher education for teacher training, the various higher normal institutions should continue to overcome the bustling phenomenon, set up the essential working system and intensify the study of discipline. They should especially grasp the central link of pedagogical reform and use the Marxist stand, viewpoint and method to transform the old pedagogical contents,

organization and methods in order to cope with the demand of national construction. When enforcing pedagogical reform, they should seriously and systematically study the advanced educational theories and experiences of the Soviet Union and closely link them to the reality of China, particularly the actual conditions of the secondary schools and the higher normal institutions. It is wrong to make formalistic and mechanical use of the Soviet experiences and educational theories without seriously studying them to comprehend their essence and without linking them to the reality of China. Pedagogical reform calls for steady progress. We must also oppose the conservative ideology which stands for the status quo and abhors change.

Pedagogical reform should pay special attention to the reform of pedagogical contents. This first calls for the determination of pedagogical plans, of pedagogical programs and of textbooks. The CPG Ministry of Education must promulgate a provisional pedagogical plan for normal institutions in the near future and must revise the provisional pedagogical plan for normal institutions some time next year. Because the conditions available to the various higher normal institutions are dissimilar, there is no way to make their pedagogical plans uniform at the moment. The various higher normal institutions should base on the provisional pedagogical plan promulgated by the CPG Ministry of Education to formulate their own pedagogical plans according to the conditions available to them and submit them to the Ministry of Education for examination and approval. The Ministry of Education should be responsible for the organization of the teachers of the various higher normal institutions to compile their pedagogical programs and textbooks in a planned and systematic manner. It must complete also the formulation of a pedagogical program and the compilation and translation of the textbooks and lectures of part of the major subjects in five years' time. Right now, the work to effect the exchange of teaching materials should be organized to facilitate teaching. Simultaneously with the revision of pedagogical contents, the pedagogical organization and the pedagogical method should be suitably reformed. The pedagogical research team is the principal form of organization for strengthening pedagocial work and an important medium to manifest collective strength and to elevate the level of the teachers and the quality of teaching. Adequate attention must be paid to make full use of the organization.

5) In order to strengthen the leadership and management of the higher normal institutions, and in order to show how the schools can be positively managed locally, the higher normal institutions should, according to the principle of united leadership and management by strata, be placed under direct local management subject to the consolidated leadership of the CPG. In placing all the higher normal institutions under its consolidated leadership, the Ministry of Education seeks primarily to control their methods, policies and plans, to guide their educational work and to determine their teaching materials. The measure of placing higher normal institutions under direct local management may be determined by the administrative regions according to the conditions of the places. They may be placed under the united management of the regional committee, or the direct management of the provincial (municipal) people's government subject to the planned consolidated supervision of the region. The Ministry of Education should base on the above mentioned principle, with due consideration given to the dissimilar conditions of the various areas, to stipulate how the higher normal institutions should be led by the educational administrations of various levels and how their duties should be divided, and communicate their decision to the GAC Committee of Cultural and Educational Affairs for approval and enforcement. The educational administrations of the regions, provinces and municipalities must designate special personnel to undertake the management of the higher normal institutions. Under the consolidated plan of the state, the various places should in future work positively for the successful operation of the normal institutions in their places and for the gradual attainment of self-sufficiency in teachers for middle schools. Because of the unbalanced development of higher

education for teacher training in the various areas, for a period of time to come, the distribution of graduates from higher normal institutions should follow the principle of local distribution and centralized adjustment. Concrete measures in this respect should be jointly devised by the Ministry of Personnel and the Ministry of Education.

6) In order to operate the higher normal institutions successfully, the educational administrations of various levels and the higher normal institutions should continue to step up their struggle against bureaucratism, subjectivism and dispersionism and work practically for the improvement of their leadership method and style. The educational administrations of the people's government above the provincial (municipal) level should strengthen their leadership, control and check up on the higher normal institutions under them. The presidents of the various higher normal institutions should, under the ideological guidance of Marxism-Leninism and in compliance with the educational programs and policies of the People's Government based on the general line and general task of national construction during the transition period, strengthen their political, ideological and administrative leadership in school work and satisfactorily combine their political leadership with their administrative leadership. They should raise their solidarity and manifest all the strength of their schools in a common effort to fulfill the educational plans of their schools.

Premier   Chou En-lai

Dated December 11, 1953.

2.6 "National Secondary Education Conference Closed"

The National Secondary Education Conference was brought to a close on January 27. Basing on the directive of Vice Premier Kuo Mo-jo of the GAC and the report of Vice Minister Lin Li-ju of the CPG Ministry of Education concerning the basic conditions of secondary education in the country and its future programs and tasks, discussions were carried out by the conference. Vice Chairman Hsi Chung-hsun and Secretary-General Chien Chun-jui of the GAC Committee of Cultural and Educational Affairs were present at the meeting to give important instructions on how secondary education should serve the general line. A report on how the NDYL organizations in schools could be brought into better coordination with the school administrations to make a success of pedagogical work was delivered by Secretary Hu Ke-shih of the NDYL Central Committee, while a report on educational work for returned overseas Chinese students was made by Vice Chairman Liao Cheng-chih of the CPG Commission of Overseas Chinese Affairs. The conference invited Soviet expert Professor Chuikov to give an account of the development of general education in the Soviet Union and of experience gained in pedagogical and school administration leadership. Finally, a summing up report was made by Vice-Minister Tung Shun-ts'ai of the CPG Ministry of Education.

After due discussion, the conference defined the nature of the present educational work and how secondary education should serve the general line. It considered that since the establishment of the People's Republic of China, our school education had

"National Secondary Education Conference Closed" (NCNA, Peking, February 1, 1954), *Survey of China Mainland Press*, No. 747 (February 13-15, 1954), pp. 27-29.

become a State Enterprise of the working class under the consolidated leadership, construction and control of the State. School education is employed as a powerful weapon by the State to educate the people and to remold the society. It adopts the cultural ideology of the working class, that is the Communist ideology, as its leading ideology. The school education of the past four years is basically consistent with the spirit of the general line for the transition period and the principle of socialist education. The future problem for the existing schools is not one of remolding but one of progress and development. Under the illumination of the general line, these schools should continue to serve the socialist construction enterprise and keep the nation supplied with a regular flow of construction personnel. At the same time, on the foundation of production development, they should work for the continued and incessant elevation of the cultural level of the people and their socialist awakening.

The future programs and tasks for secondary education were defined by the conference. The policy of the present secondary education work is to base on the general line and general task of the nation for the transition period and the foundation of reorganization and consolidation to work for the positive elevation of the quality of the middle schools, particularly of the senior middle schools, the full-course middle schools, and the rapid-course middle schools for workers and peasants. Planned and pilot development should also be made in accordance with the needs and possibilities. In order to cope with the demand for the socialist industrialization of the nation, greater importance should in principle be attached to the development of senior middle schools than that of junior middle schools and of those in the big cities and industrial and mining districts than those in the ordinary districts. Adequate attention should be paid to the culturally backward national minority areas and the places which are particularly backward in culture. Concerning the future basic policy on the subject of outlet for the senior primary and junior middle school graduates, the conference was of the opinion that on the one hand, ways and means should positively be devised to enable part of these graduates to carry on their studies so that the cultural demand of the masses might be suitably satisfied. On the other hand, steps should be taken to explain to all, simultaneously with the publicity on the general line, that since only part of the senior primary and junior middle school graduates could carry on their studies in a higher school, they should play a positive part in production labor. At the same time, the students who do not go to a higher school should be helped to find employment. Basing on the needs of the nation for industrial and agricultural production and the possible conditions governing the future development of education, the senior primary and junior middle school graduates should in the main be organized to take part in industrial and agricultural production.

According to the decision of the conference, the present task of secondary education calls for the education of the students with the spirit of the general line of the nation for the transition period with the object of having them fostered as overall developed new men to take a positive part in the socialist construction of the country and the defense of the fatherland. In order to attain this target, the conference pointed out that overall education should be carried out in the middle schools. This means the carrying out simultaneously of ideological and political education, of cultural and scientific education, and of physical culture and health education. The conference was of the opinion that the ideology of the working class must be coordinated with the reality of China and the ideological conditions of the students to give the students concrete and penetrative ideological and political education for the purpose of elevating their socialist consciousness. At the moment, main emphasis should be given to strengthen the education of the students in patriotism, labor, collectivism, and discipline. The students must be made to love their fatherland fervently and to understand that with the fatherland entering into a new epoch of socialist industrialization and socialist remolding, their tasks will be even more arduous. The youths must make a success of their studies and correctly solve the problem of their relations with the country. The individual must bow to the interests of the country, and whatever lofty ideals an individual may have must be linked with the great ideal of Socialist and Communist construction. The students must be taught to love labor and the laboring people and to comprehend correctly the lofty significance of labor. The concepts to belittle labor and the laboring people, to be careless with public property and to neglect school discipline presently prèvalent in the schools should be criticized. Ideological and political education should be realized by means of classroom teaching and extra-curricular activity. The principal way to carry out ideological and political education among the students is to foster their socialist quality. The adoption of rough and impatient measures must be opposed.

The conference also emphasized the need to improve the health of the students. During the past several years, although the health condition of the students has been improved, it is still below the standard required. This is due, according to the conference, to the inability of the educational administrations to rid themselves of subjectivism and bureaucratism. No supervision and checkup are made on their part to see that steps are taken by the school authorities to improve the health condition of the students and to ensure that the students are not over-burdened with study. The overall education concept is still vague on the part of the schools. In future, athletic sports and health education of the students must be intensified.

Concerning middle school pedagogical work, the conference was of the opinion that pedagogical reform was the central link of middle school educational reform. Pedagogical reform should center on the reform of pedagogical contents to bring about the adequate reform of pedagogical method. Pedagogical work should thoroughly implement the principle of having teaching united with production, politics and reality, and should ensure that political and ideological education is thoroughly implemented. In learning the advanced experience of the Soviet Union to improve teaching, we must unite our study with the reality of China to prevent the deviation of making mechanical use of Soviet experience. The ideological remolding of teachers is a prerequisite to pedagogical reform. By participating in the pedagogical reform, the teachers help themselves to elevate their own ideologies. Concerning the improvement of pedagogical work by the schools, the conference was of the opinion that the teachers must first be required to study the new teaching materials, to comprehend the pedagogical aim of each lesson, to grasp the central thought and contents of the teaching materials, and hence to improve the pedagogical method to ensure that the thought and contents of the teaching materials were correctly and systematically taught the students. Hereafter, the teachers must gradually be required to make use of the viewpoints of dialectic materialism and historical materialism in lectures to ensure that the scientific knowledge is correctly taught the students.

The conference was of the opinion that the teachers must be depended upon to raise the quality of teaching. Consequently, the organization of the teachers to practice sparetime study is of special significance toward elevating the level of the teachers. The conference decided that the present sparetime study of the teachers should be carried out in a planned and systematic manner in accordance with their peculiarities and needs. Teachers with a standard above that of a normal school graduate may adopt the study of political theories as the main line and the study of business as the supplementary line. Those whose standard is below that of a normal school graduate should adopt the study of the principal lessons of the normal institute as the main line and the study of current affairs and policies as the supplementary line. The various places should see that institutions for the teachers to further their studies are set up in earnest, or arrange with the normal schools to operate correspondence courses to absorb teachers with a standard below that of a normal schools graduate. During the first half of this year, all the teachers should concentrate on the study of the general line for the transition period to elevate the socialist consciousness of the teachers and to lay down a good foundation for the study of political theories in the future. The conference pointed out that the unity of the teachers must be strengthened and that the old and new teachers must respect and learn from each other to ensure mutual progress. The young teachers must learn humbly from the old teachers and the old teachers must help to foster the new teachers.

In his summing up report, Tung Shun-ts'ai pointed out with emphasis the need of advancing the leadership of the educational administrations. The various educational administrations must practically and thoroughly carry out the working directives and educational plans of the CPG. They must set up an inspection system and send out men periodically to make penetrative checkups to strengthen their concrete leadership. Concerning the division of work in respect of leadership toward middle schools, the provinces should base on the principle of consolidated leadership and level-by-level administration to pay greater attention toward political and work leadership. Apart from directly leading certain middle schools, they should leave it to the *hsien* (or municipality) to take up the direct leadership of other middle schools. The various educational administrations should pay attention to foster educational administration cadres. Tung Shun-ts'ai also called on the various educational administrations to rely closely on the leadership of the Party committees, for such leadership is a decisive link to make the work a success.

2.7 "Central People's Government Ministry of Education Issues Directive Concerning Establishment, Development and Reorganization of Normal Schools"

To ensure that secondary education for teacher training is better run and that the quality of elementary education is elevated, the CPG Ministry of Education has issued a directive concerning the establishment, development and reorganization of normal schools in the future. Apart from summarizing the development and reorganization of secondary education for teacher training made in the country during the past four years and the main current problems, the directive lays down clearcut and concrete stipulations in regard to the present task and course of work for teacher training education.

Elementary education constitutes the foundation of educational construction as a whole, while the normal schools hold the key to the successful operation of elementary education. According to the demand of the general task of the country for the transition period, how to cultivate an adequate number of teachers with the necessary qualifications for primary schools, senior classes of primary schools for adults and kindergartens in a planned manner in the future constitutes an important task for normal schools. This is also true of the work in giving the currently employed primary school teachers with a low cultural standard due elevation in a number of years. Consequently, the directive points out that in the matter of the policy of work for secondary education for teacher training, the planned development of normal

"Central People's Government Ministry of Education Issues Directive Concerning Establishment, Development and Reorganization of Normal Schools" (NCNA, Peking, June 19, 1954), *Survey of China Mainland Press,* No. 844 (July 9, 1954), pp. 33-34.

schools should be implemented in the light of the plan of development for elementary education and the possibilities. With the object of gradually enhancing the quality of elementary education, the existing junior normal schools should gradually be transformed into normal schools or centers for the training of primary school teachers by rotation in accordance with the concrete conditions of the various places. To keep the primary school supplied with teachers short course teacher training classes may also be operated apart from the normal schools. Normal schools for kindergartens should also be set up and developed in a discriminate manner.

In order to ensure the thorough implementation of the above mentioned lines, the directive points out, different measures should be adopted in accordance with the concrete conditions of the various types of normal schools as follows:

First, in the case of small normal schools, they should be enlarged in a planned manner. Generally speaking, they should be brought up step by step to 12 classes (but the number of 18 classes should not be exceeded). In places where the conditions are unfavorable for enlargement, the schools may be operated on a smaller scale (but there must not be less than six classes in a school). In places where the number of schools is too few, new schools should be set up in a planned manner in accordance with the possibilities. Normal schools with junior teacher training classes attached should plan for the cutting down of the number of students in the junior teacher training classes to make room for other students. Normal schools for art teachers, or normal schools with training classes for art teachers attached should stop to enroll students as from 1954 and take steps to have their schools changed into normal school or teacher training classes. The existing students in the normal schools for art teachers or training classes for art teachers may however carry on their study and be graduated in accordance with the original pedagogical plan. In order to ensure the single function of the normal schools and middle schools in the course of the next two or three years, all normal schools (or junior normal schools) with middle school classes attached, or middle schools with teacher training (or junior teacher training) classes attached should carry on with reorganization. Should the reorganization prove to be difficult, enrollment for one type of class should be suspended in a planned manner to make room for the development of classes of the other type.

Second, in the case of normal schools for kindergartens, these schools should be set up in a planned and discriminate manner in the industrial and mining districts and the big cities. Generally speaking, teacher training classes for kindergartens may be set up in the better operated normal schools in accordance with the needs of the various places, and students graduated from junior middle schools should be admitted.

Third, in places where the number of normal school graduates is comparatively large and there is no need to foster senior primary school graduates as primary school teachers, the junior normal schools should suspend the enrollment of students as from 1954 or 1955. This applies also to places where a large number of junior middle school graduates is available to keep the short course teacher training classes supplied with recruits, although the number of normal school graduates is small. These schools should gradually be changed into normal schools, classes for rotation training of primary school teachers, or short course teacher training classes in accordance with the concrete conditions. In view of the fact, however, that the junior normal schools have the task of elevating the existing primary school teachers whose actual cultural standard is lower than that of a senior primary graduate and who can be cultivated, the changes of their nature must be introduced gradually, and must not be effected in too great a hurry to prevent the elevation of the existing primary school teachers from being adversely affected. In the national minority areas and in places where the cultural conditions are backward and primary school teachers are short in supply, the junior normal schools should carry on with the enrollment of students (with the four year system implemented as far as possible). If necessary additional schools may also be set up.

Fourth, short course teacher training classes may be set up in normal schools or by having the junior normal schools reorganized for the enrollment of junior middle school graduates. These students should be given one year of training.

Fifth, class for rotation training of teachers may be operated to elevate the existing teachers for primary schools and kindergartens step by step. Training by rotation should first be given to the primary school teachers whose standard is lower than that of a junior normal school graduate so as to have them brought up to the level of junior normal school graduates. (In future, training by rotation should be given to the primary school teachers with the standard of a junior normal school graduate so as to have them brought up to the level of normal school graduates.) When teachers are transferred for training by rotation, their teaching work should be taken up by graduates of junior normal or normal schools.

The directive finally points out that when the work to establish, develop and reorganize the normal schools is carried out by the various places, attention should be paid to the need for developing elementary education in future when the development, enrollment and reorganization plans for normal schools are drawn up. The number of students graduated from the normal schools (including the junior normal schools, classes for rotation training of primary school teachers and short course teacher training classes) every year must be made to fall in balance with the additional teachers needed for the development of primary schools and the senior classes of primary schools for adults during the year. Practical steps should be taken to prevent the amalgamation or suspension of schools blindly. When reorganizing schools or setting up new schools, consideration should be given to the local nature of primary school teachers, with adequate attention paid to the density of population and the communication facilities. Plans for the establishment and development of normal schools for kindergartens should take into calculation the future development of kindergarten education. When changing junior normal schools into normal schools, positive conditions must be created to make sure that the change is carried out in a planned and systematic manner. Particular attention should be paid to preventing the existing teachers from drifting around. Teachers capable of being cultivated should be fostered and elevated as far as possible so that they may eventually take up teaching work in normal schools.

2.8 "Rules of Conduct for Primary School Students"

1. Endeavor to be a good student; good in health, good at study and good in conduct. Prepare to serve the Motherland and the people.

2. Respect the National Flag. Respect and love the leader of the people.

3. Obey the instructions of the principal and teachers. Value and protect the reputation of the school and of the class.

4. Arrive at the school punctually and attend the classes punctually. Never be late; never leave school before the time; and never miss a class without reason.

5. When attending school, bring all the textbooks and stationery required. Before the class begins, prepare all the things required for the lesson.

6. Be orderly and quiet and assume a correct posture during the class. When desiring to leave the classroom, ask the teacher's permission first.

7. During the class, work diligently and listen attentively to the teacher's instruction and the questions and answers by your classmates. Do not talk except when necessary; do not do anything else besides your class work.

8. During the class when you want to give an answer or to ask a question, raise your hand first. Stand up and speak when the teacher allows you to; sit down when the teacher tells you so.

9. Carefully complete in time the after-class work assigned by the teacher.

10. Perform your duties well when you are the student on duty of the day. Participate actively in after-class activities.

11. Respect the principal and the teachers. Salute your teacher when the class begins and again at the end of the class. When you meet the principal or the teachers outside the school you also salute them.

12. Be friendly with your schoolmates and unite with them and help each other.

13. When going to school or returning home, do not delay on the way so as to avoid accidents.

14. Respect and love your parents. Love and protect your brothers and sisters. Do what you can to help your parents.

15. Respect the aged. Give way and seat or any other possible help to the aged, children, the sick or anybody who may have difficulty in movement.

16. Be polite to people. Do not curse people. Do not fight. Do not make a lot of noise in public places. Do not disturb people's work, study or sleep.

17. Do not tell lies or cheat people. Do not gamble. Do not take away other people's things without their permission. Do not do anything that may be harmful to yourself or to others.

18. Take care of public property. Do not damage or dirty tables, chairs, doors, windows, walls, floors or anything else.

19. Eat, rest and sleep at regular hours. Play and take exercise frequently to make your body strong.

20. Keep your body, food, clothes, utensils, bed, and keep the place clean and hygienic. Pay attention to cleanliness and hygiene also at public places.

"Rules of Conduct for Primary School Students," Shanghai, *Wen Hui Pao,* February 26, 1955, *Survey of China Mainland Press,* No. 1067 [Supplement No. 1071], (June 17, 1955), pp. 8-9.

2.9 "Rules of Conduct for Middle School Students"

1. Endeavor to learn; learn to be good in health, good at study and good in conduct. Prepare to serve the Motherland and the people.

2. Respect the National Flag. Respect and love the leader of the people.

3. Obey the Regulations of the school. Obey the instructions of the principal and teachers.

4. Arrive at the school punctually and attend the classes punctually. Never be late; never leave school before the time; and never miss a class without reason.

5. When attending school every day, bring all the textbooks and stationery required. Before the class begins, prepare all the things required for the lesson.

6. During the class, assume a correct posture; listen to the lecture attentively; do not talk unless when necessary; do not do anything else besides your class work. When desiring to leave the classroom, ask the teacher's permission first.

7. Stand up when answering the teacher's questions. Sit down when the teacher permits you. When you want to ask the teacher a question, raise your hand first.

8. Perform your self-study carefully. Finish your work in all the subjects in time.

9. Respect the principal and the teachers. Stand up and salute your teacher when the class begins and again at the end of the class. When you meet the principal or the teachers outside the school you also salute them.

10. Be sincere and friendly with your schoolmates, unite with them and help one another.

11. Respect and love your parents. Love and protect your brothers and sisters. Help your family do house work.

12. Respect your elders. Respect the aged. Love and protect the children; take care of the sick and infirm; give them your seat on a carriage; give way to them on the road.

13. Be honest, sincere, modest and polite to people. Do not tell a lie. Do not curse people. Do not fight. Do not disturb people's work, study or sleep.

14. Do not smoke. Do not drink. Do not gamble. Do not take away other people's things without their permission. Do not do anything that may be harmful to yourself or to others.

15. Take plenty of exercises and make your body strong. Keep your body, clothes, quarters and all public places clean and hygenic.

16. Obey public order. Take care of public property.

17. Value and protect the reputation of the class and of the school.

18. Always have your student identity card with you and see that you do not lose it.

"Rules of Conduct for Middle School Students," Peking, *Kuang Ming Jih Pao,* June 18, 1955, *Survey of China Mainland Press,* No. 1094 (July 22, 1955), pp. 16-17.

2.10 "Decision of the Chinese Communist Party Central Committee and State Council Concerning Elimination of Illiteracy"

The positive elimination of illiteracy in a planned and systematic manner on a nation-wide scale to enable the broad masses to free themselves from illiteracy and to acquire modern culture constitutes a great cultural revolution in China as well as a momentous political task for China in Socialist construction. As was taught by Chairman Mao who said that the elimination of illiteracy among 80 percent of the population was work of importance for new China, the unfolding of the movement for eliminating illiteracy on a large scale at the moment in coordination with the development of Socialist industrialization and agricultural cooperation with the object of having illiteracy basically eliminated throughout the country in five or seven years of time is most essential and can very well be brought into realization.

The betterment of the life of the masses of the workers and peasants has provided them with an advantageous base for learning culture. At the same time, in the course of Socialist industrialization and agricultural cooperation, because of their need to develop production, the workers and peasants have the urgent need of learning culture. The organization of cooperatives has provided the peasants with collective strength, and it has been made possible for them to organize the learning of culture themselves. For the sake of having exertions made for the accomplishment of this arduous historical task in the course of Socialist industrialization and agricultural cooperation, the following decisions are now made:

(1) As from 1956, it is necessary to unfold the literacy campaign among the masses with vigor in close association with development of Socialist industrialization and agricultural cooperation. All places are required to eliminate illiteracy basically in five or seven years time in accordance with their conditions.

The organ cadres are required to be eliminated of illiteracy in two to three years. About 95 percent of the industrial workers in factories, mines and enterprises are to be eliminated of illiteracy in three or five years of time. The residents in the countryside and the cities should be basically eliminated of illiteracy in five or seven years. This is to say that over 70 percent of the illiterates are required to be eliminated of their illiteracy.

In national minority areas and in places where the work proves to be especially difficult, plans for eliminating illiteracy should be fixed and carried out at a rate in accordance with the concrete conditions.

The task of eliminating illiteracy is especially arduous in the countryside. This calls for all places to organize greater and more forces to have the work carried out. However, the work to eliminate illiteracy in organs, factories and mines cannot be relaxed on this ground.

People between the age of 14 and 50 should constitute the principal parties to be eliminated of illiteracy. People above the age of 50 should also be welcomed to learn to read if they themselves are willing. Members of the Communist Party and the NDYL, cadres, young people and activists on all construction fronts who are illiterate should self-consciously and positively take the leading part in learning to free themselves of illiteracy.

"Decision of the Chinese Communist Party Central Committee and State Council Concerning Elimination of Illiteracy" (NCNA, Peking, March 30, 1956), *Survey of China Mainland Press*, No. 1266 (April 12, 1956), pp. 3-7.

(2) The literacy education must thoroughly enforce the principle of "linking with reality and learning what can be used." In the countryside, the things taught should begin with the immediate need. As the first step, the urgent need of agricultural cooperation, that is the need of recording work, should be taken care of About 200 or 300 words including the names of persons, places, and cooperatives in their *ts'un* and *hsiang,* the names of farm implements, farming work and crops, numerals, terms indicating weight and measure and other urgently needed terms should first be taught. The cadres in charge of cooperation work should guide and help the local intellectuals to compile the textbooks in accordance with the need of their own cooperatives. Each place should have its own textbook which need not be sent to the educational administration for examination.

As the second step, the things taught should be enlarged to cover the things commonly seen and the terms commonly used in their own *hsien* or special administrative districts. This, even with some of the things commonly seen and terms commonly used in their own provinces and throughout the country added, calls for the learning of no more than several hundred characters. The *hsien* or special administrative district should organize the local intellectuals to edit the textbooks with the guidance and assistance of the cadres in charge of cooperation work. Such textbooks should be speedily examined by educational administrations of the special administrative district or provincial level.

As the third step, the things taught should be further enlarged to cover the things commonly seen and terms commonly used in their own provinces. This, with some of the things commonly seen and terms commonly used in the country added, calls for the learning of several hundred characters. Those textbooks should be edited by the education departments/bureaus of the provinces, autonomous regions and municipalities under the direct jurisdiction of the Central Government.

The literacy education calls for the complete learning of those three kinds of textbooks which call for the learning of about 1,500 characters. After learning these 1,500 characters, people will generally be able to read the simple-worded popular newspapers and magazines, to keep less complicated books, to write simple memorandums, and to do simple calculations with abacus. . . .

(3) In order to unfold the literacy campaign, the people must be taught by the people, and the literates must be called on to teach the illiterates. Illiteracy cannot be eliminated with full-time teachers alone. The people in the factories and mines, the countryside and the cities who are literates, the school teachers, and students studying in schools above the senior primary level, the working personnel in state organs and people's organizations and the servicemen should all be mobilized to play a part in work to eliminate illiteracy. The teaching of other people to read is a most glorious task and constitutes a concrete manifestation of serving the toiling people. All those who are literate have the obligation of taking part in the work.

The school teachers of all levels should take up the task of guiding the sparetime teachers in teaching in work to eliminate illiteracy. The sparetime teachers who take part in the literacy campaign should be encouraged constantly to make them sense the honor of serving the masses. At the same time, effective measures must be adopted to give them the necessary training and education to elevate their cultural and professional level. The government should reward those with marked contributions to work for eliminating illiteracy.

(4) Organs, industrial and mining enterprises, agricultural and handicraft producer cooperatives should all promote the literacy education positively, and vigorously organize the worker and peasant cadres and the masses of the workers and peasants who are illiterate to take part in learning. The street organizations in cities should also positively unfold the literacy campaign among the city residents. All organs, industrial and mining enterprises, agricultural and handicraft producer cooperatives,

hsiang (ts'un), and street organizations in cities should embody a concrete plan for eliminating illiteracy in the overall plans for their own units or places, and should strengthen their control in a practical manner so as to have illiteracy speedily and effectively eliminated.

(5) In organizing the masses to learn to read, the principle of voluntariness must be strictly followed and no coercion may be employed. The broad masses must be given wide and penetrative publicity and encouragement so that they may take up learning self-consciously and voluntarily. In unfolding the movement for eliminating illiteracy, it is wrong to adopt the attitude to allow the movement follow its own course without resorting to publicity and encouragement.

(6) In order to accomplish the task of eliminating illiteracy, the people must be ensured of time to learn. The Party organizations of organs, industrial and mining enterprises, cooperatives, *hsiang (ts'un)* and street organizations in cities must do away with the unnecessary meetings, and make consolidated and rational arrangements to provide them with sparetime. In organs, factories, mines and enterprises, the people seeking to learn to read must be assured of at least six hours of learning time a week and 240 hours of learning time a year. In the countryside, year-round learning must be insisted upon. Apart from learning in winter, learning must also be carried out in the three other seasons so that no less than 240 hours of time are spent in learning in a year. The sparetime learning of the peasants must be commensurate with the busy and slack seasons. The time for learning and the progress to be made should be made flexible in the light of work. The method of "learning more in the slack season, less when busy and none at all when extremely busy" should be advocated.

(7) Teaching must be carried out in a variety of forms which should be made nimble use of with due consideration given to the factors of time and personnel. In the case of organ cadres, workers and peasants and city residents who have more favorable conditions for learning, more use can be made of teaching by classes. In the case of those who cannot be gathered together with ease, teaching by classes cannot be stressed, and teaching by groups should be adopted. In the case of those whose faculty for learning is especially poor, the method of individual teaching may be adopted. In the case of ordinary peasants, more of them can gather together to attend sparetime schools in the winter. After the spring plowing, they may associate with their production organizations to learn in groups.

(8) The workers and peasants who have completed their literacy course must be helped to have their attainment consolidated. They must be constantly encouraged and guided to use what they have learned and to practice with calculation. Sparetime primary schools for workers and peasants founded on literacy education should be positively set up, and the maximum number of workers and peasants who have completed their literacy course should be enrolled to enable them to carry on with their learning so that they may have their cultural level raised to that of primary school graduates. The school system, curriculum and development plan for sparetime primary school should be separately charted by the educational administration.

The propaganda, cultural and publishing organs of all levels and other establishments concerned should organize strength to edit large numbers of newspapers, magazines and books for the literate workers and peasants. Such reading matter must have suitable contents and be written with a popular style to meet the standard and need of the workers and peasants. The distribution of books and newspapers must be vigorously improved to make sure that they are timely distributed among the masses of the workers and peasants. Particular attention should be paid to the delivery of popular books and newspapers to the countryside. The publishing organs should first make sure that an adequate supply of literacy textbooks is made available in time.

The cultural organs of all places, like the cultural palaces (stations), libraries (reading rooms) and clubs, should positively help the masses to learn culture in their sparetime in work for eliminating illiteracy. They must treat the work as an important task of their own.

(9) The elimination of illiteracy is an arduous political task. The Party and government organizations of all levels must attach weight to the work and place same on their work agenda. They must strengthen their leadership and extensively mobilize and organize the strength of all quarters to take part in this work. These decisions must be abided by when the provinces, autonomous regions, municipalities, special administrative districts, *hsien, chu, hsiang,* factories and mines and enterprises map out their plans for the elimination of illiteracy stage by stage in accordance with the local conditions. The actual development in work should also be based upon having these plans revised unremittingly. . . .

The elimination of illiteracy is a broad movement for the education of the broad masses. The organs of all places having a bearing on propaganda, education and culture should publicize on a large scale to inspire and mobilize the strength of all quarters to strive for the realization of the task for eliminating illiteracy.

2.11 "Let All Flowers Bloom Together, Let Diverse Schools of Thought Contend"

Mr. Kuo Mo-jo, President of the Chinese Academy of Sciences and Chairman of the All-China Federation of Literary and Art Circles has asked me to give a talk on the policy of the CCP [Chinese Communist Party] toward literary and art work and scientific work. The Communist Party of China stands for the blossoming of all flowers in literature and art and for all diverse schools of thought in scientific work vying with each other. This has already been said by Chairman Mao Tse-tung at the Supreme state conference. We have had some experience in the enforcement of this policy, but our experience is still limited. What I want to talk about today is my personal understanding of this policy. . . .

If China is to become wealthy and powerful, apart from the need of consolidating the people's regime, developing the economic and educational enterprises and fortifying the national defense, it is also necessary to bring prosperous development to literature, the arts and scientific work. We cannot afford to go without any of these things.

To bring prosperous development to literature, the arts and scientific work, it is necessary to adopt the policy of "letting all flowers bloom together and all schools contend in airing their views." In literary and art work, if there is "only one flower in bloom," no matter how good the flower may be, it would not lead to prosperity. Take the instance of drama before us for illustration. Several years ago, there were people who were opposed to the Peking drama. At that time, the Party resolved to enforce

Lu Ting-yi, "Let All Flowers Bloom Together, Let Diverse Schools of Thought Contend" [Speech made to a gathering of scientists, social science specialists, doctors, writers and artists on May 26, 1956.] Peking, *Jen Min Jih Pao (People's Daily),* June 23, 1956, *Current Background,* No. 406 (August 15, 1956), pp. 3-13.

the policy of "letting all flowers bloom together and the new emerge from the old" in the case of drama. Everybody is now able to see that this policy is correct and tremendously successful. Because the different kinds of dramas are free to compete with and learn from each other, rapid progress has been made in the field of drama.

In the field of scientific work, China has also its historical experience. During the epoch of the Spring and Autumn Annals and the Warring States two thousand years ago, there emerged in China the phrase of "letting all schools contend in airing their views" in the academic field. It became the golden era of academic development in the history of our country. The history of our country has proved that if there were no encouragement for independent thinking and if there were no free discussion, then academic development would stagnate. The epoch of the Spring and Autumn Annals and the Warring States was very different from the situation we are facing today. At that time, society was in a chaotic state. The contention of all schools in airing their views in the academic field was spontaneous and had no conscious, unified leadership. The people have now fought their way to a free regime, and the people's democratic dictatorship has been established and consolidated. The people want a speedy development of scientific work, therefore they are consciously drawing up an overall plan for scientific work and have adopted the policy of "let diverse schools of thought contend" to advance the progress of academic work.

We see also that in a class society, literature and arts and scientific works have after all to be used as a weapon in class struggle.

This problem is comparatively obvious in the literary and art domain. There are among literary and art works things which are obviously harmful. Hu Feng can be quoted as an example. The yellow novels which preach obscenity and lawlessness are another instance. Other instances may be found in such so-called literary works which preach "let us play mah-jongg and to hell with all State affairs" and "the moon over the United States is rounder than the moon over China." It is entirely right that all these poisonous literary and art works should be swept away like flies, mosquitoes, rats and sparrows. This can only bring advantage to literature and arts. That is why we say there are literature and arts which serve the workers, peasants and soldiers and that there are literature and arts which serve imperialism, the landlords and the bourgeoisie. What we need are the literature and arts which serve the workers, peasants and soldiers as well as the masses of the people.

Class struggle is more salient in the domain of philosophy and social science. . . .

In the domain of natural science, although natural science itself has no class status, every natural scientist still has his own political stand. Formerly, some natural scientists blindly worshiped the American way of thinking and some were inclined to be so-called "non-political." It is right that these undesirable things should be criticized. Such criticisms also mirror the class struggle.

We must also be able to see that although literature and the arts and scientific research are closely related with class struggle, nonetheless they cannot be identified with politics in an absolute sense. Political struggle is an instrument for manifesting class struggle directly. In the case of literature and arts and social science, while they can also manifest class struggle directly, they can manifest the latter too in a more devious way. It is fallacious to entertain the rightist unilateral view of "literature and arts for the sake of literature and arts" and "science for the sake of science" on the ground that literature and arts and science bear no relations with politics. On the other hand, to identify literature and arts and science with politics would also lead to another one-sided view. This is the mistake of "leftist" simplicity.

The Party's policy advocates freedom of independent thinking in the work of literature and art and in the work of scientific research, freedom of debate, freedom of creative work and freedom to criticize, freedom to express one's opinion, and freedom to maintain one's opinion and to reserve one's opinion. . . .

The freedom we are advocating is different from the freedom advocated by bourgeois democracy. The freedom advocated by the bourgeoisie is nothing more than freedom for the minority which the laboring people have little or no chance to share. The bourgeoisie is dictatorial to the laboring people. The warmongers in the United States are presently playing up their so-called "free world." In that "free world," the warmongers and the reactionary cliques have all the freedom. Nevertheless, the Rosenbergs were sentenced to death because they advocated peace. We advocate that the counter-revolutionaries should be denied freedom. We hold that we must practice dictatorship over counter-revolutionaries. But among the people we take the stand that there must be democracy and freedom. This is a political line. In politics, we must distinguish ourselves from the enemy.

The line of "letting all flowers bloom together and all schools contend in airing their views" which we advocate stands for freedom inside the camp of the people. We advocate the broadening of this freedom in accordance with the consolidation of the people's regime. . . .

There is a struggle between materialism and idealism and this struggle will be a long one. The Communists are dialectical materialists. They advocate a course of publicizing materialism and are opposed to idealism. This is something that cannot be shaken. As dialectical materialists, however, they understand the laws of social development. Consequently, they advocate that inside the camp of the people, the ideological struggle must be rightly distinguished from the struggle against the counter-revolutionaries. Inside the camp of the people, there is not only the freedom to publicize materialism but also the freecom to publicize idealism. As long as the parties concerned are not counter-revolutionaries, they are free to publicize both materialism and idealism, and both parties are free to enter into controversy.

The ideological struggle inside the camp of the people is different from the struggle carried out against the counter-revolutionaries. The counter-revolutionaries should be suppressed and brought down. A struggle should be carried out against the retrogressive idealist ideology inside the camp of the people. This struggle should also be sharp, but it seeks to unite, to overcome backwardness and to strengthen unity. The attempt to solve ideological problems with administrative orders cannot be effective. Only through open debates can materialist thinking gradually overcome idealist thinking. . . .

In short, while we advocate the drawing of a line of distinction between ourselves and the enemy in the political field, we also advocate that we must have certain freedom inside the camp of the people. The line of "letting all flowers bloom together and all schools contend in airing their views," is a manifestation of the freedom inside the camp of the people in the domain of literature and arts and sciences.

We have now every condition for the enforcement of the policy of "letting all flowers bloom together and all schools contend in airing their views.". . .

Because such conditions have been taken into consideration, the Central Committee of the Communist Party of China is now emphatically putting forward the policy: "let flowers of all seasons blossom together and let diverse schools of thought contend." This policy was aimed at mobilizing all active elements to give their best to enrich China's literature and art and to enable China's scientific work to catch up with advanced world levels.

2.12 "National Education in China"

During the past year, the national education situation, like other enterprises in the country, underwent great changes in the wake of the arrival of the high tide of the Socialist revolution. Under the leadership of the Central Committee of the Party and the State Council, definite achievements have been registered in ordinary education and normal education throughout the country.

There has first been the fulfillment of the plans for ordinary education and normal education for 1955. . . .

Secondly, some work has also been carried out in the elevation of the quality of education. . . .

In the field of the elevation of the quality of teachers and leadership cadres in schools, we have started the adoption of the measures of study while in active service and rotation transfer of the workers for full time training. . . .

In the autumn of 1955, there was established in Peking the College of Educational Administration. In many provinces and municipalities there were also organized training classes for educational administrative cadres or schools for such cadres. . . .

The Party and the People's Government show great concern over the living conditions of the teachers. For the improvement of the emoluments of teachers throughout the country, in the Wage Reform Plan passed at the 32nd meeting of the State Council on June 16, 1956, a comparatively high increase has been provided for the salary scales for teachers. According to the provisions, the average monthly salaries for teachers and staff members in the various enterprises under the Ministry of Education will, on readjustment, be raised by 28.72 percent, that is to say, from 33.92 yuan to 43.67 yuan. The raise in the salaries of primary and middle school teachers will be proportionately even greater, being 32.88 percent, or an increase from 30.2 yuan to 40.13 yuan on the average. On the basis of this new scale, the treatment for teachers is being improved compared with the past. We believe that with the further development of the national economy, the salaries of teachers will be gradually raised further.

During the past year, though our work in national education has been attended by definite achievements, nevertheless, generally speaking, its development still lags far behind the demands of socialist construction, behind the needs of production development. Today, 78 percent of the total population in the whole country are still illiterate. Only a little more than 52 percent of children of school age have been admitted to schools. Apart from these, the most marked question in general education at the moment is the insufficiency of middle school students which seriously affects the needs for national construction. . . .

I now deal with another serious question in the field of educational construction today. It is the fact that our normal education does not meet the urgent needs of general education. With the development of general education, there is growingly seriously felt the question of the insufficiency of teachers for middle and primary schools. . . .

From the second half of 1955, there emerged in our country the high tide of the socialist revolution. The great victory in socialist transformation brought basic changes to the political situation of our country. This new situation has brought sacred new tasks to various fields of our national endeavor. It has likewise brought

Chang Hsi-jo, Minister of Education, "National Education in China" (Report delivered to the 3rd session of the 1st National People's Congress on June 20, 1956), (NCNA, Peking, June 20, 1956), *Current Background,* No. 400 (July 17, 1956), pp. 19-25.

sacred new tasks to the field of national education. This calls upon us to cope with the demands of the socialist construction and socialist transformation in our country, through the realization of the cultural revolution, the elimination of illiteracy during the transition period, the universal extension of education, the universal elevation of the political and cultural levels of the masses of the people, so that the broad masses of the people in the whole country will be turned into cultured and educated people. At the same time there must also be fostered in large numbers socialist intellectuals and cadres, to meet the extensive needs of socialist construction.

On the basis of these new tasks brought to the field of national education by the new situation in the country, and in accordance with the policies directed by Chairman Mao calling for "overall planning and strengthened leadership", and "speed, quantity, quality and economy", we consider that in the field of national education, we must strive to realize the following major tasks:

(1) Beginning 1956, in accordance with local conditions in different areas, there shall be basically wiped out illiteracy in five or seven years, or in longer periods. Within the next seven to twelve years, on the foundation of literacy education, there shall be continually raised the cultural levels of cadres, workers, peasants and city residents, so that the majority of them will reach the level of primary school graduates, and some of them reach the level of junior middle school graduates.

(2) Beginning 1956, in accordance with local conditions in different areas, there shall be realized, within seven or twelve years, the universal provision of primary school education in cities, market towns and rural areas generally. In municipalities directly subordinated to the Central Government, in municipalities under provincial governments, and in industrial cities, there shall be gradually realized the universal provision of junior middle school education. On the foundation of the popularization of general education, all out efforts shall be exerted for the development of secondary education, so as to gradually meet the needs for the fostering of national construction personnel.

(3) There shall be developed with all-out effort normal education, making a good job of the task, so as to foster large numbers of teachers for secondary schools, primary schools and kindergartens. It is demanded that in the next 12 years, teachers in senior middle schools shall basically be graduates of normal colleges, teachers of junior middle schools shall basically be graduates of normal specialization institutes, teachers of higher primary schools shall basically be graduates of normal schools, and teachers of lower primary schools shall basically be graduates of junior normal schools.

2.13 "Problems in This Year's Educational Work That Merit Attention"

1957 is the last year of China's First Five-Year Plan as well as a year in which education is to be further intensified and more important problems are to be solved. The target of educational development set in the First Five-Year Plan was overfulfilled in the past four years. The quality of education was also improved year by year. All such were results of the active efforts of the educational workers. However, some problems also cropped up in the course of advancement of educational work: large-scale development of education was in some respects inappropriate; the quality of education was improved with difficulty; pedagogical plans, teaching materials, methods of teaching. . . . called for improvement; education policy was open to discussion. These problems cropped up because we had not well followed the laws of development of our education; these problems were brought up in order to discover these laws. How to solve these problems? Our work can be improved only by opposing subjectivism, bureaucratism and sectarianism as proposed by the 8th National Congress of the Communist Party and by summing up the experience of the past years. In brief, educational work this year should center on quality improvement, steady advance, summing-up of experience and discovery of laws.

How to improve the quality of education?

First, political-ideological education must be intensified.

Educational work has made great progress and the results of examination obtained by the students have been constantly bettered in the last two or three years. Successful schools and principals were leading the teaching work with care; some administrative departments of education took the results of examination as the criterion for measuring the records obtained by schools. Political-ideological education, while not being neglected, was not given sufficient attention. A number of students devoted themselves to their studies, preparing for examinations and working hard to be promoted to a higher school, and did not interest themselves in political events. Some students, whose socialist awakening remained at a very low level, could not find their bearings when important changes took place in the political events and when their personal interests were involved. In the case of those schools whose teaching work was unsatisfactory, the discipline among the students was even worse and their thinking was muddled. For this reason, all schools must intensify political-ideological education. To intensify political-ideological education does not mean launching of a shock campaign; the education must be given regular and more attention in every way.

First of all, socialist consciousness of the students should be enhanced and education in patriotism and internationalism must be intensified. To this end, current events must be studied and some lessons taken to guide the students to take a class view of things. Major events in the international sphere must be judged from the standpoint of whether they are beneficial to the working people or to the exploiting class and counter-revolutionaries; the essential distinction between the deeds of the socialist countries and the deeds of imperialist countries should be grasped from this standpoint. At the same time, our judgment of certain words and actions within the socialist camp should be based on whether they are beneficial to the working people and revolution. In giving lessons, analysing some problems of a given time and at a

Editorial, "Problems in This Year's Educational Work That Merit Attention," *Jen Min Chiao Yu [People's Education]*, No. 1 (January 9, 1957), *Extracts from China Mainland Magazines*, No. 75 (March 25, 1957), pp. 27-31.

given place and in dealing with certain vital problems of the schools and students, the students should be appropriately (without giving a forced interpretation) guided to take a class view of things. Further, the students should be regularly aroused to view with joy and rejoicings every great construction accomplishment in our fatherland and the socialist countries, taking it as a happy event among the working people.

Special care should be taken to conduct labor education. With class going to be eliminated, everybody in our country will be transformed into a laborer for transforming the world. It is wrong to take labor education merely as a temporary task. Our press articles and school education treat the labor education by fits and starts, and the reason is that the importance of labor education is not sufficiently grasped. Actually even in a communist society, each and all will have to work after graduation from universities; at present, not all students can continue their studies from primary schools up to universities; hereafter, part of the primary school and junior and senior middle school students will have to go to production posts after graduation from schools. (At these posts, they should assume not only production tasks but also the tasks of sowing the cultural seeds). All schools must conduct regular labor education among the students so that they will long for socialist production-construction and understand early the bright future of socialist construction and their important tasks.

Personality should be developed but at the same time education in discipline and collectivism must be intensified. The students should be enabled to realize that in order to develop their personality they must manifest collectivism, struggle for the interests of the people and strictly observe the discipline of safeguarding the interests of the masses. Only thus can their personality be developed in a correct way; otherwise, development of personality will only lead to development of individualism.

All the teachers must exert concerted efforts to conduct political-ideological education. The cultivation of moral character and the imparting of basic knowledge of political orientation should be linked up with the life of students and the practice of socialist construction. The schools must do everything possible to help the students before political-ideological education can be made more acceptable to the students.

Second, efforts must be made to improve teaching.

Teaching is not well done in a number of schools; even in the case of those schools with better records of teaching work, some problems remain to be solved. In order to improve teaching, it is still necessary for the school principals to strengthen their leadership. Those who neglect teaching can hardly make a good job of political-ideological education. Those principals who are not familiar with their professional duties should honestly learn from the best teachers and study together with teachers. If they learn more and hear more lessons they will naturally be able to offer opinions on how to lead the teaching work.

Many school students are now over-burdened with work while the teaching results are not satisfactory. This is not merely a question of the schools themselves but also a question of teaching plans and teaching materials. The existing teaching plans and teaching materials contain too many subjects and too much quantity. The education departments are studying how to improve the teaching plans and simplifying the teaching materials in order to give the students more time to consolidate and digest their basic knowledge and carry on some activities of self-study and independent thinking. . . . As to the question of raising the standard of teachers, their teaching hours may be reduced in the second half this year (1957) so that they can have more time to study and prepare lessons. At the same time, it is hoped that extra assignments given to schools will be cut as far as possible, that organizations and meetings inside the schools will be simplified, and that formalities (such as regular preparation of detailed teaching hour plans, too many collective discussions during preparations for lessons. . . .) which do little to increase the results of teaching but waste too much time will be reduced or done away with so that teachers will have more time to do educational work. As to how to improve the standard of teachers in other ways, it is hoped that correspondence schools, teachers' schools for advanced course and the masses of teachers will sum up their experience and put forward their concrete views.

Third, attention should be given to the health of students.

In this connection, the specific conditions of localities and schools and the nutrition and health conditions of students should be taken into consideration. Last year, owing to some improper provisions in the training system, the students "had their technical level raised but their health impaired." This must not occur again. . . .

Comrades! The First Five-Year Plan is in its last year. We educational workers must make exertions to fulfill the First Five-Year Plan successfully and make better preparations for the Second Five-Year Plan.

2.14 "Regulations Governing Certain Problems of Correspondence and Sparetime Normal School Promulgated"

The draft regulations governing certain problems of correspondence and sparetime normal schools promulgated by the Ministry of Education lay down the following provisions in respect of educational task and curricular setup.

(1) The correspondence normal school (correspondence department of normal school) and the sparetime normal school (that is, sparetime school for the advancement of primary school teachers) have the educational task of enhancing the fundamental cultural and scientific knowledge of certain primary school teachers (including kindergarten instructors and teachers of sparetime primary school for workers and peasants). They seek to raise the primary school teachers of the standard of a senior primary school graduate or of a junior normal school or junior middle school under-graduate to the junior normal school level in the matter of fundamental knowledge of culture and science. They seek to raise the teachers teaching in primary schools who are of the standard of a junior normal school or junior middle school graduate but below the standard of a normal school graduate to the normal school level in the matter of fundamental knowledge of culture and science so as to enhance their capacity for teaching.

(2) The correspondence normal school (correspondence department of normal school) and the sparetime normal school are divided into the junior teacher training class and the teacher training class (that is, the junior and senior sections of former days). The junior teacher training class is commensurate with the standard of the junior normal school and its course of study runs from three to four years. The teacher training class is commensurate with the standard of the normal school and its course of study runs from four to five years.

"Regulations Governing Certain Problems of Correspondence and Sparetime Normal School Promulgated," Peking, *Chiao Shih Pao,* October 25, 1957, *Survey of China Mainland Press,* No 1653 (November 18, 1957), pp. 20-21.

(3) The curriculums of the correspondence normal school (correspondence department of normal school) and the sparetime normal school include certain fundamental subjects of the junior normal school or normal school, and the successful study of the two subjects of language and mathematics is especially assured. In compliance with the working need of the teachers teaching in primary schools and the amount of time they can spend in study, the junior teacher training class is for the time being provided with the subjects of language (literature and Han language), arithmetic, and common knowledge of nature (zoology, botany, and physiological hygiene), as well as the two group subjects of mathematics (algebra and geometry) and history and geography (Chinese history and geography). The subjects of language, arithmetic and common knowledge of nature are compulsory, while the two group subjects of mathematics, and history and geography are optional and only one group of subjects is to be taken up. There are in addition the mobile subjects of fundamental knowledge of pedagogics and chemistry and physics, which can be introduced according to the demand of the students and the facilities available to the schools.

The teacher training class is for the time being provided with language (literature and Han language) and the three group subjects of mathematics (arithmetic, algebra and geometry), nature (physics and chemistry) and history and geography (Chinese history, world history, natural geography, Chinese geography and foreign geography). After completing the language course, the students may select and take up any two of the three group subjects. The students should take up the study of mathematics in the light of their weakness. If they are weak in arithmetic and find it difficult to teach arithmetic in primary schools, they may lay emphasis in the study of arithmetic; otherwise they may concentrate on the study of algebra and geometry. There is in addition the mobile subject of pedagogics which may be introduced if there is the need and the schools have the necessary facilities.

Concerning the question of the introduction of political course, the matter should be considered separately and centrally.

(4) Upon the completion of the study of the three subjects of language, arithmetic and common knowledge of nature and any one of the two group subjects of mathematics or history and geography by the students of the junior teacher training class and of language and any two of the three group subjects of mathematics, nature and geography and history by the students of the teacher training class, provided they pass their graduation examinations, they will be issued with certificates of graduation from the junior teacher training class or the teacher training class. Such certificates are of similar standing to the certificates of graduation issued by the junior normal school or the normal school.

Upon the completion of the study of certain subjects by the students and upon their passing their examinations, if they do not intend to continue their study, they may be issued with certificates certifying their graduation from certain subjects. In the case of the students of the teacher training class, after the completion of the language course, if they take up only one group of subjects and the results of their study are up to the standard required, they may be issued with certificates certifying their completion of the study of certain subjects (with the particular subjects specified in the certificates).

Primary school teachers who are not students but have taken up a course of private study may apply to the correspondence normal school (correspondence department of normal school) for permission to take part in final examinations for different subjects, and provided their results are up to standard, they will be issued with certificates of graduation or certificates certifying the completion of the study of certain subjects according to the circumstances.

(5) Students must be certified by the schools employing them, recommended by the educational administrations in their places and enrolled through competitive examination before they can be admitted into the correspondence normal school (correspondence department of normal school) and the sparetime normal school.

In the case of certain subjects which the students are required to study, if they are found to be up to the standard by examination or the certification of other documents, the school may recognize their completion of the study of these subjects without requiring them to take up the study of same once again. In the case of some primary school teachers of the junior normal school (junior middle school) or normal school (senior middle school) standard who are weak in certain subjects, they may also apply to the school for permission to take up the study of selected subjects.

(6) The correspondence normal school (correspondence department of normal school) and sparetime normal school are divided into two school terms of 16 weeks each every year. In principle, the time of study for the students is not less than 6 hours per week. The correspondence normal school (correspondence department of normal school) should also make use of vacations to give lectures. Its task is to guide the brushing up of study, to hold examination, to perform experiments and to study and teach new lessons. The lecturing time should in principle last from ten to twenty days in a school year.

PART
THREE

The
Great
Leap
Forward
(1958-1959)

PART THREE
The Great Leap Forward (1958-1959)

The essence of this period is dramatized by the large banners of three Chinese characters proclaiming the Great Leap Forward—"dà," "yuè," "jìn" — and the slogan of "walking on two legs." China's First Five Year Plan (1953-1957), modeled after the Soviet pattern, had initiated a series of collectivization movements to fulfill the objectives of a planned economy—agricultural collectivization, nationalization of industries, transformation of private enterprises into state-owned or joint state-private enterprises, etc.

The year 1958 was one of optimism, punctuated with slogans announcing the "Great Leap Forward" and the launching of the rural communes. Commenting on this optimism, Edgar Snow observed: "The whole party apparatus, and much of the population, was brought to a frenzy of mass enthusiasm and belief in the impossible."[1]

In August of 1958, the Central Committee of the Chinese Communist Party passed the "Resolution on the Establishment of People's Communes in the Rural Areas," which declared:

> The basis for the development of the people's communes is mainly the all-round, continuous leap forward in China's agricultural production and the ever-rising political consciousness of the 500 million peasants. . . .
>
> Although ownership in the people's communes is still collective ownership and the system of distribution, either the wage system or payment according to workdays, is "to each according to his work" and not "to each according to his needs," the people's communes are the best form of organization for the attainment of socialism and gradual transition to communism. They will develop into the basic social units in communist society.
>
> At the present stage our task is to build socialism. The primary purpose of establishing people's communes is to accelerate the speed of socialist construction and the purpose of building socialism is to prepare actively for the transition to communism.[2]

The commune system was a further development of early collectivization efforts aimed at moving China in the direction of a planned economy. Indeed, the Commune Resolution noted that: "Large, comprehensive people's communes have made their appearance, and in several places they are already widespread. They have developed very rapidly in some areas."[3] Winberg Chai identifies a series of "socialist constructions" leading to the commune system:

> The first step toward the commune system was taken in September 1957, at a Party plenum which decided to adopt the policy of "simultaneous development of industry and agriculture." The plenum also concluded that the key to agriculture development was the massive mobilization of labor power. . . .
> The second step toward the communes was the decision in March, 1958, to embark on an expansion of local industry in rural areas for the purpose of greater utilization of the under-employed labor force of co-operatives. . . .
> The third step toward the commune was the Communist attempt to create state organs for the "building of Communism."[4]

There had been widespread unpublicized organization of communes even before the official Commune Resolution. According to Edgar Snow, "When the open directive was issued in August, probably half the country-side was already in transformation."[5] By November 1958, approximately 740,000 advanced agricultural cooperatives (representing 99 percent of the peasants) had been converted to 26,000 communes. Edgar Snow noted that:

> The transfer of much of the responsibility for rural modernization directly to an all-embracing authority offered advantages of decentralization. At the same time it focused political and economy control at a level much easier for the central government to manipulate. Third, the commune administrations would theoretically provide Peking planners with the means to universalize standards of farm production, to limit consumption, and to extract savings for investment on an increased scale.[6]

The commune movement highlighted the ideological differences between China and the Soviet Union. China was attempting to use the people's communes as a vehicle for making a dramatic and rapid transformation (by comparison with the Soviet Union) from socialism to communism. The following analysis of the exacerbating effect of the commune movement on Sino-Soviet relations is provided by Edgar Snow:

> Moscow's reaction was at first cautious and then increasingly negative. Had not Russia in the earliest days tried a kind of agricultural commune and proved that it would not work? . . .
> How could China, more backward than Russia, attempt any such transition toward communism? The answer must be found in the party's belief that their people had already "changed fundamentally" even though the technology had not. In this they were to be proved mistaken, judging by the speedy retreat from claims that they were a means of *early* attainment of communism. Their appearance and continuation even in modified form, however, were to add greatly to the developing tension between Moscow and Peking. For the whole theoretical implication of the Chinese communes was that an *Asiatic form of Marxism* could develop more rapidly toward true communism that Marx, Lenin or Stalin had foreseen.[7]

However, even within China the commune movement met with considerable resistance. People's communes dramatically altered the structure of Chinese life. Peasants had been given land of their own by the Party in 1949, then lost most of it as they were forced into cooperatives, and now found themselves in the midst of a transformation from collective ownership to ownership by the people as a whole.

In any case, once officially introduced, the commune movement developed at a very rapid rate; so swiftly that neither the peasant masses nor even the cadres of peasant origin fully comprehended the technological and social implications involved in the rush "to establish 'real communism' right away."[8] Therefore, in spite of the impressive "great leap forward" in some production figures, confusion and disorder were so abundant that by the end of the year (December 1958), "the top party leadership abruptly ended the excesses and began what was to become a general retreat."[9]

Commenting on the Chinese educational enterprise, Yang Hsiu-feng, Minister of Education, singled out 1958 as a year of a "great educational revolution" in which "a great leap forward was made in education."[10] The two outstanding features of this educational revolution were: (1) implementation of the policy of "coordinating education with productive labor," and (2) implementation of the "mass line for organizing schools by the entire party and all the people and adoption of the policy of 'walking on two legs.' "[11] As a result of these, the rate and magnitude of educational development during the period between 1958 and 1959 was characterized by phenomenal growth.

In 1958, the Central Committee of the Chinese Communist Party issued a directive calling for the combination of education with productive labor and the submission of education to the political requirements of the proletariat. The essence of the educational revolution to which Yang Hsiu-feng referred centers on the relationship between education and politics; that is, the concept of putting "politics in command" in the teaching of all subjects. Such a view holds to the principle that education must serve the political ends of the proletariat. This was the central theme of the "great educational revolution" of 1958. Teachers and students alike participated in various types of productive labor—in factories and mines, at construction sites, in the rural people's communes, etc.

Schools actually operated factories and farms; similarly, factories and people's communes set up schools. These schools were divided into three categories: (1) full-day schools (in which the main business was teaching and learning with the provision that students take up some kind of productive labor and attempt to relate that labor to their special field of study); (2) half-day schools (employing the practice of working and studying half time—either half a day of manual work and half a day of study, or carrying out work and study on alternate days or alternate weeks, etc.); (3) spare-time schools for workers and peasants (in which study was carried out in the spare time and teaching was correlated with production needs). These schools were designed to "link up theory with reality," and thereby combine teaching, production, and scientific research.

It was reported that Peking University built twenty small factories in two weeks, and that Peking Teachers College established twenty-four factories in three days. Within the short period of eight months, secondary schools and institutions of higher education were said to have established 151,608 small factories and workshops and 10,319 farms, which produced 36,000 machines of various types and 1,930,000 tons of fertilizers.[12]

The second outstanding feature of the educational revolution was the concept of "walking on two legs," which called for both the simultaneous operation of schools by the state and factories, mines, people's communes, etc., and the simultaneous promotion of various forms of education (general and vocational, children's and adult, free and paid, full-day, half-day, spare-time, etc.). Perhaps one of the clearest examples of the integration of education with productive labor, and the policy of walking on two legs in educational construction work, can be seen in the development of the new agricultural middle schools on the people's communes. These were essentially half-day schools in which the work of the student was devoted part-time to farming and part-time to study, with the curriculum reflecting the unity of theory and practice.

Implementation of these guidelines generated considerable conflict, which centered first on the fundamental issue of the relationship between education and politics, and second on the relationship between "red consciousness" and "vocational expertness." In regard to the question of being "red and expert," emphasis during this period was placed on being "red," which was considered more important than being "expert."

The Party's educational guidelines encountered open resistance. There were those who opposed students' participation in labor; there were those who opposed the idea of requiring intellectuals to take up manual labor. According to Yang Hsiu-feng, implementation of the Party's educational guidelines was achieved through victories in the "sharp struggle between the two roads and the two methods," that is, between the road to socialism and the road to capitalism, and between progressive thinking and backward thinking.[13] Consequently, the leadership of the Party in educational work was consolidated and strengthened. The Party line regarding education called for achieving "more, faster, better and more economically," with the hope and expectation that this would lead to a great leap forward in the educational enterprise of the nation.

NOTES:

[1]Edgar Snow, *The Other Side of the River: Red China Today* (New York:Random House, 1962), p. 174.

[2]*Central Committee Resolution on the Establishment of the People's Communes in the Rural Areas* (Peking: Foreign Language Press, 1958), pp. 1, 8.

[3]Ibid., p. 1.

[4]Winberg Chai (ed.), *Essential Works of Chinese Communism* (New York: Bantam Books, 1969), p. 345.

[5]Edgar Snow, op. cit., p. 433.

[6]Ibid., p. 432.

[7]Ibid., p. 431-432.

[8]Ibid., p. 434.

[9]Ibid., p. 435.

[10]Yang Hsiu-feng, "China's Educational Enterprise Goes Through the Process of Great Revolution and Evolution," *Jen-min Jih-pao,* October 8, 1959, *Current Background,* No. 608 (January 8, 1960), pp. 29, 40.

[11]Ibid., p. 40.

[12]Wu Pin, "New Trends in Education," *Peking Review,* No. 21 (July 22, 1958), p. 17. Ling Lang, "Schools Run Factories," *Peking Review,* No. 39 (November 25, 1958), p. 14.

[13]Yang Hsiu-feng, op. cit., p. 40.

3.1 "Two Major Reform Measures on General Education"

During the past year our primary and middle schools have carried out major reforms under the guidance of the program, among which there are two major measures for strengthening ideological and political education and labor-production education respectively. A course in socialist education has been introduced in the middle schools, while both the middle schools and primary schools have offered a course in agricultural knowledge. Many schools have organized their students to participate in physical labor (agricultural production, handicraft work, school building work, general welfare work, etc.). In a number of places and schools the program of study combined with work (or part-time work with part-time study) has been introduced. Thus, the remedying of two long-existing basic defects in general education, namely detachment from production and neglect of politics, has started. . . .

I. WORK COMBINED WITH STUDY

To strengthen labor-production education and introduce the program of work combined with study is a great educational reform in our country. This will overcome the defect of divorcing education from production, theory from practice and brain work from physical labor, and serve to coordinate the two elements. It is a basic method to realize the socialist educational program and bring up socialist-conscious and cultured laborers and conforms to Marxist educational principles. . . .

Practice proves that schools intensifying labor-production education or enforcing work combined with study or half-farming and half-study program have achieved highly satisfactory results. Discipline through labor, first of all, dispels the erroneous thinking of the students who scorn physical labor and physical laborers and enables them to develop such virtues as the labor viewpoint, mass viewpoint, work habit, conscious discipline, collectivist spirit, capacity to work hard, frugality, etc.

Secondly, the students are enabled to acquire the basic knowledge and techniques required in industrial or agricultural production. 60 percent of the students in the middle schools in Chiu *hsien*, Hopei province have learned to thresh, while 40 percent can till and plow. The students of the school for children of handicraftsmen have learned the rudiments of spraying paint, pumping, smelting, casting, etc., totalling 26 techniques. In this manner the students turned out by our schools are no longer fragile scholars incapable of carrying a load on the shoulder pole or distinguishing the five grains, but are laborers cultured and having a productive capacity.

Thirdly, the program will consolidate, expand and strengthen the cultural and scientific knowledge acquired in the classroom and enhance the results of instruction. The students' participation in labor will enable them to gain confirmation of their book knowledge through practice and coordinate theory with actual conditions. Besides, they can also acquire some new practical knowledge not obtainable in their textbooks in the course of labor practice. The 4th Middle School of Liling, Hunan

Tung Tsun-tsai, "Two Major Reform Measures on General Education" [Written record of a talk delivered by the author at a socialism forum on March 4, 1958], *Jen Min Chiao Yu* [*People's Education*], No.4 (April 1, 1958), *Extracts from China Mainland Magazines*, No.141 (September 8, 1958), pp. 14-22.

launched the work-and-study program in 1957 and the scholarship of the students has since been raised considerably. In 1956, 5.4 percent of the students in the school failed in one subject, which dropped to 1 percent in 1957. Similar conditions are noted in many schools where the students engage in half-work and half-study. The fact proves that the combination of work with study not only will not lower scholarship but will effectively raise it.

Fourthly, the physique of the students will be improved through labor discipline. 41 percent of the students in the Third Middle School in Changke, Honan, were afflicted with stomach trouble in 1955, which dropped to 9 percent in 1956, and now there is not one such patient. At the athletic meeting summoned in the Hsuchang administrative district, the students of the school won 21 championships in 35 events. Many instances prove that in those schools where the work-and-study program has been launched, not only the incidence of diseases among the students is lower, but they often lead in athletic events.

Fifthly, the program has great economic significance. Since its introduction last year, many students have been enabled to defray their school expenses with the income from their labor. In some schools where the half-work and half-study practice is launched the students support the school with their labor. This lightens both the burden of the state and that of their families. In some schools which carry out the work-and-study program, the grant-in-aid from the state has been lopped 50 percent this year and in the coming year only individual scholarships will be offered. If the middle schools throughout the country can do the same thing, the state will save several hundred million Yuan a year. This serves to show the tremendous economic significance of the program.

The aforementioned facts indicate that the organization of the students to participate in productive labor, to combine work with study or to pursue work and studies on a 50-50 basis not only fulfills the purpose of labor-production education but also achieves the end of moral, intellectual and physical training. Labor-production education should form the basis of school education. It constitutes one fundamental measure for the upbringing of socialist-conscious and cultured laborers. As a socialist laborer one should have socialist consciousness, culture and learning and, naturally, also the capacity for production—capable of both brain exertion and physical labor. The function of the modern school is to train such a new type of laborer. Our schools are to train the new generation into laborers capable of brain exertion and physical labor through both classroom education and labor discipline. Only in this way can our school education attain the object of raising the productivity of society and actually serve our national economy. . . .

In introducing the work-and-study program there are several patterns as follows for our reference:

The first type is the combination of study and production, i.e. half-farming with half-study. Study and work go together. In some schools the students attend school half day and work half day. In rural districts they go to school during the dull season and work in the busy season, or study on rainy days and work on fine days. The curriculum consists chiefly of language, mathematics and agricultural knowledge. The students are both scholars and farmers. Many people-operated middle schools are run in this style. The one in Han ts'un, Hopei, is a typical instance. The school runs two classes. One comes in the morning and works in the afternoon, while the other has a reversed schedule. Such schools mostly count on the income of the students from their productive activities to meet the maintenance expenses. In the past, we had only state and masses-operated school; now we have a third type—the student-operated school. This type can be conveniently launched and popularized. I say such schools quite conform with Marxist educational principles, and we must not give them a low rating. Many people look down upon them and contend with profuse gesticulation that "their quality is low" and "not many courses are offered." Their attitude is not right. Some of our educators have sat at their desks several decades, but they have failed to conceive the idea of such schools which are in accord with Marxist educational principles. We should study them in seriousness and try to extend them. Why should we look down upon them?

The second type involves two different procedures to pursue work and studies. First, the students are organized to participate in productive labor at farm coops during vacation, holidays or after class hours. There is not only the advantage of participation in social production but also that of maintaining close contact with the masses, for the students to integrate themselves into the masses should also be one objective of education. Then there is the arrangement of an experimental gardening plot on a school campus to enable the students to participate in labor. Since 1952 the students of the Third Middle School in Chang Ke, Honan, have been organized to cultivate in succession 46.5 *mow* of experimantal plots, of which 3.4 *mow* is entirely for experimental purposes, while the rest is devoted to the planting of fruit trees, saplings, regular crops, etc. This represents planned and organized participation by students in productive labor. During rush seasons the students also return home to give a hand to farm cooperatives. The yield of the experimental plots in many of such schools has exceeded the highest record in the locality and claimed the attention of the masses. The adoption of either of the aforementioned procedures involves only a proper adjustment of the school calendar concerning vacations and holidays without modifying the current instructional program. This is a simple and convenient measure widely adopted among rural schools at present.

The third utilizes the instructional workshop and the experimental plot existing in a school for the students to participate in productive labor. The workshop of the First Middle School in Dairen at one time received orders from outside for simple jobs. Some schools in the cities organize their students for participation in social production during vacations, holidays or after class hours, or launch productive labor for the students through extra-curriculum research groups linked with various courses of instruction. . . .

The program of work combined with study may take varying types or patterns according to the needs of actual conditions, but in any case the following principles must be observed:

1. The coordination of education with labor is a general principle. Under the guidance of this general principle we should coordinate theory with practice and physical labor with brain exertion in the simultaneous pursuit of studies and labor, so that the intellectual elements can be welded with the mass of workmen and peasants.

2. Any type of the program of work combined with study or half-work combined with half-study must take cognizance of the need of providing ideological-political education for the students instead of seeking economic advantage alone. Ideological-political education is the soul and guide of school education, which should be borne in mind at all times.

3. The program should be carried out with due consideration of the needs of a particular locality, a particular time or particular personnel. The participation in handicraft production by the students of the school for handicraftsmen's children in Hsinhsiang, Honan, working temporarily in salt fields by the students of the Middle School in Yingk'ou, gathering oysters on the beach by the students of the middle school in Antung, picking coal by students of the middle schools in Fushun and Anshan, etc.—all this is launched on the basis of the concrete conditions of the various places where these schools are located. . . .

II. PROBLEMS RELATIVE TO SOCIALIST-POLITICAL CLASS

The socialist education course introduced in 1957 not only marks a reform in political instruction but in ideological-political education.

We have achieved enormous success in this respect in the past year. . . we have overcome the students' tendency to neglect politics, thus greatly elevating their political consciousness. . . .

The reform of solialist education chiefly lies in the coordination of real political life with the students' ideological status. In the past the political lesson was detached in two respects, namely, from real political life and from the students' ideological sentiments. . . .

The central task of the political lesson hereafter is the enforcement of ideological political education instead of the simple process of imparting knowledge. The political lesson of course will also take up such items as state policy, basic knowledge concerning the socialist revolution and construction, etc. What is the purpose of imparting such knowledge? It is to arm the students with such knowledge to blast capitalist thinking and rear socialist ideology, thereby forming the Communist conception of the world. The students, whether they have finished junior middle school or senior middle school, should be urged to cherish the noble aspiration for engaging in struggles for the promotion and construction of socialism, resolutely traversing the road of socialism. As the content of the socialist lesson continues to grow and develop, it will also enable the students to tackle problems relative to the ideological method, so that the new generation is capable of applying the dialectic materialist ideological method to deal with problems. . . .

The launching of the program of work combined with study is an essential part of the general line for socialist construction in the educational sphere, which calls for achieving more, faster, better and more economically. Apart from state-operated and people-operated schools student-operated schools have also sprung up, which represent the third type practicing the program of work combined with study. Energetic development of such schools will mean fast development. If they are developed in great numbers and at a fast pace, many good schools will come into existence. This will eventually lead to a great leap forward in the educational enterprise in our country.

Now we are in possession of the socialist educational program formulated by Chairman Mao, while new heartening developments have come to pass in educational practice. The new task now confronting us is to promote a greater leap forward in educational work. The same law calling for the overthrow of an old balance and the establishment of a new balance is also applicable to the realm of education. In the perspective of the over-all picture in the country the movement for work combined with study is yet in the offing, while our experience in socialist ideological-political education is fresh and awaits our summarization and popularization. As the old balance has been overthrown, the establishment of a new balance urgently awaits our efforts. It is hoped that the schools in those localities where some success has been achieved will continue to acquire more experience, summarize such experience and continue to forge ahead. In those areas where the practice of work combined with study and ideological political education have not yet aroused attention, the educational authorities should make haste to catch up with the revolutionary zest and create the conditions to facilitate the launching of both programs. New developments are bound to come to pass in the realm of our educational work in 1958, and there is bound to be a great leap forward.

3.2 "Onward to the Goal of 'Thoroughly Red and Profoundly Expert' "

The Peking University and other higher schools of learning are now engaged in the great debate over the question of "red" and "expert." Peking University professors have initiated criticism and self-criticism and are waging a struggle between the two paths and the two methods in connection with their functional work.

Many professors have declared sincerely their intention of devoting themselves to the people and the Communist Party. Their words and deeds indicate that the movement of ideological transformation of intellectuals in our country, especially high-level intellectuals, has now entered a new stage—a stage in which intellectuals, during the violent development of the nation-wide campaign to oppose waste and conservative ideas, have consciously demanded further and more intensive transformation among themselves to become throughly red and profoundly expert. This means a new atmosphere under the new situation in our country; and this new atmosphere is extremely valuable. . . .

The various political campaigns during the past eight years, especially the campaign for ideological transformation, have exerted a definite influence upon intellectuals. Some intellectuals are conscious of the change in situation and are determined to transform themselves and to devote their services wholeheartedly to the people and socialist construction. However, there are also a certain number of intellectuals who have not realized this point and who have failed to transform themselves consciously. Their transformation thus has remained perfunctory.

Accordingly, they continue to think in terms of personal profit and fame and of individual, narrow interests and to carry out their work according to the academic viewpoints of the capitalist class. They hold in esteem their functional work and slight political matters, pursue personal profit and fame and individual interest, sever theory from practice, and lack the feelings of workers and farmers.

In their pursuit of personal fame, certain research personnel refuse to conduct research in certain problems of production and choose to watch the country's production sustain loss. In the interests of their individual prestige and position, certain professors regard knowledge as their own private property and refuse to pass it on to students, thus intentionally ignoring student improvement. Certain engineers who have not diligently studied their functional work for a number of years still choose to play the connoisseur, with resultant damage and loss to national construction. Certain writers have not transformed their own ideology, and thus spread the poison of capitalist ideology among readers through their works.

More serious are the cases of those who pretend to be academic authorities, who steal the achievements of others, who suppress new-born forces, and who maintain conservative ideas and remain backward through self-satisfaction and complacency.

It is the greatest waste to be neither red nor expert. This sentence reveals a great truth in the research agencies, the higher schools of learning, the units of creation, the organization of medical treatment, and the departments of science and technology, when the campaign against waste and conservative ideas develops into an upsurge the spearheads will then point to the cases of serious waste and conservative ideas caused by intellectuals being neither "red" nor "expert." In this great era, intellectuals who harbor serious ideas of capitalist individualism do not promote progress, but, instead, promote regression. They have become obstacles to onward progress in the current undertakings of socialist science, technology, culture and education.

Since September 1957, the question of being red and expert were being debated

Editorial, "Onward to the Goal of 'Thoroughly Red and Profoundly Expert,' " Peking, *Jen Min Jih Pao*, March 23, 1958, *Survey of Mainland China Press*, No. 1747 (April 9, 1958), pp.1-5.

more penetratingly in many higher institutions. Through the debate, many young students had their socialist awakening raised. However, among the higher intellectuals, a clear understanding of this question has not yet been reached. Some think that so long as the higher intellectuals perform their professional jobs well, they are serving socialism. Others hold that since there is hardly time enough to become expert, it will be impossible to be both red and expert. Still others say that one who is expert but not red contributes more to the state than one who is red but not expert. These confused thoughts find expression in the attachment of greater importance to talent than to character. These people have not a clear conception of the demand for "redness," and they do not understand the truth that politics is the supreme command.

What is "red"? "Red" represents the goal wherein every intellectual has a political attitude compatible with socialist society. Undergoing one revolution, the system of private ownership in our society has changed to socialist ownership. With the foundation changed, the superstructure, too, should be changed.

The ideology of men must also undergo a revolution to do away with the ideology of capitalist individualism and to establish the concepts of collectivism of the working class. This also means that everyone should be determined to place himself wholeheartedly at the service of the people and socialism. The ideology of capitalist individualism represents a force which would guide the development of our society through division into tens of thousands of selfish individuals and small cliques which would fight against one another for their own interests, thus promoting the regression of our society into capitalist.

Is there any difficulty involved in becoming both red and expert as well as in becoming throughly red and profoundly expert? Of course there are difficulties involved. To catch up to the world level in 12 years, starting from the academic level of our country which is, after all, not very high—while also conducting ideological transformation—is truly a great difficulty. However, the primary condition for advancing to the world's level in 12 years is to be red. This red means precisely the ideology of collectivism.

It is fundamentally impossible to catch up to the world's level through individual efforts alone. Only by organizing the strength of scientists, with everyone contributing his efforts in one heart and mind as a whole, excluding the individual monopoly of research on certain minor problems, and concentrating the wisdom and strength of all to study practical problems as revealed in the process of production and livelihood and the fundamental problems of science will it become possible for us to advance and catch up to the world's level.

Regarding natural scientists: It is not our expectation that they should become both scientists and political theorists, and political activists as well. We merely wish that they may have socialist consciousness, establish ideas and working styles of collectivism, devote themselves to serving the people, and not alienate themselves from political matters

Regarding philosophers: They should have a high degree of socialist consciousness, and should know the most general objective rules governing the changes and development of the natural world, society, and cognition. They should have knowledge of both natural science and social science. Otherwise, he will say things which are meaningless, and being neither red nor expert, he is only a metaphysical ghost.

In regard to socialist scientists: They should have a definite degree of knowledge of philosophy and social science and should study their own fields of social sciences throughly from the viewpoint of Marxism.

Either being expert without being red, or being red without being expert, means the greatest waste of the manpower of the state. We oppose becoming expert without becoming red, and we likewise oppose becoming red without becoming expert. In the socialist society, everybody must promote his individual role through the great superiority of the collective force. A person who is expert but not red, because he is not red, does not rely on the collective body, but carries out his work on his subjective thinking, with his individual shortsight. He becomes a practical work who has lost his sense of direction, and he must lag behind others in academic achievement. Thus if one is not penetratingly red, one cannot be profoundly expert. A person who is red but not expert, because he is not expert, will fail to grasp the key problems in work. Comrade Mao Tse-tung had said, "Any analysis divorced from concrete facts will not lead to the understanding of the special nature of any contradiction." Politics which cannot guide actual work and living is empty politics, and such "redness" will be of no practical significance. Accordingly, one who is expert but not red is a useless person, and one who is red but not expert is likewise a useless person. The difference between the two is that the one who is expert but not red, when his individualism develops to a very serious extent, will play a role that undermines the socialist cause.

3.3 "Collectivization of the School Life of Children Realized in the Hsingchuang School District"

The building of the people's commune in Tats'un *hsiang* brings about more favorable conditions for the youth and children of the commune to receive education. The system of students collectively living in schools has been adopted by the primary schools of the commune. Collectivization of schools and free education have been realized. Such boarding primary schools have already shown their superiority in the strengthening of students' socialist and Communist education. The following is a brief introduction to what has been done and what are the superior characteristics in our school district:

I. PEOPLE DEMAND AND CONDITIONS ARE RIPE

The Hsingchuang central school district of Tats'un *hsiang* extends 15 *li* in an east-west direction. There are 21 villages and 13 primary schools in the entire school district. The service radius of the central primary school of Hsingchuang is comparatively long. The 90 students in the higher classes live in 17 villages. Some students are living at places which are nine *li* from the school. As the students live in a scattered way in different villages, their mobility is great. If there is rain, classes can not be held and, as the meal time is different in various villages, late attendance and absence are common. The discipline of students becomes lax and the elevation of educational quality is affected. Since the primary schools in various villages are in the form of one single class and multiple courses, the teachers are confronted with many difficulties manifested in lecturing, preparing of lectures, and studying themselves. Hence, the adoption of students collectively living in schools, the collectivization of schools, and the providing of free education have become the common pressing demand of the masses of the people as well as of the school teachers and students.

The flying leap forward of socialist construction makes possible the gradual

Yang Fa-tseng (of Central Primary School, Hsingchuang, Tats'un *hsiang*, Fengteng hsien, Honan), "Collectiveization of the School Life of Children Realized in the Hsungchuang School District," Honan *Chiao-yu Pan-yueh-kan* [Education Semi-monthly], No.19 (October 11, 1958), *Extracts from China Mainland Magazines*, No. 155 (January 23, 1959), pp. 45-48.

realization of the people's beautiful ideals. The building of the people's commune by the people of the whole *hsiang* has laid a good foundation and created favorable conditions for collectivization of schools and free education. Especially after the people's commune is set up and "san hua" [three changes: collectivization of living, militarization of production, and intensification of action in the form of a combat] are realized for the commune members, the schools are urged to step up the education of socialist and communist ideologies for students. In accordance with the conditions of the commune and the demands, the Party committee of the commune decided to establish new Communist schools, while mapping out the overall program for the commune, so that all students live in schools, their education on collective ideology of "all for one and one for all" is stepped up, and new men with Communist ideology are fostered.

II. PARTY COMMITTEE ATTACH IMPORTANCE, PEOPLE GIVE SUPPORT

Students collectively living in schools is carried out under the intimate concern and direct leadership of the Party committee . . . .

Under the guidance of the *hsien* Party committee Secretary, the Party committee of Tats'un *hsiang* held three conferences of cadres, which explained the superiority of having students live collectively in schools, implemented the *hsiang* Party committee's plan for boarding schools, studied how to rely on the masses to fully develop their activism in work, and appointed . . . a Party branch secretary to take up concrete leadership in this work. The extensive propaganda and mobilization were conducted among the masses. They actively supported the working method and set out to work instantly. In the evening of August 19, the people vacated their houses and delivered cooking utensils to the schools. On August 20, the people in various villages sent carts loaded with desks, chairs, and other furniture. Under the active assistance of the masses and the hard working of students and teachers, all the students and teachers of 13 primary schools came to live together in just one day's time.

III. ADJUSTMENT OF ORGANIZATION, UNIFIED ROOM AND BOARD

The entire central school district has 22 teachers (including seven teachers of primary schools of the people) and over 1,000 students. They all gather now at Shihpei *Ts'un*. Led by the commune Party committee, they study, live, and labor together. A reclassification is carried out according to students' age and the number of students in each class. The teachers are given courses to teach according to their professional knowledge. In addition, pedagogical research teams were set up for various academic fields. Tuition fee and living expenses of students are provided by the commune in a unified way. Food supplies for students are all delivered to the schools now. The commune provides food grain, fire wood, books, other miscellaneous expenses, and cooks. Half of the subsidiary food is provided by the commune and the other half is to be solved by the schools themselves by growing their own vegetables. In order to help the schools practice the study-and-work system, and to enable the combination of education with productive labor, the commune provided some land to the schools as their farms and experimental plots, and also five *mow* of vegetable gardens and a set of production tools.

IV. UNPARALLELLED SUPERIORITY SEEN IN
COLLECTIVIZATION OF SCHOOLS

(1) As the students come to live in schools, their life is collectivized. This facilitates the strengthening of leadership of the Party over the schools. Since the schools are

much larger now and the teachers and students are more concentrated, the Party committee can more easily understand the situation of school work, grasp the ideological condition of teachers and students, direct the schools to implement the Party's policy of education in earnest, and step up the education on socialist and Communist ideologies for both teachers and students.

(2) By adopting the system of boarding schools and free education, all children can now enroll in school, thereby making primary education completely universal.

(3) The Party's education policy can more properly be implemented. As the students spend all their days in schools, they study and rest together, they eat and stay together, they take unified action, and they attend classes and labor together. This is a favorable condition for the fostering of the students' collective ideology and communist morality and quality. They are trained to work and live independently. At the same time, following the collectivization of schools, more favorable conditions are provided for the practice of the half work and half study system and productive activities, for the combination of education with production, for the training of students into indoor as well as outdoor workers, red as well as expert new laborers combining mental labor with physical labor.

(4) The teachers and students find more time to work and study. Following the collectivization of schools, there are better conditions of leadership and equipment, and better arrangement of time so that the teachers can more properly study politics, go further into their professions and improve pedagogical work, and that the students can have more time to engage in study, labor, physical training, and rest.

(5) The specialized fields of teachers can be better utilized. After the students come to live collectively in schools and the adjustment of classification of students is made, the teachers are required only to teach one or two courses. They can now study more diligently in their specialized fields and heighten their teaching quality.

(6) The relations of school teachers and students with cadres and the masses can be strengthened so that the teachers may more closely associate with the workers and peasants and learn from them. When the masses regard the school as their own, they give it more support and assistance.

(7) With students living collectively in schools, the state, commune, cadres, masses, teachers, and students are all joined together, and the expenses, time, and number of teachers required are all reduced. . . .

3.4 "Agricultural Middle Schools in Their First Year"

Agricultural middle schools, which devote part time to farming and part time to study, are a new shoot of China's educational work and a new product emerging from the big leap forward in 1958. Agricultural middle schools are growing and developing under the leadership of the Party and with the support of the masses.

In March 1958, two agricultural middle schools were first set up in Shuangle *hsiang*, Hainan *hsien*, and in Shihchiao *hsiang*, Chenchiang *hsien*, of Kiangsu

Ouyang Hui-lin [Head of the Propaganda Department of the CCP Kiangsu Provincial Committee], "Agricultural Middle Schools in Their First Year," *Hung-ch'i* [*Red Flag*], No.7 (April 1, 1959), *Extracts from China Mainland Magazines*, No.168 (May 18, 1959), pp.18-23.

province. These schools represented a red flag of agricultural middle schools in Kiangsu. Under the leadership of Party committees, this was followed by a mass movement for setting up schools, and in less than one month over 6,000 agricultural middle schools were established in the province.

The masses enthusiastically greeted the establishment of agricultural middle schools. The students were happy and their parents were satisfied. But some people took bourgeois view and cast doubt on the agricultural middle schools. Instead of enthusiastically assisting the establishment and operation of agricultural middle schools, they looked on as an disinterested bystander and found fault with the schools. They held that agricultural middle schools were not regular schools because their curricula was limited and the standard ot teachers was not satisfactory, and that students could learn little from these schools. They held that schooling came into conflict with production and that such schools had no future. We firmly and constantly repudiated and combated such rightist thinking and absurd views. In our practical work, we tackled concrete problems, set examples and used impressive facts to convince them. Thus the process of opening, developing and consolidating the agricultural middle schools has been a process of struggle between two thoughts and between two methods on the educational front over the past year. . . .

Agricultural middle schools have become a component part of the people's communes since the latter were established in the autumn of last year. . . .

The development and consolidation of agricultural middle schools are proof of the correctness of our Party's guiding principle—integration of education with productive labor and walking with two legs in education construction. . . .

This year is the second year of running agricultural middle schools. . . . With regard to further development, consolidation and elevation of agricultural middle schools, we set forth the following suggestions, basing ourselves on our last year's experience:

First, the character of agricultural middle schools. An agricultural middle school is different from an ordinary full-day middle school but is not a spare-time school; it is a half-day school which devotes part time to farming and part time to study. It has its own school system, curricula, teaching plan and corresponding administrative system. An agricultural middle school will help students learn politics, languages, mathematics and basic subjects of agriculture. Some people run agricultural middle schools like a spare-time and temporary school; class hours are not fixed and students are arbitrarily transfered. This hinders the consolidation of schools. An agricultural middle school should have its definite school system. The school term is tentatively fixed at three years in Kiangsu, and the students admitted are mainly primary school graduates. In principle, the age of students should generally not exceed 16. Students over 16 years old should not be admitted in large numbers. This age limit is intended to help the communes organize labor-power and help the schools arrange teaching work. On the other hand, some localities want to imitate the full-day ordinary middle schools regardless of concrete conditions and strive for the so-called "regularization." In some cases, it is proposed that full-day middle schools be changed into half-day schools and merge with agricultural middle schools.

It is obvious that all these methods are not practical. If things are done like this, it would mean walking with one leg. It would be impossible to popularize middle school education with more, faster, better and economical results. Moreover, it will hinder improvement of the quality of ordinary middle school education. This would be disadvantageous to socialist construction. For this reason, the character of agricultural middle schools should be repeatedly made clear to cadres and the masses: agricultural middle schools must not be run like full-day ordinary middle schools, nor like a spare-time school.

Second, popularization and elevation. Agricultural middle schools will popularize middle school education but, once they are established, care should be taken to elevate them. Comrade Mao Tse-tung said in his "Speech at the Yenan Forum on Literature and Arts": "Popularization and elevation cannot be separated. The people demand popularization and then elevation month by month and year by year." Two tendencies have been observed in running agricultural middle schools: (1) empty talks about elevation while slackening efforts to develop the schools; (2) attention to popularization while overlooking elevation. We opposed these tendencies marked by one-sidedness, persisted in the principle of elevating the schools on the basis of popularization and popularizing them under the guidance of elevation. In consequence, the agricultural middle schools were enabled to achieve a rapid consolidation and development. For instance, two different views were held on the question of curricula. Some expressed the opinion that four courses of study were too few for junior middle schools in which students were to learn basic knowledge. They suggested that agricultural middle schools should follow the pattern of full-day junior middle schools. Others were of the opinion that four courses of study were too many for agricultural middle schools becuase the hours of study were few and the standard of teachers was low. They were in favor of concentrating on one or two courses of study. Both these suggestions were one-sided. They did not understand that agricultural middle schools, which devoted part time to farming and part time to study, should not teach too many courses of study at the present stage because the number of teachers was limited but that the courses of study should not be too few either because agricultural middle schools were designed to foster students as talents with middle cultural standard and basic knowledge of agriculture. Last year's experience indicates that under the present conditions it is desirable to set four courses of study. When the schools have been developed and the number of teachers has increased and their quality improved, agricultural middle schools which possess the necessary conditions may provide additional courses like chemistry, physics and hygiene as from the second grade of the junior middle schools. Along with the economic growth, technical education may be gradually intensified by providing courses in agricultural mechanization, electrification, and rural industry.

Third, the time for teaching and labor. Arranging the time for teaching and labor is essentially a question of correctly implementing the Party policy of integrating education with labor as well as a question of fostering laborers with socialist consciousness and cultural knowledge. Last year's experience indicates that in arranging the time for teaching and labor the agricultural middle schools should strengthen the teaching of basic courses and make a good job of productive labor, thereby guarding against two tendencies—devoting the time to study without labor and devoting the time to labor without study. Labor should be performed mainly for agricultural production. Where conditions are present, the schools may set up some small plants directly to serve agricultural production. At the present moment, agricultural middle schools in general are provided with land and small plants by communes for producing insecticides, chemical fertilizer, iron and wooden wares. The students in general perform labor in schools. It is advisable to perform labor for half a day (i.e. half a day devoted to labor and half a day devoted to study) or every other day (i.e. one day devoted to labor and the other devoted to study). This will facilitate organization of teaching and labor and help to consolidate the knowledge the students have learned. It has been proved by facts that both the morning and evening class (i.e. attending class in the morning and evening and performing labor between morning class and evening class) and the one-week system (i.e. one week devoted to study and the other week devoted to labor) produce unsatisfactory results. The students are overstrained in the case of the former and the knowledge learned by the students cannot be consolidated in the case of the latter. As to the distribution of the time for the whole year, some schools devote six months to study and five months to labor; others devote five months to study and six months to labor; in both cases, the vacation period is about one month. Such arrangements are approximately appropriate. The school term is arranged by the municipalities and *hsien* according to the farming season. No unified provisions are made for the whole province.

Fourth, teachers. Right from the beginning, we took four measures to solve the problem of teachers of agricultural middle schools, stressing the tapping of latent power, achieving self-reliance and breaking down the "qualifications" theory. We selected teachers on the spot and made unified distribution. We sent cadres down to serve as teachers and appointed primary school teachers to teach concurrently in agricultural middle schools. The vast majority of these teachers were new teachers, general lacking teaching experience. We guided and fostered teachers, striving to raise their teaching level in connection with politics, languages, mathematics and basic knowledge of agriculture. We adopted the following concrete measures: (1) Designating higher normal colleges and some intermediate normal schools to open correspondence schools. (2) Setting up groups in *hsien* and municipalities to assist and guide agricultural middle schools. (3) Forming teaching research teams for each *hsiang* and commune to exchange teaching experiences. (4) Instructing full-day middle schools to help agricultural middle schools resolve their difficulties. (5) Opening short-term training courses for teachers in *hsien* and municipalities during the vacation period. All these measures have achieved excellent results. It would appear that permanent teachers must be provided in agricultural middle schools and a full-time teacher must be assigned to each class before the teaching level can be constantly raised. Teachers' participation in productive labor should be subject to appropriate control so that they will have adequate time to prepare lessons and correct students' works. The problem of wages for teachers must be fully solved. Their wages in general should not be lower than wages for local primary school teachers. Necessary help should be given to those teachers from other areas who experience living difficulties. It is important to enable teachers to rest content with their work because it will help consolidate the schools.

Fifth, school funds. From the beginning to the end we have stressed the principle of relying on the masses to run the schools by industry and thrift. Agricultural middle schools in general have been established by the masses with very little money spent. Here, attention should be paid to two questions: On the one hand, we should insist on industry and thrift and oppose unnecessary spending of money. School premises and facilities should be kept with the means of the masses and people's communes. We should make do with what are available and add facilities step by step. We cannot expect everything to be perfect. Plants set up by schools should also practice economy. On the other, necessary school expenditure (like wages for teachers, teaching expenses) should be properly provided as far as possible. Therefore, practical measures must be taken to insure fixed sources of funds.

Sixth, the school scope and the question of boarding. Should agricultural middle schools be large in size or small in size? Should the students board in schools or live in their homes and come to schools every day? On these questions there were controversies. It appears that, after establishment of people's communes, readjustment of agricultural middle schools and boarding in schools have many advantages provided the schools have the necessary premises, facilities, medical facilities and administrative personnel. This can save the time spent by the students on their way to and from schools, stabilize the attendance and help arrange the time for teaching and labor. But some schools are over-sized with all students boarding in the schools. This adds to the difficulties in administration and makes it difficult for teachers to devote themselves to teaching. Besides, with many students gathered together, contact with local masses is lost: this is disadvantageous to the popularization of advanced production technique and to the cultural and social activities. Pending the formation of new inhabitants' living quarters in the rural areas, it is advisable to scatter the agricultural middle schools. The schools should not be over-concentrated, nor should the students board in schools regardless of concrete conditions. The proper size of an agricultural middle school is to embrace about 300 persons (i.e. about 100 persons for each class). If the school is too large, difficulties will arise concerning school premises and administration.

The above are some concrete experiences we have acquired in establishing agricultural middle schools. . . . We should carefully and seriously cultivate the new shoots of educational work—agricultural middle schools—so that they will grow sturdy and bear abundant fruits and that they will shine with greater brilliance and play a greater part in the construction of socialist education in our country.

3.5 "Educational Work Achievements in 1958 and Arrangements for 1959"

In 1958, educational undertakings of our country made two outstanding strides. One was successful implementation of the policy of coordinating education with productive labor, which brought about a big and comprehensive revolution in our educational undertakings. The other was successful implementation of the mass line for organizing schools by the entire party and all the people and adoption of the policy of "walking on both legs," which enabled our country's educational undertakings to make unprecedented strides.

(1) Coordinating education with productive labor is the only method by which all round development in training can be made. It is an absolute course for training laborers both in education and socialist consciousness. In 1958, as a result of their enthusiastic participation in diligent labor-economy study, their high enthusiasm in organizing factories and farms, and their engagement in productive labor and in the mass movements for iron and steel production and steel production and for autumn harvest, farming, and sowing, faculty members and students of education institutes at various levels not only supported the big forward leaps in our country's industrial and agricultural production, but also created material wealth for the State. However, most important of all, they changed the ideology of faculty members and students. Their ignorance of productive labor and their viewpoint concerning the class which exploited the laboring people in the past have been greatly changed, their viewpoints on labor and the broad masses have been strengthened, and their socialist and communist consciousness has been enhanced. They summed their achievements as "Broken Palms, Transformed Stand, Sun-Blackened Face, And Trained Ideology." . . .

Since last year, in the course of carrying out the policy of coordinating education with productive labor, we have gained the following major experiences:

(i) Educational revolution should be carried out on the basis of ideological revolution. In the basis on their victories in the rectification campaign and anti-rightist

---

Yang Hsui-feng, Minister of Education, "Educational Work Achievements In 1958 and Arrangements For 1959" (Speech delivered to the First Session of the Second National People's Congress, April 1959), (NCNA, Peking, April 28, 1959), *Current Background,* No. 577 (May 14, 1959), pp. 10-17.

struggle, educational institutes at various levels launched a series of ideological struggles, including the "Double Anti" movement, red and expert great debates, educational policy great debates, and criticisms on bourgeois educational and academic ideology. The extensive implementation of these struggles have provided us with favorable conditions for an educational revolution. If there is no victory in ideological revolution, there will be no victory in educational revolution. . . .

(ii) In carrying out the policy of coordinating education with productive labor, we must formally include productive labor in our educational plans with its goals clearly stated. We must also exert efforts to make proper arrangements for productive labor in the daily life of students and to coordinate closely the practices of productive labor with theoretical education, so as to enable them to become a wholesome teaching method. However, this is a complicated task, for it requires overall detailed planning. . . .

(iii) Proper disposal of questions concerning the relationship between theory and practice is an important link for carrying out allround implementation of educational policies. Since the implementation of educational policies, the tendency of theory deviating from actual practice has been effectively revised. However, we must not ignore or underestimate labor as it is being looked down upon by a considerable large number of teachers and students who have the ideology of ignoring practical work. This is something we cannot overcome in a short period of time. Carrying out a struggle against such an ideology is still our long-term and difficult tasks to be carried out in the future. Meanwhile, we must try to overcome and prevent the growing tendency of unilaterally believing that theories come from practice, the tendency of stressing only practical knowledge and direct experiences, and the tendency of neglected theoretical knowledge and indirect experiences. As long as we can coordinate productive labor properly with teaching, theory, and practical work, we will be able to implement the Party's educational policy in an allround manner. . . .

(2) Our country's educational undertakings made unprecedented strides in 1958. In that one year a mammoth illiteracy eradication campaign was carried out among the 600 million people, with results far better than those of the previous 8 years. Some 30 million people enrolled in various types of spare-time schools of varying standards organized by mines and factories and people's communes. We must not deny that this is an event of great significance. Kindergarten education also developed rapidly in 1958. Some 30 million children were enrolled in kindergartens last year, showing an increase of more than 27 times over the preceding year. Enrollment in primary schools in our country last year reached 86 million persons, representing an increase of 34 percent over 1957. With regard to intermediate school education, the enrollment in ordinary intermediate schools in our country last year reached 8.52 million persons, an increase of 36 percent over 1957 while 1.47 million persons were enrolled in intermediate vocational schools, an increase of 89 per cent over the preceding year. Those agricultural and other professional intermediate schools organized in 1958 had an enrollment of some 2 million persons. The total number of intermediate school students in China last year increased by 70 percent over the year before; and the number of high educational institute students was 660,000 over last year, an increase of 50 percent over 1957. This unprecedented development of our country's educational undertakings is attributable to the successful implementation of the Party's general line for socialist construction and the policy of "walking on both legs" as well.

The all-round big forward leaps of our educational undertakings in 1958 have proven that the guiding principle of "walking on both legs" prescribed by the directives issued by the central authorities and State Council last year on educational work have opened up a broad avenue for the development of our country's educational undertakings. As long as we can raise the enthusiasm of various departments of the Central Government, of local organization and departments concerned, and of the broad masses in organizing schools, under the inspiration of the guiding principles of taking the whole nation as a coordinated chess game and of coordinating the leading cadres with the broad masses, and through proper arrangement of full-time, half-day, and spare-time schools, we will be able to develop our educational undertakings in compliance with the policy of more, faster, better, and more economical. Moreover, we will be able to popularize education and to train a large body of thousands of red and expert intellectuals from the working class in a comparatively short period in our country, a country that has a large population with a poor background. . . .

In the development of educational undertakings, we must resolutely adhere to the guiding principle of coordinating the popularization of education with raising educational standards. Neglect of either of these would make it difficult for us to expeditiously change the general outlook of our country's cultural backwardness as well as to raise our scientific and cultural standards. So long as we implement the guiding principle of walking on both legs in popularizing education and in raising educational standards partially, we will be able to eliminate the contradictions between quantity and quality. We must use the method of developing half-day and spare-time schools together with the organization of educational institutes by factories and mines to meet the needs for popularizing education, and on the other hand we must raise the quality of the full-day schools as well as raise the work quality of a selected group of these schools to a particularly high level so as to enable them to become the backbone of our educational undertakings. This way of utilizing reasonably our limited strength will not only popularize education simultaneously with raising standards, but will also give equal emphasis to quality as well as quantity, thus enabling us to have initiative in developing educational undertakings.

(3) According to Premier Chou En-lai's proposal in his report concerning work tasks on the cultural and educational form for this year, they are to mobilize all possible factors—on the basis of last year's big development—to suitably develop educational undertakings, with special emphasis on reorganization and consolidation; to further implement policies and guiding principles on educational work; and to notably raise the quality of educational work. In order to victoriously fulfill these tasks, I am of the opinion that we must carry out the following undertakings properly;

(i) Regarding the development of educational undertakings, we must make efforts to continuously develop the illiteracy eradication movement with high enthusiasm and earnestness, consolidate and develop the various types of spare-time schools, and organize all the youths and adults who have been freed from illiteracy to continue their studies in order to further consolidate our achievements in the elimination of illiteracy. The development of spare-time schools should be carried out from the viewpoint of serving production and with consideration being given to the critical labor situation in our country, so that teaching can be conducted in adherence with the coordination between production and central work tasks, thereby assuring the smooth implementation of both production and study.

In areas where primary school education has been popularized basically, we must pay special attention to the consolidation and to raising the standards of work in this phase. As in areas where the popularization of primary school education has not yet been completed, efforts should be made to carry it out with earnest zeal. All intermediate schools adopting the half-day system should further develop, consolidate, and raise their work quality. As for senior high schools and normal institutes at various levels—including higher educational institutes in areas with a weak foundation—efforts should be made to make selective developments.

(ii) With regard to schools organized in 1958, efforts should be exerted to reorganize, overhaul, and improve them. With a view to assuring the high quality of educational work of schools at various levels, organizations concerned of the government and in the provincial, municipal, autonomous region, special area, and county levels should select a group of full-day schools from the regular full-day schools at various levels for selective development. The number of schools selected for selective development should not be too large and they should be pressed for high educational work quality, so as to enable them to create new work achievements and experiences and to guide other schools in their development.

(iii) With regard to education and productive labor, higher educational institutes and scientific research institutes should make efforts to arrange their practice of productive labor and study properly and in an all round manner.

Meanwhile, I would like to summarize our experiences in carrying out educational policies during the last year and to formulate anew the guiding and teaching plans or the guiding principles for teaching plans of schools at various levels. Classes on basic theoretical studies of higher educational institutes should not be reduced, and primary and intermediate schools should try their best to raise the teaching quality of their basic courses of study, so as to practically and firmly lay down the ground work for future cultural and scientific studies.

Beginning this autumn, primary and intermediate schools should separately set up their curricula for maximum and minimum implementation in accordance with the supply of teachers. Intermediate schools which have set their curricula to the fullest extent—when the situation permits—should offer courses on foreign languages starting from junior first grade with the assurance that they will be taught properly and students will learn them as perfectly as possible.

Productive labor should be listed as a part of the regular curriculum. The time ratio between productive labor and education should be arranged differently by schools of different natures. As for schools adopting the full-day system, education should be their primary assignment and the time required for engaging in productive labor by their students should be properly arranged in conformity with the ages and other specific features of students and with reference to the practices of other types of schools at various levels and vocational schools. Generally speaking, there are three basic ways for students to participate in productive labor:

(a) In factories and farms organized by the schools,
(b) In rural areas or factories through arrangements made by the school,
(c) In definitely prescribed social welfare undertakings.

It is demanded that education and productive labor be carried out in a coordinated manner. As for education and productive labor that cannot be carried out directly in a coordinated manner, they should be conducted separately according to schedule. Special attention should be given to prevent the unilateral emphasis on education which will give rise to the tendency of looking down on physical labor. Bases for carrying our productive labor in schools should be reorganized so as to insure that productive labor will be performed effectively. Efforts should also be made to formulate, step by step, overall productive labor plans according to actual needs, and to outline the productive labor tasks of students and the necessary rating systems for their performance as well. Knowledge may be acquired through hard labor. However, a too heavy educational burden given to students will not only affect the results of their study, but will also affect their physical health. Therefore, efforts should be exerted to do away with the tendency of giving excessive assignments to students.

(4) Continuously strengthening the political work on ideology and instruction on political theory. With regard to courses on political theory, along with continuous strengthening of our study of socialist and Communist ideology and its coordination

with current political tasks and events, efforts should be exerted to step up the study of Marxism-Leninism theories in a systematic manner and coordinate this education with the education on current events and government policies as well as our daily political ideology.

(5) Carrying out the collection and compilation of teaching materials properly. The formulation of teaching plans for courses of basic study of intermediate and primary schools and textbooks for general use should be carried out in conformity with the Party's educational policy. Efforts should be made to organize the forces of educational institutes to examine and compile higher educational institutes' teaching plans and materials, so that teaching materials of high academic value can be published.

(6) Scientific research work of Higher Educational Institutes should be conducted centered around educational work. Under the guidance of socialism, on the basis of last year's forward leap spirit, efforts should be exerted to continuingly develop the policy of "blooming" and "contending." Meanwhile, we must strengthen our work cooperation inside and outside educational institutes, so as to raise work efficiency and to eliminate waste. In accordance with their educational tasks and their own special features and conditions, schools should formulate scientific research plans to coordinate with the needs for production and construction of the State and their own practices of productive labor.

(7) Increasing the training of teachers and raising their quality and establishing a vast body of red and expert school teachers play an important role in developing and consolidating educational undertakings. Therefore, we must accurately implement the Party's policies concerning intellectuals, mobilize all available teachers to serve in the interests of our socialist educational undertakings, and adopt various effective measures to systematically organize school teachers to engage in spare-time studies, so as to raise the work standard and political consciousness of teachers in our country. Meanwhile, we must also energetically train new teachers by following the guiding principle of carrying out long-term and short-term training simultaneously, and by improving the various types of normal schools at various levels, so that teachers for intermediate and primary schools and for kindergartens can be trained in large numbers. The training of teachers for Higher Educational Institutes should also be conducted in conformity with the policy of walking on both legs. With the exception of retaining some of the graduates to work as assistant professors, all Higher Educational Institutes with favorable conditions—particularly selective educational institutes for higher learning—should assume the responsibility of training graduate students and of giving advanced-training to teachers simultaneously with the continuous selection of graduates to be sent abroad for advanced studies, so as to train more teachers with comparatively higher scientific and technical standards to become the backbone teachers of our country.

To correctly handle the relationship between the teachers and students is of great significance toward improving the work of teaching and study. In teaching and study, it is necessary to promote the supervisory role of the teachers on one hand and to develop fully the enthusiasm and initiative of the student on the other hand, so that both teaching and study will be advanced simultaneously. For this reason, the teachers are required to earnestly shoulder the tasks of "preaching, giving lectures," and "clearing doubts." They should love and protect the students and insist on strict discipline from the students. At the same time, they should listen and accept the opinions of the students so as to improve both teaching and study. The students should respect their teachers and should be humble in their study. On the other hand, they may adopt suitable means or forms to put forward their suggestions and criticism. Such relationship between the teachers and students are growing among the schools in our country. It is the duty of the educational workers to see that this relationship will be developed more healthfully.

We have learned from experience that the leadership of the Party is the basic insurance for all our accomplishments. The decisive factor of the enormous achievements we attained in our educational undertakings during 1958 was in establishing and intensifying the Party's leadership at the cultural and educational front. The big forward leap in production has stirred up the cultural revolution. Our powerful and enormous resources lie in following the correct direction, moving along the mass line, coordinating dissemination and improvement, and "walking on two legs" and developing fully our enthusiasm and initiative.

Our task for 1959 requires us to make a greater step in raising work quality. Only by consistently relying on the Party's leadership, relying on the people's masses, summarizing our experiences, correcting our short-comings, and improving our work can we successfully fulfill this task.

PART FOUR

Retrenchment (1960-1963)

PART FOUR
Retrenchment (1960-1963)

On the surface, it would appear that this period of "retrenchment" was a natural result of the "mushrooming phenomenon" of the previous period of the "great leap forward," with its emphasis on unparalleled growth and the accompanying reduction in educational quality. However, one of the most important determining factors underlying the polices of the period of retrenchment was the worsening Sino-Soviet relationship and the ultimate withdrawal of Soviet assistance. In this regard, it may be helpful to trace the development of the conflict between China and the Soviet Union.

As many sources indiçate, there are numerous interpretations and explanations of the origins of the ideological differences between the People's Republic of China and the Soviet Union, and the course of developments which eventually led to an open conflict between the two nations. Chinese Communist sources identify the 1956 20th Congress of the Communist Party of the Soviet Union as the point of origin, citing the following violations of Marxism-Leninism:

> In particular, the complete negation of Stalin on the pretext of "combating the personality cult" and the thesis of peaceful transition to socialism by "the parliamentary road" are gross errors of principle.[1]

The Declaration of 1957 adopted by the Moscow Meeting of Representatives of the Communist and Workers' Parties was finally worked out as a common document acceptable to all participants. However, in working on the original draft, controversy arose between the delegation of the Communist Party of the Soviet Union (C.P.S.U.) which urged the concept of peaceful transition from capitalism to socialism, and the delegation of the Communist Party of China (C.P.C.), headed by Mao Tse-tung, which considered this a violation of basic Marxist-Leninist theory on the state and revolution.

From the Chinese viewpoint, Soviet revisionism increased following the 1957 Moscow Meeting, and the leadership of the C.P.S.U. departed farther and farther from the path of Marxism-Leninism and proletarian internationalism, specifically: seeking collaboration with "U.S. imperialism" and the settlement of world politics by the heads of the Soviet Union (Khrushchev) and the U.S. (Eisenhower); Soviet advocacy of the politics of "peaceful coexistence," "peaceful competition," and "peaceful transition"; the Soviet Government in June 1959 unilaterally tearing up the October 1957 Sino-Soviet agreement on new technology for national defense and refusing to provide China with a sample of an atomic bomb and the related technical data concerning its manufacture; siding with the "Indian reactionaries" in the Sino-Indian border incident of September 1959; Khrushchev's repeated attacks on the domestic and foreign policies of the Chinese Communist Party (e.g. insinuations that China's socialist construction was "skipping over a stage," that the people's communes were "in essence reactionary").

To defend its position, and in the hope of clearing up the ideological confusion in the international communist movement, the Communist Party of China published "Long Live Leninism," and two other articles in April 1960 which:

> . . . concentrated on explaining the revolutionary theses of the 1957 Declaration and the fundamental Marxist-Leninist theories on imperialism, war and peace, proletarian revolution and the dictatorship of the proletariat.[2]

The differences between the two countries within the international communist movement widened during the summer of 1960. At the Third Congress of the Romanian Workers' Party, held in Bucharest from June 24-26, 1960, Khrushchev launched an anti-China campaign (to which the Albanian Party of Labor took exception). In July, the Soviet Government recalled all Soviet experts in China. Consequently, Sino-Soviet conflicts brought the Meeting of the Representatives of the 81 Fraternal Parties, held in Moscow in November 1960, to the brink of rupture:

> It was a struggle between the line of Marxism-Leninism and the line of revisionism and between the policy of preserving principle and upholding unity and the policy of abandoning principle and creating splits.[3]

Conditions worsened following the Moscow meeting. According to the Chinese, the 22nd Congress of the C.P.S..U., in October 1961:

> . . . marked a new low in the C.P.S.U. leadership's efforts to oppose Marxism-Leninism and split the socialist camp and the international communist movement. It marked the systematization of the revisionism which the leadership of the C.P.S.U. had developed step by step from the 20th Congress onward.[4]

The Program adopted by the 22nd Congress was viewed as "out-and-out revisionism," totally violating the fundamental theories of Marxism-Leninism. In August 1962, the U.S.S.R. notified China that the Soviet Union would conclude an agreement with the U.S. on the prevention of nuclear proliferation. (The Chinese Communists considered that the Soviet Union had capitualated to nuclear blackmail by the U.S. in the 1962 Cuban missile crisis, and that Cuban sovereignty had been violated.) By the summer of 1963, the Soviet Union, the U.S. and Britain had signed a treaty on the partial halting of nuclear testing. Thereafter, the Soviet press launched a strong anti-China campaign.

However, from the Chinese Communist viewpoint the origin of the Sino-Soviet conflict can be traced back to the 20th Congress of the C.P.S.U. in 1956, and the subsequent line of development of the differences between the leadership of the C.P.S.U. and the C.P.C. was essentially that of ideological "revisionism" — departure from the fundamental theories of Marxism-Leninsim and the international communist movement.

So far, we have presented the Chinese Communist viewpoint in considerable detail because of the integral relationship between the Party line and educational policy. There are, of course, other interpretations of the Sino-Soviet conflict. In this respect, Robert C. North notes that an analysis of Chinese Communist and Soviet Russian policy statements during 1960 and 1961 reveals a number of very significant differences:

> . . . the Chinese were almost twice as hostile toward the West; the Chinese were far more dissatisfied with the status quo; the Chinese tended to perceive the general environment as considerably more threatening than did the Russians.[5]

According to the editor of *Current Scene*, at the heart of the Sino-Soviet conflict was "the central fact of Communist China's refusal to remain subordinated to the Soviet Union," which was related partly to Chinese culture and history, and partly to political ideology.[6] Traditionally, China had always perceived herself as the "Middle Kingdom" (i.e. central), the only nation with true civilization. Although the Western powers with their superior armed forces destroyed this self-image during the nineteenth and twentieth centuries, the ancient concept of being the "hub of the universe" remained, and was recollected as the power and prestige of the People's Republic increased.

This view holds that an integral component of Mao Tse-tung's philosophy is that international communism should rely primarily on indigenous, rather than foreign, agencies to achieve political control over the underdeveloped world. This was in direct opposition to the Soviet line. Maoist strategy, according to *Current Scene*, is based on the following four convictions:

> 1. Neither indigenous nationalists nor the West will abandon vital political interests and surrender political influence in the underdeveloped world to communists without a struggle—communists will have to fight to realize their ambitions for controlling the underdeveloped world.
> 2. Nationalism, the elemental revolutionary force in underdeveloped areas, is largely an expression of anti-foreign sentiment . . . .
> 3. Communism cannot initially attract decisive political support in the underdeveloped world; local communists, therefore, must build political strength as champions of "patriotic" anti-foreign struggle, and gradually usurp the leadership and control of the nationalist movements in their respective areas . . . .
> 4. Because the Chinese Communists have discovered and successfully applied the formula for combining communist with nationalist revolution in an underdeveloped area, obviously Peking, not Moscow, should direct and guide the international communist offensive in the underdeveloped world.[7]

As a consequence of the open break with the Soviet Union, the withdrawal of Soviet technicians from China, and the public attacks on Soviet revisionism, Soviet influence decreased and Maoist thought became the model for Chinese Communism.

In addition to the international controversy resulting in the loss of Soviet assistance, there were also important internal factors which had serious consequences for the "great leap forward" and the rural commune movement. As North pointed out:

> By mid-1959 it was becoming painfully evident, however, that the Chinese Communists had grossly miscalculated, and by mid-1960 the evidence pointed to a national disaster. The products of the native heavy industry programme had proved almost worthless. The hoped-for increase in agricultural production had not materialized. The 1959 and 1960 crops had fallen short of even 1957 estimated production. Food and raw materials were getting more and more

scarce. Peking blamed natural calamities for the failure to fulfill agricultural production quotas. But faulty planning, bungling and mismanagement, together with lack of incentive associated with the commune system undoubtedly played the greater part in the fiasco. The Communique of the Ninth Plenary Session of the Party Central Committee, issued in January 1969, admitted publicly the failure to fulfill agricultural production plans for 1959 and 1960 and announced the programme of industrial retrenchment brought on by this and by shortages of other raw materials.[8]

The unfulfilled expectations in agriculture and the general economy were so severe that the entire national construction policy had to be re-examined. It appears that the harvest failures, economic disasters, and the withdrawal of Soviet aid gave the old class of capitalists and functionaries an opportunity to attack Mao Tse-tung's ideology. As a matter of fact, some of the leading Party members were said to have been responsible for the attack. They made use of the public communication media to propagandize revisionism on the Khrushchev model, and drew up many political proposals which disclosed a tendency to restore capitalism.

Responding to this challenge, Mao Tse-tung in 1962 launched his "socialist education campaign" to "purify and to rectify revisionist tendencies" and to "re-establish socialist, collective controls over the economy, especially in the rural areas."[9] Along with this, new guidelines were re-established for the period after the "great leap forward." They were "adjustment, strengthening, soundness, and high-quality."[10] There is no question that these guidelines applied to education as well, for as Robert D. Barendsen noted:

> By the beginning of 1961 it was abundantly clear that the "great leap forward" had stumbled to a halt. The party and government now began explicitly espousing policies of "adjustment" and "consolidation" which had in fact already been the operating guidelines for a good part of the previous year. The regime was deeply preoccupied with efforts to restore critically lagging agricultural production, and it realized that investments in other areas, including education would have to be held in check.[11]

As indicated previously, during the period of the "great leap forward," in keeping with the Party line of developing education with "greater, faster, better and more economical results," and the slogan of "walking on two legs," tens of thousands of schools of many different types were rapidly established in various localities. Considering the complexity of educational development, the over-night creation of schools was bound to generate many problems, one of which was the relationship between quantity and quality in education. As Barendsen observed:

> It would appear that the cumulative effects of the stress placed on productive labor and political activism under the 1958 educational reforms had seriously affected standards of teaching and learning in the nation's schools, particularly at the upper levels. These conditions gave rise in the spring of 1961 to renewed official concern with the quality of education.[12]

Another factor contributing to the low standard of education was the heavy emphasis placed on being "red," rather than on being "expert," in the "red and expert" question. The Chinese press of the period cited numerous examples of school administrators, teachers, and students who had obviously neglected academic work in order to carry out political and labor activities.

In response to the problem of educational quality, efforts were made to bring about a new shift in educational policy. The first indication of this shift was a slowing down of the "greater and faster" emphasis, as illustrated by the national enrollment figures, which were about one million less in 1960-1961 than in 1959-1960.[13] Secondly, a balance of "red and expert" was announced. In a speech to the 1962 graduates of Peking's higher institutions, Ch'en Yi stated:

> The relationship between "redness" and "expertness" is the same as that between politics and one's speciality . . . . For socialist construction, we need all kinds of personnel. . . . Ordinary higher institutions are concerned mainly with instruction in other specialities so that their students may become experts of various kinds. Thus, politics is the main subject studied in political schools, and other specialities are the main subject studied in ordinary schools.
>
> We must attach importance to both politics and our specialities . . . . We must combine them together. There is never anything like abstract politics. Politics always asserts itself through other specialities.[14]

Reflecting the change in priorities (or at least in emphasis), the time periods previously allocated for participation in political activities and physical labor were reduced to provide students and faculty with more time for academic study.

Given the nature of the Sino-Soviet conflict, and the withdrawal of Soviet scientific and technical assistance, one of China's major problems was the critical shortage of scientists and technicians. Under the circumstances, China made the decision to conduct a large-scale effort to train their own scientific and research personnel. Whereas earlier educational reform had proceeded along the lines of studying and learning from the advanced experiences of the Soviet Union, the educational reform movement during this period adopted the theme of carrying out "large-scale experimentation."[15] In sharp contrast to the optimism of the "great leap forward" period, Party leaders now acknowledged that the reform program would require "a prolonged trial-and-error process," and cautioned against attempting to "draw final conclusions prematurely."[16]

The major thrust of the new school reform now centered around efforts to: (1) raise the general standard or quality of education; (2) reduce the number of years spent in schooling (adopting a 5-year primary and a 5-year middle-school pattern to replace the 12-year organization; and (3) control the amount of time devoted to study.

The curriculum was to be "streamlined" by transferring certain courses to lower grades, merging, condensing, and reducing the redundancy in others. Outdated and insignificant materials were discarded in favor of more practical (i.e. functional) materials. Interestingly, not only were Soviet-oriented subjects and teaching materials either reduced or eliminated, but the study of English now received official encouragement.

Although the curriculum was revised, a complete revision of the texts probably did not materialize because no further details on the new school system were released at this time. Moreover, perhaps because the political leaders were reluctant to give up political indoctrination, the curriculum swung back to a program where political studies were again given more emphasis than others. As Barendsen pointed out:

> Although efforts to improve the academic quality of school instruction continued during 1962 and 1963, they were gradually overshadowed by a re-emergence of the regime's preoccupation with political indoctrination . . . . By the spring of 1963, the pendulum had swung back so far that the central party daily, *Jen-min-Jih-pao,* singled out the strengthening of ideological training as the foremost requirement for improving the quality of education in the nation's schools.[17]

Political indoctrination meant the acquisition of a firm proletarian outlook, a Marxist-Leninist class viewpoint, and the inheritance and development of the revolutionary traditions of the Chinese Communist Party.

The idea of productive labor was also revived. By the summer of 1963, physical labor was once again extolled as the best form of "class education." Schools were ordered to see that students and teachers participated in "productive labor," especially on the people's communes and in neighboring industrial enterprises. The coordination of education with productive labor became the central task of educational reform.

NOTES:

[1]Editorial Departments of *Renmin Ribao* [*People's Daily*] and *Honqi* [*Red Flag*], "The Origin and Development of the Differences Between the Leadership of the C.P.S.U. and Ourselves," *Peking Review*, No. 37 (September 13, 1963), p. 7.

[2]Ibid., p. 13.

[3]Ibid., p. 14.

[4]Ibid., p. 16.

[5]Robert C. North, "The Sino-Soviet Controversy," *This Is China,* ed. Francis Harper (Hong Kong: The Green Pagoda Press, Ltd., 1965), pp. 333-334.

[6]The Editor of *Current Scene*, "The Sino-Soviet Dispute: China's View," Ibid., p. 339.

[7]Ibid., p. 341.

[8]Robert C. North, op. cit., p. 331.

[9]Winberg Chai (ed.), *Essential Works of Chinese Communism* (New York: Bantam Books, 1969), p. 402.

[10]Chao Tzien, "Twenty Years of Communist Education," [Hong Kong] *Min Bao*, S.M. Hu (trans.), September 26, 1969, p.3.

[11]Robert D. Barendsen, *Education in China: A Survey* [Reprint from *Problems of Communism*], VIII, No. 4 (Washington, D.C.: Office of Education, n.d.), p.8.

[12]Ibid., p.9.

[13]Ibid.

[14]Ch'in Yi, "Speech to This Year's Graduates from Peking's Higher Institutions, *Communist China Yearbook, 1962* (Hong Kong: China Research Associates, 1963), p. 429.

[15]Lu Ting-yi, "Our Schooling Must Be Reformed," NCNA, Peking (April 9, 1960), *Current Background,* No. 623 (June 29, 1960), p. 2.

[16]Ibid., p. 6.

[17]Robert C. Barendsen, op. cit., p. 9-10.

4.1 "Actively Carry Out the Reform of the School System to Bring About Greater, Faster, Better, and More Economical Results in the Development of Education"

I.

Since 1958 when the CCP Central Committee and the State Council issued the "Directive on Education Work," and stimulated by the successes of the general line, the tremendous forward leaps, and the people's commune campaign, and under conditions of greatly strengthened leadership of the Party, we have fully carried out the educational policy of the Party, enormously developed our educational program, carried out a thoroughgoing revolution, and fulfilled the targets provided in the Second Five-Year Plan three years ahead of schedule. . . .

Although we have achieved tremendous successes in our educational work, it still does not satisfy the demands of the state for the rapid development of socialist construction. The present very favorable situation for technical innovation, technical revolution, and the development of people's communes has posed a set of new demands on education.

Faced with this new development and these new tasks, it has become most urgent for us to further extend the general line of the Party on socialist construction, the educational policy of the Party, and the work of developing our education program with greater, faster, better, and more economical results. To do so, we should adopt the spirit of the permanent revolution in improving and reforming all fields, particularly in reforming our middle and elementary schools.

II.

Since the founding of our country, we have continually carried out the reform of the school system in our full-time schools. Generally speaking, we have achieved better results in the reform of our higher education and vocational education, although there are still many problems to be solved. With regard to general education, although we have also achieved much success in the reform, we have not yet carried out the necessary radical reforms in the school system, the curricula, and padagogical methods in order to satisfy the demands of the state for the development of socialist construction. A serious situation characterized by smaller, slower, poorer, and less economical results still exists in these major fields of our education program.

What are the most serious conditions contributing to smaller, slower, poorer, and less economic results in middle and elementary school education today? They are the unnecessarily long period of schooling — 12 years — and the low academic standards set for those schools. The present school system is characterized by the division of elementary and middle school education into four sections, the inclusion of too many courses, the lack of emphasis on the relatively more important courses, and poor

"Actively Carry Out the Reform of the School System to Bring About Greater, Faster, Better, and More Economical Results in the Development of Education" (Speech by Minister of Education Yang Hsiu-feng), (NCNA, Peking, April 8, 1960), *Current Background*, No. 623 (June 29, 1960), pp. 11-19.

selection in the contents of the curriculums — all of which adversely affect the mastery of the most important courses by the students. Much of the mathematics, physics, and chemistry now taught in middle schools, in particular, is old stuff from the 19th century which in no way represents the science and technology of today. This backward situation is not in harmony with the socialist construction program being carried out in our country, nor with the development of the intelligence of our youth.

III.

I have so far discussed a number of important questions in general education. Now I will elaborate on the following points with regard to the ways and means of fulfilling our tasks satisfactorily this year:

(1) Actively develop full-time higher education and vocational education, and raise the standards to much higher levels. In accordance with the policy of coordinating large-scale development with over-all arrangements, we should quickly include the most advanced sciences and technology needed by our country in the curricula of our full-time higher education institutions. In the meantime, we should pay special attention to the development of such basic sciences as mathematics, physics, chemistry, biology, and electronics, in order to lay a good foundation for the development of our sciences and technology and raising them to higher levels.

We should rearrange our curricula, add new courses, and revise our curricular materials. Under the premise that pedagogy is to be treated as the main task, an effort should be made to strengthen scientific research, to place politics in command, to coordinate schooling with reality, to adhere closely to the mass line, to pay constant attention to the coordination of schooling with productive labor and scientific research, to develop the communist cooperative spirit, and to strengthen cooperation between educational institutions and other quarters.

Pedagogy in liberal arts colleges and scientific research in higher institutions should be further reformed to condemn the bourgeois ideology and modern revisionism, to expand and consolidate the position of Marxism-Leninism, to promote the development of philosophy and social science, and to speed up the growth of theoretical forces. Concentrated efforts should be made to establish a number of selected higher institutions to provide post-graduate departments for training large numbers of students. An active effort should be made to develop middle-school level vocational schools to train intermediate level construction personnel.

To lend great support to the development to agriculture and to speed up the training of specialized personnel for modernizing our agricultural operations, we should increase the number of students majoring in agricultural courses and strengthen the courses related to the mechanization of agricultural production. A great effort should be made to develop and properly operate agricultural middle schools to speed up the universalization of junior middle school education to benefit the development of agricultural production and the modernization of agricultural operations.

2) The universal development of spare-time education for workers and peasants is the fundamental way to rapidly turn large numbers of workers and peasants into intellectuals. It is also one of the most important methods of training personnel for all fields of construction. . . .

On the basis of this development, if we can first eliminate illiteracy and then universalize spare-time elementary school education and develop spare-time middle school education and higher education on a large scale, what an enormous technical force we shall possess in from three to five years! We can anticipate that by the time of the Third Five-Year Plan or a little longer, we shall have millions upon millions of students in spare-time higher educational institutions and middle-school level vocational schools. This is a matter of very great significance to us.

Spare-time education should be developed according to local conditions. Night schools, correspondence schools, radio classes, and television classes should be set up wherever possible. Under conditions where production tasks are guaranteed, the policy of of "coordinating education with production, coordinating over-all arrangements, providing education for the gifted, and flexible education methods" is adhered to, we shall most assuredly be able to direct the masses to continue their study on a lasting basis, and to continually consolidate and raise the levels of our spare-time education program. Reform of the school system is also needed in spare-time schools. Due attention should be paid to this matter.

3) Actively develop child education in order to raise the next generation properly. This is also a matter of great significance to the total emancipation of our women for state economic construction and to the consolidation and development of rural and urban people's communes. To carry out child education properly, it is necessary to formulate proper plans, to actively develop the teacher training programs in child education, to open large numbers of short-term training classes for these teachers, and to step up the training of qualified teachers and nurses for nurseries.

4) Develop the operation of schools by the entire Party and the entire nation on an even larger scale. Urge all quarters to develop fully their enthusiasm for this work. All factories, mines, enterprises, scientific research institutes, government organizations, people's organizations, units of the armed forces, people's communes, and urban street governments can open their own schools. They can open spare-time and part-time schools and also full-time schools; and they can operate institutions of higher education. Middle-school-level vocational schools, as well as regular middle schools, elementary schools, and kindergartens. Those schools can formulate flexible education plans according to their specific needs.

In the course of developing education on a large scale, we should adhere to the policy of coordinating the universalization of education with the raising of our educational standards. On the one hand, we should establish as many schools as we can in an effort to universalize education and, on the other hand, we should try our best to raise the standards of selected schools to higher levels. Both the central and local authorities should perfect the operations of a number of selected schools of different categories at different levels, where particular attention is being paid to the promotion of their educational standards in order to gain experiences for wide adoption by other schools.

5) Actively participate in the nation-wide technical innovation and technical revolution campaign, and introduce this campaign into schools. Recently, several hundred thousand teachers and students of the higher education institutions and middle-school-level vocational schools in the various localities have enthusiastically participated in the upsurging technical innovation and technical revolution campaign. In the course of this campaign, they have tightened their ties with workers and peasants, developed the communist spirit of thinking and acting boldly and the communist cooperative spirit, come forward with many inventions and creations and undergone severe ideological training. In the meantime, they have also launched a campaign for the renovation of pedagogical equipment. In the spirit of relying on one's own efforts, the great masses of teachers and students coordinated their productive labor with scientific research, experimented in the production of new products, produced various apparatuses and other modern pedagogical equipment, and created and renovated other pedagogical facilities in their schools.

With the assistance of related authorities, the educational authorities at the various levels are making preparations for the construction and expansion of laboratories and scientific and educational movie and slide studies in an effort to electrify pedagogical operations.

Large scale participation in production by schools greatly benefits the task of coordinating schools with production units and scientific research units, the development of the most advanced branches of sciences, and the task of raising the educational and scientific standards in our country. The great mass campaign of cooperation between schools and other units and between intellectuals and the masses of workers and peasants has combined the ideological, technical, and cultural revolutions into one. This is a matter of tremendous significance to the extension of the educational revolution, the reform of our school system, and of the development of our education program with greater, faster, better, and more economical results.

The basic guarantee for the success of our work lies in our reliance on the leadership of the Party and in our persistence in placing politics in command. In the face of the new development and new tasks all educational personnel in our country should rely more closely on the leadership of the Party, place politics in command, diligently study Marxism-Leninism and Mao Tse-tung's works, resolutely adhere to the mass line, and actively reform pedagogical work, in order to develop our education program with greater, faster, better, and more economical results.

4.2 "Our Schooling System Must Be Reformed"

In 1960, two upsurges have developed in our country. One is the upsurge in the technical innovation and technical revolution campaign. This is a nationwide upsurge whose large scope and quick development are unparalleled in our history. The other is the upsurge in the campaign for the building and improving of community dining halls, nurseries, and kindergartens by the rural people's communes, and for the developing on a large scale of commune-operated industry, neighborhood industry, suburban agriculture, public welfare facilities, and an organized economic livelihood of the urban residents by the urban people's communes, which are being established in large numbers. This upsurge will be very beneficial to the work of increasing production, fully emancipating women, improving the livelihood of the people, and raising the communist consciousness of the people.

These two upsurges have posed a series of new problems to those of us who are engaged in academic, ideological, cultural, and educational work. At present the great masses of workers and peasants are demanding the study of Marxism-Leninism; the study of Comrade Mao Tse-tung's works; the development of education, culture, public health, and physical culture; the care of the children, and the further condemnation of the bourgeois and modern revisionist ideologies in the fields of culture, knowledge, and ideology. We should do our best to satisfy these demands. . . .

Here, I would like to talk on one issue: our schooling system must be reformed.

We plan beginning now, carry out a large-scale experimentation on reducing the number of years spent in education, raising the standards, controlling the study

"Our Schooling System Must Be Reformed" (Speech by Lu Ting-yi, Vice Premier of the State Council, at the Second Session of the Second National People's Congress), (NCNA, Peking, April 9, 1960), *Current Background*, No. 623 (June 29, 1960), pp. 1-10.

hours, and increasing physical labor to a suitable extent in our full-time middle and elementary schools. . . .

We can now adopt this goal in our struggle: a great effort must be made to complete in the main the elimination of illiteracy among our young and adult workers and peasants, and to provide universal elementary school education to all school-age children in the period of the Second Five-Year Plan. A great effort must also be made, through the adoption of the policy of "walking on two legs," to provide junior middle school education to all the youths of appropriate age; greatly develop senior middle schools, vocational schools, and higher education institutions; establish a number of short-term college level vocational schools, develop spare-time educational institutions of all categories, and train for the state a great force of red and expert scientific and technological personnel and Marxist-Leninist theorists in the period of the Third Five-Year Plan.

Since 1958, educational reform personnel in our country have carried out experiments on the reform of the schooling system, of the curricula of middle and elementary schools, and of teaching methods in the various localities. Although it has not been very long since these experiments were carried out, it can now be seen that the reform of our schooling system is a realistic project, not a dream. I would like now to cite a few instances with regard to the experiments:

1) The present schooling system stipulates that pupils in kindergartens should not be taught reading and arithmetic. However, experiments carried out in Hopei, Shansi, Liaoning, Heilungkiang, Shensi, Kansu, Tsinghai, Shanghai, Kiangsu, Shantung, Fukien, Hupeh, and Honan show that even large kindergarten classes are able to learn now to spell Chinese words with the alphabet and to learn to read from 80 to 100 Chinese words. Experiments carried out in Heilungkiang, Kansu, Kiangsu, Honan, and Liaoning show that large kindergarten classes are able to calculate figures up to 20. The adoption of the methods of learning through playing is not only harmless to the health of the children concerned, but also makes the kindergartens more attractive to the children and their parents.

2) The prevailing schooling system stipulates that only children who have reached the age of seven can be admitted. But experiments in Peking, Kirin, Kansu, and many other localities show that it is practicable to admit children of six. It seems that it is practicable to admit children of six, six and half, and seven years of age into schools according to the development of the child concerned.

3) Beginning in September 1958, with the assistance of a work team of the Psychology Research Institute of the China Academy of Sciences, the CCP committee of Heishan *hsien* in Liaoning carried out an experiment on language study with the method of "collective study and collective exercise" at Peikuan Elementary School in the *hsien*. In five weeks, the committee completed the first volume of the language text book published by the Education Ministry of the Central People's Government — containing 233 new words — for teaching students of the first grade. By the end of the first semester, the committee had taught the students 1,700 words, with each student mastering an average of 1,115 words — with the best students mastering all 1,700 words, and the worse students mastering 400. This shows that in one semester students of the first grade may progress to the level of the second grade stipulated by the Education Ministry. . . .

In addition, the students are able to write short essays and to keep diaries. This experimental class has now progressed to the second grade. On January 10 of this year, Deputy Governor Che Hsiang-chen paid a visit to that school. Liu Yin, a student of this experimental class, wrote a poem in his honor: "Uncle Che is a busy man, yet he has time to see us in person. He listens to a lecture and takes some pictures. We shall never forget him." Please note that this is a poem written by a student of the second grade. . . .

4) The Psychology Research Institute of the China Academy of Sciences carried out an experiment in teaching arithmetic in coordination with algebra in two classes of the fifth grade in the No. 2 experimental elementary school in Peking with good results. At a unified examination in arithmetic held among all elementary schools in Hsicheng *ch'ü,* Peking, the grades of the students in these two classes averaged better that 94.

The institute holds that by teaching arithmetic in coordination with algebra, some of the curricular materials for middle schools may be introduced to elementary schools in line with the reform of our schooling system. By mastering algebra, a student will be able to solve difficult problems in arithmetic very easily.

5) Fifteen provinces and municipalities — Hopei, Shansi, Liaoning, Kirin, Heilunghiang, Shensi, Kansu, Tsinghai, Shanghai, Kiangsu, Anhwei, Kiangsu, Hupeh, Honan, and Kweichow — are experimenting on the five-grade unified elementary school system. Because many localities have extended elementary school education to all school-age children and have combined their junior and senior elementary school education; and also because the curricular material of elementary schools are too repetitious (in the case of arithmetic, for instance, the calculating method is repeated 7 times, covering figures below 10, then those below 100, then those below 1,000, then those below 10,000, then those below 100 million and finally round figures) — making it an easy matter to streamline these materials — comrades in charge of education in many localities hold that it should not be difficult to adopt the five-grade unified elementary school system. [In 1960, elementary schools in Communist China have six grades, the first four grades being junior elementary school, and the last two grades senior elementary school.]

6) Six provinces — Kirin, Shensi, Kansu, Kiangsi, Honan, and Tsinghai are experimenting on the five-grade unified middle school system or the three-year middle school and two-year senior middle school system. [In 1960, the prevailing system specified three years each for junior and senior middle schools.]

7) Peking and Honan are experimenting on the 10-year unified elementary and middle school system.

8) Heilungkiang is experimenting on the nine-year unified elementary and middle schools sytems.

There are experiments in many other categories which I will not enumerate here. A relatively long time will be needed to carry out the reform of our schoolipg system on an experimental basis. We should not try to draw final conclusions prematurely. However, it can definitely be said that if only we can properly reform our teaching methods, revise our texbooks, strengthen the leadership of the CCP committees attached to schools and organize large-scale coordinated cooperation between teachers to change their present practice of each tending his own business without coordination, it will be quite possible for us to suitably shorten the number of schooling years, raise the education standards, tighten control over study hours, and increase physical labor. . . .

It is our preliminary intention with regard to the new school system to reduce the number of years to full-time middle and elementary school education and approximately 10, and to raise the standards of the graduates to that of freshmen of our present colleges. Why do we advocate "approximately 10 years"? Because it takes approximately 10 years for children who start schooling at six or seven years of age to grow to the age of 16 or 17, when they will be considered as full manpower units. It is relatively easy to provide 10 years' full-time aducation to our children after we have completed in the main our agricultural capital construction program and have mechanized our agricultural production operations, inasmuch as such an educational program takes away little or no full manpower units from production. . . .

All students in our present senior middle schools now are full manpower units. For this reason, we cannot afford to extend our present senior middle school education to too many persons. We are graduating only several hundred thousand students from senior middle schools each year. Even if greater efforts are exerted in this work, the best we can do will be to graduate a little over 1 million students from senior middle schools each year. Should we try to increase this number, we would take away too much manpower from production.

On the other hand, if we put the new school system in our mind into practice, we shall be able to graduate more than 10 million senior middle school students a year, without taking too much manpower away from production. This can be done because we have annually more than 10 million youths attaining the age of 16 or 17.

With the supply of such a huge number of young senior middle school graduates who are of high educational standards, we shall be able to direct each of our more than 1,700 counties to establish one or more full-time and part-time higher educational institutions, and to direct all factories, mines, enterprises, government organizations, and people's communes to open some spare-time higher educational institutions, in addition to the higher educational institutions established by the Central People's Government, and the provincial, municipal, and special administrative area authorities. In this way, we shall be able to let all our youth above 16 and 17 years of age receive higher education by adhering to the policy of walking on two legs. This highlights the spectacular development of our educational program in the future. By that time, our needs for technical and theoretical cadres will be better satisfied, our technical innovation and technical revolution campaign will develop at an increasingly high speed, and the difference between mental and manual labor will be reduced to the minimum.

This will be beneficial to the state as well as to the individuals concerned. This plan is within the capacity of our efforts and its advantage is so obvious. In the interests of the great majority of our people and of our society as a whole, we must step on this road. . . .

We fully believe that after experimentation, a new schooling system, a new pedagogical system, and new textbooks will emerge in a coordinated manner from actual practice, and new pedagogical and psychological theories will be derived therefrom.

4.3 "Launch Mass Campaigns and Carry Out Communist Cooperation On a Large Scale in the Struggle for Reform of Curriculums for Middle and Primary Schools."

WORK SET IN MOTION WITH THE TRANSFORMATION OF THE OLD CURRICULAR SYSTEM

The curricular reform was this time set in motion with the transformation of the old curricular system. Thanks to criticisms made by the masses, and the analysis of the lesser, slower, poorer and more expensive results achieved in education work, it was found that these shortcomings sprang from the old curricular system. This is because the old curricular system has not got rid of the influence of the educational viewpoint of the bourgeoisie, and the contents of its teaching materials are unconnected with reality, and are antiquated, trifling, and repetitive. In order to advance the teaching standards with greater, faster, better and more economical results, this essential problem must be grasped before reform can be carried out with thoroughness. According to our analysis, there are three problems in the old curricular system.

(1) The old curricular system has not rid itself of the ideological influence of the bourgeoisie who advocate "education for the sake of education" and "science for the sake of science." The object involving the materials adopted in different courses is rather vague. An abundance of things which can be put into application are not taught. . . .

In the light of these conditions, when building a new curricular system, we give great emphasis to the need of accelerating the development of socialist economic construction and the scientific and cultural undertakings, and firmly adhere to the principle of integrating theory with practice. In mathematics for example, the subject of drawing is added. In algebra and elementary functions, the contents of linear plants are enlarged, and such mathematical subjects as mathematical analysis, theory of probability, mathematical statistics, and ABC of calculus which are essential to modern production and scientific research are added. In chemistry, the basic facts in respect of inorganic industry and metallurgical industry are added, a great proportion of the total number of teaching hours is used for experiments, and the set requirements are greatly raised. In the teaching of foreign languages, a new pedagogic system based upon the practical need of languages is also set up to make language theories serve practical languages and to foster students capable of making skillful use of foreign languages.

(2) The old curricular system in natural science is seriously influenced by the metaphysical viewpoint of the bourgeoisie. Its characteristic involves the use of static, isolated, and one-sided viewpoints to deal with scientific truth, and a disregard for the movement, development, and change of things, and their internal links. . . .

The new curricular system brings a change to this state of affairs. The new system reflects the movement and change of things, and their internal links. In mathematics

---

Liu Fo-nien (Representative of the Shanghai Curricular Reform Committee for Middle and Primary Schools), "Launch Mass Campaigns and Carry Out Communist Cooperation On a Large Scale in the Struggle for Reform of Curriculums for Middle and Primary Schools," Peking, *Jen-min Jih-pao*, June 7, 1960, *Current Background*, No. 630 (August 8, 1960), pp. 11-18.

for example, we closely combine arithmetic, algebra, geometry, and plane trigonometry to build a new system. After the students understand the concept of real quantity, and the linear and quadratic equations, teaching is carried out with functions as the center. In physics, we pay attention to the way of elucidating the internal links of the different physical phenomena. The kinematic viewpoint in respect of material particles is for example used to explain the nature and the inter-transformation of the three states of matter. The unified theory of magnetic waves is used to sum up radio magnetic waves, visible light, infra-red rays, ultra-violet rays, and X-rays.

(3) The old curricular system underestimates the receptive power of the students. It one-sidedly emphasizes the bourgeois pedagogic principle of teaching according to ability, but overlooks the intellectual development of the young people and teenage-youth in our socialist society today and man's subjective initiative. Because of this, little mention of modern scientific and technical achievements is made in the old teaching materials. . . .

The old teaching materials have also the characteristic of being repetitive and unnecessarily complicated. . . .

We studied and built our new curricular system on the foundation of thoroughly exposing the old curricular system. This new curricular system is guided by the thought of Mao Tse-tung. This is also to say that teaching materials are placed under the command of and dealt with according to the educational guideline of the Party, the viewpoints of dialectical materialism and historical materialism, and the principle of linking theory with practice, to enable the new achievements of modern science to be reflected in the curricular contents. . . .

Teaching carried out in accordance with the new curricular system is expected to yield the following results:

(1) A proper advancement in standard. After the antiquated, overlapping complicated contents are removed from the original curriculums, and the achievements of modern science are added, the standard of the middle school graduates can be raised to that of the second year students in an engineering university in mathematics, and also to that of the students of the departments of physics and chemistry in a contemporary university in physics and chemistry. Considerable advancement will also be made in the standard of other courses.

(2) A proper reduction in the total number of teaching hours and the number of teaching hours per week, and a proper increase of time for productive labor, with the students provided with more time for private study and extra-curricular reading at the same time. In this way, teaching can be integrated with productive labor more satisfactorily, the principle of linking theory with practice can be better implemented, and the students can be fostered more satisfactorily to acquire the ability of taking up work independently.

(3) Proper shortening of the number of years in study on the premise that advancement in quality is assured. Our proposed system of a five-year course for the primary school section and another five-year course for the middle school section cuts down the total number of years in study on the premise that advancement in quality is assured. Our proposed system of a five-year course for the primary school section and another five-year course for the middle school section cuts down the total number of teaching hours compared with the original system of a six-year course for each of these two sections. From the primary school to the middle school, a total of 2,498 hours of study is cut. Calculating on the basis of 28 hours of study per week, the cut is equivalent to 89 weeks or two school years. In this way, the number of school years is shortened, the standard is raised, and a foundation for the universalization of

senior middle education among all young people and teenage youth is thus laid down.

THE PROCESS OF ESTABLISHING THE NEW CURRICULAR SYSTEM REPRESENTS A COURSE OF STRUGGLE BETWEEN THE PROLETARIAN EDUCATIONAL THOUGHT AND THE BOURGEOIS EDUCATIONAL THOUGHT

The process involving the abolition of the old curricular system and the establishment of the new curricular system represents a course of struggle between the proletarian education thought and the bourgeois educational thought. This ideological struggle finds main manifestation in two aspects: one being the struggle with the principle of teaching according to ability in bourgeois pedagogics, the other, the struggle with the metaphysical curricular system in natural science. . . .

THE VICTORY OF THE PARTY'S MASS LINE, THE VICTORY OF COMMUNIST COOPERATION

The curricular reform work for middle and primary school this time stands for the victory of the Party's mass line and the victory of Communist cooperation. . . .

Before the curricular reform was carried out, for example, the Municipal People's Council organized more than 100 persons to form an educational standard investigation group to investigate the educational standard of schools of all kinds at different levels. . . .

In the process of compiling and examining the pedagogic outlines and teaching materials, mass campaigns were also launched on a large scale. The methods of "carrying out the four processes of compilation, examination, revision, and fixing the draft side by side" and of "effecting the integration of the universities, middle schools and primary schools, the teachers and students, those inside and outside the schools, and the leadership and the masses" were adopted. This is to say that all of the pedagogic outlines and teaching materials were collectively examined. . . .

THE USE OF THE NEW TEACHING MATERIALS CALLS FOR A BETTER STUDY OF THE THOUGHT OF MAO TSE-TUNG

The teaching materials which we compiled have now been published. . . .The broad masses of the teachers study them in real earnest, and actively prepare new conditions for the enforcement of the reform plan. . . .

The broad masses of teachers also understand that in order to make use of the new teaching materials, they must properly reform the pedagogic methods and renovate the teaching apparatuses. At present, although the reform of teaching materials has not been carried out with thoroughness, yet the broad masses of teachers have put the spirit of reform into application to improve the teaching methods. They study the teaching materials in real earnest to acquaint themselves with their essence and key points. They make their teaching to the point, give the students more time to take up all kinds of experiments and field work, and make the students acquire the ability to work independently. They also innovate different kinds of electrical teaching apparatus to enable the students to learn faster and with greater thoroughness. . . .

The curricular reform work for middle and primary schools in Shanghai has just begun. In the next school year, the reform plan can be experimented with only in a small number of schools. But we are pretty certain that the direction of reform pointed out by the Party is correct in every respect, and is a correct way to developing the educational undertaking and raising the teaching standard with greater, faster, better, and more economical results. . . .

4.4 "Several Problems of Pedagogic Reform for Workers' Education"

NEW CHARACTERISTICS OF NEW STAGE

In the wake of the scientifically correct and rapid development of the technical revolution, education for the workers and staff members in industry in the city of Tientsin has likewise entered upon a new stage of remarkable development, great universalization, and great improvement. This new stage is noted for the following characteristics:

First, with initiative provided by the Party, schools of various categories and at all levels are being built on a huge scale. Illiteracy among young and middle-aged workers and staff members has been eliminated basically. . . .

Second, leadership in most of the factories is now able to lay hold of the objective law of having production guide education and having education promote production, thereby forming a new rule of double leap forward in production and education. . . .

THE POLICY AND PRINCIPLE OF TEACHING REFORM

During the past ten years, workers' education has undergone several changes, and great achievements have been made. But since bourgeois educational ideas and teaching viewpoints still linger so that the phenomena of education being isolated from politics, production and reality and of smaller, slower, poorer and more expensive results in education still exist and become more conspicuous in the course of the great storm of the technical revolution. We must of necessity carry out a teaching reform now. By means of the teaching reform, we shall further implement the Party's educational policy and the principle of the Party for the workers' education calling for "coordination between education and productive labor, unified arrangements, teaching in accordance with local conditions, and adopting flexible and adjustable forms." This then is the guideline for the teaching reform. . . .

(1) We should closely coordinate with the technical innovation and technical revolution movement, absorb the achievements of the technical revolution, and revise the contents of teaching in accordance with the characteristics of the adult workers and staff members. . . .

(2) We must strive vigorously to reform the schooling systems, rationally arrange the curriculum, reduce the number of years of study, and raise the quality of teaching in order to meet the requirements of the high-speed development of socialist construction.

(3) We should get rid of the old schooling systems and institute new schooling systems with specialization as the core and with fundamental subjects (culture and techniques) serving specialization. We should also incorporate the advanced scientific knowledge and new techniques in textbooks of specialized subjects, in order to meet the requirements of the development toward a higher level, precision, and improvement, as well as the needs of diversified economic undertakings and multi-purpose utilization of material resources, so as to train with greater, faster, better and

Li Chih-min (Vice Director, Industrial Department, Tientsin CCP Municipal Committee), "Several Problems of Pedagogic Reform for Workers' Education," Peking, *Kuang-ming Jih-pao*, July 6, 1960, *Survey of China Mainland Press*, No. 2316 (August 12, 1960), pp. 26-29.

more economic results scientists and technicians who are specialized in one field but have knowledge in many other fields.

The reason why we lay down these three principles for teaching reform is mainly because spare-time education for workers and staff members is introduced principally to the producers who are engaged in some particular fields of industry on a relatively permanent basis, and the purpose of their study is to meet the requirements of present and future production so that they may quickly become red and expert technicians in their fields.

STEPS, METHODS AND DEMANDS OF TEACHING REFORM

The teaching reform is still in the experimental stage at the moment. Being short of experience, we must select some points for experiment. . . .

The process of the teaching reform is also the process of the mass movement and the ideological revolution. For this, the following jobs must be well done:

Both cadres and teachers should first of all seriously study Chairman Mao's "On Practice," "On Contradiction" and "Reform Our Study," Lu Ting-yi's "Education Must Be Combined with Productive Labor" and "Teaching Must Be Reformed" as well as the important documents of the National Conference of Heroes in Culture and Education. They must also study some advanced experiences gained from the teaching reform. Leadership cadres in the factories should not only take the lead in study, but also carry out propaganda and education for the workers and staff members. Second, we should arouse the masses to action and, through the big contending, big blooming and the holding of big debates, thoroughly expose and criticize the bourgeois ideas and viewpoints in education and teaching. We should urge all concerned to contribute new ideas and put forward plans for teaching reform for comparison and evaluation. Third, we should send the teachers and cadres to the workshops to learn from the workers and staff members, to organize on-the-spot teaching, and to undertake scientific research on a large scale. Meanwhile, we must investigate extensively into the characteristics of the workers in general and the apprentices in particular. When performing the above three jobs, we must coordinate them, so that while we are compiling teaching programs and textbooks, we may give lessons on a trial basis, and evaluate the results of such trial teaching. This then makes it necessary that the study of documents should be combined with the going into reality, with the ideological revolution and teaching reform. We should, on the basis of the spirit of "unity-criticism-unity" and through the holding of debates and the practice of labor and teaching reform, assist the teachers to raise their understanding, develop the new out of the old, establish the proletarian attitude and eliminate the bourgeois attitude, and carry teaching reform to the end.

With regard to the reform of teaching programs and teaching materials, we must do the following things: We must get rid of all old, outdated and trivial subjects; eliminate the old systems and old teaching methods; simplify the contents of those subjects which are not directly related to the particular trades of the students; merge the repetitive portions and relevant portions of a subject that is taught in the elementary, secondary and higher schools; and incorporate new and modern scientific and technical knowledge in the textbooks.

4.5 "Teaching of English in Kweiyang Middle School Improved Through Penetrating Investigation and Research"

Kweichow Jih-pao on August 4 published a survey report on how Kweiyang 5th Middle School raised the quality of the teaching of English. The report said five English teachers of this school had investigated into the causes of indifferent results of the majority of students in the study of English, changed their previous belief that the students lagging behind in English lessons lacked interest in the English subject, and realized that most of them had encountered varying degrees of difficulty in their study efforts, thereby giving rise to the feeling of willing to learn on the one hand and afraid of doing so on the other. Having thus realized the different difficulties of the students, the teachers respectively adopted various methods. After two months of efforts, most of the students had made marked progress in the subject of English.

Of the five English teachers of this school, three had majored in the English language in universities and one had studied in America, their average length of teaching service being over nine years. Despite their efforts in teaching work and their extensive preparations in their spare time, as well as their constant attention to the advanced teaching methods employed in other schools, the results achieved by most of the students were fairly bad. Taking the third class of the first year students of a junior middle school as an example, three tests given during April this year showed that students scoring three or two marks made up 65.53 per cent, while excellent students getting five marks only comprised 9.2 per cent. Under these circumstances English teachers who thought they had made good efforts attributed the poor results of the students to their lack of interest in the subject of English. Someone said: "Even though Mei Lan-fang sings his best in operas, it will be of no avail if one does not bother to listen."

Different views were given when the school brought up this question for discussion. Some held that it was necessary to get all the facts and go deeper into the problem instead of groping around superficial phenomena. All the five English teachers each chose a class as the object of their investigation and research. By asking the students to fill out survey charts, holding forums and individual talks (altogether 70 times) and using other methods, a check was made of 210 students. The main idea was to find out how the students came to know about the purpose of studying English, whether or not they were afraid to do so, what difficulties they had encountered, how they had approached the problem of learning, and what opinions and demands they had made of the teachers.

Findings of the survey showed that of the 210 students, 197 expressed fondness or willingness for learning English and 13 expressed reluctance to do so. The percentage was 93.8 against 6.2.

If 93.8 per cent of the students were willing to learn, why then were so many of them not attentive to lectures? Further analysis, therefore, was necessary to find out the hidden problems and the real causes of the not very high quality of teaching.

Findings of a further analytical survey of the 93.8 per cent showed that 57 students, making up 27.1 per cent, had all along been fond of English. This constituted the

---

"Teaching of English in Kweiyang Middle School Improved Through Penetrating Investigation and Research," Peking, *Kuang-ming Jih-pao*, August 19, 1961, *Survey of China Mainland Press*, No. 2574 (September 8, 1961), pp. 14-16.

minority group of students who achieved excellent results in the study of English. Fifty-five others, making up 26.2 per cent, were formerly fond of English but later gradually disliked the subject because of mounting difficulties. Thirty-three others, making up 15.7 per cent, were willing to catch up and learn English as a subject although they were not particularly fond of it. Thirty-four others, making up 16.2 per cent, were willing to learn but due to great difficulties their results were poor and therefore they lost confidence. Adding up, these three cases totaled 122 students. They were all willing to learn but because of difficulties they were afraid of studying the subject. This constituted the majority of the students who scored poor results.

The problem, therefore, came into clear focus. Those achieving good results and showing great interest in the subject of English were confined to a few, while those unwilling to learn the subject constituted a very small minority. Most of the student were willing to learn English but were afraid of learning the subject or, in the words of the students themselves, "like and dislike the subject," and "sometimes like and sometimes dislike it." The key to the problem was that they had encountered difficulties in their studies.

During the survey, there appeared an opposite situation. Eighteen students who were formerly not fond of English displayed great zeal in their study efforts after overcoming difficulties through help given by others with the result that they made better progress in their studies. This situation prompted the teachers to give the matter deeper thought: If the teachers knew how to guide the majority of the students toward overcoming their difficulties, would most of them not be able to raise the quality of their English study as the 18 students had done?

The findings were obvious. Unwillingness on the part of students to learn was due to difficulties blocking their path to progress. As soon as the English teachers realized this point, they made further efforts in their investigation and research to find out the specific difficulties confronting the students and how they came about.

The prevailing difficulties confronting the students were their unsuccessful efforts to remember and memorize new words and their failure to understand completely the construction of sentences. In the words of some of them, "I cannot read when the teacher is not around," and "memorizing simple words does not help understanding phrases and sentences."

Why had there been such difficulties? In teaching new words, the teachers had thought of many ways, studied the advanced experiences of other places in "groupings of new words," and explained over and over again various sentence patterns. Could it be that the methods adopted were not good enough? What were the underlying causes? English teachers again called an investigation meeting centering on these questions. Students who had been poor in their learning results reflected the situation saying: "Before old lessons have been understood new lessons start coming. Our teacher cares only for speed and does not bother whether we understand or not." Others said: "The teacher rarely bothers about students whose study results are poor." These views and demands have long been neglected by English teachers. Since the majority of the students have not been good in their results, will teaching not depart from realities if it fails to meet the actual levels and demands of the majority of students? It is precisely this departure from realities that the difficulties met by students in their learning efforts and not understood by the teachers have accumulated. As a result, the study activism of the students has been impaired. As the teachers have only taken note of the tendency of students displaying reluctance to learn, they have neglected methods of improving their teaching. This is the root cause of why the teaching quality of English classes has not been high.

With the underlying causes traced, English teachers untied the ideological "knot" that had long plagued them. Feeling awakened, they started examining the numerous problems found in their work. For instance, although the propagation of the advanced experience in the combinations of new words and sentence patterns — a successful experience in helping students master basic grammar — found favor with the students, the too broad scope of the combination of difficult words and involved sentences put to good use had proved confusing to the students. Moreover, failure to understand where the difficulties of the students lay often led to partial solutions and misplaced emphasis.

By conducting investigation and research on the one hand and finding on-the-spot solutions on the other, English teachers improved their teaching. They also strengthened contacts with students, helped them to set their understanding right, and encouraged those lagging behind to catch up with greater efforts. Before conducting classes, English teachers prepared lessons, taking into consideration the realities of the students and appropriately slowing down their teaching speed. They also asked in advance for the views of those students whose study results had been mediocre or poor. When a new lesson was introduced in the class, old lessons were reviewed and referred to as much as possible so as to give students more chances for practice. A long lesson was divided into several sections to enable students of medium ability to grasp outright the combinations of difficult words and sentences and those of poorer standards to comprehend basically various sections of the lesson. At the same time students whose results were poor and who had encountered more difficulties were given guidance by the teachers when doing their work which was corrected and graded right away. Various spare-time tutorial methods were also employed to help a few students who had encountered greater difficulties.

After making these efforts, the number of students willing to learn English grew day by day. With their study activism raised and the classroom in better order, the relations between teachers and students became more harmonious. Students who were formerly upset by English lessons now looked up tutors on their own initiative. Following these changes, the English study results of the students showed universal improvement. Taking the third class of the first year students of a junior middle school as an example, a survey conducted in June showed marked differences compared with the one taken in April. In three tests, the ratio of those students with medium and poor results dropped from 65.58 to 27.59 per cent (the number of those who failed was reduced by three-fourths), while the number of students who scored excellent results rose from 9.2 to 36.78 per cent.

4.6 "Concerning the Question of Study"

To study in earnest is an important task entrusted by the Party and the State to our fellow students. In running schools, the State wants you to make a success of study with your concentrated energy so that you may serve the building of socialism well in the future. . . .

We are very strong politically, but are still backward economically. Because of this, the Party and Chairman Mao have formulated the general line of building socialism which indicates to the people throughout the country the great goal of

---

Fu Chen-sheng, "Concerning the Question of Study" [Part of a speech delivered by Fu Chen-sheng to students of institutions of higher education in Changchun], Peking, *Kuang-ming Jih-pao*, October 17, 1961, *Survey of China Mainland Press*, No. 2612 (November 3, 1961), pp. 1-9.

building China into a socialist power with modern industry, modern agriculture, and modern science and culture as fast as possible. In order to realize this great goal, it is necessary to build a powerful army of intellectuals of the proletariat, for in so big a country as ours it will not do if this army is small in size. We need thousands and tens of thousands of able and learned experts to serve socialism. . . .

THE QUESTION OF RELATIONSHIP
BETWEEN REDNESS AND VOCATIONAL PROFICIENCY

The question of relationship between redness and vocational proficiency is in fact a question of relationship between politics and one's business. Chairman Mao has taught us that we must be red and vocationally proficient. This has always constituted the direction of our endeavors. The viewpoint of placing politics in command can never be shaken. As far as the university students of today are concerned, perserverance in the direction of redness and vocational proficiency calls on them to acquire the patriotic and internationalist spirit and observe communist ethics, to support the Communist Party and the cause of socialism, and to serve the socialist cause. Ideologically, by way of studying Marxism-Leninsim and the works of Mao Tse-tung, of participating in productive labor to a certain extent, and of tempering themselves in practical work, the students are required to establish and strengthen gradually the viewpoint of the working class, the viewpoint of labor, the viewpoint of the masses, and the viewpoint of dialectical materialism. In the field of vocational proficiency, they must strive to make a success of study in their specialities and to acquire the fundamental theoretical knowledge and basic skills. The students' process of study in school is a process of making continued advancement in these two respects. They must make advancement in these two respects before they can make sound and rapid progress and become personnel needed in socialist construction. . . .

Redness which refers to the political stand of people comes first and is of primary importance. The redness of a person is not determined by the number of meetings he attends and the number of Marxist-Leninist formulae he is able to recite, but primarily by whether he stands politically on the side of revolution.

We say that supporting the leadership of the Communist Party and socialism comes first and is of primary importance. This is because our country is a socialist country built by the people of the whole country under the leadership of the Party. If the university students fostered in our schools do not support the leadership of the Party and socialism, it will be difficult for them to develop a fervent love for their own socialist motherland and to make useful contributions to the cause of building socialism.

In emphasizing vocational proficiency, we mean to say that university students must acquire specialized knowledge and capacity for practical work. Otherwise, what are you going to use to serve the proletariat politically and socialist construction? Young students, and especially university students, must not be satisfied with listening to lectures in class. They must take up private study painstakingly after class. Apart from doing a good job in the study of textbooks and lecture notes, a good university student must read more books and reference books of relevance to broaden his field of vision and to absorb useful knowledge systematically. At the same time, university students must be encouraged to develop the capacity for studying and working independently, so that they can carry out their work with greater success after they leave school.

Redness and vocational proficiency know of course no bounds, and ideological consciousness should be heightened continuously. In regard to redness, we first require the university students to support the leadership of the Party and socialism, but we can never be satisfied with this and call ourselves to a halt. You must endeavor to foster your own proletarian world outlook, deeply comprehend the law of evolution of nature and society, and cultivate a high degree of socialist and communist consciousness on this initial foundation of redness. The young students who are ambitious in rendering greater contributions to the motherland should set for themselves a higher-goal in struggle. But it must be pointed out that ideological remolding and the firm establishment of the world outlook of dialectical materialism can never be carred out in one day. We must go through a protracted course of study with arduous efforts, and carry out self-remolding continously in practice before we can accomplish this gradually. It is a life-long undertaking.

Our fellow students must know that redness is not something vague but something tangible. The object of our institutions of higher education is to foster red personnel specialized in different fields for the working class, and to foster our own research personnel and teaching personnel. We cannot demand all university graduates to become Marxist-Leninist, nor can we foster every university student as a political activist. Part of the university students can of course be trained as political experts who specialize themselves in political work. The majority of them should, however, become personnel specialized in different fields. The agricultural students for example must be well versed in agricultural science. They must grasp the laws of agricultural development in China and become agriculturalists of outstanding contributions. The water conservancy students must grasp the subtle techniques of water conservancy engineering and become water conservancy engineers. The medical students must find the best way to combine modern medicine with the medical legacy of China, and become the doctors of the people. The mathematical students must become mathematicians well versed in mathematics. The educational students must become educators. Students who study dancing must become dancers.

Young people should have ambitions. As long as your object and attitude of study are correct, your ambition to win fame and to establish a school of thought cannot be opposed as a rule. It is of course wrong for you to adopt an individualistic attitude in study and to look upon specialized knowledge as a means to meet your personal desires, to glorify your ancestors, to win advancement in official rank and to make yourself rich. In establishing the desire to win fame and to establish a school of thought for the sake of socialism and of realizing the general line, you should receive support and encouragement.

Redness and vocational proficiency, politics and business, are united, interpermeating, and complementary. There is never any business which is not integrated with politics, nor is there any politics which is not integrated with business. Through doing a good job in the study of politics and heightening their consciousness the students will be able to have a clearer understanding of the object of study and to strengthen their self-consciouness in study, thus engendering a strong driving force for storming and taking the bulwark of culture and science. On the other hand, through doing a good job in the study of business and increasing their ability, the students will be able to broaden their horizon of knowledge, and to understand the intricate phenomena of nature and society, thus helping them to establish firmly the revolutionary world outlook at a faster rate, and insuring that their noble desire to serve the people will not come to nought. This is one aspect of the integration of politics with business.

Looking at things from another aspect, politics is made manifest through different kinds of specific business. An agricultural student should of course study politics, but speaking in terms of what the State demands of him, he is chiefly required to specialize in the study of agricultural knowledge and techniques. The primary requirement is not for him to become an ordinary political cadre, but to become an able agricultural expert. The political consciousness of a student should find expression in adopting the building of socialism as the driving force to heighten continously the quality of the line of study he is specialized in and to render great contributions to agriculture after graduation. Students in other specialities are also required to do the same in their study.

There are in our institutions of higher education several hundred kinds of specialities the overwhelming majority of which are connected with some business. If all our students become specialized personnel who meet construction needs after graduation, this proves precisely the success of our politics. If this is not the case, then politics becomes something that cannot be cashed. We hold therefore that the political consciousness of the students should be high and should be manifested in study. Although we cannot assert that a student who is good in study is bound to be ideologically advanced, yet a student with a high degree of political enthusiasm has inevitably a high degree of enthusiasm for study. This kind of enthusiasm must be protected and encouraged.

4.7 "On the Correct Handling of the Relations Between Teaching, Productive Labor, and Scientific Research"

The correct handling of the relations between teaching, productive labor and scientific research is a vital link in the thorough execution of the Party's educational policy and raising the quality of teaching in full-day institutions of higher education. Like other things, teaching, productive labor and scientific research are inter-related and restrict one another. Both production and scientific practice are important aspects in improving the teaching quality and can be integrated with teaching. However, we must recognize that teaching, productive labor and scientific research are after all different things: each has its own particularities. There are similarities as well as dissimilarities between them, and to see their similarities but not their dissimilarities or vice versa will not enable us to execute the Party's educational policy completely and correctly.

I. OVER-ALL ARRANGEMENTS WITH TEACHING AS THE CORE

Three years of practice has furnished us with numerous experiences and lessons in respect of arrangements made for teaching, productive labor and scientific research.

How, then, can we set teaching, productive labor and scientific research in their proper places? To do this, as is confirmed by the experiences gained in the past three years or more, we must work out over-all arrangements with teaching as the core. First, we must arrange teaching in compliance with the scientific law; second, we must adapt productive labor to the course of teaching; and third, we must develop scientific research in coordination with the needs of teaching. To unify the laws of teaching, production and science into an integral whole, and to draw up plans integrating education with productive labor as the basis for the organization of teaching, productive labor and scientific research—this is a problem which we must

K'ang Ti (Vice President, Northwest Agricultural College), "On the Correct Handling of the Relations Between Teaching, Productive Labor, and Scientific Research," Peking, *Kuang-ming Jih-pao*, January 7, 1962, *Survey of China Mainland Press*, No. 2668 (January 29, 1962), pp. 11-15.

urgently solve, as well as an important task facing us at present.

II. ORGANIZE TEACHING IN ACCORDANCE WITH LAW

Taking teaching as the core, higher agricultural colleges must on the one hand comply with the law of agricultural science in formulating teaching plans and organizing productive labor and scientific research, so as to advance progressively and go deeper step by step to meet the needs of teaching and productive labor. On the other hand, bearing in mind the course of learning on the part of the students, we should arrange the various teaching links to bring about a coordination between theory and reality and improve the quality of teaching. Agricultural science is a science that studies living animals and plants. It is considerably restricted by natural environments. The course of agricultural production embodies intricate and complicated connections among many subjects. For instance, a mastery of the law of the growth of farm crops involves not only certain subjects relating to. . . agriculture but also the fundamental and theoretical subjects of physics, chemistry, and others. Hence, to bring to light the various laws of agricultural science, we must apply the fundamental theoretical knowledge of physics, chemistry, and mathematics. Some people think that fundamental theories have nothing to do with agricultural science. If they do not misunderstand agricultural science, they must be ignorant of it. In fact, all specialities ranging from fundamental subjects to specialized subjects have a complete set of scientific system, according to which teaching must proceed.

For this reason, we must first attach special importance to basic theoretical science. When we revise teaching plans, we should give fundamental subjects a considerable number of study hours and put them in a relatively suitable position. Even in 1958, at a time when students of the college were sent to the countryside on a large scale to take part in labor, the first-year students were permitted to stay in the college because they had to study fundamental subjects. The second-year students of the Department of Agricultural Machine-Building were called back to the college after having been sent to the fields where it was discovered that they were so insufficiently equipped with basic theoretical knowledge that they could not carry out production properly, and were then made to continue their study of fundamental subjects. In the draft teaching plan which we recently drew up, the teaching of fundamental subjects for first-year and second-year students has been strengthened, and the amount of productive labor which they are required to do is small. This will help the students to lay a relatively strong foundation for the further study of agricultural science. Secondly, we have paid much attention to the order and coordination of fundamental subjects, basic specialized subjects and specialized subjects. The timetable of study is arranged entirely according to a scientific system, and not according to the course of productive labor. Nor can this timetable be disrupted because of other reasons. Thirdly, we must strengthen the definite connections between various subjects and maintain the independent system of various subjects and should not change the curricular system at random. The appearance and development of a science has its own historical background, and is dictated by social needs. By his struggle with nature, man comes to understand its objective laws and gradually make them perfect and systematic to form a science. It is the natural outcome, not of subjective wish, but of the development of productivity.

The course of development of teaching should reflect the course of learning of scientific knowledge on the part of students. Whether or not this can be done, the key question lies in correct handling of the relations between perceptual and rational knowledge. Speaking generally, productive labor in most cases belongs to the sphere of perceptual knowledge acquired by the students, while theoretical teaching mostly belongs to the sphere of rational knowledge. Viewed from the course of learning of the students, they may have perceptual knowledge first and rational knowledge later, or the other way round. Basing themselves on perceptual knowledge, the students can make a deeper study of theories, and if they first learn theories and then go into realities to verify them, they can make a still more thorough study of theories. If we rigidly insist on going for practice first and theories later and perceptual knowledge first and rational knowledge later, thereby over-emphasizing direct experience and perceptual knowledge, the result can only be that the students will be restricted to a certain extent from acquiring complete knowledge. If the students do not study the indirect experience in books but take part in practice personally in every field, can they complete the 20 or 30 courses within the four or five years in the university? Nevertheless, while emphasizing the importance of book learning, we do not mean that direct experience is not important. It is both necessary and important for the students to take part in practice personally.

In implementing the policy of combining education with productive labor and theory with reality over the past three years or more, we have basically adopted two courses: One is that the teachers and students have twice been sent to the countryside to participate in productive labor while continuing teaching and learning in connection with production practice; the other is that productive labor and scientific research are carried out on the experimental bases both inside and outside the college in the light of the teaching needs so that the teaching tasks can be fulfilled and aid provided for the agricultural front simultaneously. The first course is an effective measure for closing the gap between education and productive labor, between theory and reality, and between intellectuals and workers and peasants, which appeared for some time. The second course is a necessary step for carrying out the teaching plan and training all-round personnel.

III. PRODUCTIVE LABOR TO MEET APPROPRIATE DEMANDS

Productive labor represents an important aspect in the execution of the Party's educational policy and for the realization of the goal of training all-round personnel. If we neglect productive labor, we would fall into a quagmire of bourgeois educational thought. However, we cannot but recognize that education is after all education and production is after all production, and that production cannot replace education any more than education can replace production. There are similarities and distinctions between them. If we see only their similarities but not their distinctions or vice versa, we cannot implement in an over-all manner the policy of combining education with productive labor. For this reason, we must unify the course of teaching with the course of production. On the one hand, arrangements for labor should be made in the light of the process of production; on the other, arrangements for produciton should be connected with the course of teaching. In the former case the needs of various sorts of specialized labor may be satisfied, while in the latter case the complete system of teaching may not be disrupted. It is not only possible but also conducive to the improvement of teaching quality to combine productive labor with teaching in higher agricultural colleges.

Apart from having the common characteristics of higher education in our country, higher agricultural colleges have their own particularities. What are these peculiarities? First, agriculture is the foundation of the national economy and our current task is the large-scale development of agriculture and grain production; second, the conditions of agricultural production are complicated and are considerably influenced by seasonal changes and local factors; third, there are very rich experiences in agricultural production but the level of agricultural science is very backward; fourth, the level of the teaching staff, the material conditions and equipment in higher agricultural colleges cannot catch up with the development of the objective situation. In the light of these particularities and the concrete conditions in our country, we have studied the following three problems:

First, the varieties of productive labor and the number of hours for various specialities. The combination of education and productive labor is a complicated question, which raised different demands in keeping with the changes of the objects of research by the various specialities. There should be neither excessive nor inadequate productive labor. If productive labor is inadequate, the quality of the cadres in training would be affected, but if productive labor is excessive, theoretical teaching would be hindered. This boundary line is drawn not according to subjective wishes but according to objective needs. For instance, the varieties of labor demanded by the agricultural speciality, with regard to the seasons, consists of spring plowing, summer hoeing, autumn harvesting, and winter storage; with regard to measures, the construction of water conservancy projects, accumulation of manure, soil improvement, the improvement of strains, close planting, plant protection, manufacture of work tools, and field management; and with regard to crops, the production of grain, cotton, oil-bearing crops and hemp and other food and industrial crops. To compose these sorts of labor together in accordance with local, specific conditions in order to master the objective law of the growth of crops and to take the initiative to adopt measures to promote production increase, we must of necessity work out over-all arrangements for all types of labor.

Second, the arrangement of productive labor in various specialities. Owing to the fact that the object of concrete training in various specialities is different and the course of teaching is different in them, there are different arrangements for productive labor. Speaking generally, to take seasonal changes into consideration, we should give balanced thought to the needs of the four seasons, with priority arrangements for special seasons. To combine theory with reality, we should, before undertaking the study of specialized subjects, possess the necessary perceptual knowledge, and after studying the specialized subjects, we should link them with reality. To meet the needs of teaching, we should reduce the amount of productive labor during the study of fundamental subjects and increase it during the study of specialized subjects.

Third, the locations of productive labor of various specialities. In our opinion, higher agricultural colleges should have a comprehensive experimental farm and a laboratory workshop complete with relatively satisfactory equipment, and the people in charge of them should have relatively rich experience. The farm and the laboratory workshop should be operated in such a way as to suit the needs of various specialities. At the same time, however, students should go to people's communes, State farms or other factories to do a definite amount of productive labor within a certain period of time in order to acquire the practical ability to engage in production. We have always paid more serious attention to the combination of experimental bases inside and outside the college. In addition to making a success of the experimental farm in our own college, we have established long-term connections with people's communes outside the college.

We think that productive labor in higher agricultural colleges can be carried out in accordance with the specialities and teaching, except for those specialities of theoretical nature. However, several problems may be attended to: First, chief emphasis must be placed on teaching. One-sided emphasis on production should not be tolerated, and production should not be carried out during theoretical studies. Second, local conditions must be taken into consideration. Our country is vast in territory and conditions are complicated. Accordingly, there may be different plans for different areas. Third, experiences must be summed up. Since much of the rich experience in agricultural production has not yet been elevated to the theoretical level, we must therefore go among the masses to learn from them and sum up their production experiences in order to improve teaching quality. Fourth, the needs of specialities must be taken into account. In higher agricultural colleges, productive labor may be arranged in connection with certain specialities. Besides, there should be arranged certain non-specialized productive labor in the public interest. In this way, dispersal can be unified with centralization, activities inside the college with those outside it, and specialized labor with non-specialized labor. Starting from reality, a good coordination between education and productive labor can be effected.

IV. SCIENTIFIC RESEARCH SHOULD BE COORDINATED WITH TEACHING

Scientific research is an important measure for raising the level of the teachers and improving the quality of teaching. As far as the whole college is concerned, it is an indispensable task. Like productive labor, there are also similarities and distinctions between scientific research and teaching. To the teachers, scientific research and improvement of teaching quality are consistent with each other. But if the tasks of scientific research are improperly set and if the subjects of research are unrelated to teaching, teaching work can be hindered. To the students, their principal duty is acquisition of over-all basic knowledge and of basic techniques in various fields of scientific research. Scientific research can enable the students to receive a more profound training on a certain point, but it also imposes certain localized restrictions on their over-all development. For this reason, while scientific research may become an effective means to raising the quality of teaching, if it is handled unsatisfactorily, it may become a factor affecting the over-all development of students. The key problem in this connection lies in the fact that the scientific research of the students must be conducted in proper coordination with the needs of teaching.

We think that scientific research work by students can be carried out in two ways. On the one hand, basic training in scientific research should be carried out in keeping with the work of devising various teaching methods for various subjects. On the other hand, in conformity with the demands of the various links of teaching such as the writing of the annual theses (the subject of designing) and the graduation theses (designing), certain specialized research projects may be undertaken, and certain methods of scientific research should be systematically studied. In the case of the teachers, they should additionally engage in research into the methods of compiling textbooks and teaching in order to suit teaching more directly and to serve it.

Our scientific research undertaken in the past has produced good results, which have a certain effect on the improvement of the quality of teaching. And experience shows that a proper coordination between scientific research and teaching will help improve teaching quality; otherwise, the quality of teaching will be affected. We must grasp this link well in the future.

4.8 "Firmly Adhere to the Guiding Principle of Walking on Two Legs, Actively Develop and Consolidate People-Operated Primary Schools"

Since liberation, people-operated primary schools in Hupeh Province have made uninterrupted headway in development, consolidation and improvement under the leadership of the Party committees at different levels. There are at present 16,000 or more people-operated primary schools with more than 1,300,000 students on enrollment in the whole province. This plays a great role in meeting the demand of the children of workers and peasants for schooling and in the universalization of primary school education.

During the past 12 years, the development of people-operated primary schools in our province followed a winding course. From the early days of liberation to 1951, with the agrarian reform movement in progress throughout the province, a surging tide for the masses to set up schools swept the whole province. At that time, people-operated primary school students made up 70 per cent of the total number of primary school students in the whole province.

Beginning in 1952, however, because a large number of people-operated primary schools was taken over by the government, the activism of the masses in establishing schools was affected. As a consequence, the development of primary school education was checked to some extent. Later, with the advent of the tide of agricultural cooperation, especially in 1958, the activism of the masses in establishing schools was brought into play again under the illumination of the three red banners of the Party's general line, the big leap forward, and the people's commune, and people-operated primary education was developed once more on a large scale.

What experiences have we gained and what lessons have we learned from the course followed by our province in the development of people-operated primary schools?

First, how we should understand the question of running schools by the masses themselves. The educational undertaking is an undertaking of the masses of the people, and primary school education is also the fundamental education. Apart from requiring the State to establish schools energetically, the masses should also be mobilized to set up schools themselves to make up what is beyond the means of the State, before the demand of the masses for schooling can be better met. The administration of school education in the past 12 years tells us that in order to make fast progress in the development of primary school education and even middle school education, and in order to meet the demand of the masses for schooling to the maximum, it is necessary to implement firmly the guiding principle of "walking on two legs." Right now, people-operated primary schools and the students enrolled in them have an enormous role to play in meeting the demand of the masses for schooling and the universalization of primary school education. . . .

Experience thus tells us that we must arouse the activism of the masses to the full extent in the establishment of schools, courageously hand the right to receive education and especially to develop education to the masses, and translate the wishes of the masses into action. In the course of developing education, the principle of

Liu Lin (Deputy Director of Hupeh Provincial Education Department), "Firmly Adhere to the Guiding Principle of Walking on Two Legs, Actively Develop and Consolidate People-Operated Primary Schools," Peking, *Kuang-ming Jih-pao*, February 4, 1962, *Survey of China Mainland Press*, No. 2686 (February 27, 1962), pp. 7-10.

voluntariness must be firmly adhered to. Through leaving everything to the masses, including the estimation of the capital outlay, the engagement of teachers, and the management of schools, the schools not only can be set up quickly but also can be run successfully. The educational undertaking can thus be developed with greater, faster, better and more economical results, and the demand of the masses for schooling and cultural improvement can also be met.

Second, people-operated primary schools are a cultural and educational undertaking of the masses. In order to allow the masses to set up school themselves, we should proceed from the reality of the local populace and comply with local conditions. Flexible and diversified steps should be adopted. We cannot insist on uniformity, much less require the schools run by the masses to comply with the requirements set for government schools. Dissimilar demands should be set in accordance with the natural and economic conditions and the cultural standard of different areas.

At present, it is precisely because people-operated primary schools are in general formed according to the practical demand of the masses that they enjoy the warm welcome of the masses. Their salient features are:

The schools are small and dispersed and within easy reach of the neighborhood, thus giving the masses convenience and benefiting production. Usually, there is one people-operated primary school in every village, or one school for two or three villages in the neighborhood. It serves an area within a radius of one or two *li*, and at most not more than four *li* (six *li* in the mountainous area). The students can attend school even in stormy weather, and are seldom absent. The masses say: "With a school close by for their children, parents have less to fear and are able to exert themselves in production."

The things taught are in conformity with reality, and the form of teaching is flexible and diversified. The masses want the students to learn things which are needed in the countryside and can be put into application. They expect their children to be able to write and good in arithmetic after several years of study (including the ability to prepare name-rolls, to write things of practical use, to record wage points and to measure earthwork). Many people-operated primary schools have absorbed the views of the masses in this connection. They intensify the teaching of language and arithmetic (especially the use of abacus) on the one hand, and strictly require the students to write more, read more and recite their lessons more. On the other hand, they teach the students some supplementary knowledge including assorted characters, the 24 solar periods, figures written in full [for documentation], and simple bookkeeping. The students are in general able to achieve good results in study, thus winning the praise and approval of the masses.

Third, the local recruitment of teachers for people-operated primary schools is a most important experience. One of the chief reasons why many people-operated primary schools are able to gain consolidation and the affection and respect of the masses is that they engage intellectuals in their communes or brigades as teachers with the approval of the masses. These teachers have on the one hand extensive and close connections with the local populace, and are trusted by the masses. The masses have confidence in their ability to teach their children, and as a consequence, the schools can be run successfully and the students can be taught well. On the other hand, the livelihood arrangements for the teachers themselves and their family relations can be satisfactorily solved.

Fourth, on the premise that the activism of the masses can beneficially be brought into play in the establishment of schools, the strengthening of management and leadership is an important key to the sucess of people-operated primary schools. In the course of establishing schools, some *hsien* have developed a kind of management method based upon "leadership by the commune, control by the brigade, supervision by the school district, and establishment of schools by the masses." This is worthy of note. This method upholds centralized and unified leadership at the *hsien* level, clearly defines the specific task of the commune, the brigade and the school district, and arouses the activism of the commune, the brigade, and the masses in the establishment of schools.

In regard to the concrete division of work, the *hsien* educational administration department formulates the plan for the development of people-operated primary schools in the whole *hsien* and the plan for concrete work in accordance with the educational guidelines, policies and decrees of the Party and the government, and supervises the enforcement of same. The commune is responsible for the work of imparting political and ideological education to the teachers of people-operated primary schools and planning the distribution of private education within the commune. The production brigade organizes the people-operated primary school management committee to carry out democratic management in these primary schools, and, with the central full-course primary school as the center, exercises unified leadership in arranging the teaching work of the people-operated primary schools in that district, and giving guidance in production work. With management graded in this way, with over-all arrangements made, and with equal treatment extended to all, the development and consolidation of people-operated primary schools are fundamentally guaranteed. . . .

In order to meet the needs of the circumstances for development, and in order to implement better the guiding principle of "walking on two legs" in education, people-operated primary schools must in future be developed and consolidated in accordance with the spirit of "exercising control after relaxation." Leadership must be strengthened, development must be carried out with a free hand, consolidation must be conducted energetically, and improvement must be effected gradually. This is to say in places where schools have not yet been established, the masses must first be allowed to set up such schools, and gradually consolidate and improve them afterward. Where schools have already been established, the quality must be raised continuously in accordance with the concrete conditions, and the masses must be agitated continuously to set up more schools on this foundation. "Relaxation" does not mean the encouragement of free development, but is a means for agitating the masses. "Control" also does not seek to stifle their initiative but is exercised on the assumption that it is beneficial to arousing the activism of the masses in the establishment of schools as well as to their development. Both relaxation and control constitute a positive kind of leadership method.

4.9 "Some Suggestions Concerning the Unfolding of Research Work in Educational Psychology"

PRIMARY TASK OF RESEARCH
IN EDUCATIONAL PSYCHOLOGY HEREAFTER

We are in the process of boring more systematically and discriminately into pedagogic reform work in secondary and primary schools. We should also take another step forward in unfolding research work in educational psychology in accordance with the practical circumstances and on the basis of work already accomplished. On the one hand, it is necessary to gain depth in development by discussing and exploring psychological laws embodied in the practice of new educational work in China to raise the quality of experimental work in pedagogic reform. Some research work must be repeated or experimented with on a broader scale, so that psychological theories may be reinforced or summed up through carrying out further tests. On the other hand, it is necessary to widen the field properly so as to fill up the blanks or to strengthen the weak links of psychological research work essential to pedagogic reform.

There are many problems, and as we go deeper into experimental work, many more new problems will be encountered continuously. Therefore, it is not easy to list all the psychological problems which must be studied in effecting pedagogic reform in secondary and primary schools. As things stand at the moment, we can only explain broadly the problems of some aspects of primary importance for use as examples. These explanations represent but our initial views, and are rather imperfect.

(1) Psychological problems in the aspect of moral education. China's socialist education is designed to "foster laborers with socialist consciousness and culture." In such education, moral education is of primary importance. We must gradually train the younger generation to acquire the virtue of loving the socialist motherland, loving the laboring people, loving the Communist Party, loving the leaders, loving labor, loving science, and taking good care of public property, to acquire the patriotic and internationalist spirit, to support the leadership of the Party, to serve socialism and the people with willingness, and to establish gradually communist morality, the viewpoint of the working class, the mass viewpoint, the labor viewpoint and the dialectical materialistic viewpoint. It is necessary for educational psychology to analyze the students' psychological structure of morality, and to study the psychological laws governing the students' grip on moral ideas and the formation of their moral belief, moral sense, and moral behavior and habits, as well as the interrelations between them. It is necessary to study the process of development of the will of the students and of the formation of the communist style. It is necessary to study the collective role of the students in the process of forming their moral qualities, the psychological feature of self-conscious discipline and its process of formation. We have carried out very little research in these aspects. In the past few years, we carried out only a small amount of investigation and research of a general nature and experimental research of an exploratory nature. A good job must be done in intensifying research work in this connection.

P'an Shu, "Some Suggestions Concerning the Unfolding of Research Work in Educational Psychology" [Part of a speech delivered by P'an Shu at a meeting of educational psychologists convened by the Chinese Psychological Society], Peking, *Kuang-ming Jih-pao*, March 13, 1962, *Survey of China Mainland Press*, No. 2709 (March 30, 1962), pp. 1-6.

The different aspects of education are closely interconnected. Moral education and other aspects of education like intellectual education, physical education, aesthetic education and especially labor education are related. Consequently, psychological research in one aspect of education must be properly connected with research in other aspects. They can even be closely integrated in part.

(2) Psychological problems of labor education. A fundamental substance of the educational guideline of the Party is "the integration of education with productive labor." Productive labor has formed an important component part of school education. This is a basic feature of China's socialist education. The carrying out of scientific research in problems of this kind is of great significance to the implementation of the educational guideline of the Party and the carrying out of educational reform. Over the past few years, China has, in the practice of education, supplied a good deal of practical data for the analytical study of psychology in this connection, but has not summed up or re-processed them satisfactorily and derived psychological laws from them. Over these years, we have conducted certain investigation work and a small amount of practical work. This work is limited only to the partial and preliminary revelation of some educational features of labor, some educational factors in labor, and some conditions for carrying out labor education among children of the low-age group, but is still unable to go deep into many fundamental psychological problems of labor education. In future, it is necessary to study these problems further. For example, what is the psychological feature of labor as a special form of activity for students? Through what process does participation in productive labor play the role of advancing the moral qualities and especially the labor viewpoint of the students? How can the students' participation in productive labor and their acquirement of scientific knowledge be made to work for the advancement of each other? How do different categories and forms of labor affect the psychological development of the students? What are the salient features formed by the students' skill and proficiency in labor? How is labor education adapted to the individual difference and age characteristics of students? — This series of problems must be discussed and explored with greater thoroughness.

(3) Psychological problems of teaching work. Teaching activity takes up the greatest part of time for school activity, and is also divided into a great number of subjects. Consequently, the number of problems that have to be studied in this field is also great. Psychological problems in this field can be divided into two sections. One section concerns the general psychological problems of teaching, such as problems of interest in study and motive of study which have a bearing on the students' activism in study, the problem of acquirement and application of knowledge by students, and the problem of shaping the skill and proficiency of students and of developing their capacity for thinking. The other section concerns psychological problems having a bearing on the teaching of different subjects.

Over the past few years, we have done considerable work in this connection. For example, in regard to literacy teaching, much pedagogic and research experience has been accumulated by different places throughout the country. Up to the moment, however, the psychological theories embodied in different kinds of experience have not yet been sum up for the supplementation of one another to bring about common advancement. It is still necessary for us to do a good deal of work to find out what should constitute the fundamental requirement in literacy according to the psychological characteristics of the students in the lower classes, and what is the most effective way for carrying out literacy teaching.

Concerning the teaching of mathematics for example, some good experience and research results have also been obtained. But in order to solve the problem of reforming the teaching of mathematics properly, it is still necessary to study thoroughly how many cycles should be considered as essential to the matter for teaching arithmetic, what is the way to enable the children to master the laws of calculation and to achieve proficiency in calculation, which class should begin to learn such mathematical knowledge, as functions, rational numbers and geometric concept, and how is the matter for teaching mathematics and especially geometry to be arranged before the system of mathematical knowledge itself and the psychological characteristics of the students can be met and the intellectual power of the students can be developed.

Apart from this, there are also problems relating to shaping the students' ability to read and write the [Chinese] language, the students' psychological characteristics in learning foreign languages, and the psychological characteristics and laws pertinent to the learning of natural science by students under new educational conditions, and especially under the condition of combining education with productive labor. All this requires us to conduct a lot of penetrating research.

There are in teaching work also many other psychological problems which are very extensive in content. Broadly speaking, however, they amount to nothing more than exploring the organization of matter for teaching and the psychological basis of teaching methods for facilitating the carrying out of teaching more effectively. Concrete research work must be carried out in accordance with the subjects taught. It is also necessary to pay attention to connecting and coordinating the different subjects, and when necessary, to connect it with research in other fields.

(4) The psychological problem concerning the distribution of years of study. This problem includes three aspects, namely, the question of the age of admission into school, the question of stages of study, and the question of linking school education with pre-school education. These three aspects are united. For example, pre-school education and school education are distinctly different but are also interconnected in essence. If we can keep the children better developed psychologically and give them proper fundamental knowledge in pre-school education, thus organically linking pre-school education with school education, the quality of school education can certainly be raised.

Research work concerning the distribution of years of study and research work in other fields are also interdependent. The results of research in certain other aspects must be based upon before the problem of distribution of years of study can be provided with a better psychological basis. In determining the distribution of years of study according to the conditions of society and the students' characteristics of psychological development, the proper adjustment of the educational contents of the whole school will also be called for. Consequently, it is necessary for us to study the process of all-round development of pre-school child psychology and its laws, and to study what kinds of activity are suitable for them at a certain age period, what kinds of knowledge ought to be learned, what is the requirement in respect of quantity and quality, and what educational measures should be adopted before their psychological characteristics can be met, and their psychological development can benefit to the greatest extent. All these psychological problems concerning the distribution of years of study must be studied with greater thoroughness.

(5) The psychological problem of individual difference of children. The problems of several aspects studied in the above refer to the general circumstances. There also exists in every problem another aspect, that is the aspect of individual difference of children which should be considered. The individual difference of children is an outstanding fact. Under the new pedagogic conditions in particular, facts of this kind cannot be ignored, and proper measures should be adopted to deal with them. Under the new pedagogic conditions, the phenomenon of a vast difference in the results of students in the same class (so-called "differentiation of two classes") is often liable

to occur. Consequently, to study the manifestation of individual differences and the laws governing their occurrence and development so that they may be handled properly is a very important problem. The study of this problem should also include two aspects. One aspect is to spot special talents from among the students like a talent for literature and arts and a talent for science, and to study how they should be fostered properly. The other aspect is the need to analyze the causes of the bad conduct or poor results of some students and to give them proper assistance separately. In this way, our education will set an identical demand on the students, and will enable the individuality of the students to develop according to what is possible or as it should.

(6) The systematical study of the psychological development of children. Every psychological problem concerning education involves the peculiar manifestation of psychological laws in different study activities and also the question of development of child psychology. In educational work, the question of development of child psychology is more fundamental. As explained in the above, our educational measure must be based upon the psychological characteristics of the children and young people, and must also further or guide their psychological development. As a consequence, educational workers have recently a more eager demand for knowledge of the psychological and age characteristics of children which mark conspicuously the development of child psychology. During the past few years, a small amount of our research work concerning pre-school children gave a partial study to this field. Some research work concerning pedagogic reform in primary schools has also something to do with this problem. These kinds of work are of course far from adequate for summing up the psychological and age characteristics of our children and young people or a more complete range of laws of psychological development to meet the needs of educational work. As a matter of fact, we are still devoid of data in this connection. We must start from the beginning and make greater efforts to unfold systematically research work in this field.

The systematic study of the psychological development of children is an important task of educational psychology and at the same time the central task of child psychology. Educational psychology and child psychology are interlaced at this point. This is because the psychological development of children is brought into realization in the process of education. It is necessary therefore to go deep into the reality of the educational process to conduct research. But at the same time, it is also necessary to carry out essential discussion from a wider angle deeper into theories in coordination with research directly integrated with educational practice. This must be done before the psychological development of children can obtain more complete and more penetrating scientific data befitting the demand of educational practice in China. Consequently, research in the psychological development of children is also an important part of psychological work which is currently coordinated with pedagogic reform.

4.10 "Peking Young Communist League Committee and Young Communist League Committee of Tsinghua University Call Separate Forums on 'Redness' and Expertness"

The Universities Committee of the Peking Municipal Committee of the Young Communist League Committee of Tsinghua University recently called separate forums on the question of "redness" and expertness with a view to providing better guidance to students in becoming both "red" and expert and obtaining all-round development. Most of those taking part in the forums were senior students who were more successful in solving the problem of "redness" and expertness, elected by various universities. Basing themselves on their own experience, they expressed, their views on the question of "redness" and expertness.

BECOMING BOTH "RED" AND EXPERT IS A GOAL SET FOR US BY THE ERA OF SOCIALISM

All agreed that becoming both "red" and expert was a sacred mission given the youths of the present generation by the era of socialism. This is because the purpose of the training conducted by the Party and the State is not only to make us ordinary scientists but, what is more important, to make us firm revolutionary warriors and successors to communism. Such persons must be both "red" and expert. "Redness" and expertness are harmonious. It would be wrong to neglect either. One who is expert but not "red" is like a ship without a course and will eventually lose one's way. One who is "red" but not expert will become at most a good-for-nothing "empty politician." For this reason, it is only by following the "red" and expert road firmly and unwaveringly that one can train oneself and become a useful person needed by the Party and the State and can have an infinitely bright future for oneself. . . .

IN ORDER TO BECOME "RED" AND EXPERT, ONE MUST FIRST ANSWER THE QUESTION, "TO WHOM SHOULD ONE BELONG?"

The students all said that in order to train oneself and become both "red" and expert, one must first answer the question "To whom should one belong?" Wang Chih-yüan, a 5th-year student of Peking Agricultural University, said, "To whom should one belong? When this question has been solved, the rest, such as what one should do, what one should not do, and why one should study, are easy to solve. I began to like horticulture when still in middle school. So I made up my mind to go to an agricultural university. But as soon as I entered it, I came across a problem. In consideration of the needs of the State, the university placed me in the Vegetable Speciality. At the time, I was not interested in this speciality. Later, helped and educated by the Party, I gradually came to realize the purpose of study and solved the problem 'To whom should I belong?' after a period of hard work, I became keenly interested in the Vegetable Speciality. I began to study it energetically, the more so

"Peking Young Communist League Committee and Young Communist League Committee of Tsinghua University Call Separate Forums on 'Redness' and Expertness," Peking, *Chung-kuo-nien Pao*, December 8, 1962, *Survey of China Mainland Press*, No. 2889 (January 2, 1963), pp. 2-5.

because I thought that its foundation was weak as people had not attached sufficient importance to it in the past, and felt that I had the duty to add new content to this branch of science." Ts'ao Yün-yen, a 5th-year student of Tsinghua University, said, "In order to train oneself and become both 'red' and expert, one must first solve the problem of direction of one's life, that is, the problem 'For whom is one studying?' With this problem unsolved, it will be senseless to talk about the rest. Old, bourgeois thoughts try to influence us in different ways. One's family, for instance, will pose a number of demands on one even before one has graduated, such as asking one to go to one place and not to any other place and now to do this and now that. This being so, what should the criterion for one's actions be? This is a very serious quesiton. If one does not solve the problem 'Why should one study?' and 'To whom should one belong?' one will be in danger of going astray. For instance, some students did rather well in their studies, but, at the time of graduation, they haggled with the Party or even opposed its request, thus embarking on an incorrect road."

All said that the problem "To whom should one belong?" was a basic problem concerned with one's being revolutionary or non-revolutionary. A genuine revolutionary should belong first to the revolution and the people. His thoughts, words, and acts should proceed from the needs of the Party and the revolution. In face of the interests of the Party and the revolution, he does not consider his personal gains or losses. In order to solve the problems "For whom should one study?" and "To whom should one belong?" one must continuously wage firm struggles against bourgeois individualist thoughts. Individualism is the root of all evils. It is also the most dangerous stumbling stone in the way ahead of intellectuals.

ONE MUST HAVE A GREAT AMBITION
AND A SPIRIT OF STUDYING HARD

The students said that in order to train oneself and become both "red" and expert, one must have the great ambition of studying for the socialist and communist cause and a spirit of studying hard and practically. Without an ideal or aspiration, one will be a vulgar kind of man who has no vigor and no sufficient driving force. However, when one has formed a great ideal or aspiration, one must safeguard it with a spirit of studying hard and practically. The deeds of every one of the students taking part in the forums show that provided one combines the two together properly, one can become both "red" and expert. . . .

When they talked about ideals and aspirations, the students said that some people lacked great ideals or noble ambitions, went after immediate comfort and ease in life, and, even before they left university, began to fill their brains with considerations for working conditions and pay and even premature considerations for marriage, with the result that their energy was distracted and they could not study well. This is very noteworthy. . . .

SHOWING CONCERN FOR THE GROUP,
TRAINING ONESELF IN GROUP LIFE

All agreed that, in order to train oneself and become both "red" and expert, one must not boast but must set high standards for oneself in all matters in everyday life and train and temper oneself in concrete practice. One question in everday life is always noteworthy. It is the question of relationship between the individual and the group and the masses. The quality which a revolutionary must possess is that he should show concern for the group and for the masses. For this reason, while studying, one must pay attention to the cultivation of this quality. If one does not show concern for the group but always disagrees with it while in school, one will find it very difficult, when working in society later on, to become a person serving the masses conscientiously. Concern for the group and for the masses must be cultivated through everyday acts no matter how trivial they may be. One should actively take part in all activities organized by one's school and in doing all things beneficial to the group and to others. If others want one to do social work, one should actively and seriously undertake to do it. Almost all of the students taking part in the forums had social work to do. They all felt that doing appropriate social work was very useful to one in cultivating the thought of serving the masses and in training one's organizing ability. Provided one divides one's time reasonably, concentrating on one's work when working and on one's studies when studying, participation in social work will not affect one's studies. The students said that facts about past graduates showed that those who did social work in school were as a rule able to make rapid progress after they left school and began to work.

PHYSICAL HEALTH HAS VERY IMPORTANT BEARING ON "REDNESS" AND EXPERTNESS

All the students taking part in the forums agreed that, in order to train oneself and become both "red" and expert, one must have good physical health. Without good physical health, one would find it difficult to become "red" and expert. Lu Kuo-pao, a 6th-year student of Peking University, said, "Physical health has a very important bearing on 'redness' and expertness. Take myself for instance. My health was very poor when I was in middle school. This affected my studies. Later, I began to pay attention to physical training. For several years, I kept on doing physical exercises and such things as long-distance running. In this way, my health has been able to give me considerable help. In the university, I have been working for a Party branch for several years. I often work and study till very late, but I never feel tired. Even after studying throughout the night, I would still feel quite energetic when I go to class the following day. My experience shows that, in order to train oneself and become the kind of useful person needed by the Party, one must pay attention to physical training." . . .

Chung-kuo Ch'ing-nien Pao editor's note: To be firm revolutionary warriors and "red" and expert successors is the demand of the Party and also the vow of the broad masses of the students. But how can one train oneself and become both "red" and expert? This is a question over which the students now feel very concerned. The account of important points discussed at forums is published in our paper today for their information. We hope that the broad masses of students still studying in school and those who have already graduated will write to us for publication about their forums or discussions on, and personal views of, this question.

4.11 "Primary and Middle Schools in Peking and Wuhan Guide Students To Compare the Bitterness of the Old Society With the Sweetness of the New Society, Receive the Stimulation of Class Education, and Sow the Seeds of Revolutionary Thought"

(NCNA Peking, July 13) A dominant feature of this term's ideological and political education conducted among primary and middle schools in Peking municipality has been the adoption of diversified and lively forms in educating pupils to develop the class and class struggle viewpoints. Calling this method "conducting education by the roots," teachers have all recognized this as an important way of bringing up and training the next generation into staunch revolutionaries.

Students have warmly welcomed the methods of asking veteran workers, veteran poor peasants, and veteran Communist Party members to relate their sufferings of oppression and exploitation in the old society and stories of revolutionary struggles, and of carrying out education among the student by using such materials as factory histories, mine histories, cooperative histories, village histories, and the family histories of the laboring people. In the past two months, a group of junior-grade students of Tayu Middle School in the neighborhood of Ment'oukou Colliery launched the activity of "walking about, looking around, listening and thinking." Led by Pai Pao-ch'un, a retired veteran mining worker, who was very familiar with changes that had taken place in the colliery and who suffered greatly in the old society, the students were shown around the mine, so that they could look at real people and listen to accounts of real happenings and real things given by the veteran mining worker. Before a row of low sheds now reconstructed and used as depots and vegetable cellars, the veteran worker told the students: "This is the place where mining workers of the old society lived. I was put up in Room No. 51, which accommodated scores of people. It was so crowded that those living in it could hardly turn around." He also explained the ballad then popular with the miners: "A broken brick serves as a pillow, worn-out straw matting is laid on the ground, gunny bags serve as a blanket which cannot even cover the feet, and food consists of black loaves." Pointing to the "Pit For Ten Thousand People" below a small ridge, the veteran worker said to the students: "In the past, capitalists did not look upon workers as human beings. As the shafts often collapsed or were flooded with water, large numbers of miners were either knocked down unconscious or drowned. Some gravely ill workers breathing their last were dragged out and thrown into the fields to be bitten to death by wild dogs and jackals." Having heard these accounts, the chidlren were full of hatred for the vicious capitalists. Accordingly, they arrived at this conclusion: "The hearts of capitalists are blacker than coal." By taking the students to the villages to interview poor villagers and find out their sufferings, Chunghsin Primary School in Lulits'un in the suburbs of Peking changed the concept of many students of the landlord, who previously had appeared to them to be one with "a big belly." They also found out that landlords prospered and became rich by ruthlessly exploiting [tenant farmers], and realized how the peasants, under the

---

"Primary and Middle Schools in Peking and Wuhan Guide Students To Compare the Bitterness of the Old Society With the Sweetness of the New Society, Receive the Stimulation of Class Education, and Sow the Seeds of Revolutionary Thought" (NCNA, Peking, July 13, 1963), Peking, *Jen-min Jih-pao*, July 14, 1963, *Survey of China Mainland Press*, No. 3036 (August 9, 1963), pp. 13-15.

leadership of the Party, had fought the landlords.

Another very significant activity extensively launched by various schools is to "compare childhood." Many schools have guided students to compare their own . . . childhood with that of veteran workers and veteran poor peasants and tenant farmers, thereby making them understand that class exploitation and class oppression are the root-cause of the sufferings of the laboring people of the old society. A number of schools have collected pictures and drawings about teenagers and children living under the capitalist and colonial systems. After watching these pictures on display at school exhibitions, students say: "Although we live happily today, we must never forget that there are still tens of thousands of teenagers and children the world over who are living miserably."

Diverse and manifold activities launched on revolutionary occasions and days in memory of the death anniversaries of martyrs have also made it possible for students to receive lively and rich class education and education in revolutionary traditions. One of the classes of First Middle School for Girls not long ago organized a Young Pioneer meeting of which the central theme was the "Internationale," at which students were told the story of the struggle waged by the Paris Commune and how the first red banner of the proletariat was hoisted. The students said: "We will hold high this red banner, so that it will keep on fluttering forever." Other activities conducted after classes, such as screening of lantern slides, reciting poems, reading of books on revolution, telling stories of revolution, and singing revolutionary songs, have also become very popular in various schools. . . .

According to an NCNA dispatch from Wuhan dated July 13, many primary and middle schools in Wuhan municipality have adopted diverse and diversified forms, such as using the method of comparing the history of the new society with that of the old society to educate youths and adolescents.

Since the beinning of this term, nearly 50 middle schools in Wuhan municipality have one after another organized over 10,000 students to go to the countryside. In the course of visiting the production teams of rural people's communes, the students participated in farm labor on the one hand and on the other interviewed veteran poor peasants and tenant farmers to find out about their conditions in the days before the introduction of land reform. They ate, lived and did farm labor together with these peasants, listening to their pathetic stories of how in the old society they were ruthlessly exploited by landlords. When the students found many scars on the bodies of some poor peasants and tenant farmers — evidence of maltreatment by landlords, some shed tears. The students said that in the past they only learned from books what exploitation meant, but now they realized in a concrete manner how landlords exploited peasants. Many schools have also organized students to interview veteran workers, veteran Red Army fighters, and veteran revolutionary cadres. The affiliated primary school of Wuchang Experimental Normal School organized its students to interview twenty-nine parents, including veteran Red Army fighters, veteran workers, and veteran peasants in the suburbs. These people told the children the sufferings they had experienced in the past. Upon their return to school, exhibitions of pictures prepared by the children themselves were held, and discussion meetings sponsored by the children themselves were called. Activities such as these have greatly helped to strengthen the children's class viewpoint and class feelings.

Some schools have made good use of the historical background and special features of Wuhan municipality to conduct vivid class education among youths and adolescents, by organizing them to visit certain landmarks in this city. For instance, the teachers of a primary school in Lutuch'iao, Wuhan municipality, recently took a number of students to the former "British Settlement," French Concession," "German Concession," and "Japanese Settlement." In the course of visiting these old relics, the teachers told the children how in the past imperialists ran amuck and imposed a tyrannical rule on Chinese territories. Having listened to what had been related by their teachers, the chidlren were very angry and said the visit to the former settlements made them realize the crimes committed by imperialism and the happy life they led today. Some schools held Young Pioneer meetings after visits and interviews were over, to "denounce the evils of the old society." At these gatherings, the children used the materials they had gathered from interviews to educate one another, thereby making them acquire a deeper understanding of the evils of the old society.

Influenced by class education, the thinking and feelings of students have progressively undergone changes. Many middle school students, in the course of participating in productive labor in the countryside, have displayed zest and made determined efforts to do various jobs willingly and to uphold the interests of the collective. Accordingly, they have been praised by commune members. The students of Shuikuhu Middle School in Wuchang, who in the past were not inclined to study their lessons well, have recently made considerable improvement in their study records. The results of their mid-term examinations universally were much better than those of previous tests. Quite a good number of the students of this school recently became League members or Young Pioneers.

4.12 "Energetically Train a Force of Red and Expert Teachers"

RAISING THE IDEO-POLITICAL AND VOCATIONAL LEVELS OF TEACHERS IS A VERY IMPORTANT PART OF OUR SCHOOL'S WORK HENCEFORTH OF RAISING QUALITY AND THE SCIENTIFIC LEVEL

As a result of implementing the Party's education policy and carrying out a series of ideological revolution, educational revolution and practical work, our university has in recent years brought about a fundamental change in the ideo-political appearance of the teachers and a notable rise in their vocational level. It has, moreover, accumulated some initial experience in the training of teachers. This has laid a good foundation for the training of a force of red and expert teachers by the university to meet the needs of the development of work. We must avail ourselves of these favorable conditions in adopting measures for more effectively raising the ideo-political and vocational levels of our teachers and accelerating the growth of the teaching force.

The vocational level of the teachers of our school, in spite of the marked rise in recent years, is still not high enough to meet the requirements of work. The proportion of professors and assistant professors in the total number of teachers at present is comparatively small and there are insufficient teachers of high academic attainments. The growth of intermediate level teachers still lags behind requirements. Among them some require urgent improvement in specialized knowledge and in their ability to undertake scientific research. In some cases, basic work also needs

Lu P'ing (President, Peking University), "Energetically Train a Force of Red and Expert Teachers," Peking, *Kuang-ming Jih-pao*, September 12, 1963, *Survey of China Mainland Press*, No. 3078 (October 11, 1963), pp. 1-9.

strengthening. For lack of intermediate level backbone teachers, some units are confronted with a situation in which "the old crop will all be consumed before a new crop can be reaped." Quite a sizable number of young teachers have not gained a sufficient command of fundamental theories, basic knowledge and basic skill. Obviously this state of affairs cannot satisfactorily meet the needs of current work. From a long-term point of view, in order to enable the various subjects of study in our school to reach the modern scientific level, we must have a force of red and expert teachers who are at the same time outstanding scientists and specialists.

Although our teachers have made big strides in their ideo-political standing, yet many problems still remain and there is need for continual improvement. The basic task of our socialist universities is to implement the policy of making education serve proletarian politics and integrating education with productive labor and to bring up laborers with socialist consciousness and culture. In order to fulfill this task, our teachers should ideologically and politically support the Party and uphold socialism, whole-heartedly serve the people and vigorously struggle for the cause of socialism and communism. It is only by relying on such a force of teachers that the Party can bring up intellectuals of the working class and train up a younger generation willing to serve the people and strive for the victory of socialism and communism in China and throughtout the world. From another standpoint, if our vocational level is to be raised quickly, we must also raise our ideo-political consciousness. Take social sciences for example. They are sciences with a class character and a Party character. If those studying these sciences do not possess a set proleterian world outlook and do not apply Marxist-Leninist viewpoints and methods to the direction of their pursuits, then it will be next to impossible to really solve any problem of a substantial character and it may even lead to mistakes in theory and direction. Although natural science has no class character, its workers, if able to apply the viewpoints and methods of dialectical materialism consciously, can be certain of gaining a better understanding and grasp of the laws of nature's development, thereby giving an impetus to their own work and enabling our scientific level and research work to improve at a faster speed.

To summarize what has been said above, vigorously raising the teachers' ideo-political consciousness and vocational level and building a force of red and expert teachers who understand politics as well as their calling and who answer to the requirements of the development of work is a very important task for our university from now on. . . .

4.13 "How Should We Educate Our Children?"

A MESSAGE TO OUR READERS ON WAYS
OF INITIATING DISCUSSIONS
ON "HOW SHOULD WE EDUCATE OUR CHILDREN?"

Dear Workers and Comrades:

In the past few months we have received letters from a number of parents reflecting certain problems related to and their views on the education of their children. Some parents, both being workers, think they are too preoccupied with work to have any

The Editor, *Kung-jen Jih-pao*, "How Should We Educate Our Children?", Peking, *Kung-jen Jih-pao*, August 20, 1963, *Survey of China Mainland Press*, No. 3061 (September 17, 1963), pp. 5-7.

time for teaching their children, or they have too many children who make too much demands on their time. Other parents think since they themselves suffered a great deal in the past, they should now let their chidlren live comfortably. Accordingly, they will not let their children do this and that, and try in every possible way to let them have good food and fine clothes. Some parents think since their children were born into a working class family in the new society, they will be imbued with the thought of the working class without the need of educating them at all. Others even think that it does not matter much if their children have defects when they are still young, for they will change and develop good habits when they are grown up. Although some parents have been very strict in educating their children, they have not achieved good results, due to the use of improper methods when teaching their children. Some parents aim to educate their children and train them so that they may become engineers, experts, or artists, instead of teaching them how to become an ordinary laborer with culture, with the result their children belittle physical labor and only wish to specialize in something they have set their mind on.

Due to various reasons mentioned above, some children have early in their life developed the bad habit of living in a disorganized manner, fearing nobody, beating and cursing people, and acting waywardly. Some children have been so pampered by their parents that they are keen on food but lazy in doing work. Accordingly, they are not diligent in studying their lessons and their study records are poor. Whenever they sit for graduation or entrance examinations, their parents are often the first to get excited about their children's chances of success. In some cases, children are found to have developed the bad behavior of telling lies, acting selfishly, and seeking small gains at the expense of others. There are also cases in which some children, being clever and alert, and having done their lessons well, have been fondly cherished by their parents and frequently commended by their teachers. With the added advantages of affluent family life and an ample supply of good food and fine clothes that are not normally available to most children, they have consequently developed a feeling of superiority and are inclined to be very haughty when they are together with their schoolmates and other children around them.

The mind of teenagers and children is simple, pure and innocent. When they become sensible enough in their early childhood, they find everything around them new and exciting. They are by nature curious and are very fond of imitating others. When they are not attending school — primary or secondary school, they spend most of their time at their own homes. Their parents are their first teachers. In their eyes, their parents are their examples. The words and deeds of parents produce a direct influence on the children. This shows that parents have the major responsibility of educating their children.

In the old society, parents educated their children for the purpose of securing some means of support in their old age. In the new society, no worker need worry about his old age, although sons and daughters have the obligation to support their parents when they are too old to work. Hence, the upbringing of children in the new society is not merely a personal matter or a private family affair, but is for the cause of socialist construction. This point is entirely consistent whether it concerns the personal interests of each worker or the future of one's children. In this aspect, our Party and State have pinned great hopes on our children, and expect them to become fine successors to the revolutionary cause.

Although our children were born into working class families, and have been brought up in the new society, they will not necessarily develop spontaneously socialist concepts. As far as the children themselves are concerned, they after all have been brought up in a peaceful environment. Accordingly, they are not immune to attacks by old ideas, old practices, and the force of old habits prevailing in society. Judging from letters sent us by readers and manuscripts submitted by contributors, although parents all fondly cherish their own children and hope they will become useful persons in the future, not everyone can fulfill parental obligations. Even though parents realize their own obligations, they are not necessarily familiar with the methods of educating their children. Like other things, the problem of educating children is now in the state of going through drastic changes, such as those taking place in our country, since the practices left over by the old society are no longer found suitable, while the practices prevailing in the new society have not yet been properly mastered by all. It is necessary, therefore, for our workers and their families to discuss and solve certain problems concerning the education of children. Putting it more specifically, these problems are: Is it not necessary for children brought up in the new society to pay attention to education? Will these children spontaneously develop socialist awareness? Will children born into working class families not change their character and become bad? Can we not become "irresponsible parents" and get away from educating our children? Is it right for us to shirk the responsibility of educating our children and pass it on to school and society? How important is family education? What kind of next generation should we bring up and train? How should we educate and train children to adopt a correct attitude toward ideals and future prospects? Why should we avoid pampering our children? If parents are inconsistent in their words and deeds, talking only but doing nothing, how will they influence their children? What should be done when children have done something wrong? How should parents collaborate with the school in educating their children? Regarding problems such as these, all may have their own views and ideas, as well as personal observations and experiences in varying degrees. Whatever efforts made by us to discuss thoroughly and get these problems straight will be of help to the upbringing and training of our next generation. In order to help parents to find solutions to these problems, this paper will begin, from today, a new section called "How Should We Educate Our Children?" It is hoped that all will express their views heartily.

The Editor

PART FIVE

Two-Line Party Struggle (1964-1965)

PART FIVE
Two-Line Party Struggle (1964-1965)

During the period of retrenchment (1960-1963), and especially following the withdrawal of Soviet technical assistance and the disasterous crop failures, Liu Shao-chi, who had been appointed the successor to Mao Tse-tung as President of the People's Republic of China, urged a series of reforms; he was further joined by other high government officials and members of the Chinese Communist Party in pressing for economic reforms: monetary incentives to individuals for agricultural production; the extension of agricultural plots for private use; the extension of opportunities for individuals to sell their products in a free market situation; increasing the number of small enterprises run on the principle of private profit; fixing output quotas on the basis of households rather than on the basis of production brigades, etc.

All these policies came into conflict with Mao Tse-tung's concept of the "superstructure of proletarian socialism which requires acquisitiveness to be replaced by a spirit of service."[1] As a result, the stage for a direct ideological confrontation was set; the two-year period (1964-1965) of internal two-line Party struggle eventually led to the "Great Proletarian Cultural Revolution" which began in 1966 when Liu Shao-chi (referred to as the "Chinese Khrushchev") and his followers were openly attacked as Rightists who were following the counter-revolutionary capitalist road—i.e., imitating the Soviet model.

The following statement from the *Peking Review* is illustrative of the charges which were later to be leveled against Liu Shao-chi, "the top Party person in authority":

> Before the socialist transformation of agriculture was in the main completed, he did his utmost to protect and develop the rich peasant economy and oppose the socialist collectivization of agriculture. And after the basic completion of that transformation, he made big efforts to restore capitalism and disintegrate the socialist collective economy. He madly sabotaged the socialist revolution in the countryside, and came out against the masses of poor and lower-middle peasants. He pursued an out-and-out counter-revolutionary revisionist line, a

line which represented a vain attempt to restore capitalism in the rural areas, a
line which would, in fact, allow the landlords, rich peasants, counter-
revolutionaries, bad elements and Rightists to make a comeback.[2]

The Rightist point of view was analyzed by Joan Robinson, in *The Cultural
Revolution in China,* in a somewhat more sympathetic fashion; she states:

> It was something like this: Mao's ideas were fine for leading a peasant army
> but they are not appropriate to running a modern State. The Great Leap of 1958
> was an irresponsible adventure, for which a heavy price was paid in the three
> bad years that followed. . . .
> The Rightists insist upon the need for organization and authority. Every
> army and every industry in the world is run on the basis of a chain of command
> from the top downwards. That those in a higher grade in the hierarchy should
> have a more comfortable standard of life than those below is not only excusable
> but desirable, since it adds prestige to authority. The workers need tutelage;
> obedience and diligence are required of them; they are none the better for
> having their heads full of political wind. The task of industrialization must be
> carried out fast. It is nonsense to wait till the mass of the population are
> educated. We must build up a corps of managers and civil servants quickly;
> that means that we must draw upon the old lettered class, even if they were
> landlords or reactionaries in the past. In the arts, the dominance of politics
> produces a dreary philistinism and in literature a stupid black and white
> morality, smothering all the subtlety and grace of Chinese traditions.[3]

With the top leadership, led by Liu Shao-chi, this rightist platform seemed to gain
strength. Nevertheless, "to the people at large Mao *was* the government,"[4] even
though he had formally yielded the position of President to Liu Shao-chi and was
nominally only Chairman of the Central Committee of the Communist Party of
China. Furthermore, beginning in 1962, China's harvests had improved and the
nation was overcoming the technological gulf created by the earlier withdrawal of
Soviet technical assistance, thus strengthening Mao Tse-tung's position.

In the fall of 1962, at the Tenth Plenary Session of the Eighth Central Comittee of
the Chinese Communist Party, Mao Tse-tung urged that the Party must "never forget
class struggle." The "socialist education" campaign of 1963 and 1964 was launched
to clean up problems in four areas: politics, ideology, organization, and the economy.
In 1964, responding to the call to turn "intellectuals into laborers and revolutionaries," more than 300,000 educated youth in the nation's cities went to the rural
areas and mountain regions to participate in rural socialist construction.[5]

However, Mao's "rectification" campaign, that is the "four clean-up" movement, was somehow deflected to the purposes of the Rightists. Later, in August 1966,
Mao was to refer to this as "the wrong tendency of 1964 which was 'Left' in form but
Right in essence."[6] To get the "rectification" campaign back to the Leftist line, Mao
Tse-tung authorized (January 1965) what has been referred to as "the 23-article
document" (officially titled, "Some Current Problems Raised in the Socialist Education Movement in the Rural Areas"), which clearly stated that:

> The main target of the present movement is those persons within the Party who
> are in authority and are taking the capitalist road.[7]

The challenge was reiterated in September 1965, during the Working Conference
of the Party's Central Committee, when Mao Tse-tung raised the following question:

> What are you going to do if revisionism appears in the Central Committee? This
> is highly likely. This is the greatest danger.[8]

Thus the confrontation between revisionism and Maoism was accelerated, although it was not brought into full public view until 1966.

The political conflict of 1964-1965, the period of the "two-line party struggle," was reflected in the field of education. In view of the growing discord within the Party headquarters (sometimes referred to in Chinese sources as the "two command headquarters" to illustrate the struggle between the two lines of thought), the re-emphasis on political education and productive labor—a carry-over from the previous period—gained momentum. This culminated in the decision of December 1965, calling for the transformation of the educational system to one based on the concept of "half-work and half-study."

According to Robert D. Barendsen, the "half-work half-study" school had its origins in the period of the "Great Leap Forward," during which time the government had committed itself to a rapid expansion of educational facilities, to the eventual universalization of junior middle-school education by 1967, and the extension of opportunities for higher education to all by 1972. Unable to afford the economic expenditures required to achieve these educational objectives, the central government delegated considerable responsibility for establishing and operating schools to local collective agencies, and at the same time encouraged the establishment of part-time schools, in which students divided their time between studying and participating in productive labor. Income from student labor was to be applied to meet the operating expenses of the schools and therefore play a major role in achieving the educational objectives of the "Great Leap Forward."[9]

The half-work half-study schools did not, however, become the universal educational pattern; nor did they resolve all the financial difficulties associated with the ambitious educational goals of the "Great Leap Forward." The half-work half-study schools were also the object of much criticism regarding the quality of students' schoolwork and level of academic achievement. A so-called two-track educational system of schools was developed, in which there were both a system of state schools devoted to full-time study and a system of half-work half-study schools. Outstanding students were admitted to the full-time schools. This was the "two-track educational system and two kinds of labor" advocated by Liu Shao-chi.

The Rightists (Liu Shao-chi, Lu Ting-yi, etc.) were later to be accused of introducing the "little treasure pagoda" system of revisionist education, in which schools and educational institutions were divided into two categories: (1) the school of the "little treasure pagoda" which concentrated on giving training to an educational elite, future cadres, technicians, engineers, and professional personnel; and (2) the other schools in general which were to produce industrial and agricultural workers.

The "little treasure pagoda" concept contended that it was important for China to establish certain schools of special quality, which would form the backbone of schools in general and thereby be sort of a "capital construction in education." Provinces and municipalities were directed to select a number of key full-time schools and establish a "little treasure pagoda." Thus, within the system of full-time schools there existed a division between the "little treasure pagoda" schools, training students for advanced study (sometimes referred to as being "elevated to heaven") and full-time schools in general, whose students would become a labor reserve. The "little treasure pagoda" schools also received special allocations of state funds and equipment, selected teachers, etc.

In any case, while the two-line Party struggle was carried on internally, Liu Shao-chi used his power and influence to insist on his educational ideas. He travelled through nineteen provinces and made more than twenty reports to publicize and gain support of his "two-track educational system and two kinds of labor," which the Leftists considered a replication of the "double-track" system of capitalist education.[10]

The Leftists attacked these schools on a number of grounds: putting professional abilities in command, rather than putting politics in command, thereby enabling bourgeois intellectuals to assume the leadership of schools; enlarging the gap between mental and physical labor; and pushing China's youth toward the "slough of revisionism."[11]

In particular, Mao Tse-tung criticized the existing school curriculum, the teaching methods and the system of examinations, charging that: courses were too numerous, imposing undue pressure on students; lecture methods were poor and inefficient; and the examination system treated students as enemies. He called for a sweeping educational reform. Yet the Rightists, including Lu Ting-yi, cautioned against overhaul of the general educational framework, and urged that educational reform should be carried out only after proper experimentation.

Interestingly, during this period China introduced, on a trial basis, the "open-paper" examination in higher education; students were permitted to consult textbooks, lecture notes, or reference materials while taking the examination in a selected number of subjects. The emphasis was placed on having students understand and apply the knowledge they had acquired, rather than on rote learning and repeating information. One such "open-paper" examination problem given to second-year physics students at Shanghai's Chiaotung University (specializing in engineering) tested the ability of students to devise methods of determining the wavelengths of visible and ultraviolet rays, on which there had been no specific teaching. The head of the welding teaching research group stated:

> We do not regard examinations simply as a method of checking up on how many facts a student has acquired. More important, they should help him to grasp the knowledge better and to use it practically.[12]

Whereas the Rightists stressed the education of an elite group—technicians, engineers, Party officials, etc.—with academic standards protected by a system of formal examinations, the Leftists (Maoists) stressed training successors to the proletarian revolutionary enterprise, as illustrated in the following selection from a *Peking Review* article entitled, "Bringing Up Heirs for the Revolution":

> The matter of bringing up worthy heirs to the proletarian revolution—of raising new generations who will steadfastly carry the socialist revolution through to the end, occupies an important part of the attention of the Chinese people today. . . .
> Raised with special authority by Chairman Mao Tse-tung, this question is one of the utmost historical importance. It is a question, in the final analysis, of how to ensure that the revolution, won by the older generation at the cost of such sacrifices, will be carried on victoriously to the end by the generations to come; that the destiny of our country will continue to be held secure in the hands of true proletarian revolutionaries; that our sons and grandsons and their successors will continue to advance, generation after generation, along the Marxist-Leninist, and not the revisionist, path, that is, advance steadily towards the goal of Communism, and not to retreat to make room for a capitalist restoration.[13]

In the field of education, the two-line Party struggle culminated in the Spring 1964 decision to revitalize the earlier half-work half-study program and the public announcement, in December 1965, of the plan to eventually "make the half-work half-study system universal in China and apply it to well-functioning full-time schools . . . ."[14] The ideological basis of this decision, according to Donald J. Munro, was:

> . . . to eliminate the difference between mental and manual labor, between the viewpoint of bourgeois intellectuals and workers. The students who emerge

from half-work half-study schools theoretically will be intellectuals and workers at the same time. Thus the danger of revisionism coming forth is meant to be obviated.[15]

Supporters of the half-work (farming) half-study schools also pointed out that since the introduction of these new schools, the proportion of female students attending school had increased significantly. A number of factors were cited by way of explanation: many poor and lower-middle-class peasants had financial burdens and heavy household chores which required the daughter's help at home; some parents still attached greater importance to sons than to daughters, and didn't consider their daughters' study too important, etc. The new school charged a small fee which was not too difficult to pay, and provided time for daughters to participate in the household chores as well as study.[16]

The ''irregularity'' of the half-work half-study schools, which previously had been one of the criticisms leveled against the system and one of the reasons given for the continuation of the two-track educational system, was now pointed to as a unique feature which facilitated the extension of schools to rural and remote areas. Some remote areas such as Inner Mongolia even received ''travelling'' or ''mobile'' work-study schools (sometimes referred to as *ai-li* schools, after the Mongolian word for yurt). Children of nomadic herdsman's families in these stockbreeding communes engaged in classroom study for seven months a year (in summer and winter) and productive labor during the spring lambing season and autumn harvest. The school set up tents or yurts and actually followed the herds around, equipping the children ''with knowledge much needed in the pastoral areas . . . [as well as being certain] to foster a socialist devotion to manual labor and the interests of the collective.''[17] Similar mobile schools were established in some pasture areas of Sinkiang, Tsinghai, and Tibet.

For the student, the claimed advantage of the half-work and half-study schools was that lessons were practical and related to life; for the government, it was the availability of a much larger labor force and the idea of training intellectuals and workers at the same time. The concept of work-study schooling thus dominated official thinking on academic development, and the practice spread quickly; as reported in *Current Scene:*

> The work-study practice soon extended outwards and upwards. From the communes it spread to the cities, where training in the new style involved factory work. From the middle school the idea penetrated to the university.[18]

The first half-work (farming) and half-study schools had been introduced in the countryside and on the people's communes; these were then followed by vocational or technical half-work half-study schools in urban areas. Sponsors included municipal government departments (e. g. building, town planning, public utilities, etc.); electrical, mechanical, chemical, textile, and radio factories; various mining enterprises, etc. Operating expenses were met, either completely or in part, by the school itself, with teachers being recruited locally—usually by applying the principle of regarding the ''capable as the teacher.''[19] The students' study was directly related to the practical and often highly-technical knowledge needed in the industrial or mining enterprise, and production levels were increased.

While the half-work half-study practice was catching on, Mao's teachings were by no means neglected. An April 11, 1964 *Peking Daily* editorial entitled ''Cultivate a Lively, Active Climate of Study on One's Own Initiative,'' reminded its readers of Mao Tse-tung's statement on educational policy and students' all-round development—''Our educational policy must enable everyone who gets an education to develop morally, intellectually, and physically and to become a cultured, socialist-minded worker''—and then presented the following analysis of the ''dialectical relationship'' between teaching quality and the reduction of students' burdens, and the necessity for strengthening students' extracurricular activities while at the same time lightening their burdens:

> The relationship between the improvement of teaching quality and the reduction of the burdens on students is an opposite but unified dialectical relationship. In order to improve teaching quality, it is necessary to reduce the students' burdens; in order to reduce the the students' burdens, it is necessary to improve teaching methods and teaching quality. By correctly handling the relationship between these two tasks, we shall be able to improve teaching quality on the one hand and reduce the students' burdens on the other. But, if poorly handled, the task of improving teaching quality will result in an aggravation of the students' workload, or the reduction of the students' burdens will turn out to be a degeneration in teaching quality.
>
> Therefore, the reduction of the students' burdens is a positive measure rather than a negative one. It means that educational workers are required to do more instead of less. Without improving our teaching methods, the reduction of the students' burdens will not improve the quality of teaching. In order to improve teaching work and teaching quality, we should reduce the students' burdens and, in the meantime, strengthen their extracurricular activities. The relations between curricular and extracurricular activities should be correctly handled by the schools and teachers.[20]

Young Communist League (YCL) organizations in schools were directed to implement Chairman Mao's directives, and urged to attain a complete understanding of the educational policy of the Party, rather than to ''one-sidedly pursue a high percentage of admissions of our students into institutions of higher learning or adopt improper methods of teaching.''[21]

As part of Mao Tse-tung's stress on ''students' all-round development,'' physical culture became an important aspect of school education, particularly at the primary and middle-school levels, and was considered as a means of carrying out both political and ideological education:

> . . . it [the physical culture movement] will enable the students to better complete their study task so that in the future when they participate in productive labor, enter into military service, or join other construction enterprises, they will be vigorous and firmly determined to shoulder the heavy task.[22]

According to Liu Ai-feng, then Vice Minister of Education, the improvement of school physical education called for doing a good job in three ways: (1) to ''handle the physical training course properly . . . according to pedagogic plans,'' that is, to correctly understand the significance of physical training; (2) to ''make the students persistently and painstakingly do morning exercises and intermission exercise''; and (3) to ''actively unfold the extracurricular physical training activities among students,'' so as to fit in with their timetable for work, self-study, and recreational activities.[23]

Military sports were also considered an important means of intensifying ''proleterian consciousness,'' defined as:

> . . . an intense comprehension of enemy activity and national defense and constant awareness of the fact that class and class struggle exist throughout the transitional period, that class enemies and new and old bourgeois elements at home and elsewhere are always attempting a restoration of capitalism.[24]

YCL organizations were encouraged to develop mass activities of military sports (firing practice, mountain climbing, military camping, grenade throwing, swimming with a heavy load, etc.), so that the youth of the country could be made "to know that they must be ever ready to fight as long as class enemies exist."[25]

In view of the intensification of the "struggle between the two lines" and the "two command headquarters," political education reached an all-time high level of activity. The Rightists recommended the reduction of students' political activities and "class education." Maoists accused them of adopting the policy of "motherly love education," which holds that young children are incapable of accepting class education, that class struggle is a cruel topic and would hurt the souls of young children.[26]

Eventually, the turmoil of this political revolution—which called for a thorough reform within the Party, in politics, the economy and culture—would force the school system to come to a complete halt; China's schools were unable to function and had to close when then Cultural Revolution broke out in 1966. The phenomenon of the Cultural Revolution was unprecedented in the history of China, and indeed perhaps in the history of the world.

NOTES:

[1] Joan Robinson, *The Cultural Revolution in China* (Baltimore, Maryland: Penguin Books, 1969), p. 12.

[2] Editorial Departments of *Renmin Ribao* [*People's Daily*], *Hongqi* [*Red Flag*], and *Jiefangjun Bao* [*Liberation Army Daily*], "Struggle Between the Two Roads in China's Countryside," *Peking Review,* No. 49 (December 1, 1967), p.11.

[3] Robinson, op. cit., pp. 16-17.

[4] Ibid., p. 83.

[5] "More Than 300 Thousand Educated Youth Head for Rural Areas and Mountains," *Shih-shih Shou-ts'e* [*Current Events*], No. 5 (March 6, 1965), *Extracts from China Mainland Magazines,* No. 469 (May 17, 1965), p.30.

[6] Mao Tse-tung, "Bombard the Headquarters—My Big-Character Poster" (August 5, 1966), *Peking Review,* No. 33 (August 11, 1967), p.5. [The English translation was published in *Peking Review* to commemorate the anniversary of the appearance of the poster.]

[7] Ibid., p. 7.

[8] Ibid.

[9] Robert D. Barendsen, *Half-Work Half-Study Schools in Communist China* (Washington, D.C.: U.S. Government Printing Office, 1964), p.2.

[10] Wang Hsuan-tze, "General Review of Culture and Education in Communist China in 1969," S.M. Hu (trans.), *Studies on Chinese Communism,* No. 12 (December 31, 1969), p.80.

[11] Revolutionary Rebel Command H.Q. of Shantung Provincial Department of Education, "Demolish the 'Little Treasure Pagoda' System of Revisionist Education," *Jen-min Jih-pao* (December 17, 1967), *Survey of China Mainland Press,* No. 4100, (January 16, 1968), pp. 1-4. The Red Guard Corps of the 4th Middle School of Peking, "Five Major Charges Against the Old Educational System," *Jen-min Jih-pao* (December 17, 1967), Ibid., pp. 9-11.

[12] "Radical Change in Examination Methods Introduced at Chinese University" (NCNA-English, Shanghai, March 21, 1965), *Survey of China Mainland Press,* No. 3424 (March 25, 1965), p. 18.

[13] "Bringing Up Heirs for the Revolution," *Peking Review,* No. 30 (July 24, 1964) p. 19.

[14] Donald J. Munro, "The Current Anti-Intellectual Campaign in Perspective," *Current Scene,* No. 2 (June 1, 1966), p. 5.

[15] Ibid.

[16] Editor's postscript, "A Question Absolutely Deserving Close Attention," *Jen-min Jih-pao* (May 7, 1965), *Survey of China Mainland Press,* No. 3463 (May 24, 1965), p. 8.

[17]"Remote Areas of Inner Mongolia Get Travelling Work-Study Schools" (NCNA-English, Huhehot, April 9, 1965), *Survey of China Mainland Press*, No. 3438 (April 14, 1965), p. 26. [For a fascinating detailed account of the "mobile" school, the editors recommend, "Schools That Follow Mongolian Yurts," written by the Pastoral Area Education Investigation Work Group of the Editorial Department of *Practice* Magazine and the Educational Bureau of Inner Mongolia—which originally appeared in *People's Daily* (May 27, 1965), and was translated in *Survey of China Mainland* Press, No. 3484 (June 24, 1965), pp. 12-15.]

[18]Maurice Kelly, "The Making of a Proletarian Intellectual," *Current Scene,* No. 19 (October 21, 1966), p. 4.

[19]Editorial commentary, "The Promising Future of Schools Run on a Half-Work and Half-Study Basis," *Jen-min Jih-pao* (July 30, 1964), *Survey of China Mainland Press,* No.3276 (August 11, 1964), p. 7.

[20]Editorial, "Cultivate a Lively, Active Climate of Study on One's Own Initiative," *Jen-min Jih-pao* (April 11, 1964), *Survey of China Mainland Press,* No.3207 (April 28, 1964), pp. 13-14.

[21]Editorial, "Guide the Students to Develop in an All-round Way," *Chung-kuo Ch'ing-nien Pao [China Youth Daily]* (April 14, 1964), *Survey of China Mainland Press,* No.3226 (May 26, 1964), p. 1.

[22]Liu Ai-feng, "Do School Physical Culture Well and Develop Students' Physique," *Hsin T'i-yu* [New Physical Culture], No. 7 (July 6, 1964), *Extracts from China Mainland Magazines,* No. 434 (September 14, 1964), p. 34.

[23]Ibid., pp. 35-36.

[24]Editorial, "Promote Revolutionization of Youths by Vigorously Developing Military Sports," *Chung-kuo Ch'ing-nien Pao [China Youth Daily]* (March 25, 1965), *Survey of China Mainland Press,* No.3435 (April 8, 1965), p. 7.

[25]Ibid.

[26]"Strengthen Class Education Among Children," *Kiangsu Chiao-yu [Kiangsu Education],* No.2 (February 25, 1965), *Extracts from China Mainland Magazines,* No.482 (August 3, 1965), pp. 18-21.

5.1 "A Hundred Examples of Liu Shao-ch'i's Speeches Opposing the Thought of Mao Tse-tung"

Liu Shao-ch'i's reactionary, revisionist speeches are directly opposed to the thought of Mao Tse-tung. In order to expose his revisionist features, we have selected a hundred examples from a mass of revisionist fallacious speeches made by Liu Shao-ch'i (mostly after the liberation), and contrasted them with the directives of Chairman Mao, Comrade Lin Piao, and the Party Central Committee. The thought of Mao Tse-tung is used here as a weapon to distinguish fragant flowers from poisonous weeds. . . .

VI. TAMPERING WITH CHAIRMAN MAO'S EDUCATIONAL POLICY

Tampering with the Goal of Training in the Name of Developing "Two Kinds of Education System"

(56) Those who graduated from intermediate technical schools and from part-work, part-study schools are new people for us. They are capable of not only mental labor but also of physical labor. Such kind of people are our future, the future of our country.
(At a meeting of Cadres of Kwangsi, 1964)

(56) Chairman Mao proposed five conditions for training a successor to the proletarian revolutionary cause.
(1964)

(57) Recently, we thought out a method: Opening part-work, part-study schools. . . . In this way, it will not be easy for our factory and government organ leaders to become bureaucratic. If a factory director becomes a bureaucrat, the university students in that factory will ask him to step down because many workers may and can work as factory director. Corruption is also made difficult because university students among the workers are capable of reckoning accounts.
(Talk with Sung Shuang, 1963)

(57) Class struggle, production struggle and scientific experimentation are the three great revolutionary movements for building a mighty socialist country; they are a sure guarantee that Communists shall be freed from bureaucratism, revisionism and dogmatism shall be avoided, and we shall be in an invincible position forever. . . .
(*Quotations*, p. 36, 1963)

"A Hundred Examples of Liu Shao-chi'i's Speeches Opposing the Thought of Mao Tse-tung," Peking, *Ching-kang-shan* [Chingkang Mountains], (February 1 & 8, 1967), *Survey of China Mainland Press*, No. 173 (April 4, 1967), pp. 1, 11-13.

(58) If junior middle school graduates are always asked to go to the countryside to be peasants, they would be unwilling to go. If, after arriving at the countryside, they can go to school, say, the part-work, part-study or part-farming, part-study schools, then they may be willing to go.
(A talk on the two kinds of education system, 1964)

(59) Claiming the credit for himself, Liu bragged that the part-work, part-study system was his "invention." He said: "In 1958 I visited Tientsin and gave a talk there. At that time they were very enthusiastic, and with a bang schools sprung up."
(Speech at a Meeting of Cadres of Kwangsi,1964)

(58) Organizing middle school students and senior primary school graduates to participate in the work of cooperativization deserves special attention.

The countryside is a vast world where one finds great possibilities.
(60 Points on Methods of Work, 1958)

(59) In January 1958 Chairman Mao wrote the "60 Points on Methods of Work." Point 49 states: "Students should divide their time between work and study."
(A selection of editor's notes to Socialist Upsurge in China's Countryside, 1955)

Opposing Bringing Politics to the Fore,
Opposing Reform of Teaching

(60) Our Party members, League members and revolutionary intellectuals must study hard, seriously engage in professional research, properly master all kinds of technical and scientific knowledge. Wherever possible, they should strive to make themselves "red and expert"—Red specialists.
(In Commemoration of the 40th Anniversary of the October Revolution, 1957)

(61) Speaking to students going to study in Russia, he said: "First of all, you must learn the Russian language well before going to Moscow, and secondly you must prepare youselves politically.
(1952)

(60) The tendency not to interest oneself in politics must be criticized. On the one hand we must oppose empty-headed politicians; on the other we must also oppose realists who lose their bearings.
(60 Points on Methods of Work, 1958)

(61) Without a correct political viewpoint, one has no soul.
(*Quotations*, p. 124, 1957)

(62) Liu Shao-ch'i thought that revolutionary successors were cultivated by schools. He said: " A small number should study literature, politics, government and law, and finance and economics . . . because some people will still be needed to work as Party committee secretaries, to run and manage enterprises, and to be writers and artists."

(At a meeting of cadres
in Shanghai, 1957)

(62) Successors to the proletarian revolutionary cause are born in the midst of the mass struggle and grow up tempered by the great storms and waves of the revolution. We should observe and judge cadres and select and cultivate successors during the prolonged mass struggle.

(*Quotations,* p. 242, 1964)

(63) Industrial construction is confronted with a host of difficulties. China has money, manpower, and machines, but no engineers.

(Talk with Sung Shuang, 1963)

(63) Political work is the lifeline of all economic work. This is especially so during the period when the social-economic system undergoes a basic change.

(*Quotations*, p. 119, 1955)

(64) Liu Shao-ch'i underrated Chairman Mao's directive concerning education work during the "Spring Festival." At the enlarged session of the Political Bureau of the CCP Central Committee held in November 1965, he said: "Let's hold one more meeting. If we don't see the target clearly, we must not command blindly!"

(64) The present educational system, curriculum, methods of teaching, and methods of examination must be changed for they torture the students.

(At forum on education work
during the Spring Festival, 1964)

(65) Addressing the students studying in the Soviet Union, he said: "I wish you will return upon graduation with five marks. Four marks is fair, but three marks will be too bad."

(1952)

(65) As far as study is concerned, we should not bother with five marks nor with two marks. Three or four marks would be all right. To demand five marks would be to impose an unbearable burden. We shouldn't learn too many things for they would only ruin us.

(Talk with Wang Hai-yung, 1965)

5.2 "Give the Students Education in the Revolutionary World View, Starting with Class Education"

I. *The Question of the Aim of Study Is a Concentrated Expression of Students' View of the World and the Focal Point of Struggle between the Bourgeoisie and the Proletariat to Win Over Young Students*

Why does one go to college? For whom does one study? Whom does one serve? What kind of man should one be? On these questions, each student has his own definite views. According to our survey, the students may generally be classified into three categories: First, a considerable number of the students have a correct aim of study. They are able to integrate their studies with the socialist revolution and socialist construction and are determined to be red and expert successors to the revolutionary cause. Second, the majority of the students are prepared to dedicate their knowledge to the cause of socialist construction but they lack a great revolutionary ideal and are not mentally prepared for the revolutionary burden. The students in this category are generally influenced by bourgeois individualism in varying degrees. Third, a small number of the students are seriously imbued with the bourgeois idea of winning personal fame and fortune for themselves. They study so that "man may leave fame in the same way as a wild goose leaves its cackle" and that they may have "beautiful wives," and live a "comfortable life," and can "glorify their ancestors" and "repay their parents for their care.". . .

The students' aim of study is a concentrated expression of their world view. It has a far-reaching effect on the road of life ahead of them. The students' aim of study is the general thought guiding their words, actions and conduct in their five or six years of study. Without setting a correct aim of study, the students cannot consciously cultivate and steel themselves in the direction laid down in the education policy of the Party. We are therefore deeply convinced that to enlighten the students on the revolutionary world view and guide the students to set a study aim of serving the people with all their heart is an important question having bearing on the implementation of the Party's education policy in school and on the moral, intellectual and physical development of the students as successors to the proletarian cause.

II. *Guide the Students, on the Basis of Class Education, to Solve Several Fundamental Questions of Thinking and Understanding Concerning the Aim of Study.*

We have all these years attached importance to conducting education for the students concerning the world view. We have done quite some work and achieved a certain success. Following the 10th Plenary Session of the 8th CCP Central Committee, we studied Chairman Mao's directive on intensification of class education and education in class struggle. This directive gave us a great enlightenment. In the spirit of the 10th Plenary Session and according to this directive of Chairman Mao, we summed up our past work experiences, investigated the students' political thinking on many occasions, and gradually came to understand that education in the world view must be guided by Chairman Mao's thinking and based on class education and must be conducted by grasping the aim of study, the most important living idea. . . .

Over the past year and more, we have educated students in the following three respects with reference to several fundamental questions of thinking and understand-

---

Chinese Communist Party Peking University Committee, "Give the Students Education in the Revolutionary World View, Starting with Class Education," Peking, *Kuang-ming Jih-pao*, June 14, 1964, *Survey of China Mainland Press*, No. 3252 (July 7, 1964), pp. 1-7.

ing concerning the aim of study:

(a) *Guide the students to raise their knowledge about classes and class struggle and to set the political bearings of a revolutionary.*

An important reason why a wrong aim of study is set is because many students know nothing about classes and class struggle and nothing about class oppression and class exploitation and lack the revolutionary ideal of fighting for the great revolutionary cause of the proletariat. They think that now that revolution has ended in victory [for the proletariat] in our country, their only task is to study and the only important thing to do is to acquire specialized knowledge.

When we first intensified class education and education in class struggle, a number of students were lethargic and were unable to take a clear view of the situation of class struggle. It was only after the situation of class struggle was explained and particularly after the students were urged to take a direct part in the practice of class struggle that they gradually came to know that acute class struggle existed in the international arena and at home. In order to help the students gain a deeper knowledge of classes and class struggle and to hate class oppression and class exploitation and in order to raise their revolutionary awareness, we guided the students to understand many living facts of class oppression and class exploitation during the socialist education campaign in the rural areas and through the activity of visiting the poor peasants, making friends with poor peasants and lower middle peasants and writing village and family histories. On this basis, we expanded self-educating activities of reckoning the accounts of exploitation, recalling national sufferings and class sufferings, finding the differences [between the advanced and the backward] and the cause of such difference and examining the dangers [to oneself]. Reckoning the accounts of exploitation and hearing and seeing the accusations made by the peasants who told of the way their families were ruined in the old society, the students gained a concrete impression of the bitter life of the working people who were exploited and oppressed in the past. They realized that "class exploitation is the greatest irrationality in the world," and began to have a concrete and realistic understanding of why revolution must be made, why it must be carried through to the end, and why the revolutionary struggle of the world people must be given firm support.

At this juncture, helped by favorable circumstances, we led the students to ponder over seriously the question: For whom does one study and serve? A number of students consciously examined their wrong throughts about their aim of study, and made up their mind to set up the political direction for a revolutionary. They said this: "It is not that there is no class struggle, but it is that we have no notion of class struggle; it is not that there is no revolutionary task, but it is that we lack a great revolutionary ideal." "The sufferings of poor peasants and lower middle peasants in one village and the hatred they nursed remind us of the sufferings of the whole exploited class and the hatred they nursed, of the fact that two-thirds of the working people in the world have still to be set free, and of our heavy task of carrying through the proletarian revolution to the end." They were determined to "carry the heavy burden of the Chinese revolution and world revolution and link their studies with the revolutionary struggle to overthrow all the exploiting classes and systems of exploitation."

(b) *Guide the students to take a correct attitude to the question of who supports whom, to break the idea of private ownership of knowledge, and to establish the thought of serving the working people.*

Over the past year, the great masses of students have taken part in the practice of class struggle and productive labor, eating, living, laboring and fighting together with the poor peasants and lower middle peasants. They have gone a step further to strengthen their class viewpoint, labor viewpoint, mass viewpoint, and realized that "the fruits of labor do not come easily," and gained a practical understanding about the truth that "labor creates the world." A number of them begin to understand the question, who supports whom, and realize that "it is the working people who feed us with their sweat and blood." When the students had such thinking, understanding and feeling, we guided them to go a step further to ponder over the question of for whom were they studying and whom were they to serve, and aroused them to examine their notion of private ownership of knowledge and their idea of personal fame and fortune in study. Quite some students made these painful remarks: "We eat grain grown by the working people. We learn knowledge accumulated by the working people in their practice of class struggle and production struggle. It is the working people who nurse us. If we do not serve the working people well and if we take knowledge as our private property and bargain with the people, we would be very ungrateful to them." They declared their determination to learn more knowledge in the interests of the working people and return their knowledge to the working people!

With a view to helping the students establish the thought of serving the working people, we assisted them in taking a more correct view of the working people and in correctly understanding the object of their service — the working people. We countered the students' knowledge about the peasants, which were brought to light, by guiding them to compare awakening, contributions, knowledge, and life with the poor peasants and lower middle peasants, to examine their wrong views of the working people, the danger of these views and their cause, and to analyze why the peasants also have certain shortcomings and how to deal with them correctly. Through this education, many students began to correct their view of the working people and to know that it was due to the influence of the thought of the exploiting class that they disliked the peasants because they were "rustic" and "dirty" and thought they were "ignorant and backward." We followed up this work by urging the students to read once again Chairman Mao's directive that intellectuals must combine with the workers and peasants. A number of the students felt that the directive "is particularly applicable to them" and that they comprehended something new from it.

(c) *Guide the students to examine consciously the wrong ideological effects their families and society have on them, to improve their ability to know and criticize bourgeois thought, and to increase their consciousness for transforming the world.*

Having identified the reactionary and exploiting character of their families, many students who came from families of the exploiting classes felt that "the ideological effect their families have on them must not be underestimated, and they must completely revolt from the exploiting classes ideologically and politically." They brought to light and criticize the effects their families had on their aim of study and their road of life. They expressed their "determination to break up with these thoughts of the exploiting classes and to serve the working people — their really beloved ones — assiduously and conscientiously for life. Further, they examined their wrong thought in the past: Handicapped by the idea that their "family background was not good and they had no political future," they slackened their ideological remolding and were only interested in finding a professional job. They came to realize that "since they were deeply influenced by the exploiting classes, they should all the more make up their mind to remold their thought with redoubled efforts and over a longer period of time.

Many students who came from families of bourgeois intellectuals improved their ability to see clearly the effects of bourgeois thought their families had on them. The parents of a 1st-year student at the department of chemistry often told him: "Natural science is an iron rice-bowl; with the knowledge of mathematics, physics and chemistry, one can go anywhere in the world without worry.'' Recently, his class consciousness raised, he came to understand that ''there is also class struggle in his family and in his mind. This finds concrete expression in his aim of study. He said: ''The Party teaches me to follow the red-and-expert road. Some relatives pull me to the 'iron rice-bowl' road — 'with knowledge of mathematics, physics and chemistry, one can go anywhere in the world without worry.' Is not this a class struggle?'' Further, he came to understand that 'going anywhere in the world without worry' means this: I have knowledge and, if you give me good pay I will serve you. It is delivery of goods against cash.'' He was determined to ''fight this extremely wrong thought and to follow the red-and-expert road pointed out by the Party and to serve the working people with all his heart.''

Many students who came from the families of the working people came to realize that they must elevate their study aim of ''showing gratitude to their parents and serving their families'' to the plane of the ''great ideal of serving the revolutionary cause of the exploited and oppressed working people all over the world.'' Some children of the revolutionary cadres began to understand that ''blood relations may be inherited but the revolutionary stand and viewpoint cannot be inherited,'' and realized that they themselves ''are also in need of labor steeling and ideological remolding.''

With the favorable situations developed in the international arena and at home, with modern revisionism further exposed and criticized, with the steeling in the great socialist education campaign in town and country, and with the education in the revolutionary world view intensified on the basis of class education, the ideological awakening of the students in our school has shown a marked improvement over the past year and more. A number of students have gained a clear understanding about the aim of study they should set. ''Be red and expert successors to the revolutionary cause,'' ''carry both the burden of revolution and the burden of construction,'' ''become one with the worker and peasant masses,'' and ''serve the working people for life,'' — these slogans have become a strong motivating force for painstaking studies and ideological remolding on the part of the student masses. A number of ideologically backward students have made marked progress and some of them have shown a great change. They have completely and consciously criticized their wrong thoughts and are more determined to reform their minds.

With their consciousness universally raised for reforming their world view, many students consciously and regularly persist in flexible study and application of Chairman Mao's works. They have voluntarily set up many teams for study of Chairman Mao's works. They use the thought of Mao Tse-tung for solving their ideological and study problems. They take interest in the important events at home and abroad. The practice of political studies is getting ever stronger. The mind of the students is very active. They dare to set forth their views, to expose thoughts and practice criticism and self-criticism. A new high tide of ideological revolution begins to appear among the students. . . .

5.3 "Some Experiences in Implementing the Principle of 'Less But Better' in Pedagogical Work"

(1) PROCESS OF WORK

Implementing the principle of "less but better" [the Chinese phrase "shao erh ching" means literally small in quantity but more refined in quality] is important to the launching of pedagogical reform and the raising of the quality and quantity of education.

We have generally passed through the following three stages from the inception of our implementing the principle of "less but better" to the present.

The first stage was one of enlightenment. Beginning from the first half of the 1961, with a view to implementing the Party policy of "adjustment, consolidation, filling out, and raising standards," our school has, under the direct leadership of the Party committee, made investigations and research on the quality and quantity of teaching. . . .

The second stage was one in which the principle of "less but better" was adopted to adjust the pedagogical plan and pedagogical program. . . .

The third stage was one in which the contents of teaching were selected carefully, the various phases of teaching were arranged centrally and pedagogical methods were revamped. . . .

(2) INITIAL RESULTS

In the last two years, we have already garnered the following initial results in the area of implementing the principle of "less but better."

(1) Most of the teachers have realized ideologically that implementing the principle of "less but better" is not only the crucial point in raising the quality of pedagogy and reducing the burden of the students, but also the main measure to enable the students to make vivid and active development morally, intellectually and physically. . . .

(2) In the process of implementing the principle of "less but better," most of the teachers have also realized that this is a huge, complex and exacting work. . . .

(3) The study load on students has dropped and the chaos and passiveness which used to prevail have been rectified. Most of the students have also become more stringent in demanding their own completion of the courses and exercises. More people are now reading Chinese and foreign-language reference books outside of their classes; many of them have achieved advancement in their study ability as well as their ability to read foreign languages. In the meantime, the time for the students to study Chairman Mao's writings and current events has also increased and their cultural and athletic activities have also become more brisk.

(3) SOME EXPERIENCES

(1) Under the centralized leadership of the Party committee, there must be close coordination between the Party and the government in meticulously and intensively carrying out ideological work. It is also necessary to correctly recognize the following three relationships in pedagogical thinking as well as to gradually establish the following three viewpoints.

The Pedagogical Research Office of Sian Chiaotung University, "Some Experiences in Implementing the Principle of 'Less But Better' in Pedagogical Work," Peking, *Kuang-ming Jih-pao*, December 5, 1964, *Survey of China Mainland Press*, No. 3380 (January 19, 1965), pp. 12, 17-20.

THREE RELATIONSHIPS

1. The relationship between implementing the principle of "less but better" and improving the quality and quantity of teaching. Some teachers are skeptical about the principle of "less but better" or even disagree with it. Their reason is that, in a word, "less but better" cannot raise the quality and quantity of teaching. We maintain that solution of this cognitional problem depends on the correct understanding of the quality and quantity of teaching. First, the educational policy of the Party is very clear, that is, we must "enable those who are educated to develop morally, intellectually and physically so that they may become laborers with socialism and culture." Thus, if we should merely seek the improvement of work quality and quantity but neglect all-round development, this would not train the talents needed by socialist revolution and socialist construction. In order to train talents of all-round development, we must implement the principle of "less but better" in pedagogical work. Next, from the standpoint of improving the quality and quantity of teaching, we deem that the objective norm with which to gauge the quality and quantity of teaching is that it must insure that the students are able truly to learn the most essential knowledge and technology during the stipulated time and to learn and apply them flexibly. Some teachers take the view that it is better to teach more than less and that it is only by teaching more and what is deep that it will be possible to improve the quality and quantity of teaching. However, as has been proven by pedagogical practices, because the teachers did not proceed from practice and because they aimed only at comprehensiveness and profundity, the result was that the load on the students was increased. This has not only affected their all-round development, but also prevented them from learning the basic contents of their courses. Thus, in order to improve truly the quality and quantity of teaching, it is necessary to resolutely implement the principle of "less but better" in teaching work.

2. The relationship between implementing the principle of "less but better" and "comprehensive and specialized learning." Some teachers take the view that the students trained by us must be "comprehensively learned and expert" before they can satisfy the growing needs of scientific enterprises in China. They are skeptical if there is not any contradiction between "comprehension and expertness" and "less but better." Our view is that from a business standpoint, the purpose of the school in training talents is that after a longer period of time and on the basis of their solid foundations at the school, they will gradually attain the status of being "comprehensively learned and expert" through continuous studying and practice. Being "comprehensively learned and expert" is a result of the accumulation, expansion and deepening of knowledge. In order to achieve this goal, we must implement the principle of "less but better" in the methodology of study, especially in pedagogical work at the school. This is because "less but better" is a principle of scholarship with which to accumulate, increase, broaden and deepen knowledge. Because of the vastness of knowledge, our subjective strength at a specific time is bound to be limited. So it is necessary for us to observe the principle of "less but better" to increase and broaden our knowledge so that it may progress from "less but better" to "comprehensively learned and expert." The period of training in the school is limited to five years. There must be a process for the students to amass knowledge and they cannot learn everything all at once. This is to say that the study of the students must be in keeping with the objective law before they can really learn something on a solid basis. Thus, the purpose of firmly implementing the principle of "less but better" is just to enable the student to achieve the goal of being "comprehensively learned and expert" gradually.

3. The relationship between implementing the principle of "less but better" and raising the level of teachers: Some teachers take the view that in order to raise the

quality and quantity of teaching, the crux is that the academic level of teachers must be raised. When this is done, it will be possible to improve pedagogy without mentioning what is "less but better." There are others who say that to implement this principle is the task of those teachers who have a higher level, and since their own level has not been raised, there is no use to talk about "less but better." Or they would say that one must raise one's own level first before he deals with the principle of "less but better." There are still others who maintain that this kind of implementation cannot help raise the level of teachers. Our view is that the basic task of the teacher is to train talents based on the demands of the educational policy of the Party. While it is necessary to raise the academic level of teachers, it does not mean that once this is done, the quality and quantity of teaching will be improved necessarily. There is in it also the problem of pedagogical methodology. If the teaching method is improper, it will still be impossible to raise the quality and quantity of teaching. Thus, in order to become a good teacher, one must raise one's ideological and political level, academic level, as well as pedagogical level. It is only thus that he will be able to fulfill comprehensively the tasks of a teacher. . . .

THREE VIEWPOINTS

1. We must advocate proceeding from practice and stress real results, but oppose subjectivism and greediness. In teaching, there are two aspects of "practice": the conditions of acceptance on the part of the students (work, foundation, acceptance ability, study time) and the objective law of studying. Investigation data show that whereas the level of students is usually below what is estimated by the teacher, their load of study is nevertheless often higher. To advocate that one must proceed from the practice of the students does not mean to lower our demand on them, but is merely to coordinate the subjective wish of the teacher with the objective practice of students in order to enhance the effects of teaching.

2. We must distinguish between what is primary and what secondary, insure key points and oppose the principle of averages. There should be such distinction not only for all courses in the pedagogical plan, but also for each course and even during each class lecture. It is necessary to highlight the main aspects instead of trying to be comprehensive and spending one's energy evenly.

3. We must advocate the viewpoint of the whole and oppose the one-sided viewpoint. (a) There is the whole of all-round development morally, intellectually and physically. Unless one proceeds from this whole, it will be impossible to handle their relationships correctly, nor will it be possible to raise the quality and quantity of teaching with the correct methodology. (b) There is the whole of pedagogical planning. This planning serves the goals of training; the position and functions of each course in the planning must be subordinated to the goals of training. (c) There is the whole of the various phases in each course. These phases must be coordinated closely in order to develop their respective functions. (d) There is the whole of teaching diverse types of students in keeping with their talents. In each class, there are bound to be many types of students. Besides using common norms for them, it is also possible to present varying demands on them.

We deem that in order to correctly recognize these three relationships and to gradually establish these three viewpoints, we must firmly adopt the proletarian stand and continuously eradicate the influences of bourgeois educational ideology and revisionism. . . .

5.4 "Curricula for Half-Work (Farming) Half-Study Schools"

In the provision of curricula for half-work (farming) and half-study schools, it is absolutely necessary to give full attention to three sides — the political course, the cultural course, and the industrial and agro-technical course, to prevent the tendency to attach importance to the cultural course to the neglect of knowledge in industrial and agricultural production. While we oppose the mechanical duplication of the whole-day system, we must also prevent the excessive weakening of fundamental knowledge.

1. *Several situations in the provision of curricula of half-work half-study schools.*
In a half-work half-study school, the ratios among the political, cultural and technical courses, on the basis of total teaching hours, are as follows:
political courses — about 10 to 15 per cent;
cultural courses — about 30 to 35 per cent;
technical courses — about 50 to 60 per cent (including basic technical courses and specialization courses.)

(i) In the Tientsin Photographic Films Works Half-Work Half-Study School, the three-year program consists of 2,160 teaching sessions. In political education, apart from the regular political and ideological education activities, 240 class-hours or 11 per cent of the total, are provided for the teaching of political theory; 900 class-hours or 42 per cent of the total are provided for the teaching of cultural courses; which as much as possible enable the young students to acquire more basic cultural knowledge to lay the foundations for further elevation in the future. Technical basic courses and specialization courses are provided according to the needs of different specializations, and they total 1,020 class-hours, being 47 per cent of the grand total.

(ii) In the Tientsin Municipality Electronics Instruments Works Half-Work Half-Study School, the ratios of different kinds of courses provided are as follows:
Political courses, 15 per cent. They include the study of the works of Mao Tse-tung, the History of the Chinese Communist Party, basic knowledge of philosophy, and the moral advancement of youths.
Cultural and basic courses, 50 per cent. They include language, physics, chemistry, algebra, geometry, trigonometry, and higher optics.
Specialization courses, 35 per cent.
The total number of class-hours range from 2,400 to 2,600. If the time taken up is demarcated in a broad manner, during the first two years in this school, cultural courses constitute the major subjects of study, while during the last two years, teaching is concentrated in basic courses and specialization courses.

2. *Situation in the provision of curricula of half-farming and half-study schools.*
On the basis of investigations carried out, the agricultural middle schools in various localities have brought forward the following principles: teach whatever the people's communes want taught; teach whatever is needed locally; teach whatever the masses lack knowledge of; teach whatever farming operations are being carried out during the current farming season; teach first what is urgently needed for use; and

"Curricula for Half-Work (Farming) Half-Study Schools," *Kiangsu Chiao-yu* [Kiangsu Education], Nanking, No. 2 (February 25, 1965), *Extracts from China Mainland Magazines*, No. 485 (August 16, 1965), pp. 9-10.

study in order to put the acquired knowledge into application.

The curricula provide in the main politics, language, mathematics, and agricultural knowledge. The political courses are centered around the study of Chairman Mao's works generally, and there is carried out education in the Party's guidelines and policies, and the ideal of happiness in farming, the fostering of the four viewpoints, and participation in the important political movements in the rural areas. The language courses have such added subjects as documents for daily usage, miscellaneous characters often met with in the rural areas, and calligraphy. The mathematics courses have such added subjects as bookkeeping, statistics, and the use of the abacus. The agricultural knowledge courses include "crop cultivation," "soil and fertilizer," "plant protection," and "animal husbandry and veterinary surgery" and such subjects relating to knowledge and technical operations.

(i) In Nieh-chi Agricultural Middle School, Ts'ao Hsien, Shantung province, the major requirement is the proper study of the four departments of politics, language (including documents of practical usage in the rural areas, and writing with the brush), mathematics (including general knowledge of accounting, and the use of the abacus), and agricultural knowledge. The ratios of the teaching hours for the different courses are: politics, 8 per cent of total; language, 36 per cent; mathematics, 26 per cent; and agricultural knowledge, 30 per cent (including the teaching time for general knowledge of chemistry and physics.)

(ii) The Tieh-tung Agricultural Middle School in Anhwei Province provides six departments: politics, language, mathematics, agricultural knowledge, physics and chemistry, with such added subjects of practical knowledge, practical usage, bookkeeping, calligraphy, the use of the abacus, and surveying and drawing. In the field of agriculture, on the basis of needs, the school emphasizes teaching of the technique of cotton planting.

(iii) The Ho-tzu-yuan Horticultural School in Erh-tao-ho, Kirin province, provides courses in such basic cultural subjects as language, politics, botany, and chemistry, as well as vegetable and fruit cultivation, good strains culture, plant protection, soil and fertilizer, and the use of the abacus, which are included as specialization technical subjects.

The above described courses are provided separately in the different grades of the schools according to needs.

5.5 "Rural Farming-Study Primary Schools in Kirin"

In accordance with the spirit of the directive of the CCP Central Committee on the implementation of the two educational systems and the two labor systems, and due to the earnest implementation of the guideline of "walking on two legs," today in the extensive rural areas of Kirin province, farming-study schools of many forms are developing on a large scale, and a new atmosphere has emerged in rural primary education. We have truly achieved the state in which education serves the poor and lower-middle peasants, and education is promoted in a lively manner. For the future consolidation and elevation of the farming-study primary schools, we herewith bring forward the following preliminary views on such problems as teaching plans, study periods, and the training and elevation of teachers.

I. THE DIRECTION TO BE FOLLOWED IN THE OPERATION OF FARMING-STUDY SCHOOLS AND GOAL OF DEVELOPMENT

There should be the same direction of operation and goal of development for both farming-study primary schools and other primary schools. The Party's educational guidelines must be correctly implemented thoroughly and workers with socialist consciousness and cultural accomplishment fostered. The major aim in the operation of farming-study schools is the active creation for the children of poor and lower-middle peasants conditions for schooling facilities locally, and the popularization of rural primary education. Accordingly, in the form of school operation, the provision of curricula, the content of teaching, and the arrangement of study time, the characteristics of the rural areas must be completely complied with, local expediency must be considered, and the demands of the poor and lower-middle peasants must be fully met in order to serve agricultural production, and to foster the new generation for socialist construction.

II. ENROLLMENT, STUDY PERIOD AND SCHOOL REGISTER

The enrollment and the study period for the farming-study primary school should be based on the characteristics of the rural areas and the needs of agricultural production, and the principle should be the facilitation of the attendance of the students. Accordingly, apart from the enrollment of students in the fall, on the basis of actual conditions, enrollment may also be undertaken in the spring, to provide even more convenience for the admission of children of poor and lower-middle peasants. For children less than seven full years of age, so long as their parents urgently desire to place them in schools, and when it is possible, they should also be taken care of. Priority should also be given to children who have exceeded the normal schooling age.

The study period of the farming-study primary school may be longer or shorter as necessary. According to conditions of the farming-study primary schools in our province, there are generally three types in regard to the study period.

(1) The lower primary school. Generally the study period is four years, but it may also be only three years. On the completion of the study period, if a student's attainment in language and arithmetic reaches the standards prescribed by the teaching plans, he may proceed to the higher primary school of the whole-day

---

"Rural Farming-Study Primary Schools in Kirin," *Kirin Chiao-yu* [*Kirin Education*], Changchun, No. 3 (March 25, 1965), *Extracts from China Mainland Magazines,* No. 482 (August 3, 1965), pp. 24-27.

system. A graduate of the three-year course may enter the fourth grade of the whole day system. Individual students with ouststanding achievements may be exempted from the study period restrictions and allowed to skip grades.

(2) The higher primary school. Generally the study period is two years, but it may be only one year. Enrollment is made principally among graduates of lower primary schools who cannot regularly attend the higher primary school of the whole-day system, as well as graduates of the lower primary school of the farming-study system. On the completion of the study period, those who attain the standards of, or equivalent to, graduates of the higher primary school of the whole-day system may sit for the entrance examination to a State operated junior middle school of the whole-day system,or else they may enter the half-farming half-study agricultural middle school, for continued studies.

(3) The all-through primary school. Where facilities are available, the farming-study primary school may be operated right through to the completion of the higher primary section. Graduates may likewise seek admission to a State operated whole-day junior middle school, or enter the half-farming half-study agricultural middle school for continued studies.

Where facilities permit, parents and students who desire continued studies in the same school in the same locality, the study period may be further extended by one or two years, to take up courses as taught in the half-farming half-study junior middle schools, and then a transfer may be effected to an agricultural middle school. On reaching the standard of a graduate of the agricultural middle school, a student may seek admission through examination to a State operated agricultural technical school, or a rural half-farming half-study agricultural technical school.

In the matter of study periods, in addition to the above three types of schools, there may also be operated literacy classes for teenagers. These will admit children of an older age not placed in ordinary schools, for study for one or two years, principally in the language course, concentrated in the acquisition of a knowledge of characters, with 2,000 characters as the goal, thereby having their illiteracy wiped out. In arithmetic, the demand is only for the mastery of the four operations in their simple form, or the study may be concentrated in the use of the abacus, enabling them to read or write up wage points and ordinary journals.

The management of the register of a farming-study primary school should not be stereotyped. The students of such a school, apart from those given the regular annual promotions to the next higher grade, may be allowed to skip grades in the same school if their achievements are particularly outstanding. Students suspending studies or withdrawing from the school on account of illness or other reasons, if later making an application for re-admission, should be welcomed and placed in the appropriate grades. If necessary, separate sections may be created, to give them opportunities to continue their studies. Students of a farming-study primary school may transfer to, or be placed in the appropriate grade of, a rural primary school of the whole-day system. Concrete measures for the management of school registers should be considered and formulated by the various *hsien* (municipalities).

III. TEACHING CONTENT AND CURRICULA

The teaching content and the provision of curricula of farming-study primary schools should be guided by the general spirit of consideration for the needs of rural production and livelihood, and the satisfaction of the demands of poor and lower-middle peasants, and arrangements should be made after listening to the view of the masses, and stemming from actualities. For this reason, in the provision of courses and teaching content, we cannot just duplicate the teaching plans of the whole-day primary school. The number of courses cannot be "numerous and varied." Generally there may be provided courses in language, arithmetic (the abacus), and current affairs and policies. The major object is to make a good study of language and arithmetic. The examination of study results should also be restricted to these two subjects.

In the provision of language and arithmetic courses, the old frames must be taken down. In the lower grades, only the language course may be studied, and arithmetic only taken up in the second or third grade. In the language course of the primary school, the phonetic alphabet may be dropped, or else it may be taken up during the medium grades. The teaching of the use of the abacus may be taken up at the lower primary stage, or else it may be taken up at the higher primary stage. It may also be studied in a concentrated form, or in stages. Education in the current affairs and policies should principally be linked up with the actual ideological state of the students, and there should be developed among them education in class struggle as well as ideological and political education.

The textbooks used should be those for farming-study schools compiled by the provincial authorities, but the *hsien* (municipalities) may also undertake the self compilation of some textbooks and supplementary textbooks. In the selection and compilation of textbooks, various localities must break down the old frames of the existing textbooks in use in the whole-day system. They should meet the demands of rural production and livelihood, and give consideration for the characteristics of the children. They should conform with current rural production levels, and also have consideration for the needs of the future development of the "four transformations" of agriculture. Farming-study primary schools of all types may, on the basis of the provincial compiled textbooks of those self selected, and linking them with the actual conditions of the locality and of the school itself, formulate concrete teaching plans.

classes, in groups, and individually. Formalism should be thoroughly overcome.

IV. TEACHING FORMS AND METHODS

To enable the children of poor and lower-middle peasants both to study in the school and to participate in labor, expediencies of the school and the people may be taken into account, and there may be conducted independent or multiple classes; morning, afternoon and evening classes; mobile primary schools; and teaching teams which underwrite all teaching work. Many and varied teaching forms may be adopted. There should be the flexible employment of the three forms of teaching — in classes, in groups, and individually. Formalism should be thoroughly overcome.

There should be the resolute implementation of the principles of linking theory with practice and of putting acquired knowledge into application, in the active improvement of teaching methods in the farming-study primary schools. Teaching activities must stem from the actualities of the students, and be in keeping with their capacities. Because the children in the rural areas do not enter school at a uniform age, and also because there are differences in their basic knowledge of the language and or arithmetic, it is therefore necessary, proceeding from actualities, to make adequate arrangements, and conduct teaching in accordance with their varying capacities. On the one hand, students with approximately the same levels of accomplishment in both language and arithmetic may be organized into a class or a group; while on the other hand, those with greater differences in their levels may be organized in different groups or classes for the teaching of language and arithmetic separately. In a class in a farming-study primary school, there are always several grades in the levels of the students, and so the primary teaching method should be that of the conduct of multiple classes. Generally speaking, there should be a great reform of teaching methods, the characteristics of different localities have to be considered, "regularity" cannot be forcibly sought, and teaching methods adopted should be of benefit to the studies of the students.

V. THE QUESTION OF THE SCHOOL CALENDAR

In a farming-study primary school, teaching, the commencement of classes, and holiday arrangements must be based on the living customs and production needs of the masses. In the general arrangement of timetables, in the lower grades, from eight to nine months in the year should generally be devoted to studies. In the higher grades, the students may have from seven to eight months for studies, and about one month should be set aside for rest (principally during the new year and festival periods.) As to the time for the commencement of classes, the agricultural seasons and local production characteristics should be conformed with. Concrete arrangements should be made by the people's commune or the production brigade.

VI. TRAINING AND ELEVATION OF TEACHERS

The active elevation of the standards of the army of teachers of farming-study primary schools is of decisive significance for the consolidation of these schools. In dealing with the problem of teachers, in addition to their proper selection and appointment, and the earnest settlement of the problem of their treatment, the major task is to strengthen ideological and political work among them and to raise their capacity for teaching. Today the teachers in the farming-study primary schools in our province are principally intellectual youths in the rural areas, possessed of great zeal, but lacking in teaching experience. The teaching work which confronts them, moreover, is very complex and varied, and it is necessary to help them raise properly their teaching capacity. In the elevation of the standards of the teachers, we should base our efforts on actual conditions obtaining in different localities, go through many and varied channels, with planning and with measured steps. Whatever the form adopted, we must be mindful of the characteristics of the farming-study primary school, and refrain from the mechanical duplication of the measures used for the whole-day primary schools. In the future, the educational administrative departments and the institutes for the advanced training of teachers in all localities must put on their agenda the task of the elevation of the teachers of farming-study primary schools.

The farming-study primary school is a new thing. Educational cadres of all localities must overcome bureaucracy and subjectivism, regularly penetrate realities and penetrate the masses. In their work they have to pay special attention to summing up experiences of operation and teaching in the farming-study primary schools, foster models, and establish samples, using the good samples to promote work, and thence enable the various forms of primary schools now in operation in the rural areas to develop in an animated manner and without interruption.

5.6 "Problems Revealed by Two Statistical Tables"

Last year, we investigated the development of elementary education, percentage of students among schoolage children, and scales and distribution of schools in the whole *hsien* in the past few years. In this investigation, we specifically obtained some

Cultural and Educational Bureau, Yanghsin *hsien,* Hupeh province, "Problems Revealed by Two Statistical Tables," Peking, *Jen-min Jih-pao,* May 18, 1965, *Survey of China Mainland Press,* No. 3475 (June 11, 1965), pp. 13-14.

statistical data on the changes before and after running part-farming and part-study primary schools in varied forms. These data sufficiently demonstrated the important problems on rural elementary education.

The following are two of the statistical data obtained:

(1) *Comparison of percentages of students among school-age children before and after farming-study primary schools were opened in Yanghsin hsien* (Statistics up to November 10, 1964)

PERCENTAGE OF CHILDREN IN SCHOOL

Year	1956	1958	1963	1964
Category of schools				
Publicly-run full-time schools	34.32%	43.24%	31.25%	41.64%
Privately-run full-time schools	3.11%	10.7%	11.36%	17.21%
Farming-study school				20.76%
Total	37.43%	53.94%	42.61%	79.61%

(2) *Comparison of percentages of students among children of poor and lower-middle peasants in Huakuo commune, Yanghsin hsien* (Statistics up to the end of 1964)

Category of schools Percentage of school attendance	Publicly-run and privately-run	Farming-study schools	Total
Percentage of students in total number of school-age children	62.5	32.79	95.29
Percentage of students in total number of school-age children of poor and lower-middle peasants	45.17	49.1	94.27

What are the problems revealed in these two statistical tables?

(1) Elementary education had developed before farming-study primary schools were established, but this development was still far behind the demand for universal education. In our *hsien*, the percentage of students among school-age children was the highest in 1958, being 53.94 per cent, and dropped in 1963. However, a new situation appeared in elementary education after farming-study primary schools had been established. The percentage of students among school-age children rapidly rose to over 79. This demonstrated that only by running farming-study primary school would it be possible to speed up universalization of education.

(2) The statistical data obtained from Huakuo commune revealed that, before farming-study primary schools were established, the percentage of children of poor and lower-middle peasants attending full-time primary schools was less than 50. This meant that: Even if we could expand the accommodation of full-time primary schools and conduct education still better, it would be very difficult to solve completely the problems concerning schooling for children of poor and lower-middle peasants, if we did not integrate education better with productive labor. The above situation basically changed after we established farming-study primary schools in various forms. The percentage of students among children of poor lower-middle peasants rose to over 94. Facts proved that only by firmly implementing the guideline of running schools by the "walking on both legs" method, would it be possible to accommodate the broad masses of children of poor and lower-middle peasants.

The problems revealed by these two statistic tables merit the deep thoughts of educational workers!

5.7 "Steadfastly Promote the Part-Farming and Part-Study Education System"

(NCNA May 28) At the National Conference on Rural Part-Farming and Part-Study Education held recently, the Ministry of Education noted that the part-farming and part-study education system introduced on an experimental basis in recent years in various localities paved the way for popularization of primary education and expansion of secondary education in rural areas with greater, faster, better and more economical results. . . .

The conference stressed that operating the part-work and part-study as well as part-farming and part-study education system on an experimental basis while conducting full-time schools well was another thorough revolution in our education. This was significant because it could popularize primary education and develop secondary education with greater, faster, better and more economical results. Additionally, from a long-range point of view, it tended to gradually eliminate the differences between mental and physical labor. It was, moreover, one of the fundamental measures for cultivating successors to the cause of the proletarian revolution and preventing capitalist restoration in our country. Therefore, the conference observed, this was a great and glorious task which should be tackled by all revolutionary education workers. . . .

This was the first time since the new China was founded that a conference was specially convened to study the revolutionary system of part-farming and part-study education. . . .

The conference was convened in the highly favorable situation of extensively developing part-farming and part-study schools in the whole countryside. Since the beginning of last year many localities — in accordance with Chairman Liu Shao-ch'i's instructions and apart from continuing to reform existing full-time schools — have energetically conducted large numbers of part-farming and part-

"Steadfastly Promote the Part-Farming and Part-Study Education System," Peking, *Jen-min Jih-pao*, May 30, 1965, *Survey of China Mainland Press*, No. 3481 (June 21, 1965), pp. 1-5.

study primary schools and agricultural middle schools on an experimental basis in rural areas. . . .

The conference enumerated the following major experiences in operating part-farming and part-study schools on an experimental basis in the past years:

One, relying on Party leadership, persistently putting politics in command. On the educational front, developing the struggle between two roads, two ideologies and two methods. In addition, uniting all forces that can be united and mobilizing the positive factors in all spheres. This is the most important experience.

In the course of operating half-farming and half-study schools in various localities on an experimental basis, many obstacles have been encountered. Most of them were due to the influence of bourgeois ideas about education and the force of habit. As a consequence, there was inadequate knowledge and understanding of the important significance and superiority of part-farming and part-study schools.

Attaching first importance to this round of educational revolution, Party committees at all levels on the one hand organized appropriate personnel to study Party educational guidelines and Chairman Liu Shao-ch'i's instructions on two labor systems and two educational systems—in this way solving the problem of ideological understanding.

On the other hand, Party committees gave vigorous support to those who would operate half-farming and half-study schools well. They cited convincing facts and experiences to educate all education workers. In this way an upsurge in operating schools was very rapidly whipped up in the countryside with the whole Party and all the people taking part.

Two, in the course of setting up schools, all localities have put into practice the method of the mass line—by combining cadres, teachers and the masses under Party leadership. This is a new development in education work in our country.

Before experimentally operating schools, education workers in many localities mobilized the masses, particularly the poor and lower-middle peasants, to tell about their sufferings from lack of culture and discuss the problem of holding the seal of power. After heightening their ideological understanding, education workers then consulted with them about the type of school they would operate, what curricular subjects would be taught and how they would solve the various problems that might arise in the course of running schools. They also actively sought the support of basic-level rural cadres. In this way, the past practice of relying merely on a few persons for running schools was changed. In this way it was possible to operate schools in a dynamic manner and in accord with practical needs.

Three, in the course of experimentally operating this kind of new-type schools, education workers have paid attention to conducting investigation and study according to actual conditions. In a manner suited to local conditions, they have first conducted experiments and acquired experience before popularizing their experiences step by step and running schools properly. . . .

Four, in operating half-farming and half-study schools well, it is also necessary to train and build up a revolutionary contingent of teachers. Numerous facts provided by various localities prove that teachers who have been revolutionized will run schools with strong class feelings. They will defy all sorts of difficulties, resolutely relying on the Party and the masses and energetically endeavoring to operate schools well.

Five, experiences gained in various localities in experimentally operating half-farming and half-study schools prove that we must learn from the Tachai spirit and run schools self-reliantly and with industry and thrift. Part-farming and part-study primary schools as well as agricultural middle schools set up in many localities are run along simple lines and built with materials available locally. All of these schools have been established by local inhabitants with the help of teachers and students.

The conference attached first importance to the above-mentioned experiences in running part-farming and part-study schools. It regarded this experience as one of the fine traditions of the revolutionary educational undertaking in our country.

The conference also seriously studied certain other problems that must be solved in regard to further developing the half-farming and half-study education system in the future.

The conference noted that in enforcing two educational system, the relationships between part-work and part-study or part-farming and part-study schools on the one hand and full-time schools on the other must be correctly viewed and handled. In this respect, the former was a kind of new-type educational system—the direction for long-range development of socialist and communist education.

As far as secondary or higher education was concerned, the conference observed, the new-type educational system would become the mainstay of our country's education system in the future. As far as primary schools were concerned — although more full-time primary schools would be set up in the future — the present emphasis on operation of part-farming and part-study primary schools was in keeping with the method of "walking on two legs" and, therefore, one of the important means for popularizing primary education with greater, faster, better and more economical results.

The conference recognized that under Party leadership full-time schools since liberation had been reformed in many ways — in this way becoming schools of a socialist character. However, the conference found many shortcomings in full-time schools which must be thoroughly rectified in the future. In this way full-time schools should be better able to implement Party educational guidelines and serve socialism.

Because these two systems of running schools had to be enforced simultaneously over a fairly long period in the future, the conference stressed that both must be conducted well. In this regard, teachers and cadres of both types of schools should learn from one another and encourage each other to make progress — in this way learning profitably from the other's merits to make up for one's shortcomings for joint improvement.

PART SIX

The
Cultural
Revolution
(1966-1969)

PART SIX
The Cultural Revolution (1966-1969)

According to most accounts, the year 1966 officially marks the beginning of the Chinese "Cultural Revolution"—also referred to as the Great Socialist Cultural Revolution, or the Great Proletarian Cultural Revolution (GPCR). In his often-quoted essay, "On New Democracy," Mao Tse-tung had written: "A cultural revolution is the ideological reflection of the political and economic revolution and is in their service."[1] The Marxist-Leninist dialectical conception of history contends that socialist revolution is an on-going process, and that ideological revolution should be carried out by a series of class struggles, and that these class struggles should be led by the proletariat:[2]

> . . . without arousing the masses and without supervision by the masses, it is impossible to exercise dictatorship over the reactionaries and bad elements or effectively to reform them; they will continue to make trouble, and there is still the possibility of a restoration. We should be vigilant on this question, and comrades should think about it carefully.[3]

The earlier periods, and especially that of the "struggle between the two lines," were preludes to the Cultural Revolution, the principles of which were set forth in the Circular of the Central Committee of the Chinese Communist Party (May 16, 1966), drawn up under the personal guidance of Mao Tse-tung. Official Chinese sources cite the Circular as:

> . . . an epoch-making document for charting the great proletarian cultural revolution; it is a militant call to the proletariat and the broad masses of revolutionary people, under the conditions of socialism, to march against the bourgeoisie and all other exploiting classes.[4]

Although the Circular is credited with establishing the theory, Party-line, principles, and policies for continuing the revolution under the dictatorship of the proletariat as advocated by Mao Tse-tung, the Cultural Revolution had its origins in the field of art and literature. Earlier, Wu Han (a writer and Vice-Mayor of Peking) had produced a number of literary works set in the historical period of the Ming Dynasty (1522-1566) dealing with the character of Hai Jui, portrayed as an honest and courageous court official who was dismissed because of his outspoken opposition to the Emperor's handling of state affairs. Wu Han related this to the 1959 dismissal of Marshal Peng, who spoke out against the Party's adoption of the "great leap forward" program.

Wu Han and a number of other writers who held important positions in the government or in the Party wrote several other articles which satirized, ridiculed, or generally attacked (in various disguises) Mao Tse-tung and the program of the "great leap forward." Therefore, the Central Committee of the Chinese Communist Party appointed a Cultural Revolution Group to study the question of the nature of art and literature in a socialist culture. The "Outline Report on the Current Academic Discussions Made by the Group of Five in Charge of the Cultural Revolution," prepared under the direction of Peng Chen (a top Party official and also Mayor of Peking), was attacked by the Central Committee of the C.C.P. as an attempt to protect Wu Han from the criticism personally leveled against him by Mao Tse-tung.

Thus, the Circular of the Central Party of the Chinese Communist Party was actually a repudiation of the Outline Report of its Cultural Revolution Group: it revoked the Outline Report, dissolved the Group of Five, and set up a new Cultural Revolution Group. The Circular identified ten main errors of the Outline Report, and concluded that:

> In short, the outline opposes carrying the socialist revolution through to the end, opposes the line on the Cultural Revolution pursued by the Central Committee of the Party headed by Comrade Mao Tse-tung, attacks the proletarian Left and shields the bourgeois Right, thereby preparing public opinion for the restoration of capitalism. It is a reflection of bourgeois ideology in the Party; it is out-and-out revisionism. Far from being a minor issue, the struggle against the revisionist line is an issue of prime importance having a vital bearing on the destiny and future of our Party and state, on the future complexion of our Party and state, and on the world revolution.[5]

In addition, the whole Party was directed to follow Comrade Mao Tse-tung's instructions:

> . . . hold high the great banner of the Proletarian Cultural Revolution, thoroughly expose the reactionary bourgeois stand of those so-called academic authorities who oppose the Party and socialism, thoroughly criticize and repudiate the reactionary bourgeois ideas in the sphere of academic work, education, journalism, literature and art and publishing, and seize the leadership in these cultural spheres.[6]

Following the dissemination of the Circular, unrest in the academic community grew and became more open. On May 25, 1966 several members of the Philosophy Department of Peking University put up the famous "big-character poster" (da-zi-bao) criticizing the President of Peking University and the suppression of the debates on literature.[7] The publication of this poster in the June 2, 1966 issue of *People's Daily* has been referred to as "the first shot fired in the Cultural Revolution."[8] The movement was quickly picked up by other higher institutions, then spread more widely to middle schools, factories, and other enterprises.

The initial victories were won by the Maoists; the Central Committee of the C.C.P. reorganized the Peking Party Committee, the President of Peking University was dismissed, new editors and editorial boards of certain Peking papers were appointed to replace the "Rightists," and some publications were temporarily suspended. In the meantime, the Rightists not only counter-attacked but actually gained strength. Mao, who had been out of town (the much-publicized swim in the Yangtse), returned to Peking at the end of July 1966. The Eleventh Plenary Session of the Eighth Central Committee of the C.C.P. met in Peking from August 1 to 12, 1966. It was the occasion of an intense struggle between Mao Tse-tung with his supporters, and Liu Shao-chi with his supporters—who were at first in the majority.

On August 5, 1966 Mao Tse-tung dramatically put out his own "big-character poster" entitled "Bombard The Headquarters," criticizing those leading comrades—from the central Party headquarters down to the local levels—who had adopted the reactionary stand of the bourgeois; for in so doing:

> . . . they have enforced a bourgeois dictatorship and struck down the surging movement of the great cultural revolution of the proletariat. They have stood facts on their head and juggled black and white, encircled and suppressed revolutionaries, stifled opinions differing from their own, imposed a white terror, and felt very pleased with themselves. They have puffed up the arrogance of the bourgeoisie and deflated the morale of the proletariat. How poisonous! Viewed in connection with the Right deviation in 1962 and the wrong tendency of 1964 which was "Left" in form but Right in essence, shouldn't this make one wide awake?[9]

It appears that Mao's big-character poster was a highly significant weapon in the struggle against Liu Shao-chi and the Rightists; official Chinese sources make frequent reference to it as "a most brilliant revolutionary document," which laid down the general principles of the Great Proletarian Cultural Revolution:

> "Bombard the Headquarters" blasted the lid off the struggle between the proletarian revolutionary line and the bourgeois reactionary line and between the proletarian headquarters and the bourgeois headquarters which had existed in the Party over a long period. It made the entire Party and people understand more clearly the main object and task of the great proletarian cultural revolution.[10]

On August 8, the Central Committee adopted the "Decision of the Central Committee of the Chinese Communist Party Concerning the Great Proletarian Cultural Revolution," announcing a new stage in China's socialist revolution:

> Although the bourgeoisie has been overthrown, it is still trying to use the old ideas, culture, customs and habits of the exploiting classes to corrupt the masses, capture their minds and endeavour to stage a come-back. The proletariat must do the exact opposite: it must meet head-on every challenge of the bourgeoisie in the ideological field and use the new ideas, culture, customs and habits of the proletariat to change the mental outlook of the whole society.[11]

The August 8 Decision set forth sixteen points (the document is often referred to as the "Sixteen Point Decision") which became the guidelines for the Cultural Revolution.

The revolutionary movement quickly gained momentum; student groups organized as "Red Guards" launched fierce attacks against revisionism and bourgeois ideology, against old habits, old ideas and old culture. When the Red Guards first appeared in small numbers in the summer of 1966, they were seen as a "reactionary organization" by the Rightists. However, Mao recognized the enormous vitality of this revolutionary youth organization, gave it his support and praised the Red Guards as courageous, daring, vigorous and intelligent. Within a short period the Red Guards increased in number to millions, spread throughout the nation, and developed organizations in schools, factories, and rural areas. According to *People's Daily,* the mission of the Red Guards was to destroy the old and establish the new:

The revolutionary Red Guards set about destroying the "four olds" (old ideas, culture, customs, and habits) of the exploiting classes on a large scale and extensively fostered the "four news" (new ideas, culture, customs, and habits) of the proletariat. Playing the role of the vanguard, they stand foremost in the criticism and repudiation of the bourgeois reactionary line.[12]

To carry out the mission of "destroy the old and establish the new," the Red Guards were encouraged to go to the people and make a mass revolution, and also urged to learn the revolutionary spirit from the People's Liberation Army. Various Red Guard organizations formed a Congress of the Red Guards of Universities and Colleges in Peking (February 1967), adopted the Declaration of the Congress of the Red Guards, pledged their loyalty to Mao Tse-tung and the Party, and proclaimed their determination to carry the Cultural Revolution to the end. In this struggle, the Red Guards were armed with the "most powerful weapon," Mao Tse-tung's thought. As the *Liberation Army Daily* stated:

Mao Tse-tung's thought is our political orientation, the highest instruction for our actions; it is our ideological and political telescope and microscope for observing and analyzing all things. In this unprecedented great cultural revolution, we should use Mao Tse-tung's thought to observe, analyze and transform everything. We should use Mao Tse-tung's thought to storm the enemy's positions and seize victory.[13]

With great speed and flourish, the study of Mao Tse-tung's thought (quotations, speeches, writings, etc.) became a national movement. The "Sixteen Point Decision" had clearly stressed that:

In the great proletarian cultural revolution, it is imperative to hold aloft the great red banner of Mao Tse-tung's thought and put proletarian politics in command. The movement for the creative study and application of Chairman Mao Tse-tung's works should be carried forward among the masses of the workers, peasants and soldiers, the cadres and the intellectuals, and Mao Tse-tung's thought should be taken as the guide to action in the cultural revolution.[14]

An astronomical number of copies of *Quotations From Chairman Mao Tse-Tung* were prepared in a red plastic-covered pocket-book form and distributed to the great masses throughout the nation. Lin Piao's foreword to the second edition reiterated the significance of Mao Tse-tung's thought as the guide to action; he wrote:

. . . the most fundamental task in our Party's political and ideological work is at all times to hold high the great red banner of Mao Tse-tung's thought, to arm the minds of the people throughout the country with it and to persist in using it to command every field of activity. The broad masses of the workers, peasants and soldiers and the broad ranks of the revolutionary cadres and the intellectuals should really master Mao Tse-tung's thought; they should all study Chairman Mao's writings; follow his teachings, act according to his instructions and be his good fighters.[15]

The entire nation was stirred to revolutionary excitement and action. The "Sixteen Point Decision" had warned that the Cultural Revolution, since it was a revolution, would meet with strong and stubborn resistance "from those in authority who have wormed their way into the Party and are taking the capitalist road." New revolutionary organizations were established to combat the "bourgeois reactionary line" and to seize political power from those top Party authorities who were "taking the capitalist road."[16]

The Cultural Revolution was an historic event of such magnitude that it virtually changed (or at least significantly affected) the outlook of a quarter of the population of the world—to say nothing of its world-wide impact. Joan Robinson's analysis is particularly incisive:

> The conception which underlies the Cultural Revolution is that the reconciliation of democracy with good order can be made by imbuing the whole nation with the ideology expressed in the phrase "serve the people." Ideology is necessary in any administration. It is impossible for every detail to be covered by a book of rules. There must be an accepted attitude which makes everyone know which is the proper way to decide individual cases. The overpowering emphasis on the Thought of Mao Tse-tung, in education, propaganda, entertainment and art is intended to develop an attitude of mind and habit of work that will put, as it were, a ratchet behind the achievements of the Cultural Revolution and prevent them slipping away. (Mao himself is realistic, however, and cheerfully remarks that it may well be necessary to have another Cultural Revolution after fifteen or twenty years.)[17]

The actions and activities of the Red Guards had a tremendous impact upon educational policy. Section ten of the Sixteen Point Decision established the guiding principle for educational reform during the Cultural Revolution. The old educational system, as well as the old principles and methods of teaching were to be transformed (the theme of continuing reformations and transformation should now be a familiar one). All schools were directed to apply Mao Tse-tung's policy of "education serving proletarian politics and education being combined with productive labor." Specifically, schooling was to be shortened, courses reduced in number and improved in quality, and teaching materials thoroughly transformed. In addition to their school studies, students were also expected to learn industrial work, agricultural and military affairs. They were to "take part in the struggles of the cultural revolution to criticize the bourgeoisie as these struggles occur."[18]

In the early phase of the Cultural Revolution, these struggles were to occupy the major attention of students and teachers who became caught up in the activities of criticizing and eliminating revisionists and their ideas. It was impossible to carry on formal classes under these conditions; the schools actually closed down after the summer vacation in 1966. On June 13, 1966 the Central Committee of the C.C.P. and the State Council formally announced the decision to abolish the old system of entrance examinations and enrollment of students in higher educational institutions and to postpone that year's enrollment of new students for half a year:

> . . . so that, on the one hand they [higher institutions] and the senior middle-schools will have enough time to carry out the Cultural Revolution thoroughly and successfully and, on the other hand, there will be adequate time for making all preparations for the implementation of a new method of enrollment.[19]

Large numbers of teachers and students left their homes and schools and flocked to Peking, Chingkang Mountains, Yenan, and other revolutionary shrines to participate in the "exchange of revolutionary experience." Thus implementation of the new educational reform policies of the Sixteen Point Decision had to await future developments.

The absence of formal schooling does not necessarily mean the cessation of learning or of teaching. Indeed, some educational analysts may view this non-schooling phase as one of the educational highpoints of the Cultural Revolution—a time in which revolutionary students and teachers united in the struggle to change the mental outlook of the masses. Maud Russell observed that it was only schooling that the Red Guards lost, not education; she commented:

> What those millions of Red Guards got from their activities in the cultural

revolution was indeed education—a kind of education no textbooks, no teachers, no schooling could have given them—revolutionary education for sharing in the building of their socialist society. . . .

These youth have been the shock troops of the cultural revolution; they have been out among the people; they have worked with the farmers in the fields; they have traveled the length and breadth of their country; they have initiated mass expression and discussion with their encouraging of "big-character-posters"; they have experienced the deceptions, the brutalities, the exploitations of the counter-revolutionaries; they have been through factional struggles with each other; they have tested out much of the Thought of Mao Tse-tung, they have matured in struggle.[20]

Some may find Maud Russell's observation too romantic. Undoubtedly, this was a time of great frenzy and confusion, action and destruction, vandalism and violence. It was a time characterized by the call to "destroy the old and establish the new"; indeed, it was a revolutionary struggle! In any event, it is not unreasonable to assume that the youth who participated in the struggles of the cultural revolution may have obtained (and internalized) an entirely new mental outlook which seemed to prepare them for the new educational system that was soon to develop.

In January 1967, a more detailed plan of educational reform was drafted; specifically, it recommended the following: (1) abolition of all examination systems (This was considered a heavy blow to the Rightists' cause and an encouragement of the Leftist students. The new method of enrollment of students for senior middle-schools and institutions of higher education was based upon the recommendation of students for their outstanding moral, intellectual and political qualities. The old entrance examination was criticized for having closed the door of further schooling to many outstanding children of workers, poor and lower-middle-class peasants, revolutionary cadres, etc.); (2) further shortening of the cycle of schooling; (3) expeditious implementation of the half-work half-study system; (4) provision for military training in all schools; (5) placing special emphasis on "Mao Tse-tung thought" in the curriculum; (6) placing politics in command in the school; and (7) abolition of summer and winter vacation (to increase students' participation in productive labor).[21]

The Central Government, in February 1967, issued a call to the teachers and students participating in this exchange of revolutionary experience, urging them to return to their own places and schools to make revolution and participate in the "struggle-criticism-transformation."[22] Newspapers published articles and editorials calling upon teachers and students to respond to Chairman Mao's instruction to resume classes while continuing the revolution. Getting millions of teachers and students who had spread out to distant points throughout the country to return home, to re-open the schools, to overhaul their organization and to resume classes was a task of great magnitude. Some teachers and students would return only to shortly leave again after a few days. It took quite some time before classes and studies were fully resumed.

Interestingly, the elimination of grades and examinations during this phase would eventually be re-assessed in 1969, when it was claimed that this had created a chaotic situation which had hampered the implementation of Mao's directive that "all colleges, secondary schools and primary schools must resume classes to make revolution."[23]

To fully implement and coordinate the back-to-school movement, Mao eventually had to turn to the PLA. His famous "March 7" (1967) Directive stated:

The army should give political and military training in the universities, middle schools and the higher classes of primary schools, stage by stage and group by group. It should help in re-opening school classes, strengthening organization, setting up the leading bodies on the principle of the "three-way alliance" and carrying out the task of "struggle-criticism-transformation."[24]

Lessons were resumed, subject matter and teaching materials were transformed. Committees consisting of students, teachers, workers, and cadres, revised the curriculum so that emphasis was given to political development; both teachers and students gave lectures; cramming and rote learning was replaced with teaching and studying methods emphasizing "inquiry and reasoning things out."[25]

The period of the Cultural Revolution, especially in its early phase, was a particularly difficult time for teachers. Their status and role, as well as the part they had played in the old educational system, were the subject of intense criticism. Teachers were severely attacked, both verbally and physically. Many teachers who were formerly paid by the state, found themselves being paid by the commune production brigade which was now managing the schools. These rural teachers were paid on the basis of work points—as the peasants were paid—plus a small allowance from the state. Work points were given on a day-to-day basis; there was also a semi-annual assessment of the performance and a year-end general assessment. This had the effect of establishing a new relationship between the professional teacher and the peasants.[26]

The Revolutionary Committees of some communes "remolded" and "re-educated" primary and middle-school teachers by requiring that the teachers "eat, live, labor, study and make criticism together with the poor and lower-middle-class peasants." Old poor peasants who had "suffered" in the past were "assigned the task of helping each teacher." Teachers who were alienated from reality and labor were "patiently taught . . . techniques of agricultural production." Some teachers showed "relapses" before they had thoroughly transformed their "bourgeois world outlook," which was interpreted as evidence of the "lengthiness and complexity" of the class struggle in areas of ideology and politics.[27]

Under the circumstances, some teachers, fearing that they would be accused of following Liu Shao-chi's revisionist line, went to great lengths to repudiate the idea of "intellectual education first" or "professional work in command"; they were fearful of imposing requirements on students or of assigning academic homework, etc.[28] Reports indicate that many teachers now seriously regretted having chosen teaching as a profession; the phrase, "It is bad fortune to be a teacher," was frequently cited. It may well have taken unusual daring to have been a teacher during this time.

Tentative programs of educational reform were written in November 1967, and were based upon the educational policies stipulated in the 1966 Sixteen Point Decision, and Mao's Directives of "May 7" (1966) and "March 7" (1967). Mao now stated that in carrying out the proletarian educational revolution:

> . . . it is necessary to rely on the broad masses of revolutionary students, revolutionary teachers and revolutionary workers in schools, and on the activists among them, namely, the proletarian revolutionaries who are determined to carry the great proletarian cultural revolution to the end.[29]

Intellectuals and other so-called "academic authorities" came under heavy attack. Yao Wen-yen, a Party leader, echoed Mao's instructions: "As long as there is a group of intellectuals, whether it is a school or other units, workers and liberation army must go in to break the intellectual's domination of everything."[30] The objective was to build the educational system into a great school of Mao Tse-tung thought.

Consequently, fresh proletarian personnel entered the schools and assumed leading roles in educational decision-making. These "worker-peasant-soldier" teams seized control over many educational institutions (from primary schools to universities) and cultural establishments (science and research centers, art and literature institutes, publishing houses, etc.). Through study and discussion, members of the worker-peasant-soldier teams were expected to develop respect for one another and to develop their understanding of class struggle and the thought of Mao Tse-tung. The hope was that such joint participation in the educational revolution would assure that the nation's youth would be remolded as proletarian successors of the revolution, and lead to the emergence of a group of outstanding worker-cadres not only capable of managing the schools, but also of strengthening all aspects of various state organizations and Revolutionary Committees. The following news report (this particular one from Shuiyuan Commune in Yingkou County) is typical of the period:

> . . . the commune revolutionary committee decided to abolish the former system of giving the school principal sole responsibility, and to set up in each school a committee for the educational revolution, consisting of representatives both of the poor and lower-middle-class peasants and of the revolutionary teachers and students.[31]

Another clearly identifiable line of educational policy was the popularization of locally established primary and secondary schools. In addition to official pronouncements urging the local authorities to found these "May 7" type schools—so-called after the principles in Mao's May 7, 1966 directive—*People's Daily* established a special column (beginning in November, 1968) for the exchange of opinions and discussion of the idea that all State-run primary schools in the countryside should be put under the control of the commune's production brigades and run by them. The idea and its implications then spread to the industrial and urban areas, initiating a movement to have schools (higher-level schools as well as primary schools) placed under the direction of, and operated by, factories, mines, business enterprises, neighborhood revolutionary committees, etc.—or run jointly by combinations of these (factories and communes; factories, communes and neighborhood organizations, etc,). In these jointly-run schools, students participated in *both* industrial and agricultural labor, in addition to their related classroom studies.[32]

Encouragement of the creation of locally established and managed schools appears to have been predicated upon the claims that such schools would: (1) save educational expenditures; (2) destroy the capitalist intellectuals' domination of the schools; (3) popularize education; (4) re-educate intellectuals; and (5) coordinate education so that the nation's youth would develop the proper attitude toward productive labor and the proletarian viewpoint.[33]

On May 12, 1969 *People's Daily* published a proposal for the operation of the middle and primary schools in Kirin Province. Subsequent issues of this and other leading Chinese newspapers devoted space to an extensive discussion of the proposal, which, with certain modifications to meet particular local needs, could very well be considered a prototype recommended as a model for the nation's primary and middle schools in the rural areas, directly managed by the poor and lower-middle-class peasants.[34]

In the initial stages of the Cultural Revolution it was the students and teachers who left their homes and schools to go to the factories, rural communes, etc. to "exchange revolutionary experience." In the later stages of the Cultural Revolution it was the workers and peasants who were now encouraged to go to the schools to participate in the mass movement of "struggle-criticism-transformation." Mao's directive stated that: "The leading role of the working class in the great cultural revolution and in all fields of work should be brought into full play." Workers were instructed to enter the engineering institutes to participate in revolutionary mass criticism and repudiation; "bare-foot doctors" were instructed to enter medical colleges to smash the revisionist stereotypes.[35]

A unique institution created during this period was the "May 7 Cadre Schools," which are to be distinguished from the "May 7" primary or middle schools. The May 7 cadre schools, most of which are located in remote areas, were established to implement Mao's directive that: "Sending the broad masses of cadres to lower levels for manual labor gives them a good opportunity to study anew.''[36] Edgar Snow described the cadre schools as "reform schools for reformers.''[37] Cadres were "sent" to school for varying periods of time, generally from a minimum of six months or a year, up to two or three years. During that time they studied Marxist-Leninist ideology (including "Mao Tse-tung thought"), participated in class struggle (criticizing the bourgeoisie and engaging in political movements), and worked (mainly agricultural production, but also forestry, small industrial production, etc.).

The motto of the cadre schools was (and continues to be) "Plain living and hard struggle [and] self-reliance.''[38] Cadres go among the workers, learn from them, work with them, and participate with them in investigations and activities. The object of these activities is to raise the cadres' ideological level and eliminate bourgeois attitudes. After graduation they return to their original positions or are transferred to new work.

When the primary and middle schools returned to a more normal operation in 1968—the colleges, generally, did not resume normal operations until 1970—the number of years of pre-university schooling was cut down to a total of nine or ten years (depending upon local circumstances) and the number of subjects was reduced accordingly. The curriculum was reorganized so that concentration was given to only five major areas of study: political theory and practice; language; mathematics; military and physical training; and industrial and agricultural production. Mathematics and language were the only subjects retained from the traditional curriculum, but the scope of their content was no longer as comprehensive as it had formerly been. To revolutionize education, Mao Tse-tung thought or Maoism was incorporated into every subject. A typical problem in an arithmetic text read:

> Chairman Mao is the reddest "red sun" in our heart; it is most fortunate to be able to see Chairman Mao. In 1968 on the national birthday, there were 150 representatives of capital workers, liberation army, Maoist propaganda teams, and the poor, lower-middle class peasants, to visit Chairman Mao; there were also 67 representatives of Red Guards and revolutionary public. How many representatives in total were there to visit Chairman Mao?[39]

Examples of Maoist influence on the curriculum were so ubiquitous that they were featured by many English-language newspapers; the following report which appeared in *The New York Times* is illustrative:

> Here [Canton's No. 32 Middle School] more than a quarter of the formal curriculum is dedicated specifically to studying the thoughts of Chairman Mao, and the political content of the school's total program is much higher. . . .
> The new curriculum as outlined by Mrs. Chen, a Chinese language teacher and head of the teachers group, was as follows: Politics (the study of Mao Tse-tung thought), eight periods a week; mathematics, six periods; physics, two; chemistry, two; Chinese, five; English, two; history and geography, one; military training, two; agricultural knowledge, two; and revolutionary literature and arts, one. . . .
> This is not all. The school week is six days long and there are seven 45-minute periods daily. Time not spent on the formal curriculum is given over to further study of revolutionary literature and arts, criticism, and repudiation of the "revisionist education line". . . .[40]

Considerable emphasis was also given to the creation of locally-developed curriculum materials (suited to specific local needs) which were locally tested, evaluated, and then revised accordingly.

In the kindergarten, children studied and learned to recite passages from the "three often-read articles"[41] and the sayings of Chairman Mao Tse-tung, participated in mass political activities (such as the celebration of China's successful explosions of nuclear and hydrogen bombs, the denunciation of "China's Khrushchev," the condemnation of "U.S. imperialists" for their "crimes of aggression" against Vietnam, etc.), and were organized into children's propaganda teams for "Mao Tse-tung thought" (which included putting on performances for workers, Red Guards and foreign visitors, as well as making broadcasts on the Central People's Radio Broadcasting System).[42]

The basic principles set down for curriculum reform at the kindergarten, primary, and secondary school levels also applied to higher education as well. Courses in the colleges and universities were reduced in number, course content was simplified along practical lines, and political studies became more important than professional course work. On July 22, 1968, Mao stated:

> It is still necessary to have universities; here I refer mainly to colleges of science and engineering. However, it is essential to shorten the length of schooling, revolutionize education, put proletarian politics in command and take the road of the Shanghai Machine Tools Plant in training technicians from among the workers. Students should be selected from among workers and peasants with practical experience, and they should return to production after a few years' study.[43]

Mao's directive was aimed at those intellectuals and students who had only book-knowledge but no practical experience; he urged them to see their own defects, to put on a humble attitude, and to cast away their lofty airs. The directive launched a new movement to reform higher education, to break the monopoly of the "bourgeois intellectuals" and "academic authorities," and to establish "socialist universities." Science and engineering colleges operated factories; colleges, universities and research institutes hooked-up with factories, mines, etc. and actually ran these enterprises, thereby implementing Mao's principle of uniting theory with practice. The hallmark of a "socialist university" was that it combined education and production.[44]

In Peking University, for instance, students who were studying liberal arts were required to learn industrial work, farming, and military knowledge; Chairman Mao's works formed the basis of the curriculum materials, which were supplemented with literature, history, philosophy, politics, law, and other specialities. Two-thirds of the schooling period was allocated for students to go out to learn from workers, peasants, and soldiers.[45]

At Peking's China Medical University, the former Western-style 8-year course of medical education (including 3 years of pre-med training and one year of internship) was attacked as being crammed with many unnecessary courses, as emphasizing professional proficiency to the detriment of "proletarian politics," and "lop-sided theoretical" training to the neglect of the practical needs of the worker-peasant masses. The Revolutionary Committee of China Medical University cited the following ditty as a portrayal of the revisionists' educational line:

> In the old Medical University one has to study eight years,
>   It has really ruined many a student.
> In the first three years he is not anywhere near medicine.
>   In the next five years he is not anywhere near a patient.
> After eight years of study he is not anywhere near the worker-peasant
>   masses.[46]

It is interesting to note that in addition to the specific provision for course-work in military training, a completely military pattern of organization was applied to the school system itself. Beginning in 1968, the traditional names of principal, dean, director, and the like gradually disappeared from the listings of educational administration; they were replaced with terms such as sergeant, lieutenant, and major. The new school organization was modeled after the system used in the People's Liberation Army (PLA). Even the traditional class and director system were reorganized according to the military structure of squad, platoon, etc. Schools changing their original organizational structure were cited for special mention and praised in the Chinese press.[47]

The Cultural Revolution dramatically brought Chinese education into a new phase of development—admittedly not without a great deal of disorder, violence, and the loss of life. This was after all a revolution, and the order of the day was "break down the old and establish the new." It should be remembered that China's youth—those under the age of twenty—had not actually previously experienced any revolutionary conflicts or themselves participated in revolutionary class struggles. A continuing pattern of "struggle-criticism-transformation" is at the center of Marxist-Leninist (and Maoist) ideology, and the Cultural Revolution should be seen in this context. According to Mao Tse-tung thought, successors to the revolutionary cause of the proletariat "are born in mass struggles and grow up through training in big tempests of revolution."[48]

NOTES:

[1]Mao Tse-tung, "On New Democracy" (January 1940), *Selected Works of Mao Tse-tung*, II (Peking: Foreign Language Press, 1967), p. 373.

[2]Editorial Departments of *Renmin Ribao* [*People's Daily*], *Hongqi* [*Red Flag*] and *Jiefangjun Bao* [*Liberation Army Daily*], "Quotation from Chairman Mao Tse-tung," *An Epoch-Making Document* (May 17, 1968), (Peking: Foreign Language Press, 1968), [p. i].

[3]"Quotation from Chairman Mao Tse-tung," Ibid., [p. ii].

[4]Ibid., p. 1.

[5]K. H. Fan (ed.), *The Chinese Cultural Revolution: Selected Documents* (New York: Monthly Review Press, 1968), pp. 131-132.

[6]Ibid., p. 132.

[7]"What Are Sung Shih, Lu Ping and Peng Pei-yun Up To in the Cultural Revolution," *Peking Review*, No. 37 (September 9, 1966), pp. 19-20. [This is a re-publication of the "big-character" poster which appeared on May 25, 1966.]

[8]Joan Robinson, *The Cultural Revolution in China* (Baltimore, Maryland: Penguin Books, 1969), p. 18.

[9]Mao Tse-tung, "Bombard the Headquarters" (August 5, 1966), *Peking Review*, No. 33 (August 11, 1967), p. 5.

[10]Ibid., p. 6.

[11]*Decision of the Central Committee of the Chinese Communist Party Concerning the Great Proletarian Cultural Revolution*, *Peking Review*, No. 32 (August 12, 1966), p. 6.

[12]*Renmin Ribao*, S. M. Hu (trans.), January 1, 1967, p. 3.

[13]*Jiefangjun Bao*, S. M. Hu (trans.), June 7, 1966, p. 1.

[14]*Decision of the Central Committee of the Chinese Communist Party Concerning the Great Proletarian Cultural Revolution* (Peking: Foreign Language Press, 1966), p. 13.

[15]*Quotations From Chairman Mao Tse-tung* (Peking: Foreign Language Press, 1966), Foreword.

[16]*Decision of the Central Committee of the Chinese Communist Party Concerning the Great Proletarian Cultural Revolution*, p. 2.

[17]Robinson, op. cit., pp. 43-44.

[18]*Decision . . . Concerning the Great Proletarian Cultural Revolution,* p. 10.

[19]"Notice on Reform of Enrollment for China's Institutes of Higher Learning," NCNA-English, Peking (June 18, 1966), *Current Background,* No. 846 (February 8, 1968), p. 1.

[20]Maud Russell, *The Ongoing Cultural Revolution in China* (New York: Faculty Press, Inc., 1968), p. 11.

[21]Wang Hsuan-tze, "Educational Reforms in Communist China," S. M. Hu (trans.), *Studies on Chinese Communism,* No. 2 (February 28, 1967), pp. 80-82.

[22]Editorial, "Let Revolutionary Teachers and Students of Middle Schools Quickly Go Back to School to Resume Class and Make Revolution," *Wen-hui Pao,* Shanghai (February 17, 1967), *Survey of China Mainland Press,* No. 170 (March 23, 1967), p. 16.

[23]Propaganda Team Stationed in Ch'anghsintien *Chen* Central Primary School, Peking Municipality and the Revolutionary Committee of Ch'anghsintien *Chen* Central Primary School, "Establish a New Proletarian System of Examination and Assessment," *Kwang-ming Jih-pao,* Peking (August 31, 1969), *Survey of China Mainland Press,* No. 4504 (September 26, 1969), p. 7.

[24]"Chairman Mao's 'March 7' Directive Guides Cultural Revolution in Peking Schools," NCNA-English, Peking (March 7, 1968), *Survey of China Mainland Press,* No. 4139 (March 13, 1968), p. 14. [Although the text of the "March 7" Directive stated that it was to be distributed to the whole country to be acted upon accordingly, it was not until a year later, March 8, 1968, on the occasion of the first anniversary of its issuance, that *Renmin Ribao* published for the first time the full text of the "March 7" Directive.]

[25]Ibid., p. 16.

[26]"Salaries of Rural Teachers May Be Paid by the People with State Aid," *Jen-min Jih-pao* (January 6, 1969), *Survey of China Mainland Press,* No. 4346 (January 27, 1969), pp. 6-8.

[27]Correspondence Group of Ch'angte *Hsien* Revolutionary Committee, *Hunan Jih-pao* Reporter, Reporter of Hunan People's Radio, and *Jen-min Jih-pao* Reporter, "Carry Out Policy and Raise Enthusiasm of Middle and Primary School Teachers," *Jen-min Jih-pao* (May 30, 1969), *Survey of China Mainland Press,* No 4435 (June 12, 1969), pp. 5-8.

[28]"Educate the Teachers and Students to Teach and Learn Socialist Culture Well," *Jen-min Jih-pao* (June 21, 1969), *Survey of China Mainland Press,* No. 4450 (July 8, 1969), p. 9.

[29]*Jen-min Jih-pao* (November 3, 1967), *Survey of China Mainland Press,* No. 4116 (February 12, 1968), p. 1.

[30]Editorial, "China Mainland Schools Under Management of the Working Class," S. M. Hu (trans.), *Studies on Chinese Communism,* No. 10 (October, 1968), p. 1.

[31]News Section, *Peking Review,* No. 39 (September 27, 1968), p. 21.

[32]"Movement of Press Discussions in Various Places" [Concerning the question of how schools should be run.], *Jen-min Jih-pao* (December 27, 1968), *Current Background,* No. 870 (January 27, 1969), p. 43.

[33]Wang Chun, "An Analytical Study of the Chinese Communist Decision to 'Down Grade' Middle and Primary Schools for the Operation of the 'People,'" S. M. Hu (trans.), *Studies on Chinese Communism,* No. 2 (February, 1969), p. 65.

[34]"Draft Program for Primary and Middle Schools in Chinese Countryside," NCNA-English, Peking (May 13, 1969), *Survey of China Mainland Press,* No. 4418 (June 19, 1969), pp. 9-15.

[35]Editorial, "Working Class Must Supervise Education," *Wen-hui Pao* (August 17, 1968), *Survey of China Mainland Press,* No. 4254 (September 10, 1968), pp. 13-14.

[36]"Discussion on How to Operate 'May 7' Cadre Schools Well," *Jen-min Jih-pao* (August 18, 1969), *Current Background,* No. 899 (January 19, 1970), p. 1.

[37]Edgar Snow, *The Long Revolution* (New York: Random House, 1972), p. 118.

[38]"The 'May 7' Cadre School," *Peking Review,* No. 19 (May 12, 1972), p. 6.

[39]Hai Feng, "The Present Stage of Children's Education in Communist China," S. M. Hu (trans.), *China Monthly,* No. 66 (September 1, 1969), p. 23.

[40]*The New York Times* (December 2, 1969), p. 15.

[41]The "three often-read articles," sometimes also known as the "three constantly read articles" are: "In Memory of Norman Bethune" (December 21, 1939); "Serve the People" (September 8, 1944); and "The Foolish Old Man Who Removed the Mountains" (June 11, 1945). The complete text of each of these three articles, including editorial notes and explanatory notes can be found in *Selected Readings From the Works of Mao Tse-tung* (Peking: Foreign Language Press, 1967).

[42]Yuhsiang Kindergarten of the Air Force of Peking Military Region, "Nurture the Revolutionary Next Generation With the Thought of Mao Tse-tung," *Kuang-ming Jih-pao* (December 23, 1967), *Survey of China Mainland Press,* No. 4106 (January 24, 1968), pp. 5-11.

[43]Editorial, "Combat Program of Proletarian Revolution in Education," *Wen-hui Pao* (July 22, 1968), *Survey of China Mainland Press,* No. 4249 (September 3, 1968), p. 13.

[44]"How Should Socialist Universities Be Run?" *Jen-min Jih-pao* (March 29, 1969), *Current Background,* No. 881 (March 26, 1969), p. 1.

[45]Chung Hua-ming, "The Current Educational Revolution in Institutes of Higher Education in Mainland China," S. M. Hu (trans.), *China Monthly,* No. 67 (October 1, 1969), p. 8.

[46]Revolutionary Committee of China Medical University, "Thoroughly Criticize and Repudiate the 8-Year Course Promoted by China's Khrushchev," *Jen-min Jih-pao* (December 17, 1967), *Survey of China Mainland Press,* No. 4100 (January 16, 1968), p. 8.

[47]Wang Chun, "Military Training and Military Control of Primary and Middle Schools in Mainland China," S. M. Hu (trans.), *Studies on Chinese Communism,* No. 7 (July 10, 1969), p. 73.

[48]Editorial, "Raise High the Great Red Banner of the Thought of Mao Tse-tung, Be Fresh Troops for the Great Cultural Revolution of the Proletariat," *Chung-kuo Ch'ing-nien* (China Youth), *Extracts from China Mainland Magazines,* No. 537 (August 15, 1966), p. 8.

6.1 "May 7th Directive, 1966"

Comrade Lin Piao:

I acknowledge the receipt of the report from the General Logistics Department which you forwarded on May 6. I think this plan is quite good. You are requested to decide whether it is possible to send this report to all military regions, and ask them to call together cadres at the army and divisional levels to discuss it and submit their views to the Military Commission, so that proper instructions may be issued to the whole army subject to the consent of the Central Committee. So long as there is no world war, the armed forces should be a great school. Even under the conditions of a third world war, it is also quite possible to form such a great school, and apart from fighting, the armed forces can also perform various kinds of work. Wasn't this what we did in the various anti-Japanese bases during the eight years of the Second World War? In this great school, our armymen should learn politics, military affairs and agriculture. They can also engage in agricultural production and side occupations, run some medium and small factories and manufacture a number of products to meet their own needs or exchange with the state at equal values. They can also do mass work and take part in the socialist education "four cleanups" movement in the factories and villages. After the "four cleanups" movement, they can always find mass work to do, in order to insure that the army is always as one with the masses. They should also participate in each struggle of the cultural revolution as it occurs to criticize the bourgeoisie. In this way, the army can concurrently study, engage in agriculture, run factories and do mass work. Of course, these tasks should be properly coordinated, and a difference should be made between the primary and secondary tasks. Each army unit should engage in one or two of the three tasks of agriculture, industry and mass work, but not in all three at the same time. In this way, our army of several million will be able to play a very great role indeed.

While the main task of the workers is in industry, they should also study military affairs, politics and culture. They, too, should take part in the "four cleanups" movement and in the criticizing of the bourgeoisie. Where conditions permit, they should also engage in agricultural production and side occupations, as is done at the Tach'ing oilfield.

While the main task of the peasants in the communes is agriculture (including forestry, animal husbandry, side occupations and fishery), they should at the same time study military affairs, politics and culture. Where conditions permit, they should collectively run small plants. They should also criticize the bourgeoisie.

This holds good for students too. While their main task is to study, they should in addition to their studies, learn other things, that is, industrial work, farming and military affairs. They should also criticize the bourgeoisie. The school term should be shortened, education should be revolutionized, and the domination of our schools by bourgeois intellectuals should not be allowed to continue.

Where conditions permit those working in commerce, in the service trades and Party and government organizations should do the same.

The above is no longer any new idea, creation or invention, since many people

---

"May 7th Directive, 1966," *Chairman Mao on Revolution in Education* (Kuangtung: People's Publishing House, April, 1969), *Current Background*, No. 888 (August 22, 1969), p. 17.

have acted in this way for many years, although this has not been popularized. As to the armed forces, they have acted in this way for several decades, but this has now been further developed.

Mao Tse-tung
May 7, 1966

6.2 "Decision of C. P. C. Central Committee and State Council On Reform of Entrance Examination and Enrollment in Higher Educational Institutions"

The Central Committee of the Chinese Communist Party and the State Council issued a notice on June 13 announcing that, to ensure the successful carrying out of the cultural revolution to the end, and to effect a thorough reform of the educational system, a decision had been made to change the old system of entrance examination and enrollment of students in higher educational institutions and to postpone this year's enrollment of new students for colleges and universities for half a year.

The full text of the notice follows:

Considering that the great cultural revolution is only now developing in the colleges, universities and senior middle schools, a certain period of time will be needed in order to carry this movement through thoroughly and successfully. Bourgeois domination is still deeply rooted and the struggle between the proletariat and the bourgeoisie is very acute in quite a number of universities, colleges and middle schools. A thorough-going cultural revolution movement in the higher educational institutions and senior middle schools will have most far-reaching effects on school education in the future. Meanwhile, though it has been constantly improved since liberation, the method of examination and enrollment for the higher educational institutions, has failed, in the main, to free itself from the set pattern of the bourgeois system of examination; and such a method is harmful to the implementation of the guiding policy on education formulated by the Central Committee of the Party and Chairman Mao, and to absorption into the higher educational institutions of a still greater number of revolutionary young people from among the workers, peasants and soldiers. This system of examination must be completely reformed. Therefore, time is also needed to study and work out new methods of enrollment.

In view of the above-mentioned situation, the Central Committee of the Chinese Communist Party and the State Council have decided to postpone for half a year the 1966 enrollment into the higher educational institutions so that, on the one hand, they and the senior middle schools will have enough time to carry out the cultural revolution thoroughly and successfully and, on the other hand, there will be adequate time for making all preparations for the implementation of a new method of enrollment.

In order that enrollment and the opening of a new semester in the senior middle schools shall not be affected, the students graduating from senior middle school this term in schools where the cultural revolution is still under way should be properly

"Decision of C.P.C. [Communist Party of China] Central Committee and State Council On Reform of Entrance Examination and Enrollment in Higher Educational Institutions" [June 13, 1966], *Peking Review*, No. 26 (June 24, 1966), p. 3.

accommodated and their time-table arranged by the school authorities so that the movement may be carried out thoroughly and successfully; in the case of students in schools where the movement is completed before enrollment into the higher educational institutions has begun, their schools should organize them to participate in productive labour in the countryside or in the factories.

6.3 "Chinese Communist Party Central Committee's Notification (Draft) Concerning the Great Proletarian Cultural Revolution in Primary Schools" (February 4, 1967)

(FOR DISCUSSION AND TRIAL ENFORCEMENT)

(1) Primary schools form an important front in the great proletarian cultural revolution. They must firmly carry out the proletarian revolutionary line represented by Chairman Mao and thoroughly criticize and repudiate the bourgeois reactionary line. They must act according to the "Decision of the CCP Central Committee Concerning the Great Proletarian Cultural Revolution."

(2) Primary schools in all places shall resume classes after the Spring Festival. Primary school teachers and pupils who have gone to other places to exchange revolutionary experience should return to their own schools to play an active part in the great proletarian cultural revolution, to carry out struggle-criticism-transformation and to organize studies for the pupils.

(3) Primary school pupils may organize Red Little Soldiers. Those in the 5th and 6th year classes and graduates of 1966 should, in conjunction with the great cultural revolution, study quotations from Chairman Mao, the three most widely studied articles, the three main rules of discipline and the eight points for attention, and the sixteen articles of the cultural revolution, and learn to sing revolutionary songs.

Those in the 1st, 2nd, 3rd and 4th year classes should be organized to study quotations from Chairman Mao and learn to read characters and sing revolutionary songs with the revolutionary teachers and pupils in senior classes acting as their supervising personnel.

During the period of the great cultural revolution, primary school pupils must also be taught some general arithmetic and scientific knowledge.

(4) Cultural revolution committees and cultural revolution groups in primary schools shall be brought into being by teachers and pupils in senior classes through democratic elections. Revolutionary teachers and pupils in senior classes should form the main body in these organizations.

School administration should be strengthened or re-elected through mass discussion to take good care of the life of teachers and pupils.

(5) In the great cultural revolution, no leaders shall be permitted to adopt various

"Chinese Communist Party Central Committee's Notification (Draft) Concerning the Great Proletarian Cultural Revolution in Primary Schools" (February 4, 1967), *Collection of Documents Concerning the Great Proletarian Cultural Revolution, Vol. I* (Peking: Propagandists of Mao Tse-tung's Thought, Peking College of Chemical Engineering, May, 1967), *Current Background*, No. 852 (May 6, 1968), p. 62.

means to hit back in revenge on the ground that the masses have criticized them or exposed their problems. Revolutionary teachers and pupils who have been branded as "counterrevolutionaries," "pseudo-leftists but genuine rightists," "little monsters and demons," etc., in the great cultural revolution must be vindicated.

(6) A handful of Party persons in authority taking the capitalist road should mainly be attacked in the great cultural revolution. Meanwhile, those landlords, rich peasants, counterrevolutionaries, bad elements and rightists (not referring to their family background) among the teachers and staff members who firmly cling to the reactionary stand should be purged, and the educational organs should arrange for their reform through labor in their own places.

This notification may be posted in urban and rural basic-level units and primary schools throughout the country.

Dated February 4, 1967

6.4 "Notice of the Chinese Communist Party Central Committee and the State Council Concerning [Urban] Educated Youths Working in Rural and Mountainous Areas Who Go Out To Exchange Revolutionary Experience, Make Revolution, or Call on People at Higher Levels" (February 17, 1967)

The great proletarian cultural revolution, personally started and led by Chairman Mao, has already entered a new stage of great alliances and great seizure of power by proletarian revolutionaries. The vast numbers of educated youths working in rural and mountainous areas who have gone out to exchange experience, make petitions and call on people in high places are actively returning to their own units to participate in the struggle for power seizure and in agricultural production in response to our great leader Chairman Mao's call "to grasp revolution and promote production." However, at the moment, there are still a small number of people who remain indefinitely in the cities under various pretexts. With a view to finding a satisfactory solution to this question, the following regulations are hereby laid down:

1. All those educated youths working in rural and mountainous areas, youths who have gone to the border regions to help with construction, farm workers and all personnel who have gone out to exchange experience, make petitions and visit people in high places should immediately return to their own units to take part in the great cultural revolution and do a good job of production. All liaison stations set up by them should be abolished without exception.

2. Some educated youths working in rural and mountainous areas who have been

"Notice of the Chinese Communist Party Central Committee and the State Council Concerning [Urban] Educated Youths Working in Rural and Mountainous Areas Who Go Out To Exchange Revolutionary Experience, Make Revolution, or Call on People at Higher Levels" (February 17, 1967, *Collection of Documents Concerning the Great Proletarian Cultural Revolution, Vol. I* (Peking: Propagandists of Mao Tse-tung's Thought, Peking College of Chemical Engineering, May, 1967), *Current Background,* No. 852 (May 6, 1968), p. 82.

influenced by the bourgeois reactionary line and counter-revolutionary economism and who have done some things damaging to the interests of the State and the people shall not be prosecuted if they return to their own units to make serious self-examinations and correct their mistakes.

3. Among educated youths working in rural and mountainous areas, youths who have gone to the border regions to help with construction, and farm workers who have gone out to exchange experience, make petitions and visit people in high places, there are a few wicked elements who act mysteriously, do not give their real names and work units, practice deception everywhere they go, disrupt social peace and order and damage the property of the State. These elements must be thoroughly investigated and punished according to law.

4. The problem of placement should be dealt with in accordance with the third article of the CCP Central Committee's "Notice Concerning Opposition to Economism": "Those people who several years before were sent down to rural areas to participate in agricultural production and educated youths who have gone from urban areas to work in rural and mountainous areas should participate in agricultural production with contentment and participate in the great proletarian cultural revolution in the rural areas. Problems in connection with placement should be solved gradually by Party committees at various levels."

5. The problem of placement for those who several years before were retrenched and were sent down to the countryside and who are now living in cities and towns should also be handled in the spirit of point No. 4 above. They shall not return to their original industrial and communications enterprises or business units and demand reinstatement.

This notice may be posted in rural areas and cities.

The CCP Central Committee
The State Council

Dated February 17, 1967

6.5 "Chinese Communist Party Central Committee's Opinion on the Great Proletarian Cultural Revolution in Middle Schools" (February 19, 1967)

(FOR DISCUSSION AND TENTATIVE IMPLEMENTATION)

1. While making the great proletarian cultural revolution, middle schools (including intermediate technical schools and schools run on part-work and part-study or part-farming and part-study basis) must resolutely execute the proletarian revolutionary line represented by Chairman Mao and thoroughly criticize and repudiate the bourgeois reactionary line. They also must carry out struggle, criticism and trans-

"Chinese Communist Party Central Committee's Opinion on the Great Proletarian Cultural Revolution in Middle Schools" (February 19, 1967), *Collection of Documents Concerning the Great Proletarian Cultural Revolution, Vol. I* (Peking: Propagandists of Mao Tse-tung's Thought, Peking College of Chemical Engeneering, May, 1967), *Current Background,* No. 852 (May 6, 1968), pp. 87-88.

formation in line with the "Decision of the CCP Central Committee on the Great Proletarian Cultural Revolution."

2. As from March 1, middle school teachers and students (including students who expect to graduate in 1966 but have not yet graduated) must stop going to other places to form ties. They should, as a rule, return to their schools. Those who have gone to the countryside or factories are also required to return to their schools, where they must attend their lessons on the one hand and make revolution on the other. In order to strengthen their revolutionary spirit, scientific approach and concept of organization and discipline, the middle school teachers and students must, by groups and by stages, go through a short-term military and political training.

3. Revolutionary Red Guards are vanguards of the great proletarian cultural revolution in middle schools. Red Guard organizations should be reorganized, consolidated and developed during the movement. Red Guards should be formed mainly of revolutionary students born of families of laboring people (workers, peasants, soldiers, revolutionary cadres, and laborers engaged in other fields). Students who were not born of families of laboring people may also join the Red Guards providing they cherish deep feelings for Chairman Mao, have the proletarian revolutionary spirit and have consistently behaved themselves comparatively well politically and ideologically.

Establishment of reactionary organizations in schools is forbidden. Reactionary organizations, such as the United Action Committee and the Red Terror Team, must be disbanded as a rule. Students who have been hoodwinked and joined the reactionary organization must go through intensive political and ideological education and be allowed and helped to rectify their mistakes.

4. The situation of domination of our schools by bourgeois intellectuals must not be allowed to go on any further. On the basis of proletarian revolutionary great alliances in middle schools, cultural revolution committees should be democratically elected by the revolutionary students, revolutionary teachers and staff members and revolutionary leading cadres. These committees will be responsible for leading the great cultural revolution in schools, making concrete arrangements for teaching of lessons and properly supervising the life of teachers and students. In those schools where such committees cannot be elected for the time being, a provisional leading group may be set up through consultation among representatives of various groups.

5. In middle schools, teaching of lessons must be closely combined with the great cultural revolution. Effort must be made earnestly to study Chairman Mao's works and the Party Central Committee's documents concerning the great cultural revolution, and criticize and repudiate bourgeois teaching materials and the pedagogical system. It is also necessary to devote some time to reviewing mathematics, physics, chemistry, foreign languages and other essential courses of study. During the busy farming season, the teachers and students may be organized in a planned manner to participate in labor in the countryside and to learn things from the poor and lower-middle peasants. It is not compulsory for students of part-work part-study schools which are assigned with productive tasks by the State to participate in labor in the countryside.

6. Nobody is allowed to retaliate upon those revolutionary students and revolutionary teachers and staff members who make criticism and disclose problems. Effort must be made earnestly to vindicate those revolutionary students and revolutionary teachers and staff members who were branded "counter-revolutionaries" and "rightists" during the initial period of the great cultural revolution. The majority of teachers and cadres in middle schools are good or compara-

tively good. Do not reject and overthrow everyone.

During the great proletarian cultural revolution, struggles between one group of the masses and another must be opposed resolutely. Divergent opinions among the masses must be settled correctly by the method of marshalling facts and reasoning things out.

We must resolutely uphold struggle by reasoning and forbid violent struggle. We must follow Chairman Mao's directive "learning from past mistakes to avoid future ones and curing the sickness to save the patient" and actively supervise those who have made mistakes and help them rectify their mistakes, so that they will return to the proletarian revolutionary standpoint represented by Chairman Mao.

7. The ranks of teachers must be reorganized and purified seriously. Those land-lord, rich-peasant, counter-revolutionary, bad and rightist elements (referring to themselves and not their families) who cling to their reactionary standpoint and refuse to be remolded must be purged from the ranks of teachers and staff members. This is an important requirement for the proper running of a school.

8. Chairman Mao's directive "practice economy while making revolution" must be implemented earnestly and State property protected. Equipment in schools must wholly be maintained by their own effort. Those who have destroyed State property must be educated or given disciplinary punishment according to the severity of their offense, and must make amends for the damage done.

This document may be put up in urban and rural areas and middle schools all over the country.
Dated February 19, 1967

6.6 "Chinese Communist Party Central Committee's Regulations (Draft) Governing the Great Proletarian Cultural Revolution Currently Under Way in Universities, Colleges and Schools" (March 7, 1967)

(FOR DISCUSSION AND TRIAL IMPLEMENTATION)

1. In the course of the great proletarian cultural revolution, institutes of higher learning must firmly implement the proletarian revolutionary line represented by Chairman Mao and thoroughly criticize and repudiate the bourgeois reactionary line. They must also carry out "struggle, criticism and transformation" in accordance with the "CCP Central Committee's Decision on the Great Proletarian Cultural Revolution."

2. Revolutionary teachers and students who have gone to factories and the countryside or gone to other places to establish ties (including those who participate

---

"Chinese Communist Party Central Committee's Regulations (Draft) Governing the Great Proletarian Cultural Revolution Currently Under Way in Universities, Colleges and Schools" (March 7, 1967), *Collection of Documents Concerning the Great Proletarian Cultural Revolution, Vol. I* (Peking: Propagandists of Mao Tse-tung's Thought, Peking College of Chemical Engineering, May, 1967), *Current Background,* No. 852 (May 6, 1968), pp. 99-100.

in the seizure of power in other units or are stationed in liaison posts in other localities) must, as a rule, return to their institutes before March 20 and take part in the great cultural revolution there.

3. Revolutionary teachers and students of all institutes of higher learning must creatively study and apply Chairman Mao's works and rectify their thinking, styles of work, and organization. In accordance with unified arrangements, they must carry out short-term military and political training by stages and by groups.

4. In accordance with their concrete situations, all institutes of higher learning must profoundly criticize, repudiate and struggle against the handful of Party persons in authority taking the capitalist road and the bourgeois reactionary academic "authorities" politically, ideologically and academically. They must study ways to reform the old educational system, policy of teaching, and methods of teaching.

5. In all institutes of higher learning, with the handful of Party persons in authority taking the capitalist road and the reactionary academic "authorities" excepted, leading cadres at all levels, professors, lecturers, assistant lecturers and other members of the teaching staff should be united with and educated, and invited to join in the great cultural revolution, and arrangements made for their work. Those who have made mistakes should be treated in accordance with the principle of "learning from past mistakes to avoid future ones and curing the sickness to save the patient." They must be allowed to turn over a new leaf and encouraged to make amends, providing they are not anti-Party and anti-socialist elements, do not persist in their mistakes and do not refuse to correct their mistakes after repeated education.

6. In each institute of higher learning, revolutionary students, revolutionary teachers and staff members and revolutionary leading cadres must form a provisional organ of power to lead the great proletarian cultural revolution and exercise the power of the institute. In an institute of higher learning, if the organization of students of the revolutionary left has grasped the leadership, effort should be made to accept revolutionary members of the teaching staff and revolutionary leading cadres into this organization. When the conditions ripen, a general election should be held to formally establish a cultural revolution group, a cultural revolution committee, a cultural revolution congress, or an organization of a similar type, which is to be regarded as the formal organ of power leading the great cultural revolution.

7. The revolutionary Red Guards of institutes of higher learning are vanguards of the great proletarian cultural revolution. Red Guard organizations should be rectified, consolidated and developed in the course of the revolution. They should take revolutionary students born of families of laboring people (including workers, peasants, soldiers, revolutionary cadres, and laborers engaged in other fields) as their mainstay. Students who were not born of families of the laboring people may also join these organizations, providing they have deep affection for Chairman Mao, have the revolutionary spirit of the proletariat and have consistently behaved themselves comparatively well politically and ideologically.

8. Factories, enterprises and scientific research units under the institutes of higher learning must firmly carry out the directive of grasping revolution and promoting production given by Chairman Mao and the Party Central Committee, and earnestly implement the "CCP Central Committee's Ten Regulations (Draft) Concerning Grasp of Revolution and Promotion of Production."

This document may be posted in all universities, colleges and schools throughout the country.
Dated March 7, 1967

6.7 "Decision of the Military Commission of the Chinese Communist Party Central Committee Concerning the Enforcement of Military Control in Higher Military Academies and Schools" (April 19, 1967)

In order to implement and carry out better the instructions of out great leader Chairman Mao and the Military Commission of the Central Committee concerning the great proletarian cultural revolution in military academies and schools, and in order to safeguard the carrying out of the great proletarian cultural revolution with greater success, the Military Commission of the CCP Central Committee hereby decides to enforce military control in the higher military academies of the Chinese People's Liberation Army and to set up the Military Control Committee. . . .

1. The Military Control Committee must hold high the great red banner of Mao Tse-tung's thought, bring proletarian politics to the fore, energetically publicize the thought of Mao Tse-tung, firmly support the proletarian revolutionaries, unite and rely upon the broad revolutionary masses and the revolutionary cadres, direct the spearhead of struggle at the top Party persons in authority taking the capitalist road, and thoroughly accomplish the task of first struggle, second criticism and third transformation.

2. The great proletarian cultural revolution and teaching and administrative work shall be carried out in higher military academies under the leadership of the Military Control Committee. It is imperative to carry out and implement resolutely the "Decision of the CCP Central Committee Concerning the Great Proletarian Cultural Revolution," the January 28 "Order of the Military Commission of the Central Committee," the June 6 "Order of the Military Commission of the Central Committee" and other relevant instructions and rules of the Military Commission.

3. The mass organizations of higher military academies must seriously carry out the rectification campaign, and overcome anarchism, the small group mentality, individualism and other non-proletarian thoughts. They must strive to realize the great alliance of the proletarian revolutionaries and the revolutionary "three-way combination." They must earnestly advocate struggle by reasoning and firmly curb struggle by force. Should struggle by force occur again, the murderers and their instigators should be disciplined or punished as required.

4. The guards, communications and transportation detachments of higher military academies shall be under the command of the Military Control Committee, which shall take over the control of wired broadcasting equipment.

5. All personnel must creatively study and apply Chairman Mao's writings, eradicate "self-interest" and establish "public interest" in a big way, firmly guard their work posts, work energetically, observe discipline, submit to command, and set up a good revolutionary order. The orders and decisions of the Military Control Committee must be firmly carried out.

The Military Commission of the CCP
Dated April 19, 1967.   Central Committee

"Decision of the Military Commission of the Chinese Communist Party Central Committee Concerning the Enforcement of Military Control in Higher Military Academies and Schools" (April 19, 1967), *Collection of Documents Concerning the Great Proletarian Cultural Revolution, Vol. I* (Peking: Propagandists of Mao Tse-tung's Thought, Peking College of Chemical Engineering, May, 1967), *Current Background,* No. 852 (May 6, 1968), p. 121.

6.8 "*Jen-min Jih-pao* Editorial on Importance of Transforming Chinese Educational System"

The *Jen-min Jih-pao* today carries a frontpage editorial on the significance of the announcement made by the Central Committee of the Chinese Communist Party and the State Council on June 13 of the decision to change the existing entrance examination method of enrolling college students.

The editorial is entitled "Carry Out the Cultural Revolution Thoroughly and Transform the Educational System Completely."

The text of the editorial follows:

On June 13 the Central Committee of the Chinese Communist Party and the State Council announced the decision to transform the existing entrance examination method of enrolling students in institutes of higher learning and to postpone the enrollment for 1966 by half a year. This decision is an important measure for carrying out thoroughly the great cultural revolution in the field of education and completely transforming China's educational system.

Today the vast numbers of revolutionary students, administrative and other staff and teachers in many universities, colleges and middle schools in Peking and other places are holding aloft the great red banner of Mao Tse-tung's thought, breaking through all the obstacles and restraints imposed by the bourgeois royalists and directing a fierce barrage of fire at the black anti-Party and anti-socialist line in the field of education. However, this struggle has only just begun and there are still many stubborn bourgeois strongholds which have not yet been breached. If the entrance examination of enrolling new students went ahead as usual just now, this would undoubtedly bring the great proletarian cultural revolution in the field of education to a stop half way, cripple the revolutionary enthusiasm of the Left students and encourage the counter-revolutionary arrogance of the bourgeois Right. The decision of the Central Committee of the Chinese Communist Party and State Council is an enormous help to the development of the great proletarian cultural revolution, a tremendous encouragement to the Left students and a heavy blow for the bourgeois Right.

For a long time now the workers, peasants and soldiers, and revolutionary students and teachers have made it clear that they are very angry about the old entrance examination system of enrolling students and have been urgently demanding that it should be scrapped once for all. The two letters to the Central Committee of the Party and Chairman Mao which are carried in our paper today, one written by students of the fourth class in the senior third grade at Peking's No. 1 Girls' Middle School and the other by students of the fifth class in the senior third grade at Peking's No. 4 Middle School, and the many other unpublished letters which have come in from the

---

"*Jen-min Jih-pao* Editorial on Importance of Transforming Chinese Educational System" (NCNA-English, Peking, June 18, 1967), *Current Background,* No. 846 (February 8, 1968), pp. 2-5.

masses strongly demand the abolition of the old system of admitting students. The two letters are full of sincerity and loyalty to the Party and the people, they are brimming over with revolutionary spirit, they demonstrate the spirit of daring to think, to speak, to act, to break through and to make revolution which imbues the revolutionary youth of the Mao Tse-tung era; they reflect the desire of the great numbers of revolutionary teachers and students and speak with the voice of the revolutionary masses.

The Central Committee of the Chinese Communist Party and the State Council took the decision to abolish the existing entrance examination method of enrolling students in institutes of higher learning in accordance with Chairman Mao's instructions and the demands of the masses. Beginning this year, a new method of enrollment, a combination of recommendation and selection, in which proletarian politics are right to the fore and the mass line is followed, will go into effect; the best students will be admitted, selected from among those recommended for their outstanding moral, intellectual and physical qualities. The same method will be used in enrolling students of senior middle schools.

Again and again, the Central Committee of the Party and Chairman Mao has pointed out that the old bourgeois educational system, including the enrolling of students by examination, must be thoroughly transformed. This old examination system of enrolling students is most dangerous and harmful to the socialist cause. It places not proletarian but bourgeois politics in command, it places school marks in command. This system is a serious violation of the Party's class line, shuts out many outstanding children of workers, former poor and lower-middle peasants, revolutionary functionaries, revolutionary armymen and revolutionary martyrs and opens the gates wide to the bourgeoisie to cultivate its own successors. This system is a great obstacle to the revolutionizing of young people's minds and encourages them to become bourgeois specialists by the bourgeois method of "making one's own way" and achieving individual fame, wealth and position.

For a long time now, a handful of anti-Party and anti-socialist bourgeois representatives have opposed the educational policy of the Party and Chairman Mao and used the old entrance examination system as a weapon of class struggle against the proletariat, of dictatorship over the children of workers and poor and lower-middle peasants. And in the current great cultural revolution, these bourgeois royalists have been attacking the proletarian Left and suppressing and sabotaging the mass movement in the great proletarian cultural revolution, once again using the pretext that they were interfering with lessons and wasting study time" and the threat that they "would not pass up and be admitted to a higher school."

The facts show that the old examination system of enrollment has become a stumbling-block in socialist education and the great proletarian cultural revolutionary movement.

It is through schools that the proletariat trains and cultivates its successors for the proletarian cause and through schools, too, the bourgeoisie trains its successors for purposes of a capitalist come-back. There is sharp class struggle here, between the proletariat and the bourgeoisie, to win over the younger generation. The Party's Central Committee and Chairman Mao Tse-tung have always placed great weight on proletarian education and the revolutionary transformation of the educational system. Chairman Mao has put forward the policy that education must serve proletarian politics and must be combined with productive labor; he has pointed out that "our educational policy must enable everyone who gets an education, to develop morally, intellectually and physically and become a cultured, socialist-minded workers." The series of instructions given by Chairman Mao on proletarian education light the way in China's socialist and communist cause like a great beacon.

The representatives of the bourgeoisie who have insinuated themselves in the educational world and are against the Party, against socialism and against Mao Tse-tung's thought, hate the socialist revolution bitterly and are deeply antagonistic to the cultural emancipation of the worker, peasant and soldier masses. Using the positions they have occupied in the various fields of education, they have persistently carried out a bourgeois and revisionist educational line and done everything within their power to impede and sabotage the educational line of the Party's Central Committee and Chairman Mao. Unless this black anti-Party and anti-socialist line is eliminated, it is impossible to carry out the educational line of Chairman Mao.

The transformation of the present entrance examination system represents a true break-through in the struggle to apply Chairman Mao Tse-tung's educational line consistently and eliminate the bourgeois educational line thoroughly. That will be the beginning of a complete revolution in the whole of the old educational system. It is not only the system of enrollment that requires transforming, all the arrangements for schooling, for testing, for passing up or not passing up and so on, must be transformed, and so must the content of education. Further investigation must be made as to how to implement the policy of combining education with productive labor. We must relegate to the morgue all the old teaching material that goes against Mao Tse-tung's thought, that seriously departs from the three great revolutionary movements of class struggle, the struggle for production, and scientific experimentation, or that inculcates an exploiting class world outlook. New teaching material must be compiled under the guidance of Mao Tse-tung's thought and the principle of placing proletarian extracts from Chairman Mao's works and the senior classes can study more of them and also some of the articles including "Serve the People," "In Memory of Norman Bethune" and "The Foolish Old Man Who Removed the Mountains." Middle school students can study "Selected Readings from Mao Tse-tung's Works" and articles related to these readings. College students can study "The Selected Works of Mao Tse-tung." The study of Chairman Mao's works should be listed as a compulsory course in all schools, whether primary or intermediate or institutions of higher learning.

This revolution in the educational system, beginning with the change in the system of enrollment, is a tit-for-tat struggle between the proletariat and the bourgeoisie, between the road of socialism and the road of capitalism. It is a revolution that will destroy the bourgeoisie's "nursery" and eradicate the poisonous roots of revisionism. As the letter from the revolutionary pupils of the Peking No. 4 Middle School declares: "What we are out to smash is not just an examination system but the cultural shackles imposed on the people for thousands of years, the breeding ground in which intellectual aristocrats and high-salaried strata are nurtured, the stepping stone to modern revisionism. Our revolutionary actions will deal the bourgeoisie a fatal blow." The transformation of the educational system in the final analysis affects the question of what sort of successors we shall produce, the question of whether we shall pass on Mao Tse-tung's thought from generation to generation, the question of whether our Party and country will change color.

A thoroughgoing revolution in the educational system will destroy the influence of the old, exploiting class educational ideas which have dominated for several thousand years, ever since Confucius, and will extirpate one of the important seats of power of the bourgeois "authorities" and scholar-tyrants in the field of ideology. Those anti-Party, anti-socialist representatives of the bourgeoisie, and the monsters and demons of all sorts, will not reconcile themselves to being defeated. They always stubbornly defend their reactionary positions, fight every inch of the way and never willingly retreat a single step. If we don't hit them, they won't fall, and after they fall they try to stand up again. Therefore, the transformation of the educational system will certainly be a process of sharp and complex class struggle. We must at all times be ready to meet every challenge presented by the reactionary classes and their representatives, and to deal them resolute and destructive blows.

We must warn those high and mighty anti-Party and anti-socialist bourgeois "authorities" who are occupying positions in the educational world: the food you eat is provided by the working people, the clothes you wear are provided by the working people, and yet under the signboard of "serving the people" you are doing mischief against the people and the revolution. You have taken the offsprings of the reactionary classes to your bosoms and in a hundred and one ways have thwarted, spurned and attacked the children of the working people. You have collaborated with and encouraged the anti-Party and anti-socialist bourgeois "specialists" and "professors" to spread bourgeois and revisionist poison. With so much wickedness to your account, with such a debt you owe the people can we possibly allow you to continue your misdeeds without exposing you, without criticizing you, without fighting you? Don't imagine that you will remain on your "thrones" just because you have established a group of royalists, don't dream that you will be able to carry on and get by or that after a time you will revert to your former state and resurrect your reactionary class "hereditary treasures." This is absolutely out of the question. Responding to the fighting call of the Central Committee of the Chinese Communist Party and Chairman Mao Tse-tung, the masses of the workers, peasants and soldiers and of the revolutionary cadres and revolutionary intellectuals have made up their minds to expose all you monsters, to uproot you, to rid you of all your "imposing airs" and smash your bourgeois "hereditary treasures" to pieces.

The transformation of the educational system is a complicated and difficult task. So long as we, in firm accordance with Chairman Mao's instructions, have full confidence in the masses, rely on them, mobilize them fully, and energetically develop the mass movements, we shall destroy the strongholds of the bourgeoisie and win complete victory for the revolution of educational system.

Let the great red banner of Mao Tse-tung's thought fly, forever high, over our proletarian educational front!

6.9 "Loud Cheers for the Results of Paichiachuang Middle School in Military Training"

In marking the 10th anniversary of the publication of Chairman Mao's *On the Correct Handling of Contradictions among the People,* we wish to recommend to all the experience of the Paichiachuang Middle School in forging its revolutionary great alliance. . . .

In his great work, *On the Correct Handling of Contradictions among the People,* Chairman Mao points out: "The proletariat seeks to transform the world according to its own world outlook, and so does the bourgeoisie. In this respect, the question of which will win out, socialism or capitalism, is still not really settled."

No school can be a place of vacuum. If the proletariat does not occupy it, the bourgeoisie will certainly do so. If the proletarian revolutionary line does not rule it, the bourgeois reactionary line will certainly do so.

"Loud Cheers for the Results of Paichiachuang Middle School in Military Training," Peking, *Tsao-fan Chih-sheng* [*Voice of Rebels* (Published by Ch'aoyang *Ch'u* Committee, Red Guard Congress of Metropolitan Middle Schools)], (June 30, 1967), *Survey of China Mainland Press,* No. 212 (November 29, 1967), pp. 1-3.

Who occupies a school? Who rules it? This is an important question bearing on which class will train up successors, on whether or not Mao Tse-tung's thought can be handed down from one generation to another for milleniums, and on the future of China and the fate of the world.

It is from this high altitude that the PLA comrades carrying out military and political training at the Paichiachuang Middle School proceed to understand problems, perform their tasks and educate the masses. That is why they have gained a wealth of experience and set a brilliant example.

The experience of the Paichiachuang Middle School teaches us: "To forge a revolutionary great alliance proletarian revolutionaries must firmly grasp the general orientation of struggle in close coordination with the work of struggle, criticism and transformation in their respective units."

Chairman Mao teaches us: "We are confronted by two types of social contradictions—those between ourselves and the enemy and those among the people themselves. The two are totally different in their nature."

To mix up these two types of contradictions of different nature will shift the general orientation of struggle and allow the enemy to escape. What is called the general orientation of struggle refers to the need to point the spearhead at the handful of top Party persons in authority taking the capitalist road and at the bourgeois reactionary line represented by them.

It goes without saying that criticism and repudiation on such a big scale cannot be carried out in separation from the struggle-criticism-transformation of one's own unit. The two form an organic unity. When one carries out criticism and repudiation behind closed doors in separation from the general orientation of struggle, one would resemble a blind man riding a blind ass and would lead astray the struggle between lines. When one does not carry out criticism and repudiation in coordination with the struggle-criticism-transformation of one's own unit, it would likewise be impossible to basically remove the remnant poison of capitalist restoration. Nor would it be possible to isolate to the greatest extent the Party persons in authority, large and small, who take the capitalist road. And the revolutionary masses would also be unable to get real training. We must never assume an air of pedantry and over-simplify the complex class struggle.

The experience of the Paichiachuang Middle School teachers us: "To forge a revolutionary great alliance calls for the correct treatment of the befuddled masses. Proletarian revolutionaries must be broad-minded. They must be good at uniting not only with the people whose views are identical with their but also with those whose views are different from theirs. In addition, they must be good at uniting with the people who had once opposed them and who have now been proved in practice to have committed mistakes. We must deal with the befuddled masses sternly but give them warm-hearted assistance and strive to take the initiative. We must do penetrating, meticulous, patient and hard ideological work.

Chairman Mao says: "All problems of an ideological nature and all problems involving disputes among the people can only be solved by democratic means, through discussion and criticism and by methods of persuasive education. They cannot be solved by force, coercion or suppression."

In regard to those members of the public who are willing to remold themselves and are determined to stand on the side of Chairman Mao's revolutionary line, a warm welcome should be extended to them and active steps should be taken to unite them. At no time should the spearhead be directed at the masses. Otherwise, it will turn upside down the relationship between the enemy and ourselves, confuse the principal contradiction with secondary contradictions and thus lead to the commission of gross mistakes.

Naturally we must thoroughly expose and resolutely struggle against the die-hards who have up to now still refused to come to their senses, regarding themselves as being of a "noble breed," singing the praises of the bourgeois reactionary line and instigating the masses to fight among themselves.

The experience of the Paichiachuang Middle School teaches us that in a school where the struggle between two lines is extremely sharp a factor of key importance contributing to the formation of a revolutionary great alliance within a short time is the correct and satisfactory support of the PLA for the Left. PLA soldiers take the stand of the Left and have the ideas and feelings of the Left. They regard the crises facing the Left as their own. They think in the same way as the Leftists.

When the Leftists temporarily constituted a minority and were attacked on all sides by conservative influences, they stepped out without the slightest hesitation to give resolute support to the Leftists. When leftist organizations encountered new problems, they promptly used Chairman Mao's thought to help them find the right direction. With unswerving determination they fought together with the Leftists, won victories together with them and assisted them to seize power successfully and hold it firmly in their hands.

The experience of the Paichiachuang Middle School teaches us: "In order to forge a revolutionary great alliance we must have the steadfast revolutionary Leftists as the core of leadership in the alliance." The reason is that the Leftists, having fought their way out of the struggle between two lines, have an unbounded measure of fervent love for Chairman Mao. They worship him without reserve. They understand most profoundly and implement most resolutely his proletarian revolutionary line.

They may have committed mistakes and shown shortcomings of this or that kind, but the general orientation they have been pursuing has been correct from beginning to end. They dare to think, to speak, to blaze the trail, to charge at the enemy and to criticize the old world. They have a strong spirit of revolution and rebellion. When power is held in the hands of such steadfast, revolutionary Leftists, it stands for proletarian authority, for the best consolidation of this authority.

The forging of a revolutionary great alliance at the Paichiachuang Middle School is inseparable from the work of the PLA comrades. These comrades hold high the great red banner of Mao Tse-tung's thought, lead military training with political training and adhere to the proletarian revolutionary line represented by Chairman Mao. They go deep into reality, conduct investigation and study in a thorough-going way, hear the views of many quarters and cooperate closely with the broad mass of revolutionary teachers and students. They regard themselves not only as a revolutionary force but also as a revolutionary target. In the course of the struggle between two lines they educate themselves as well as the masses.

We should therefore make a good effort to learn from the PLA comrades. Just as Chairman Mao points out: "Sending troops and cadres to train revolutionary teachers and students is a very good method. There is a big difference between little training and no training. Through training the teachers and students will be able to learn from the PLA politics, military affairs, the Four Firsts, the "3-8" Style of Work, the Three Main Rules of Discipline and the Eight Points for Attention. They will also be able to strengthen their sense of organization and discipline."

The experience of the Paichiachuang Middle School is very good, indeed. Facts have proved that without a revolutionary great alliance there can be no revolutionary "three-way alliance," no seizure of power to speak of and no struggle-criticism-transformation in one's own unit to carry out. This is the key of keys and the foundation of foundations.

The broad mass of revolutionary teachers, revolutionary students and Red Guard fighters, we should to the fullest extent act according to Chairman Mao's instruction of "March 7," actively respond to his great call for supporting the army and cherishing the people, correctly apply the formula of unity-criticism-unity, correctly deal with the contradictions among the people, closely cooperate with the PLA successfully carry out military and political training and carry through to the end the great proletarian cultural revolution in middle schools.

6.10 "Universities and Middle and Primary Schools Must Resume Classes While Making Revolution"

Following is the full text of a *Jen-min Jih-pao* editorial of October 25, entitled: "Universities and Middle and Primary Schools Must Resume Classes While Making Revolution":

To resume studies while making revolution is an urgent need of the great proletarian cultural revolution at the present stage; it is also the common wish of the broad masses of revolutionary teachers and students and the vast revolutionary masses.

The "Decision of the Central Committee of the Chinese Communist Party Concerning the Great Proletarian Cultural Revolution," namely, the 16-point decision which was formulated under the personal direction of Chairman Mao, points out: "An extremely important task of the present great proletarian cultural revolution is to reform the old education system and'the old guidelines and methods of teaching."

On May 7, 1966, in a programmatic directive, Chairman Mao indicated the basic direction for the educational revolution: "Students, while taking studies as the main task, should learn other things as well, namely, besides learning literature, they must also learn industry, agriculture, and military science, and they must also criticize the bourgeoisie. The duration of courses of study should be shortened and education must be revolutionized. The situation in which bourgeois intellectuals rule our schools cannot be allowed to continue."

At the moment, the great proletarian cultural revolution has won a decisive victory. After a year and more of the great proletarian cultural revolution, a handful of counter-revolutionary revisionists on the educational front have been dragged out, and the revisionist educational line represented by China's Khrushchev has been subjected to mass criticism. This paves the way for reform of the old educational system and the old guidelines and methods of teaching.

Under these circumstances, it is entirely possible and necessary for schools of all types to turn from suspension of classes for making revolution to resumption of classes for making revolution, and the broad masses of revolutionary teachers and students should concentrate their strength on struggle, criticism and transformation in their own schools.

It is an arduous task to proceed with struggle, criticism and transformation and to complete the reform of teaching in one's own school. For this, it is imperative to trust and rely on the masses, freely mobilize the masses, bring the enthusiasm and creativeness of the broad masses of revolutionary teachers and students into full play, hold high the revolutionary red banner of Mao Tse-tung's thought, and let all exercise their brains and think out methods.

Editorial, "Universities and Middle and Primary Schools Must Resume Classes While Making Revolution," *Jen-min Jih-pao,* October 25, 1967, *Current Background,* No. 846 (February 8, 1968), pp. 15-17.

Reform of teaching must be integrated with the practice of teaching. Teaching and reform should go hand in hand. Without practice of teaching, one will not know how to carry out reform. Chairman Mao teaches us: ". . . If you want to acquire knowledge you must take part in the practice of changing reality. If you want to know how a pear tastes, you must change the pear, that is, put it into your own mouth and eat it." Only by taking part in the practice of teaching and through mass discussion, criticism, revolution and creation shall we be able to implement Chairman Mao's idea on the educational revolution, get to know the law of educational revolution under the socialist system, and gradually put forward plans for revolutionizing the system and content of teaching.

Resuming studies while making revolution and making a success of the struggle, criticism and transformation in schools is a struggle between two classes, two roads and two lines. It is a struggle between two kinds of world outlook. All schools must seriously execute Chairman Mao's great directive concerning struggle against selfish ideas and criticism of revisionism, and must teach every revolutionary teacher and student to wage a fierce struggle against the "self-interest" in his mind and, with a high sense of proletarian revolutionary responsibility, thoroughly criticize the revisionist educational line represented by China's Khrushchev and set up in a big way the proletarian educational line of Chairman Mao. All revolutionary comrades must be constantly on their guard against the destructive activities of the class enemies.

To grasp this basic issue—struggle against selfish ideas and criticizing revisionism, it is necessary to grasp tightly the political and ideological work of the revolutionary teachers and students and grasp penetrating criticism of the revisionist educational line. In this way, a good job can be done of resuming classes while making revolution, and the educational revolution will be realistically effected.

In the course of resuming classes while making revolution, revolutionary mass organizations and revolutionary Red Guards in all schools must observe Chairman Mao's "March 7" directive, study the experience of Yenan Middle School of Tientsin, and, on the revolutionary principle and according to the system of classes, grades and departments, realize a revolutionary great alliance, help the revolutionary cadres and teachers to come out, and set up a leadership group of revolutionary three-way combination.

While studies are being resumed in the midst of revolution, both revolutionary teachers and revolutionary cadres should constantly remind themselves that the work in which they are engaged has a great bearing on the cultivation of successors to the proletarian revolution. They should have the courage and the determination to thoroughly criticize the old educational system and completely break with their own bourgeois world outlook. They should realize that they are both educators and the educated, and that their students are wiser than they in many respects. They must go to the students, mingle with them, and establish a new-type teacher-student relationship of socialism.

In the matter of resuming studies while making revolution, the principle of achieving rejuvenation through self-reliance and practicing industry and economy must also be observed. Expedient measures should be taken, and all should help solve the problems relating to material and equipment. The students should be taught to cherish State property, and parents too should step up political and ideological education of their children in cooperation with the school.

It is a proud and great undertaking to fulfill the task of the proletarian educational revolution. We must use Chairman Mao's idea on educational revolution as a weapon, and become brave pathfinders for the educational revolution, getting rid of all stumbling blocks. Fearless, courageous, resourceful, and undaunted, we must be bold enough to eliminate those bourgeois old conventions which are against the thought of Mao Tse-tung, and propose a new socialist educational system, new content and methods of teaching that conform to the thought of Mao Tse-tung. In the recurrent process of practice, knowledge, more practice and more knowledge, in the course of repeated revolutionary practice, we must continue to sum up experience and build up a brightly red proletarian educational system glittering with the light of Mao Tse-tung's thought.

6.11 "The Road for Training Engineering and Technical Personnel Indicated by the Shanghai Machine Tools Plant"

THE ROAD FOR TRAINING ENGINEERING AND TECHNICAL PERSONNEL INDICATED BY THE SHANGHAI MACHINE TOOLS PLANT

(Report of an Investigation)

Renmin Ribao Editor's Note: We recommend this investigation report to proletarian revolutionary comrades throughout the land, to the broad masses of workers, poor and lower-middle peasants, students, revolutionary intellectuals and revolutionary cadres. It vividly illustrates the tremendous changes of the great proletarian cultural revolution in a particular sphere, that is, in the ranks of engineering and technical personnel. It shows the robust vitality of new socialist things. The report is entitled "The Road for Training Engineering and Technical Personnel Indicated by the Shanghai Machine Tools Plant", but at the same time it has also set forth the orientation for the revolution in education in schools and colleges.

In these penetrating words Chairman Mao recently pointed out:

> It is still necessary to have universities; here I refer mainly to colleges of science and engineering. However, it is essential to shorten the length of schooling, revolutionize education, put proletarian politics in command and take the road of the Shanghai Machine Tools Plant in training technicians from among the workers. Students should be selected from among workers and peasants with practical experience, and they should return to production after a few years' study.

This great call of Chairman Mao's is our militant programme for carrying the proletarian revolution in education through to the end. It is a task of fundamental importance for hundreds of years to oppose and prevent revisionism. Revolutionary committees at all levels throughout the country and all genuine proletarian revolutionary comrades in factories, schools and on other fronts must resolutely carry out Chairman Mao's proletarian educational line, repudiate the revisionist educational line, smash the old, bourgeois educational system, resolutely take the road indicated by Chairman Mao—the road of integration with the workers, peasants and soldiers, and carry the revolution in education through to the end.

Scientific research institutions and leading organs should also study this report

---

Wenhui Bao and Hsinhua correspondents, "The Road for Training Engineering and Technical Personnel Indicated by the Shainghai Machine Tools Plant" [Originally published in *Renmin Ribao*, July 22, 1968], *Take the Road of the Shanghai Machine Tools Plant in Training Technicians from Among the Workers* (Peking: Foreign Language Press, 1968), pp. 1-29.

carefully. It is a sharp weapon for further repudiating the counter-revolutionary revisionist line in science and technology pursued by China's Khrushchov.

The immense historic significance of the great proletarian cultural revolution and the far-reaching effects of this revolution in various fields are just beginning to make themselves felt. The great proletarian cultural revolution is bound to create conditions for a new industrial revolution in our country. The great creative force of the masses of the people will constantly perform miracles which are unimaginable to bourgeois philistines and Right conservatives. We would like to advise those who are short-sighted but who nevertheless are not die-hard capitalist roaders to look a bit further ahead, and to advise those college students who look down upon the workers and peasants and think themselves marvellous to throw off their affected airs so that they can quickly catch up with the hundreds of millions of revolutionary people who are advancing with mighty strides.

PROFOUND CHANGES BROUGHT ABOUT
BY THE GREAT PROLETARIAN CULTURAL REVOLUTION

The Shanghai Machine Tools Plant is a large factory famous for its production of precision grinding machines. It has a technical force of more than 600 engineers and technicians which is made up of people from three sources: 45 per cent of them are from the ranks of the workers, 50 percent are post-liberation college graduates and the remainder are old technicians trained before liberation. The tempest of the great proletarian cultural revolution has brought about a profound change in the ranks of the technicians of this plant.

This great revolutionary change manifests itself mainly in the following ways:

First, the proletarian revolutionaries have truly taken into their hands the leadership in the factory, including power over technical matters. The reactionary bourgeois technical "authorities" who formerly controlled the leadership in technical matters have been overthrown. Many technicians of worker origin, revolutionary young technicians and revolutionary cadres are now the masters in scientific research and technical designing. They are proletarian revolutionary fighters with deep class feelings for Chairman Mao and the Communist Party. These revolutionary technicians, once ignored and held back, now continually display their creative power and technical ability. Boundlessly loyal to Chairman Mao's proletarian revolutionary line, they have scaled one technical height after another. In the first half of this year, they successfully trial-produced ten new types of precision grinders, four of which reached advanced international standards. This is without parallel in the history of the plant both in regard to speed and quality of production.

Second, the counter-revolutionary revisionist line pushed by China's Khrushchov in the technical sphere and the reactionary bourgeois world outlook have been sharply criticized. Politically, the reactionary bourgeois technical "authorities" have become infamous, and technically, their incompetence—the incompetence of paper tigers—has been fully exposed. In the past, the capitalist roaders did their utmost to idolize the reactionary "authorities," urging the young technicians to learn from them, "measure up" to them and "work hard in order to become engineers." The mental outlook of many of the young technicians has now undergone a marked change. They understand that the desire for fame and gain is the root cause of revisionism and that one should not seek bourgeois laurels. Many research workers in the grinder research department used to note down technical information which they regarded as their own private "property." Now they have voluntarily handed this material over to the collective, and it has been put together in the form of reference books, available for use by everyone. All the technicians have volunteered to work in the shops alongside the workers. Together they study and improve designs. While working in the shops, the old technicians pay attention to casting off their airs of superiority and learning modestly from the workers.

Third, relations between the workers and technicians have changed. The few capitalist roaders and reactionary "authorities" in the plant advocated a "one-to-one" combination, that is, one worker serving one technician. This so-called combination meant "the engineer gives the word and the worker does the job" or "the engineer has the idea and the worker carries it out." This was still the old nonsense of "those who do mental labour rule, while those who work with their hands are ruled." They also advanced the reactionary theory that "workers and technicians should act as a check on each other" and "form a pair of opposites." They put out a set of rules and regulations to control, check and suppress the workers. Every worker was expected to memorize and act on the more than 170 rules in the "Handbook for a Worker in Production." All this further widened the gap between workers and technicians. During the great cultural revolution, a "three-in-one" combination of workers, revolutionary technicians and revolutionary cadres was introduced in the plant. The rank-and-file workers now take part in designing and the technicians go to operate machines in the first line of production, closely linking theory with practice. As a result, there is a big improvement in the relations between workers and technicians.

ROAD FOR TRAINING ENGINEERING AND TECHNICAL PERSONNEL

The young technicians (including those around 35 years of age) at the plant come from two sources: college graduates (numbering some 350, of whom one-tenth are post-graduates or graduates of colleges abroad) and technical personnel promoted from among the workers (numbering around 250, a few of them with several years at secondary technical schools). The facts show that the latter are better than the former. Generally speaking, the former have a great number of backward ideas and are less competent in practical work, while the latter are more advanced ideologically and are more competent in practical work. At present, the overwhelming majority of the technical personnel of worker origin have become the technological backbone of the plant and about one-tenth of them are capable of independently designing high-grade, precision and advanced new products. The chief designers of six of the ten new precision grinding machines successfully trial-produced in the first half of this year are technical personnel of worker origin.

Selecting technical personnel from among the workers is the road for training proletarian engineers and technicians.

Here is an example of a sharp contrast between two technicians of about the same age but with different experiences,

One is a Shanghai college student who, after graduation, spent one year studying a foreign language. Then he went abroad for further study, and four years later, was there granted the academic degree of *kandidat nauk* (Bachelor of Science). In 1962, he went to work as a technician in the laboratory of the grinder research department of the plant. Although he has studied for over 20 years in schools, for quite a long time he has not made any significant achievement in scientific research because his theoretical studies were divorced from practice and he failed to integrate himself well with the workers.

The other is a worker who began as an apprentice at the age of 14. At 18, he was sent to a technical school for machine building in Shanghai where he studied for four years. In 1957, he began to work as a technician in the same research department. In April of this year, with him as the chief designer, a huge surface grinding machine was successfully trial-produced. The machine is up to advanced international standards and is urgently needed to advance China's industrial technology. It fills in a blank in the country's production of precision grinders.

Before the great cultural revolution, the handful of capitalist roaders in the Party and reactionary technical "authorities" rabidly barred the workers from undertaking designing. Around 1958, a number of workers were promoted to be technicians. But the reactionary "authorities" in the plant one after another removed quite a number of them from the designing department on all sorts of pretexts. Nevertheless, technical personnel of worker origin broke through one obstacle after another and demonstrated their rich resourcefulness and creative power. Of the new products designed and successfully trial-produced by the plant since 1958, those successfully trial-produced by technical personnel of worker origin and by young technicians in co-operation with the workers accounted for about 60 per cent in 1958, about 70 percent in 1959, and about 80 per cent in 1960. In the years following 1960, especially since the start of the great proletarian cultural revolution, nearly all the new products were designed and successfully trial-produced by them. Quite a number of these new products are up to advanced international standards. For instance, the universal cylindrical grinding machine for mirror surface grinding, the high-centre cylindrical grinding machine and other major products were all designed and successfully trial-produced by technical personnel of worker origin.

Some young technicians who are college graduates, gradually freeing themselves of the influence of the revisionist educational line, have thrown off their affected airs and are integrating themselves with the workers. After some time of practice, they have also made fairly noteworthy contributions in designing and trial-producing new products. Take a certain 1964 college graduate for example. When he came to the plant, he pored all day long over a foreign book on the thread grinding machine. (We do not mean to say that it is unnecessary to read foreign books.) Proceeding from theory to theory, he did not create anything in his work for several years. During the great cultural revolution, his class consciousness and his understanding of the struggle between the proletarian revolutionary line and the bourgeois reactionary line have been raised. He firmly resolved to take the road of integrating himself with the workers. Early this year, together with two workers-turned-technicians and a veteran worker, he succeeded in trial-producing an important electrical device needed for grinders.

Why do technicians of worker origin develop more quickly and make greater contributions?

The most important reason is that they have profound proletarian feelings for Chairman Mao and the Party and, in their advance along the road of science and technology, they seek neither fame nor gain, and defy all danger and difficulty to reach their objective. They always bear in mind the teachings of Chairman Mao and strive to overtake the imperialists, revisionists and reactionaries in speed of advance and quality. They always look for ways to economize for the state and arrange things to suit the convenience of the workers. However, some young intellectuals who had been poisoned by the revisionist educational line were for a long time divorced from the shops and the workers, chased bourgeois fame and gain and as a result achieved nothing. In his desire to win fame and become an expert overnight and surprise people, one technician did work on more than 60 subjects during the past decade and more, hopping from one new project to another, but he did not carry a single one to success and wasted much state money into the bargain. In the hope of winning fame, a 1956 college graduate experiemented with grinding heads all by himself and ruined more than 30. Later, he learnt from veteran workers and with their help succeeded. With deep understanding he said: "I suffered from making the grinding head behind closed doors and I succeeded in making it by integrating with the workers. After all, I must 'grind' my own head before I can make a good grinding head."

The contrast between technicians of worker origin and the old bourgeois intellectuals who are eaten up with the desire for personal fame and gain is even more striking. One bourgeois "expert" spent eight years trying to design a grinder and wasted a large amount of state funds, without success; but he accumulated considerable "data" as capital for his own reputation and gain. The workers say: How can we expect persons like him to have the slightest feeling for our new society?

Chairman Mao says: "The fighters with the most practical experience are the wisest and the most capable." In their long period of work in the shops, the technicians of worker origin accumulated rich practical experience. Having studied for a few years in spare-time general or technical schools, they closely link the theory they have learnt with their practical experience, thus a leap is achieved in their knowledge and soon they are able to do scientific research work and independent designing. This is a very important reason for their rapid maturing. When they study, they have specific problems in mind, therefore, they can learn and understand quickly and apply what they learn. One technician of worker origin drew on his rich practical experience and solved complicated technological problems in making a certain product. As he did the experiments, he studies the principles of metal cutting. He was soon able to raise his practical experience to the level of theory and advanced some original views on the technology of metal cutting.

Before they integrate themselves with the workers, college-trained technicians are lacking in practical experience. Their book knowledge is divorced from practice. Therefore they are scarcely able to achieve anything. Once a few college-trained technicians deficient in practical experience designed an internal thread grinding machine. The workers followed their blueprints in making the parts, but they could not be assembled. Later, some workers with rich practical experience had to reprocess some of the parts before it was possible to assemble the machine.

The combination of the revolutionary spirit of daring to think, to act and to make a break-through with a strict scientific attitude is an essential prerequisite for engineering and technical personnel in scaling the heights of science and technology. Whether or not they are able to achieve this combination is, in its turn, closely connected with their world outlook as well as their practical experience. Many technicians of worker origin, free from the spiritual fetters of working for personal fame or gain and rich in practical experience, dare to do away with fetishes and superstitions and break through all unnecessary restrictions and are the least conservative in their thinking. Take, for instance, the recently successfully trial-produced precision grinder which has reached advanced international standards. Because the technicians of worker origin courageously broke through long-standing restrictions, they cut the time needed to make the prototype from the usual 18 months to six. The surface finish was advanced four grades, and the number of parts and the total weight were both reduced by one-third. It cost only 15.5 per cent of the price of an imported precision grinder of the same type. Some technicians trained in schools do not pay attention to their own ideological remoulding. They are prone to be concerned with personal gains and losses, and fear to lose face and "prestige." Besides, because they have accommodated themselves to many regulations and restrictions, it is not easy for them to do away with fetishes and superstitions and evolve new technologies. Some of them say: "The more books one reads, the heavier the yoke becomes. And, as a result, one scarcely has any go left in him."

If faced with a choice between graduates from colleges and graduates from secondary technical schools, the workers in the Shanghai Machine Tools Plant prefer the latter because they, though with less book knowledge, are less conceited, have more practical experience and are less bound by foreign conventions. Quite a number of students in this category have made much more rapid progress than students from colleges. For example, the current designing of two highly efficient automatic production lines is led by a couple of 1956 graduates from secondary technical schools.

THE ORIENTATION FOR EDUCATIONAL REVOLUTION
INDICATED BY THE PLANT

An analysis of the different types of engineering and technical personnel at the Shanghai Machine Tools Plant and the roads they have travelled shows us the orientation for the revolution in education. From practical experience, the veteran workers and many of the young technical personnel of the plant have come to realize more deeply the unparalleled wisdom and correctness of Chairman Mao's teaching: "The domination of our schools by bourgeois intellectuals should by no means be allowed to continue." They find that the carrying out of the proletarian revolution in education in accordance with Chairman Mao's thinking on education is a matter of great importance which brooks no delay. Chairman Mao's series of instructions on the revolution in education have shown us the way forward. The question now is to act unswervingly and faithfully in line with Chairman Mao's teachings.

In accordance with Chairman Mao's thinking on education and in view of the actual conditions in the plant, the workers and technical personnel put forward the following opinions and ideas in respect to the revolution in education:

First, schools must train up "workers with both socialist consciousness and culture" as pointed out by Chairman Mao and not "intellectual aristocrats" who are divorced from proletarian politics, from the worker and peasant masses and from production, as the revisionist educational line produced. This is a cardinal question which concerns whether or not revisionism will emerge. Comrades at the Shanghai Machine Tools Plant are of the opinion that the past practice of college graduates working as cadres in factories or in the countryside right after their graduation was irrational. Integrating themselves with the workers and peasants and participating in productive labour is the essential way for young students to remould their world outlook and gain practical technical knowledge. Therefore, the comrades propose that college graduates should first take part in manual labour in factories or in the countryside and work as ordinary labourers. They should get "qualification certificates" from the workers and peasants, and then, according to the needs of the practical struggle, some may take up technical work while participating in labour for a certain amount of time. The others will remain workers or peasants.

Second, school education must be combined with productive labour. Chairman Mao teaches: "Our chief method is to learn warfare through warfare." As was seen from the case of some technical personnel at the Shanghai Machine Tools Plant, one serious drawback of the old educational system was that theory was divorced from practice and unnecessary complexity was the rule so that the students became bookworms and the more they read the more foolish they became. Only by going to practice, can one grasp theory quickly, understand it profoundly and apply it creatively. Workers and technical personnel at this plant suggest that schools should have experienced workers as teachers and let workers appear on the classroom platform. Some courses can be given by workers in the workshops. There was a young technician who worked in a research institute right after he had graduated from college. All day long he immersed himself in books, digging deep into theory and learning foreign languages. Since he was divorced from practice he felt more and more frustrated. In the initial stage of the great cultural revolution, he went to learn from some veteran workers with rich experience in the machine tools plant where he did practical work. As a result, things became quite different. Recently he and some workers made a significant creation in the field of mirror surface grinding. His understanding is particularly deep of the fact that he must have the workers as his teachers.

Third, as to the source of engineering and technical personnel, they maintain that, apart from continuing to promote technical personnel from among the workers, junior and senior middle school graduates who are good politically and ideologically and have two to three or four to five years of practical experience in production should be picked from grassroots units and sent to colleges to study. All conditions now exist for this to be done. Take the Shanghai Machine Tools Plant for example. Most of its workers have acquired an educational level equivalent to or above junior middle school education. The advantages in selecting such young people to go to college are as follows: first, they have a fairly solid political and ideological foundation; second, they have a certain competence in practical work and are experienced in productive labour; and third, junior and senior middle school graduates, averaging about 20 years of age after taking part in labour for a few years, would be able to work independently at the age of 23 to 24 after finishing another few years of higher education. But as it is now, after being assigned to their work posts, college graduates generally have to undertake two to three years of practical work before they are gradually able to work independently. Therefore, the selection of young intellectuals with practical experience for college training is in conformity with the principle of achieving greater, faster, better and more economical results.

Fourth, on the question of reforming the present technical force in factories and raising its level, they point out that large numbers of school-trained technical personnel have for a long time been poisoned by the revisionist educational line and the revisionist line in running enterprises. There is also a group of technical personnel trained before liberation. Though some of them are patriotic and hardworking, do not oppose the Party and socialism and maintain no illicit relations with any foreign country, they have many problems in their world outlook and style of work. Factories should hold aloft the great revolutionary banner of criticism in line with Mao Tse-tung's thought and organize them to participate actively in revolutionary mass criticism and repudiation in accordance with the policies laid down in the Decision of the Central Committee of the Chinese Communist Party Concerning the Great Proletarian Cultural Revolution. This will enable them to repudiate thoroughly the fallacies that "experts should run the factories" and "technique comes first" as well as the philosophies of "going-slow" and of "servility to things foreign" which China's Khrushchov trumpeted. It will also enable them thoroughly to repudiate bourgeois ideas of chasing after fame and fortune. Factories should, at the same time, help them take the road of integrating themselves with the workers and linking theory with practice by organizing now one group of them, now another, to work as rank-and-file workers, or by arranging more time for them to work in the workshops.

6.12 "Shanghai Workers' Propaganda Teams Mobilize Revolutionary Teachers and Students of Institutes of Higher Learning to Gradually Carry Out Chairman Mao's Latest Directives"

The time has come to reform education. According to the series of Chairman Mao's latest directives, the workers' Mao Tse-tung's thought propaganda teams led by Shanghai Municipal Revolutionary Committee have triumphantly entered all institutes of higher learning in Shanghai. This indicates the advent of an upsurge in the proletarian revolution in education and the tasks of struggle-criticism-transformation in institutes of higher learning, over which the working class of Shanghai is beginning to exercise leadership. . . .

The tasks for the Shanghai workers' Mao Tse-tung's thought propaganda teams entering institutes of higher learning are:

(1) To vigorously propagate Mao Tse-tung's thought and to join the revolutionary teachers, students, workers and staff members in organizing Mao Tse-tung's thought study classes and in studying and implementing in an all-round manner Chairman Mao's latest directives;

(2) To penetratingly carry out revolutionary mass criticism and repudiation and promote and consolidate the revolutionary great alliance and the revolutionary three-in-one combination;

(3) To promote cleaning up of the class ranks and purging of the Party;

(4) To promote the enforcement of the policy of "better troops and simpler administration";

(5) To carry out investigation and study well, to reform education and to create conditions for selecting students from among workers and peasants with practical experience.

To make a success of these tasks, the workers' propaganda teams organized Mao Tse-tung's thought study classes to carry out Chairman Mao's latest directives as soon as they entered the institutes. They carry out investigations intensively, promote the revolutionary great alliances, do a good job of cleaning up the class ranks, and earnestly implement the Party's directives and policies. . . .

Many workers said: "With Mao Tse-tung's thought, we are no longer 'rough and rude.' With Mao Tse-tung's thought, we can attain a high level." They declared that they would, in the new battle, implement the Party's directives and policies in a better way, learn from the Red Guard young fighters and revolutionary teachers, students, workers and staff members who were boundlessly loyal to Chairman Mao, form a revolutionary three-in-one combination of workers, PLA fighters and activists among students, teachers and workers in the institutes who were determined to carry the proletarian revolution in education through to the end, and triumphantly accomplish the proletarian revolution in education.

The entry of the working class in Shanghai into institutions of higher learning not only has begun to form a powerful mass campaign for all-round dictatorship of the proletariat on the front of institutes of higher learning, but also has caused tremendous social influence and motivated the revolution in other spheres of the super-

---

"Shanghai Workers' Propaganda Teams Mobilize Revolutionary Teachers and Students of Institutes of Higher Learning to Gradually Carry Out Chairman Mao's Latest Directives," Shanghai, *Wen-hui Pao,* August 31, 1968, *Survey of China Mainland Press,* No. 4265 (September 25, 1968), pp. 15-17.

structure. Many middle and primary schools, and units dealing with medicine, science, technology, literature and art ask the working class to join them, so as to have working-class leadership. This shows that the entry of workers' propaganda teams into institutions of higher learning in Shanghai and other units which have not yet carried out their tasks of struggle-criticism-transformation well will effectively accelerate the advent of the upsurge of struggle-criticism-transformation throughout the superstructure.

6.13 "The Question of Prime Importance in the Revolution of Education in the Countryside Is That the Poor and Lower-Middle Peasants Control the Power in Education"

Inspired by the excellent situation in the great proletarian cultural revolution, the poor and lower-middle peasants of the Chiuk'eng commune in Ch'unan *hsien* in February took over the management of schools and made transformation in the school system in accordance with Chairman Mao's brilliant instruction that "education should be revolutionized." Within the short period of six months, they have changed the phenomenon of bourgeois intellectuals dominating the schools and ushered in a new situation in proletarian education. Their view is that the question of prime importance in the revolution of education in the countryside is that the poor and lower-middle peasants control the power in education. Only when this question is settled, is it possible to insure the implementation of Chairman Mao's instructions on the revolution of education and enable Mao Tse-tung's thought to take firm hold of the educational positions in the countryside. . . .

PROFOUND CHANGES AFTER POOR AND LOWER-MIDDLE PEASANTS TOOK OVER EDUCATIONAL POWER.

Since taking over power in managing schools, the poor and lower-middle peasants of the Chiuk'eng commune have vigorously demolished the revisionist system of education and are firmly running the schools in accordance with Chairman Mao's thinking on education, thus bringing about profound changes in the schools.

1. The "blockade" against children of poor and lower-middle peasants has been smashed. The age limit for enrollment has been abolished, regular enrollment of new pupils is now done in the spring, but children can also go to school any time in the term, the old system of promoting pupils and keeping those who failed examinations in the same grade for another year has been discarded, the primary school period has been shortened from six to five years and these are no longer divided into two periods, and a two-year junior middle school course has been instituted in the

The Investigation Group of the Chekiang Provincial Revolutionary Committee, "The Question of Prime Importance in the Revolution of Education in the Countryside Is That the Poor and Lower-Middle Peasants Control the Power in Education" (Report on an investigation of the revolution in education in the Chiuk'eng Commune, Ch'unan *hsien*, Chekiang province), Peking, *Jen-min Jih-pao*, October 18, 1968, *Current Background*, No. 868 (December 31, 1968), pp. 1-5.

commune's central primary school. The curriculum is arranged so as to closely link the central task of the commune and brigades and the farm seasons, with less study during the busy seasons, more during the slack seasons and vacations during the busiest seasons. Since this school system meets the countryside's special requirements, school enrollment has considerably increased. The number of primary school pupils has jumped from last year's 521 to the present 818, the junior middle school course has enrolled 98 pupils, and almost all school-age children are now in school.

2. The study of Chairman Mao's writings is now put in first place and teaching is closely linked with the three great revolutionary practices of class struggle, the struggle for production and scientific experiment. The poor and lower-middle peasants have the warmest love for Chairman Mao, they understand his thinking on education best and are most opposed to study behind closed doors, which is divorced from politics and reality. Acting on their suggestion, the schools now use Chairman Mao's works as the basic teaching material, make it a regular system for studying Chairman Mao's works every day and work in a systematic way to get the pupils to take an active part in political activities and collective productive labor. This includes joining the poor and lower-middle peasants in discussing their experience in the living study and application of Mao Tse-tung's thought, undertaking revolutionary mass repudiation, joining the struggle against the enemy and spending one-third of their time in collective productive labor. This kind of education, say the revolutionary teachers and pupils, gives them ideological training and enables them to learn real skills in the struggle for production. During the last six months, many good pupils who love labor, are concerned with the collective, actively propagate Mao Tse-tung's thought and take a firm and clear-cut stand in class struggle have emerged. Seventy-five have been honored by the commune members as "red propagandists." The poor and lower-middle peasants are very happy over this. They say with satisfaction that pupils of this kind set down real roots, grow up well and are red in heart and will certainly be able to become reliable successors to the revolutionary cause of the proletariat.

3. The teachers have embarked on the road of integrating with the workers and peasants. Now that teaching is linked with the three great revolutionary practices, they teach in school while serving as pupils outside school. They are teachers when they give lectures but become pupils when poor and lower-middle peasants take the floor. In the past they feared contact with peasants and did not want to become soiled; now they work in mud alongside the peasants. Many teachers have come to deeply appreciate these teachings of Chairman Mao: "The lowly are most intelligent; the elite are most ignorant" and "the intellectuals will accomplish nothing if they fail to integrate themselves with the workers and peasants." They have given up the concept of looking down upon workers and peasants and have discarded their fancy airs. Many teachers have acquired class feeling and thus work enthusiastically to train children of poor and lower-middle peasants. If any pupil comes too late for class, the teacher promptly tutors him. Some teachers have used their own money to buy stationery for poor pupils or given their own cotton-padded coats to pupils who needed them. Despite illness, some have persisted in joining the pupils in study, labor and the struggle against the enemy. People say: "We can rest assured when we entrust our children to this kind of teacher."

4. The poor and lower-middle peasants are enthusiastic in running schools, considering them their own. Many old poor peasants have lectured to the pupils. Commune members offered their own furniture when the schools were short of desks. In March, when the commune's central primary school was applying to the *hsien* for an appropriation to build classrooms for the junior middle school course, an old poor peasant named Chien learned about it and made a special trip to the school to criticize

it for the mistake of demanding money from the state. He suggested using self-reliance to build the classrooms, and when the commune members lent a hand six classrooms able to accommodate a total of 300 pupils were soon built.

The changes in the Chiuk'eng commune are a graphic illustration of the fact that the poor and lower-middle peasants must manage schools and that they are entirely capable of running them well. Those who think they understand education best should themselves conscientiously take the poor and lower-middle peasants as teachers. . . .

6.14 "Hungch'i Middle School in Penhsi, Liaoning, Forms Textbook Compiling Group"

In accordance with Chairman Mao's proletarian line of education and under the leadership of the working class, the worker-PLA Mao Tse-tung's thought propaganda team stationed in Hungch'i Middle School affiliated to the No. 2 Steel and Iron Plant of Penhsi Steel and Iron Corporation, Liaoning Province, formed a textbook compiling group comprising workers, peasants and soldiers and revolutionary teachers and students. After making efforts for three months and more, this group compiled textbooks on politics, language, military physical culture and knowledge of industrial and agricultural production for trial use in four-year urban middle schools. In these new textbooks, the black goods of feudalism, capitalism and revisionism were crushed and Mao Tse-tung's thought was put in ascendancy. The principal characteristics of these textbooks were:

First, the black goods of feudalism, capitalism and revisionism in the old textbooks are crushed and Mao Tse-tung's thought is brought to the fore. For example, the textbooks of language and literature were formerly compiled in accordance with the different styles of the articles and vigorously disseminated feudal, superstitious ideas and the ideas of seeking a higher official post, getting rich and establishing one's fame. The new textbooks are compiled in accordance with Chairman Mao's viewpoint of the class struggle and viewpoint of dialectical materialism and are filled with the spirit of wholeheartedly serving the people and the internationalist and patriotic spirit.

With regard to the contents of these textbooks of language and literature, in addition to Chairman Mao's writings and poems, there are selected hymns, ballads, correspondence and special articles written by the Chinese people and the world's revolutionary people in praise of Chairman Mao. For the purpose of educating the students in the class struggle and the struggle between the two lines, the following have also been selected: The history of the No. 2 Steel and Iron Plant, the history of P'ienling commune, the family histories of old workers and old poor peasants and excerpts from the model Peking operas on contemporary revolutionary themes, such as "The Red Lantern," "Taking of the Bandit Stronghold" and "Shachiapang."

Reporting Group of Penhsi Municipal Revolutionary Committee, Reporting Group of Penhsi Military Subregional Command and Reporting Group of No. 2 Steel and Iron Plant of Penhsi Steel and Iron Corporation, "Hungch'i Middle School in Penhsi, Liaoning, Forms Textbook Compiling Group," Peking, *Jen-min Jih-pao,* May 8, 1969, *Survey of China Mainland Press,* No. 4419 (May 20, 1969), pp. 6-7.

These new textbooks sparkle with the splendor of Mao Tse-tung's thought.

Take the course of mathematics for example. Formerly, mathematics basically was not linked with politics and the students purely learned reasoning, theorems and formulas and did not know for whom they learned all this. At present, the mathematics course starts with the accounts of exploitation and emancipation of the workers and poor and lower-middle peasants, so as to strengthen the students' concepts of the classes and the class struggle and to solve the question of for whom these accounts are kept.

Second, the situation of separating theory from practice as in the old textbooks has come to an end and new contents serving the three great revolutionary movements are adopted. Take the course of language and literature for example. In an investigation, the compiling group discovered that some graduates did not know how to write articles of criticism and blackboard posters. Therefore, the new textbooks include articles criticizing and repudiating big renegade Liu Shao-ch'i, the program of the report on the ideas of the late Comrade Li Wen-chung, reports on investigations, articles for practical use, and other new contents. Added to the course of mathematics are such new contents as drawing of diagrams, rural accounting, working of an abacus, surveying, and use of measuring and weighing instruments.

Third, the tendency of seeking things foreign, famous and antique as taught in the old textbooks is eliminated and the teaching materials on things Chinese are adopted. For example, in the past, lessons on foreign apples were taught in Botany and lessons on the kangaroo and the crocodile were taught in Zoology, and these lessons had nothing to do with local, practical needs. Now, in the textbooks on "knowledge of industrial and agricultural production" are adopted first of all Chairman Mao's great directive on developing agriculture, the "eight-point character for agriculture," the "road taken by Tachai," and the history of the struggle between the two lines in the development of agriculture in red-banner bearer units in Liaoning Province. Meanwhile, the knowledge of cultivation and management of staple agricultural crops in the local area is also added to the textbook. The textbook on zoology also includes the method of breeding pigs, cattle, horse and sheep and common knowledge of veterinary science.

Fourth, scholasticism in the old textbooks is eliminated, so that the lessons taught are few but essential. Formerly the contents of the textbooks were pedantic and redundant and too many subjects were taught. Now, in accordance with Chairman Mao's brilliant "May 7 Directive," only five courses, namely, political science, mathematics, language, knowledge of industrial and agricultural production, and military physical culture, are offered. The contents of these courses have also been simplified. Take the course of mathematics for example. Formerly more than 1,000 sessions were needed to finish teaching the lessons for the junior and senior middle school sections. At present, only 500 sessions or more are needed.

The students were overjoyed when seeing this set of new textbooks compiled in line with the outlook of the working class. They said: "The new textbooks have been compiled very well. They are greatly different from those of the past! The old textbooks dealt with the black goods of feudalism, capitalism and revisionism while the new ones give lessons on Mao Tse-tung's thought. In the past, the lessons were about 'the murmur of a brook,' while at present the lessons tell us 'never to forget the class struggle.' In the past, the lessons were about seeking a higher official post, getting rich and taking the 'White and expert' road while at present we are taught to serve the people and to take the 'red and expert' road. The lessons taught in the past were about emperors, kings, generals, ministers, scholars and women, while the lessons taught at present deal with the heroic images of the workers, peasants and soldiers. The new textbooks are imbued with the invincible Mao Tse-tung's thought.

We must study them very well.''

Reporting Group of Penhsi Municipal
Revolutionary Committee,
Reporting Group of Penhsi Military
Subregional Command and
Reporting Group of No. 2 Steel and Iron
Plant of Penhsi Steel and Iron Corporation

6.15 "Draft Program For Primary and Middle Schools in Chinese Countryside"

The "People's Daily" yesterday published a programme for primary and middle school education in China's rural areas drafted by the Revolutionary Committee of Lishu County, Kirin Province. The draft programme filled the front page of the paper under the banner headline: "Discussion on Turning State-run Primary Schools Over to Production Brigades." This discussion has been continuing in the paper for many months.

In an editorial note accompanying the draft programme, the "People's Daily" wrote: "We are publishing the 'programme for primary and middle school education in the rural areas (draft)' worked out by the Revolutionary Committee of Lishu County, Kirin Province, for general discussion. The programme was drafted by the revolutionary committee of the county in cooperation with other departments. We made some modifications after consulting the poor and lower-middle peasants, teachers and students in a number of communes. Some of the differing views are put in parentheses. We hope that the poor and lower-middle peasants revolutionary teachers and students and the People's Liberation army commanders and fighters supporting agriculture throughout the country as well as the comrades concerned on the revolutionary committee in various provinces, regions and counties will take an active part in this discussion and put forward their suggestions for additions or modification. This will help us pool the wisdom of the masses, sum up experience and take into consideration the diverse conditions in various localities. We shall be able to improve and enrich the content of the programme and make it more suitable to the actual conditions in various places after it is discussed for some time and revised."

The programme reads in full:

**PROGRAMME FOR PRIMARY AND MIDDLE SCHOOL
EDUCATION IN THE RURAL AREAS**

(Draft, for General Discussion)

**CHAPTER ONE
GENERAL PROGRAMME**

The primary and middle schools in the rural areas are a new type of socialist school

"Draft Program For Primary and Middle Schools in Chinese Countryside" (NCNA-Engligh, Peking, May 13, 1969), *Survey of China Mainland Press,* No. 4418 (May 19, 1969), pp. 9-15.

directly managed by the poor and lower-middle peasants under the leadership of the Chinese Communist Party. These schools must hold aloft the great red banner of Mao Tse-tung thought, put proletarian politics to the fore and in an all-round way carry out Chairman Mao's "May Seventh" Directive: "**The same hold good for the students too. While their main task is to study they should also learn other things that is to say, they should not only learn book knowledge they should also learn industrial production agricultural production and military affairs. They also should criticize and repudiate the bourgeoisie.**"

The rural schools must resolutely carry out Chairman Mao's policy. "**Education must serve proletarian politics and be combined with productive labour,**" eliminate the pernicious influence of the counter-revolutionary revisionist line on education, criticize the remnants of old ideas culture customs and habits and ensure that Chairman Mao's proletarian revolutionary line commands the field of education politically ideologically and organizationally.

The primary and middle schools must meet the demand of the children of the poor and lower-middle peasants for schooling, open their doors wide to such children and truly serve the interests of the poor and lower-middle peasants and other commune members.

The aim of education in the countryside is to "**enable everyone who receives an education to develop morally intellectually and physically and become a worker with both socialist consciousness and culture.**" It should enable the young people to temper themselves in the three great revolutionary movements of class struggle, the struggle for production and scientific experiment and become reliable successors to the cause of the proletarian revolution loyal to the great leader Chairman Mao, to Mao Tse-tung thought and to Chairman Mao's revolutionary line and whole-heartedly serving the great majority of the people of China and the world.

CHAPTER TWO
LEADERSHIP

Article 1.   In acordance with Chairman Mao's teaching, "**In the countryside, schools and colleges should be managed by the poor and lower-middle peasants—the most reliable ally of the working class,**" the middle school should estabilsh "three-in-one" revolutionary committee which comprise poor and lower-middle peasants, who are the mainstay commune and brigade cadres and representatives of the revolutionary teachers and students. Such committee should be placed under the leadership of the party organizations and revolutionary committees of the commune and the production brigade. The primary school should be placed under the unified leadership of the brigade's leading group in charge of education. Representatives of the school who are members of the leading group are in charge of the routine work of the schools.

(Some comrades think that the commune revolutionary committee should establish a committee for the revolution in education, but some other comrades hold that such a committee is unnecessary.)

Article 2.   Following are the main tasks of the poor and lower-middle peasants in managing the schools: ensure that Chairman Mao's proletarian line and principles on education and his proletarian policies are carried out to the letter; do a good job in the school's struggle-criticism-transformation by depending on "**the masses of revolutionary students, teachers and workers in the schools and colleges and on the activists among them**"; bring about the ideological revolutionization of the teachers; and decide upon and review the expenditure of the schools.

Article 3.   In managing schools the poor and lower-middle peasants should apply the principle of democratic centralism, exercise political leadership over the schools and hear reports on the work at regular intervals. The representatives of the poor and lower-middle peasants should constantly supervise and review the work of the schools. They should study the important questions in the schools and take decisions on them. Under ordinary circumstances, they should fulfill their duty in their spare time.

CHAPTER THREE
IDEOLOGICAL AND POLITICAL WORK

Article 4.   Politics is the commander, the soul in everything. The fundamental task in the ideological and political work of these schools is to ensure that Mao Tse-tung thought take firm front in all positions of education and that the living study and application of Mao Tse-tung thought is put in first place in all the work of the schools.

Article 5.   Arm the teachers and students with Chairman Mao's theory of continuing the revolution under the dictatorship of the proletariat, constantly familiarize them with the situation and tasks and the principles and policies of the party and raise their consciousness of class struggle and the struggle between the two lines. Teach the students to have a clear aim in studying and to take the revolutionary road of integrating themselves with the workers, peasants and soldiers.

(Some comrades suggest that "educate the students always to maintain the line qualities of the poor and lower-middle peasants" should be added to the ideological and political work.)

Article 6.   Learn from the Liberation Army, give prominence to proletarian politics, persist in the "four firsts" [1] and energetically foster the "three-in-one" working style[2].

Article 7.   A new-type, proletarian relationship between the teachers and students should be established in the rural primary and middle schools: they should encourage each other politically help each other ideologically, learn from each other in teaching and study and care for each other's welfare.

Article 8.   Education by the school, society and the family should be combined, and the three sides should jointly shoulder their responsibility for doing good ideological and political work among the students.

Article 9.   Bring into full play the exemplary and vanguard role of the Communist Youth League members and Red Guards in the schools and enable them to help the party organizations and school revolutionary committees to do a good job in ideological and political work. They should actively propagate Mao Tse-tung thought, take part in extra-curricular public activities and strengthen their revolutionary spirit, scientific approach and sense of organization and discipline.

(Some comrades suggest adding "consolidate the Little Red Soldier organizations".)

CHAPTER FOUR
DISTRIBUTION OF SCHOOLS AND LENGTH OF SCHOOLING

Article 10.   All irrational rules and regulations in the old schools should be abolished. Necessary proletarian rules and regulations should be instituted in accordance with specific conditions and a revolutionary new order established.

Article 11.   In setting up such primary and middle schools, the principle of **"Make it convenient for peasants' children to go to nearby schools"** should be followed and the confines of administrative areas should be broken.

The primary school should be run by the production brigade. The middle school should be run by the commune, or branches of it set up in several villages, or run jointly by brigades, or run solely by a brigade where conditions permit. The commune of the brigades will cover the school expenses, plus state aid.

Article 12. There should be an uninterrupted nine-year system, and the division into stages can be made according to local needs and conditions.

Article 13. In accordance with the specific needs of local agricultural development counties and commune may run some agricultural technical schools enrolling students who come from and will return to their communes after graduation so as to popularize agro-technique and train agro-technicians.

Article 14. Eliminate age restrictions for enrollment, which were enforced by the counter-revolutionary revisionist line. Abolish the old systems for examination and leaving students in the same class without promotion. Allow those students who excel politically, ideologically and in their studies to jump a grade.

The enrollment for middle schools should be both by recommendation and selection giving priority to the children of workers, poor and lower-middle peasants, revolutionary martyrs and armymen.

(As regards the proper age to start primary school, some think it should be at age six while others think it should be at age seven.)

Article 15. The school year in general should start in the spring so as to facilitate over-all unified state planning.

Article 16. Those who complete rural primary and middle schools should mainly work in the countryside; they should take part in the three great revolutionary movements of class struggle, the struggle for production and scientific experiment, and work for socialist construction.

CHAPTER FIVE
TEACHERS

Article 17. "**In the problem of transforming education it is the teachers who are the main problem**." The rural primary and middle schools should strive to build up their ranks of proletarian teachers.

Article 18. Conscientiously purify and strengthen the ranks of teachers in accordance with Chairman Mao's policy of uniting with educating and remoulding intellectuals. Encourage the present teachers to serve the poor and lower-middle peasants. Clear out class enemies who sneaked into the ranks of the teachers. In strengthening the ranks of the teachers, recommend poor and lower-middle peasants, demobilized soldiers, and educated young people having been tempered in manual labour for a certain period, who hold aloft the great red banner of Mao Tse-tung thought and are qualified to teach. The appointment and dismissal of teachers should be discussed by the poor and lower-middle peasants, proposed by the revolutionary committee of the production brigade for endorsement by the revolutionary committee of the commune, and reporting to the revolutionary committee of the county.

Article 19. Recommend poor and lower-middle peasants with practical experience, revolutionary cadres, and militarymen who are activists in the living study and application of Mao Tse-tung thought, to be part-time teachers or to form lecturers' groups.

Article 20.   In line with Chairman Mao's teaching that **"Being educators and teachers, they themselves must first be educated**," the teachers should take an active part in the three great revolutionary movements, and, by taking part in labour in the production teams at regular intervals and in other ways, consciously accept re-education by the poor and lower-middle peasants so as to remould their world outlook.

Arrangements should be made to ensure that the teachers have adequate time needed to raise their educational level and study problems related to their work. Help the teachers constantly raise their professional competence by making arrangements for them to study at their posts or get special full-time training in rotation.

Article 21.   The production brigade should take over the management of state-run primary schools in the rural areas. The teachers should be paid instead by the brigade on the work-point system, supplemented by state subsidies. In general, this new wage system should not lower the present living standards of the teachers. The work points received are to be reckoned annually. Men and women teachers are to receive equal pay for equal work.

(With regard to the pay of middle school teachers, one view is that they should be paid according to the work-point system plus a state subsidy; another view is that the methods should be fixed after further study and that the work-point system should not be adopted.)

Article 22.   Before the promulgation of the regulations, the existing regulations should be carried on with regard to sick leave and maternity leave for teachers, free medical care for them with the cost borne by the state, and burial expenses. For teachers who have not been transferred to work in the production brigades where their homes are, leave should be granted for them to visit their families.

Article 23.   The appropriate number of students in each class in the rural primary and middle schools should be between 30 and 50. As for the size of the teaching staff, on the average there should be 2.5 teachers to each middle school class (the exact number can be fixed by the commune or production brigade according to the school grade), and 1.3 teachers to each primary school class.

CHAPTER SIX
TEACHING

Article 24.   In arranging the curriculum, adhere to the principles of giving prominence to proletarian politics, of combining theory with practice and of making the courses fewer and better. This is in line with Chairman Mao's teaching that **"Courses should be fewer and better. The teaching material should be thoroughly transformed, in some cases beginning with simplifying complicated material"** and **"While their main task is to study, students should also learn other things."**

Five courses are to be given in primary school: politics and language, arithmetic, revolutionary literature and arts, military training and physical culture, and productive labour.

Five courses are to be given in middle schools: education in Mao Tse-tung thought (including modern Chinese history, contemporary Chinese history and the history of the struggle between the two lines within the party), basic knowledge for agriculture (including mathematics, physics, chemistry and economic geography), revolutionary literature and art (including language), military training and physical culture (including the study of Chairman Mao's concepts on people's war, strengthening the idea of preparedness against war, and activities in military training and physical culture), and productive labour.

(Another view on the middle school curriculum is that it should include: education in Mao Tse-tung thought, general knowledge about agriculture, mathematics, physics, chemistry, language, revolutionary literature and art and military training and physical culture.)

With regard to the importance of the various courses, politics is of primary importance and should be put first in order, relative to productive labour and general knowledge and culture. But in arranging time, more periods should be given to courses in general knowledge and culture. It is appropriate for these courses to account for about 60 per cent of the periods for study in middle school and not less than 70 per cent in primary school.

Article 25.   With regard to arranging teaching time for the whole school year, schools should open classes for about forty weeks of the year (including the time taken up by courses in productive labour) and the students given about 35 days of leave during the busy farming seasons. The length at time can be increased or reduced in accordance with the specific conditions in the locality and the age of the students.

(Some poor and lower-middle peasants proposed that one and a half to two months leave is needed during the busy farming seasons.)

The school should give about 35 days of winter and summer vacations, according to local climate.

(Some comrades suggest that this should be decided by areas in line with local climate.)

Article 26.   In accordance with Chairman Mao's instruction, "**Teaching material should have local character. Some material on the locality and the villages should be included.**" Aside from the teaching material compiled by the state, localities should organize workers, peasants and soldiers and revolutionary teachers and students to compile teaching material on the area as supplementary teaching material.

Article 27.   In teaching theory should be combined with practice. Chairman Mao's "ten teaching methods" should be applied by encouraging the students to investigate for themselves, relating what is near to what is far and what is elementary to what is advanced so that the initiative of the students is stimulated for study.

The method of teachers and students teaching each other and commenting on their teaching and study should be followed. The methods of combining teaching both in the classroom and on the spot and teaching by both full-time and part-time teachers should be used so as to link study closely with practice.

In the upper grades of the primary schools and in middle schools, students should be encouraged to undertake self-study and discussion, and to learn to use Mao Tse-tung thought to distinguish fragrant flowers from poisonous weeds. Students should be given time to read, think, analyze, criticize and study problems.

Article 28.   A reasonable amount of homework should be assigned to students and a certain number of tests and examinations should be given. Open book tests and practical skills are methods to be used in raising and testing the students' ability in analyzing and solving problems. The teachers should conscientiously mark and correct the homework and test papers of the students.

CHAPTER SEVEN
RUN SCHOOLS ON A PART-TIME WORK, PART-TIME STUDY BASIS

Article 29.   The road of relying on our own efforts should be firmly followed and diligence and frugality should be practiced in running schools so as to lighten the burden on the poor and lower-middle peasants. Extravagance and waste and the tendency to seek grandeur and what is bourgeois should be opposed.

Where conditions permit, the primary and middle schools should set up bases for production and labour in agriculture, forestry, animal husbandry, fishery and side-line occupations. Where circumstances allow, scientific research should be conducted.

Article 30.   Follow Chairman Mao's teaching, "**Rural students should make use of their vacations, week-ends and holidays and spare time to return to their own villages to take part in production.**" The primary way is for students to participate in production in the people's commune, the production brigade and the production team, while their participation in labour arranged by the schools is supplementary, the main form of participation in production conducted by schools should be productive labour classes.

All income from such production should be taken care of by the people's communes and production brigades.

NOTES:
[1]"Four firsts" means:.1. As between man and weapons, give first place to man; 2. As between political and other work, give first place to political work; 3. As between ideological and routine tasks in political work, give first place to ideological work; 4. In ideological work, as between ideas in books and the living ideas currently in people's minds, give first place to the living ideas currently in people's minds.

[2]The "three-eight" working style: the "three" refers to a firm and correct political orientation, and industrious and simple style of work, and flexible strategy and tactics; the "eight" refers to the eight characters which mean unity, alertness, earnestness and liveliness.

6.16 "Some Suggestions Concerning the Running of Middle Schools by Factories"

In conformity with Chairman Mao's teaching that "the school term should be shortened and education should be revolutionized," we hereby put forward some suggestions concerning reforms in urban middle schools for the discussion of revolutionary comrades.

1. The leadership of the working class in schools should be strengthened, and organs of power based on "three-in-one" combination should be established. Under the leadership of the Party organization and revolutionary committee of the factory, a school revolutionary committee should be formed by factory workers in conjunction with revolutionary teachers and students, but with the factory workers as the mainstay. Under the leadership of the Party organization and revolutionary committee of the factory, the school Party organization and revolutionary committee should make unified arrangements for political and teaching work in the school. The important problems of the school should be examined and determined by the factory

The Workers' Mao Tse-tung's Thought Propaganda Team and the Revolutionary Committee of the Work-Study School of the Shanghai State-Owned Cotton Mill No. 16, "Some Suggestions Concerning the Running of Middle Schools by Factories," Peking, *Jen-min Jih-pao,* December 10, 1969, *Current Background,* No. 870 (January 27, 1970), pp. 15-16.

revolutionary committee. To strengthen its leadership in the school, it is suggested that an educational group should be set up in the factory revolutionary committee to lead the school in concrete work.

2. The school should regard the study of Mao Tse-tung's thought as higher, greater and more important than everything else. By way of education, the students should solidly establish the class struggle viewpoint, the viewpoint of the struggle between the two lines, the viewpoint of uninterrupted revolution under the dictatorship of the proletariat, the viewpoint of serving the people, the mass viewpoint and the labor viewpoint. The working class should constantly give the students class education and continuously raise their political consciousness. The students should criticize and repudiate revisionism together with the workers and resolutely take the road of building the school politically.

3. The policy of distributing graduates in "four directions" should be firmly implemented. We are of the view that this should be boiled down to the concrete not only in the thought of the teachers and students, but also in the target of cultivation, the arrangement of curriculums, and each and every teaching link. At the same time, considering the extent of development in industrial technical revolution and rural mechanization and electrification under the strong impetus given by the great cultural revolution, the training of the students in basic skills should be strengthened to meet the need of large-scale development of industrial and agricultural production.

4. Under the leadership of the factory revolutionary committee, there should be established a workers' regiment of teachers and a teaching group based on "three-in-one" combination (of workers, students and teachers). Together with the students, the capable persons should serve as teachers, so that "the officers may teach the fighters, the fighers may teach the officers, and the fighers may teach each other," and so that they may teach and learn from each other for the mutual advancement of the teachers and students. On-site teaching should be strengthened and vocational knowledge should be learned in production practice and brought back to production. The workers, students and teachers should be organized in line with the army; the old class master system, the teaching research group system and the promotion and repeat system should be abolished; and the system of holding instructors responsible should be enforced. This is of advantage to implementing the policy of "making preparations for war, for famine and for the people." The students should be appraised by the workers, peasants and soldiers at the time of graduation.

5. The question of school system and the forms of schools to be run. It is suggested that pupils who have finished primary school be enrolled (as a continuation to primary school education). The course should generally last four years. These schools may take diverse forms. One is the four-year course secondary vocational school (divided into specialized courses, but when specialized courses are established, their adaptability to the city and the countryside should be considered). Schools of another kind are the ordinary schools run by factories (in which no specialized courses are provided, and generally fundamental subjects on industry and agriculture are taught with emphasis on the characteristics of the trades running such schools). Yet another kind is for the enrollment of graduates from junior middle schools, and it is appropriate to provide these schools with a two-year course.

6. Question of teachers and funds. The existing contingents of teachers (including teachers of ordinary middle schools and schools run by factories) must be reorganized, remolded and rebuilt. They must be transferred to the grassroots level by stages and groups for manual labor and for re-education by the workers, peasants and soldiers. The number of full-time teachers should be cut drastically, and workers

with high political consciousness and practical experience should be selected and sent to schools to serve concurrently as teachers, so as to change the state of accumulation of intellectuals in schools. The intellectuals from old schools who are better integrated with the workers, peasants and soldiers may also assume the task of educating the students.

7. "This holds good for students too. While their main task is to study, they should in addition to their studies, learn other things, that is, industrial work, farming and military affairs. They should also criticize the bourgeoisie." When students come to a factory to take up manual work, arrangements should be made for them to take up ordinary work or service work in the first instance. Later, their work posts should be stabilized in a relative sense, and they should be rotated from one job to another in a planned and methodical manner. Those who learn farming should be hooked up with the commune in the vicinity of the factory, and organized to give support to "summer and autumn plowing, planting and harvesting" work. During the course, poor and lower-middle peasants should be invited to give the students class education and teach them knowledge in farming. This can link the students with realities and will enable them to learn industrial work and farming. The students should be cultivated to share the feelings of workers and peasants and to overcome the thought of giving more weight to industrial work than farming. To learn military affairs, demobilized soldiers in the factory should be invited to hold classes in military physical culture. The students should study the "three-eight" style of work and the "four firsts" of the PLA for the purpose of realizing ideological revolutionization. Meanwhile, the physique of the students should be strengthened, and they should learn skill to defend the fatherland.

8. "Material of instruction must be thoroughly reformed and should be simplified first in some cases." At present, there should be set up a teaching material compilation group based on "four-in-one" combination (workers, students, teachers and technicians) which should go deep into factories and the countryside to conduct extensive surveys, and gradually compile various kinds of teaching material that bring proletarian politics to the fore and are closely linked with realities in accordance with the current conditions of industrial and agricultural production to meet the need for the development of industrial and agricultural production.

The working class leading the schools is a consistent thought of the great leader Chairman Mao. Under the rule of Liu Shao-ch'i's counterrevolutionary revisionist line in education in the past, the work-study schools run by factories did not bring proletarian politics to the fore, and their pernicious influence was rather intense. We should earnestly sum up the experiences and lessons, and make efforts to create the "May 7" type of schools for the cities.

6.17 "Establish A New Proletarian System of Examination and Assessment"

Great leader Chairman Mao taught us: "The present method of examination is a method used to handle the enemy, which takes him by surprise with odd and out-of-the-way questions. It is a method of examination used in tests on stereotyped writings." In the course of developing educational revolution penetratingly we have shattered the old system of examination and put the new system of examination on trial in accordance with Chairman Mao's thinking on educational revolution. Establishment of the new system of examination has greatly increased the teachers and students' enthusiasm of teaching and learning for the sake of revolution, elevated the quality of teaching and brought about a new situation in the movement of resuming classes to make revolution.

WHY MUST A NEW SYSTEM OF EXAMINATION BE ESTABLISHED?

Through the revolutionary mass criticism and repudiation against "intellectual education first" and "marks in command" pushed forward by big renegade Liu Shao-ch'i the broad masses of revolutionary teachers and students profoundly realized: The old method of examination is an important component part of the counter-revolutionary revisionist system of education which gravely ruined the physical and mental health of the children and youths. Since the beginning of the proletarian cultural revolution we have conscientiously implemented Chairman Mao's proletarian revolutionary line of education and abolished the old method of examination. . . .

TWO FUNDAMENTALLY DIFFERENT SYSTEMS OF EXAMINATION

In the new system of examination. . . there are three stages. The first stage is pre-examination preparation. During this stage ideological mobilization is conducted first to make the teachers and parents repudiate the old system of examination and the bad influence of "marks in command" together to clarify the aim of examination and correct the people's attitude toward examination. Then the students are informed of the time and scope of the examination and a systematic review is conducted.

The second stage is the examination itself. For language examination, closed book examination is generally used for the lower years of the primary school. For the higher years, open book examination is adopted to test the students by means of composition, question-answer, etc. All questions are open and students are allowed to refer to books or conduct discussions.

The third stage is appraisal and assistance after examination. In this stage, first of all the students conduct a democratic appraisal of the attitude toward studies and academic achievements of their fellow students according to their achievements in studies during ordinary times and the result of examination. This is done with the squad (i.e., study groups) as the unit. Then the teachers gather the views of the masses and submit them to the platoon committee for approval after adding marks

---

Propaganda Team Stationed in Ch'anghsintien *Chen* Central Primary School, Peking Municipality and the Revolutionary Committee of Ch'anghsintien *Chen* Central Primary School, "Establish A New Proletarian System of Examination and Assessment," Peking, *Kuang-ming Jih-pao,* August 31, 1969, *Survey of China Mainland Press,* No. 4504 (September 26, 1969), pp. 7-11.

and comments on the examination (the 100-mark system is adopted). Finally ideological education is conducted with a view to the study attitude of the students and assistance in the study of cultural knowledge is given.

The following are the three fundamental differences between the new system of examination which is on trial in our school and the old system of examination:

First, the purpose of examination is not the same. The examination is the past was solely for the purpose of obtaining marks which decided whether a student repeated or was to be dismissed and the teachers used the examination to suppress the students and reject students who were children of workers and peasants. However the examination today is solely for the purpose of promoting the teachers' idea of teaching for the sake of revolution and the students' idea of studying for the sake of revolution, helping the students with their reviews and their consolidation of what they have learned, and cultivating the students' ability of analyzing and solving problems so as to improve the method of teaching and elevate the quality of teaching.

Secondly, the method of examination is not the same. In the past examination was conducted like a surprise attack using odd and out-of-the-way questions. As a result the students studied mechanically and by rote and remained in a state of permanent tension. But today the students are informed of the time and scope of the examination beforehand so that they can review the important points. The emphasis of understanding instead of rote learning brings about moral, intellectual and physical development in the students in a lively and healthy manner.

Thirdly, effects of the examination are not the same. Examinations in the past were solely for the purpose of giving marks to students. Those who got high marks became elated. Teachers extolled them, fellow students envied them, parents praised them, and even material incentive was utilized. Those who got low marks became dejected. Teachers criticized them, fellow students looked down upon them and parents scolded or beat them up. The students were preoccupied with marks all the time—before, during as well as after the examination, which made them stupid and unambitious.

But today the attitude of study is appraised first and then results of studies are assessed. Assistance is given to the students in connection with their political studies and then their cultural studies. In this way those with high achievements are encouraged to do better and those with lower achievements are encouraged to catch up. Consciousness is heightened, enthusiasm is rallied, and knowledge is increased every time an examination is administered. Students welcome such examination.

PART SEVEN

The
Post-Cultural
Revolution
(1970 to the Present)

PART SEVEN
The Post-Cultural Revolution (1970 to the Present)

In the People's Republic of China events seem inevitably to be measured against two historical benchmarks; the first and most important of these is the Liberation of 1949, and the second is the Cultural Revolution of the late 1960's. The Ninth Party Congress of the C.C.P., in April 1969, at which Lin Piao was designated as Mao Tse-tung's heir-apparent and the PLA emerged as the most dominant force in the Chinese body-politic, has been regarded as marking the end of the Cultural Revolution.[1]

Our visits to the People's Republic of China have made us even more acutely conscious of the phrase "wen ge yihou"—"after the Cultural Revolution"—and its implications for education. During the Cultural Revolution the super-structure of Chinese society—the way people think, their values, the rules they live by, their institutions, etc.—underwent an intensive "struggle-criticism-transformation movement," and Mao Tse-tung issued specific instructions on how to carry out the "revolution in education."[2] However, it is during the period after the Cultural Revolution, "wen ge yihou," that the nation has embarked on a comprehensive movement to *apply* the principles proclaimed in the new Constitution of 1975, that education must "serve proletarian politics, serve the workers, peasants and soldiers, and be combined with productive labour."[3] Thus, in the field of education the period after the Cultural Revolution is in a very real sense a period of the application of the principles of the "revolution in education."

According to Mao Tse-tung Thought, the "revolution in education" is necessary to build a Socialist country (and eventually a Communist society), to transform one's world outlook, and to achieve the all-round dictatorship of the proletariat. In the opening sentence of his famous essay, "On Contradiction" (August 1937), Mao stated, "The law of contradiction in things, that is, the law of the unity of opposites, is the basic law of materialist dialectics," and quoted Lenin's law of the essence of dialectics: "Dialectics in the proper sense is the study of contradiction *in the very essence of objects.*"[4]

Mao Tse-tung's philosophy holds that there have been only two basic conceptions concerning the law of development of the universe, "the metaphysical conception and the dialectical conception, which form two opposing world outlooks." The former evolutionist world outlook "sees things as isolated, static and one-sided." The latter world outlook contends that:

> . . . in order to understand the development of a thing we should study it internally and in its relations with other things; in other words, the development of things should be seen as their internal and necessary self-movement, while each thing in its movement is interrelated with and interacts on the things around it. The fundamental cause of the development of a thing is not external but internal; it lies in the contradictoriness within the thing.[5]

The Maoist view holds that the universality and absoluteness of contradiction is such that it "is present in the process of development of each thing from beginning to end."[6] In the world-outlook of materialist dialectics, a phenomenon such as the Great Proletarian Cultural Revolution, which engulfed China for a period of more than three years, is neither surprising nor entirely unexpected. (Again, we have the benefit of historical hindsight; many of the excesses of the Cultural Revolution would not have been readily nor easily predicted.) Similarly, if we analyze the developments in the People's Republic of China according to the world-outlook of materialist dialectics, we should not expect that the ending of the Cultural Revolution would necessarily result in the elimination of opposition and struggle between ideas, between classes, between the old and the new—even within the Party itself.

With this background in mind, let us return to the course of events following the close of the Cultural Revolution and the Ninth Party Congress (April 1969), at which Lin Piao, Minister of Defense, was officially designated as Mao Tse-tung's successor.

Foreign observers cite the Second Plenum of the Ninth Central Committee (August-September, 1970) as signaling the beginning of Lin Piao's fall from political grace. Among the problems which divided the Chinese leadership were conflicts between old and new cadres (the question of whether positions of leadership should be given to the older cadres who had actually undergone the tests of participation in revolutionary struggles, or to the "politically immature" new cadres), and conflicts between the military and the civilians (the question of reducing the power and influence of the PLA in the educational, economic, cultural and political affairs of the nation, and the new directive that the military now "learn from the people.") The result was sharp polarization between civilian and military leadership.[7]

It was said against Lin Piao that he was involved in plots to assassinate Mao Tse-tung, that he attempted to seize power using the backing of the PLA, that he had links with hostile foreign elements, and that his activities during the Cultural Revolution were "wrong in essence."[8] According to the "official" Chinese version, Lin Piao is reported to have died on Sepbember 12, 1971 (along with several "other plotters") in an air crash in Mongolia following an abortive plot against Mao Tse-tung.[9]

Following the downfall of Lin Piao and his supporters, the Party has gone to considerable lengths to reaffirm its authority over the PLA and the provincial organizations (the purge has greatly affected top leadership in the provinces; there have been many changes, suspensions, transfers, etc.)[10] Whereas formerly the Chinese people had been urged to "learn from the PLA,"now the military are being directed to "learn from the revolutionary masses." The new emphasis is on strengthening the unity between the military and the civilians, and between the PLA and the Government with "strict Party discipline and adherence to the Party's organizational chain of command."[11] The 1973 New Year's Day editorial of *People's*

Daily pointed out the necessity to grasp the "true nature" of the revisionist line of "swindlers like Liu Shao-chi," and to carry out an intensive program of repudiation. The Party line stressed that the downfall of Lin Piao was not merely an intra-Party power-struggle, but rather a matter of irreconcilable differences over policies, and notes that this revolutionary struggle between the two lines should unite the Party and the people on the basis of Mao Tse-tung thought, and therefore strengthen the revolutionary cause.[12]

Up to the end of 1972, the official line had been to accuse Lin Piao and his followers of being ultra-Leftists. Beginning in 1973, the term "ultra-Rightism" was applied to these "swindlers like Liu Shao-chi," in the anti-Lin Piao campaign. The Chinese press and radio described the counter-revolutionary conspiracies of Lin Piao, Chen Po-ta, and their supporters as having employed "tricks which were 'Left' in form but Right in essence . . . to fan up ultra-Leftist sentiments."[13] The *Kirin Daily* of January 9, 1973 (broadcast over Kirin Radio), stated:

> They [Lin Piao and his followers] appeared to be extremely "Left." In reality, "Left" was their method, while Right was their essence.[14]

Particularly revealing is the following commentator's article in the official *Szechuan Daily* (released over Szechuan Radio on January 30, 1973):

> What is the true nature of the revisionist line of swindlers like Liu Shao-chi? Some people say that it is ultra-Leftist. This is wrong. The line of swindlers like Liu Shao-chi is a counter-revolutionary line. It is ultra-Rightist. . . . By getting a clear picture of the contents and aim of the revisionist line of swindlers like Liu Shao-chi and the class interest which it represents, we can clearly see that the true nature of this line is ultra-Rightist, not ultra-Leftist.
>
> Of course, at some times and on some issues, swindlers like Liu Shao-chi stirred up and made use of ultra-Leftism. However, this was just the phenomenon, not the essence, the method, not the aim. Rightism was their true nature and their aim. If we hold that the line of swindlers like Liu Shao-chi was ultra-Leftist, it means that we have not grasped its true nature. Only by grasping tightly the true nature of the revisionist line of swindlers like Liu Shao-chi can we understand the great significance of the current struggle to repudiate the counter-revolutionary revisionist line of swindlers like Liu Shao-chi for defending and developing the fruits of the great proletarian Cultural Revolution.[15]

There is considerable speculation among China-watchers, and quite a number of different hypotheses, as to the shifting emphasis in the anti-Lin Piao campaign. Significantly, at the Tenth National Congress of the Communist Party of China, held in Peking from August 24 to 28, 1973, Lin Piao and Chen Po-ta were publicly denounced as renegades and traitors, and expelled (Lin Piao posthumously) from the Party. However, the anti-Lin Piao campaign, if carried to extremes, runs the risk of discrediting many of the policies of the Cultural Revolution—the so-called "socialist new-born things"—formulated at the very time that Lin Piao and his supporters were at the height of their power.[16] Perhaps the history of the Great Proletarian Cultural Revolution may yet have to be re-written.

Throughout the People's Republic of China—in the press and on the radio, in art and literature, in cultural activities and on banners and posters—there is an intensification of the call to work toward remodling one's world outlook. As stated by the leading Party magazine, *Red Flag:*

> . . . we must learn Chairman Mao's philosophy well and make dialectical materialism and historical materialism the powerful weapon to change the subjective and objective world.[17]

The study and application of "Mao Tse-tung Thought" plays *the* pivotal role in the education of children and youth, in the remolding of one's world outlook, and in "fostering . . . successors to the proletarian revolutionary cause and the consolidation of the dictatorship of the proletariat."[18]

Accelerated efforts have been made to popularize or universalize five-year primary education in rural areas—one of the unfulfilled proclaimed national goals of the 1950's. In places with "favorable conditions," seven-year education (i.e. 5-year primary plus 2-year lower-middle) is being popularized; however, provinces are being cautioned against stressing secondary education (7-year schools) at the expense of the realization of the universalization of a system of five-year primary education. Again, Mao Tse-tung thought is cited as the basis for policy: "No one should make plans of action unwarranted by the objective situation, or reach for the impossible."[19]

To facilitate the extension of educational opportunities in rural areas, wherever possible schools were established near the homes of the poor and lower-middle-class peasants. Some localities adopted the policy of dispersing schools, "setting up teaching points, touring schools . . . morning classes, noon classes and evening classes . . ." etc., which are highly integrated with the production schedule.[20] The policy of "walking on two legs" (running schools in various forms, etc.) is again being urged; variety is being pointed to as a definite strength of the schools, allowing them to assume forms more in keeping with the particular character of the specific locality, "tailored to the needs of the poor and lower-middle peasants."[21] The August 1972 issue of *China Reconstructs* carried an interesting article about the "school boats" or floating classrooms established to service children of Kuangtung province's New Village Fishing Harbor; the sea-going school actually follows the fleet out to the fishing grounds during the busy season (March to September).[22]

However, getting students to come to school, or in the more remote areas sending the teachers or schools to the students' doorsteps, is not the solution to all educational problems. The Cultural and Educational Bureau of Hsianho *Hsien*, Hopei Province reported the following discoveries revealed by its investigation of the universal education movement:

> Among the school-aged children, the girls were more transitory than the boys; students of higher grades were more transitory than students of lower grades; more students left at the beginning of a school term than toward the end of a school term; students who did poorly in their studies were more likely to drop out than students who did well.[23]

The notion of an "open-door" school policy (from primary through higher education) which was applied at this time is actually an applicaiton of Mao's concept of "serving the people." For example, the Education Group of Shenyang Municipal Revolutionary Committee reported:

> In accordance with Chairman Mao's teaching "serve the people wholeheartedly," . . . the primary schools have smashed the rules and restrictions of the former educational system, and have thrown the doors wide open to the children of the working people. Not only will they accept children from the age of six upward into the school, but they have also admitted more than 1,000 children, who suffer from infirmities and whose mental development is retarded, into the schools.[24]

From Kiangsi, reporting their efforts to obey Mao's teaching concerning higher education that, "Students should be selected from among the workers and peasants with practical experience, and they should return to production after a few years' study,"[25] the Education Group of the Kiangsi Provincial Revolutionary Committee noted that the enrollment of students had been affected in the following four ways:

1. The orientation of enrollment of students has greatly changed. In the past, only graduates from senior middle schools were enrolled. Now students are selected from among the workers and peasants with practical experience, really carrying out Chairman Mao's instructions.

2. The standard of selection has greatly changed. In the past, the candidates' scores in the examination were considered exclusively, regardless of their class origin. Now, attention is paid to the line and the candidates' thinking, so that education really serves proletarian politics.

3. The method of enrollment of students has greatly changed. In the past, enrollment of students was conducted in a dogmatic way, alienated from practice and dominated by bourgeois intellectuals. Now, enrollment of students is conducted in accordance with the mass line and students are selected by workers and poor and lower-middle peasants.

4. The aim of training has greatly changed. In the past, students aimed at personal fame and gain, and education was conducted to train successors to the bourgeoisie. Now, laborers with both socialist consciousness and culture are to be trained to serve the workers, peasants and soldiers.[26]

Although the operation of "open-door" schools was initially heralded as an important feature of the educational revolution, some subsequent reports indicated that there was a growing movement toward giving greater attention to enrolling "sons and daughters from the exploiting classes who have truly performed well and who can be educated."[27]

In the area of school management, this period began with a continuation of two features of the latter part of the Cultural Revolution: the poor and lower-middle-class peasants' taking control of the rural schools, and the key role of "worker-peasant-soldier teams" in school operation. The Lin Piao faction was critical of the ability and performance of the management of schools by the poor and lower-middle-class peasants. The Maoists continued to urge operation of the schools (particularly in the rural areas) by the masses, and to support the "worker-peasant-soldier teams" as a powerful force in transforming education. However, it is likely that patterns of school management will be affected by the growing concern for raising academic standards and educational quality.

The Chinese Communist Party continues to exercise its control over education, with control being exercised directly at the level of the instructional process:

> In relation to the reality of educational revolution, we conscientiously studied Chairman Mao's instruction: "Our educational guideline would enable those who receive education to develop morally, intellectually, and physically and so become cultured workers with socialist consciousness." Our socialist revolution and construction urgently needs such workers. If the Party committee does not grasp the revolution in the realm of teaching and strive to improve the quality of teaching, the growth of the successors in the cause of the proletarian revolution will be seriously impeded and education will not be able to serve proletarian politics well . . . . If ideological-political task is not combined with teaching activity in school, it will depart from reality and will not be able to play its due role of commander and guarantor in teaching work. It is completely wrong to sever ideological-political leadership from teaching work and to oppose one to the other.[28]

Party workers and Propaganda Team members enter the schools to assure that content, teaching materials, and teaching methods are compatible with the Party line — that Mao Tse-tung thought is used to transform the students' world outlook, and thereby foster successors to the proletarian revolutionary cause.

It is not only students who are in need of ideological transformation, but also teachers, as was clearly spelled out in the *Kuangming Daily*:

Chairman Mao teaches us: "The change in world outlook is something fundamental." In order to give prominence to proletarian politics in teaching, it is necessary for the teachers to vigorously remold their world outlook. In teaching a lesson, the teacher either educates the students in the proletarian ideology or poisons them with the bourgeois ideology. The deeper the reform of teaching develops, the higher are the demands imposed on the teachers for remolding their world outlook. Therefore, in the reform of teaching, the teachers must take a firm hold of the fundamental problem of remolding their world outlook.[29]

Teachers are often sent "down to the countryside" or to Cadre Schools where they are tempered so that they will give up their bourgeois world outlook and gradually develop the proletarian world outlook—the process of remolding one's world outlook is described as "a process of arduous tempering."[30]

The teacher's position in China remains a precarious one, subject to the shifts in emphasis on the "Red and expert" issue. Criticizing those comrades who had "incorrect ideas" about the "group of old teachers . . . left over from the old society," the *Kuang-Ming Daily* noted (June 19, 1971) that, "most of the teachers are still willing to serve the people and continue to make progress."[31] In general, a much more conciliatory tone has been used when referring to teachers and intellectuals. The following policy statement by the Party Committee of Wuhan University is illustrative of this changing attitude:

As long as we are able to implement conscientiously the Party's policy, boldly make use of them [teachers and intellectuals], and while using them strengthen education and transformation on them, we can turn them into an active force for the revolution in education. There is a serious difference between that and taking the "specialist line."[32]

Indeed, the CCP Committee of Chungshan Medical College went so far as to contribute an article to *People's Daily* (April 11, 1972) entitled, "Firmly Adhere to Transformation through Employment, Bring the Expertise of Intellectuals into Play."[33] Mao's statement, "The question of teaching reform is mainly one of teachers," so often cited during the Cultural Revolution, has been replaced with a different statement which lends itself to a much more liberal interpretation:

Comrades of the whole Party must understand that a correct policy toward intellectuals is an important condition for winning the revolution.[34]

The principle of combining or uniting theory with practice continues to be a major educational theme, but the application of Mao's "May 7 Directive" that "Education must serve proletarian politics and be integrated with productive labor" has undergone some significant modifications. In 1970, primary schools, middle schools, colleges and universities followed Mao's call to "regard the whole society as their workshop."[35] They set up and ran their own workshops, farms or factories, thereby implementing the "three-in-one" system of unifying teaching, scientific research, and production. Hofei Industrial University (in Central China) reported the following experiences:

Hofei Industrial University perserveringly runs a factory, unites the factory with its departments and establishes a three-in-one system combining teaching, scientific research, and production. Practice shows that a science and engineering university is a school as well as a factory and a scientific research unit, and this is a basic measure for implementing Chairman Mao's educational policy that "education must serve proletarian politics and be combined with productive labor."[36]

Wuhan University reported similar experiences:

> Chairman Mao teaches us: "All laboratories and affiliated workers of higher technical schools that can turn out products should carry out production as much as possible, after meeting the requirements of teaching and scientific research." School-run factories should be developed into being for effecting the three-in-one combination of teaching, scientific research and production . . . . In compliance with Chairman Mao's teaching, "Take study as the principal work and simultaneously learn other things," they [the students and teachers] persistently put nurturing of men on the first place in running factories in the school . . . .[37]

Indeed, the "three-in-one" principle was applied at all educational levels. The experience of Chingtuitzu Primary School (in Liaoning Province) in running a small factory was reported as follows:

> The small factory run by Chingtuitzu primary school not only furnishes favorable conditions for integrating teaching with productive labor but what is more important, cultivates the students' socialist consciousness and tempers their thinking of fearing neither hardship nor fatigue . . . . After going through the practice of labor in the small factory, the students learned not only to do industrial work, but also to make scientific experiment.[38]

By 1972, there were clear signs of a shifting attitude toward the relationship between theory and practice. While continuing to criticize the separation of theory from practice, the shift in emphasis took the form of stressing that it was also important to criticize "the wrong idea that 'theory is useless.'"[39] This was part of a new upsurge of concern for educational quality and for building up the force of "theoretical workers" needed for China's future development—it should be remembered that China's institutions of higher learning closed during the Cultural Revolution and did not re-open until late 1970. This change was most clearly seen at the level of higher education in the field of science.

> Only when one has mastered the laws of nature, that is, deeply understood the internal relations of objective things, can one put forward one's views of analyzing and solving practical problems. The concrete demand of the laws of nature is the ability to correctly understand and explain the laws of nature, apply them, and find new laws. This is to say that the task of the science faculty is to train working personnel versed in the theories of natural science who are required by current production as well as theoretical workers required by the country in its future development of production and science.[40]

By the end of 1972 and the beginning of 1973, the change in educational policy had gone as far as to openly criticize the earlier tendency which had stressed practical training and experience at the expense of book knowledge. This was now denounced as "pragmatism" and "formalism," and part of the "revisionist line of swindlers like Liu Shao-chí."[41] This represented a major policy shift; scientific research was now being encouraged as essential to production and the achievement of China's long-term needs.

The change in the Party line was that whereas basic theory had been criticized in the past as being divorced from reality, it was now held that it should not be belittled nor should one negate the importance of gradual advancement in study. Chairman Mao's statement, "take study as the main task," was used to support the new concern and growing respect for theoretical studies. *Kuangming Daily* of December 3, 1972 openly reported the less-than-successful experiences with sending students to factories for practical training before they had adequate classroom instruction:

> Because they had taken no lessons at all, and so lacked the necessary basic

knowledge, they did not know what to do. Under the circumstances, some teachers gave the students lessons on the spot, but the result was not satisfactory.[42]

This situation was contrasted with an example in which teachers of a radio technology course gave students more than two months instruction in elementary mathematics and the principles of radio operation *before* sending them to a factory for practical training. In this instance, the report stated, the "necessary foundation" for learning had been established and the students were able to achieve the principle of "an orderly and gradual advancement" in study.

Visits to the People's Republic of China by the authors in 1974 and 1975 confirmed the reports that the "revolution in education" which started during the Proletarian Cultural Revolution has in recent years developed considerable momentum and is now going on throughout China. The current campaign to carry forward the "revolution in education" is roughly the educational equivalent of the political campaigns to criticize Lin Piao and Confucius, and to study the "theory of the dictatorship of the proletariat."

Mao Tse-tung pointed out that the struggle between the two roads is a continuing struggle—between the two classes, the proletariat and the bourgeoisie, and between the two lines, the Marxist and the revisionist. Herein lies the clue to the meaning of the campaigns to criticize Lin Piao and Confucius, and the campaign to study the theory of the dictatorship of the proletariat. The relationship between politics and education is clearly set forth in Article 12 of the Constitution of the People's Republic of China adopted on January 17, 1975:

> The proletariat must exercise all-round dictatorship over the bourgeoisie in the superstructure, including all spheres of culture. Culture and education, literature and art, physical education, health work and scientific research work must all serve proletarian politics, serve the workers, peasants and soldiers, and be combined with productive labor.[43]

The on-going "revolution in education" is one of the "socialist new-born things" which had its origins in the Cultural Revolution. It represents a further transformation of the educational system and takes as its guiding principle the implementation of Mao's directive that "education must serve proletarian politics and be combined with productive labor"[44] and that "our educational policy must enable everyone who receives an education to develop morally, intellectually and physically and become a worker with both socialist consciousness and culture."[45]

The most distinctive aspects of the "revolution in education" are those associated with the length of the period of schooling, educational policies, teaching methods, teaching materials, the enrollment system of higher education, and the world outlook of teachers. Efforts are being made to increase the experimentation with shortening the period of schooling. This usually means five years for primary school, four or five years of middle school (two or three years for lower-middle and two years for upper-middle school), and two or three years for higher education at the unversity level.

Coupled with the shortening of the period of schooling is the reduction of the number of subjects and the elimination of "superfluous" subjects and "redundant or useless" teaching materials. Top priority is given to the study of revolutionary theories: — Marxism-Leninism and Mao Tsetung Thought.

The educational experience is structured to strengthen the ideological education of the students and to integrate book-learning with practical production. This is done by having the schools establish ties with nearby communes, factories, and PLA units. Some primary and middle schools, and virtually all universities, have opened their own farms or small workshops. Workers, peasants and PLA soldiers are invited to serve as part-time teachers or as "coaches." At the university level teaching and productive labor is also combined with scientific research.

Students and teachers actually go to factories or communes to take part in collective labor for a specified period of time. They are encouraged to study for the revolution and to learn to serve the people wholeheartedly. Students are encouraged to develop their initiative and there is a concerted effort to establish a new relationship between teachers and students, that of comrades *both* taking part in the three great revolutionary movements of class struggle, struggle for production and scientific experiment.

Examinations have not been eliminated, but have been thoroughly transformed. The open-book examination system has become widespread. Students and teachers discuss test questions beforehand, students may refer to books and discuss the examination questions among themselves. In several of the schools we visited it was quite common to see small groups of students working collectively on a solution to examination problems.

Curriculum materials have been re-written (often by "worker-peasant-soldier-teacher writing teams") to encorporate Mao Tse-tung's teachings on the "revolution in education" and to stress the ideology of serving proletarian politics, socialist revolution and construction, and training successors to the cause of the proletarian revolution.

The university enrollment system has been altered to reflect the principle that education must "serve the workers, peasants and soldiers, and be combined with productive labor."[46] Following graduation from middle school most students are assigned to posts in the rural areas or the communes, others become workers or PLA members. Universities generally select students from among workers, peasants and soldiers with two or more years of practical work experience who have been recommended by the masses and approved by the local leadership of the factory, commune or PLA unit. In the enrollment procedures for higher education special allowances are made and considerations given to veteran workers, poor and lower-income-middle peasants, revolutionary cadres, and members of China's national minorities. The first waves of these worker-peasant-soldier university students are now being graduated from the universities.

The "revolution in education" is part of a planned effort to integrate theory with practice, to have students and teachers alike participate in the three revolutionary movements (class struggle, struggle for production and scientific experiment), to have students make a useful contribution to the society in the course of receiving their education (while at the same time creating wealth for the state), and to contribute to the gradual lessening of the differences between workers and peasants, between town and country, and the traditional invidious distinctions between mental and manual work.

The revolution in education is more than simply a campaign designed for school children, students and teachers. As one of the fruits of the Cultural Revolution it is a comprehensive educational campaign, a nation-wide effort to remold the world outlook of the entire Chinese society. Its significance can be illustrated by the debate over educational policy which was touched off in November and December of 1975. At Peking's Tsinghua University, some leading educators questioned the policy of running schools in an "open-door way," claiming that there had been a general decline in the quality of university education, and further criticized the academic level attained by the new worker-peasant-soldier university graduates.

The point of the criticism was that unless academic standards were raised, China would not be able to achieve the goal of becoming a modern industrial state by the end of this century. This touched off a mass debate, the essence of which is reflected in the following statement that appeared in the January 1, 1976 issue of *Hongqi (Red Flag)*, the Chinese Communist Party's major theoretical journal:

In the current excellent situation, there is still the struggle between the two classes, the two roads and two lines. The erroneous trend of thought that emerged not long ago in society negating the Great Proletarian Cultural Revolution, the socialist new things and the proletarian revolution in education was a concentrated reflection of the struggle between the two classes, the two roads and the two lines. The great victories we have won since the start of the Great Proletarian Cultural Revolution undoubtedly constitute a shattering defeat for the bourgeoisie and all other exploiting classes. They will never take this defeat lying down but will invariably wait for an opportunity to stage a vengeful counter-attack in an attempt to reverse the previous verdicts passed during the Great Proletarian Cultural Revolution. Since they have stirred up a Right deviationist wind to reverse previous verdicts and come out with such revisionist trash as the absurdities spread by some people in educational circles, the proletariat and revolutionary people should naturally wage a tit-for-tat struggle against them.[47]

Following the death of Premier Chou En-lai on January 8, 1976 many (if not most) Western observers had expected that Teng Hsiao-ping would be appointed as Chou En-lai's successor. Teng Hsiao-ping was the Vice-Chairman of the Central Committee of the Communist Party of China and First Vice-Premier of the State Council. For almost two years Teng had carried out the major functions of premier while Chou En-lai was hospitalized as a result of his illness. However, contrary to the conventional wisdom of many China-watchers, Hua Kuo-feng, a relatively little-known member of the State Council, was named Acting Prime Minister.

The debate in educational circles over the revolution in education was identified as striking at the very future and destiny of the Party and the state. Teng Hsiao-ping was accused of placing the development of the national economy—specifically production and realization of the "four modernizations" (of agriculture, industry, national defense, science and technology)—ahead of class struggle, and charged with negating the Party's basic line of taking class struggle as the "key link."[48]

Following a "counter-revolutionary political incident" at Tien An Men Square on April 5, 1976, events moved swiftly. On April 7 the Central Committee of the Communist Party of China declared that the situation had turned into one of "antagonistic contradiction." Hua Kuo-feng was appointed First Vice-Chairman of the Central Committee of the Communist Party of China and Premier of the State Council; and Teng Hsiao-ping was dismissed from "all posts both inside and outside the Party."[49]

Mao Tse-tung has stated that: "There is always need for revolution. There are always sections of the people who feel themselves oppressed. . . ."[50] Premier Chou En-lai, one of the stalwarts of the socialist revolution and a major figure in the Party and state, has passed from the scene. China has recently experienced an "antagonistic contradiction" within the Party resulting in the removal of Teng Hsiao-ping and the appointment of Hua Kuo-feng as Premier. The Central Committee of the Communist Party of China announced on June 15, 1976 that Chairman Mao Tse-tung would no longer receive foreign visitors because he "is well advanced in years and is still very busy with his work."[51]

It may well be that the People's Republic of China is on the threshold of a new period of educational development, which may coincide with the beginning of a new era—one destined to achieve the status of the third major benchmark (the first being "Liberation," and the second being "The Great Proletarian Cultural Revolution") in the historical development of the People's Republic of China.

NOTES:

[1]Rajan, "Mao's Second Cultural Revolution," *China Report* (January-February, March-April, 1972), p.4.

[2]*Jing Gang Shan,* Peking, July 11, 1967, pp. 1-2.

[3]"The Constitution of the People's Republic of China" (Adopted January 17, 1965) Article 12, *Peking Review*, No. 4 (January 24, 1975), p. 15.

[4]Mao Tse-tung, *Selected Works of Mao Tse-tung*, I (Peking: Foreign Langauge Press, 1967), p. 311.

[5]Ibid., p. 313.

[6]Ibid., p. 319.

[7]"Moves to Curb the PLA and Provincial Groups," *Current Scene* (March 10, 1972), pp. 17-18; "Putting Down 'Conspirators and Careerists,'" *Current Scene* (September, 1972) pp. 20-23.

[8]Rajan, op. cit., p. 5.

[9]"Putting Down 'Conspirators and Careerists,'" loc. cit.; *The New York Times* [Reuters dispatch from Peking, June 18, 1973], June 19, 1973, p. 4.

[10]*China News Summary* (February 15, 1973), p. 1.

[11]"Moves to Curb the PLA and Provincial Groups," op. cit., p. 18.

[12]*China News Summary* (January 4, 1973), pp. 4-5.

[13]*China News Summary* (January 25, 1973), p. 5.

[14]Ibid., p. 6.

[15]Ibid.

[16]*China News Summary* (March 29, 1973), p. 1. [The phrase "socialist new born things," which appeared in the March, 1973 issue of *Red Flag*, referred to such things as "the creation and popularization of the revolutionary model theatrical works, worker-peasant-soldier enrollment in universities, educated youths going down to the countryside, the cadre masses taking part in manual labour, the development of cooperative medical schemes, medical personnel going to the rural areas, and so on."] A special issue of Peking Review, No. 35 and No. 36 (September 7, 1973) features articles and documents concerning the Tenth National Congress of the Communist Party of China (August 24-28, 1973).

[17]*Hongqi*, S.M. Hu (trans.), No. 2 (February, 1971), p. 6.

[18]*Jen-min Jih-pao (People's Daily)*, May 30, 1970, *Survey of China Mainland Press*, No. 4675 (June 12, 1970), p. 115.

[19]"Popularize Five-Year Elementary Education, Conditionally Develop Seven-Year Education," *Jen-min Jih-pao (People's Daily)*, July 8, 1972, *Survey of China Mainland Press*, No. 5179 (July 21, 1973), p. 188.

[20]"Rural Education in China Develops Vigorously Under the Guidance of Chairman Mao's Proletarian Line of Education," *Kuang-ming-Jih-pao* [NCNA dispatch of December 27, 1971], December 28, 1971, *Survey of China Mainland Press*, No. 5052 (January 12, 1972), p. 119.

[21]"Keep Running Schools in Various Forms," *Jen-min-Jih-pao (People's Daily)*, April 20, 1972, *Survey of China Mainland Press,* No. 5126 (May 4, 1972), p. 149.

[22]"Seagoing Schoolrooms," *China Reconstructs*, No. 8 (August, 1972), pp. 37-38.

[23]"Grasp the Laws and Do a Good Job of Consolidating and Improving Universal Education," *Jen-min Jih-pao (People's Daily)*, May 17, 1972, *Survey of China Mainland Press*, No. 5145 (June 1, 1972), p. 106.

[24]The Education Group of Shenyang Municipal Revolutionary Committee, "A New Type of Neighborhood Primary School Run by the Masses,' *Jen-min Jih-pao (People's Daily)*, February 25, 1971, *Survey of China Mainland Press*, No. 4854 (March 10, 1971), p. 86.

[25]Education Group Under Kiansi Provincial Revolutionary Committee, "Selecting Students from Workers and Peasants Is a Deep-Going Revolution," *Jen-min Jih-pao (People's Daily)*, August 22, 1970, *Survey of China Mainland Press*, No. 4730 (September 1, 1970), p. 42.

[26]Ibid., p. 44.

[27]*The New York Times*, July 9, 1973, p. 9.

[28]CCP Committee of Educational Bureau of Tientsin, "Effectively Strengthen Party Committee Leadership Over the Revolution in the Realm of Teaching," *Jen-min Jih-pao* (*People's Daily*), August 3, 1972, *Survey of China Mainland Press*, No. 5197 (August 17, 1972), p. 147.

[29]Revolutionary Committee of Cultural and Educational Bureau of T'angku *Ch'u*, Tientsin Municipality, "Use Chairman Mao's Philosophic Thinking to Direct Teaching," *Kuang-ming Jih-pao*, December 1, 1970, *Survey of China Mainland Press*, No. 4798 (December 14, 1970), p. 1.

[30]Committee of the General Party Branch of the Chemical Engineering Department, Hunan University, "Remold the Teachers' World Outlook in the Practice of Struggle," *Kuang-ming Jih-pao*, December 11, 1971, *Survey of China Mainland Press*, No. 5042 (December 28, 1971), p. 49.

[31]"An Effective Way for Remolding Existing Teachers," *Kuang-ming Jih-pao* (*Kuang-Ming Daily*), June 19, 1971, *Survey of China Mainland Press*, No. 4930 (July 6, 1971), p. 5.

[32]"Virgorously Grasp Line Struggle, Maintain Using and Transforming Teachers At the Same Time," *Kuang-ming Jih-pao*, March 22, 1972, *Survey of China Mainland Press*, No. 5107 (April 6, 1972), p. 105.

[33]CPC Committee of Chungshan Medical College, "Firmly Adhere to Transformation Through Employment, Bring the Expertise of Intellectuals into Play," *Jen-min Jih-pao*, April 11, 1972, *Current Background*, No. 945 (January 11, 1972), pp. 40-45.

[34]Bureau of Education, Changchun Municipality, Kirin Province, "Bring the Teacher's Role into Full Play in the Educational Revolution," *Jen-min Jih-pao*, August 16, 1972, *Survey of China Mainland Press*, No. 5214 (August 29, 1972), p. 1.

[35]Workers and PLA Propaganda Teams Stationed at Finance-Economics College of Shantung; Revolutionary Committee of Finance-Economics College of Shantung, "Fundamental Orientation for Reform of Old Liberal Arts Colleges," *Jen-min Jih-pao*, January 18, 1970, *Survey of China Mainland Press*, No. 4590 (February 3, 1970), p. 31.

[36]Workers' Propaganda Team and PLA Propaganda Team Stationed in Hofei Industrial University, and Revolutionary Committee of Hofei Industrial University, "Schools and Colleges Should Establish 'Three-in-One' System Combining Teaching With Scientific Research and Production by Running Factories," *Kuang-ming Jih-pao*, July 30, 1970, *Survey of China Mainland Press*, No. 4715 (August 11, 1970), p. 42.

[37]Workers-PLA Mao Tse-tung's Thought Propaganda Team Stationed at Wuhan University and Revolutionary Committee of Wuhan University, "Running Factories by Schools and Linking Factories With Schools to Carry Out Three-in-One Combination of Teaching, Scientific Research, and Production," *Jen-min Jih-pao*, June 27, 1971, *Survey of China Mainland Press*, No. 4935 (July 13, 1971), p. 58.

[38]"Red Young Soldiers Vigorously Run 'Children's Factory,'" *Kuang-ming Jih-pao*, July 29, 1970, *Survey of China Mainland Press*, No. 4717 (August 13, 1970), p. 145.

[39]Chou P'ei-yuan, "Some Views on Educational Revolution in the Science Faculty of Universities," *Kuang-ming Jih-pao*, October 6, 1972, *Survey of China Mainland Press*, No. 5238 (October 19, 1972), p. 113.

[40]Ibid., p. 117.

[41]*China News Summary* (January 11, 1973), p. 1.

[42]Ibid., p. 4.

[43]"The Constitution of the People's Republic of China" (Adopted on January 17, 1975), Article 12, *Peking Review*, No. 4 (January 24, 1975) p. 15.

[44]Mao Tse-tung, "A Talk Delivered in 1958," *Current Background*, No. 888 (August 22, 1969), p. 7.

[45]Mao Tse-tung, "On the Correct Handling of Contradictions Among the People" (February, 1957), *Four Essays on Philosophy* (Peking: Foreign Language Press, 1968), p. 110.

[46]"The Constitution of the People's Republic of China" (Adopted on January 17, 1975), op. cit., p. 15.

[47]Chih Heng, "Firmly Grasp Class Struggle As the Key Link," *Peking Review*, No. 6 (February 6, 1976), p. 7.

[48]"The Great Proletarian Cultural Revolution Continues and Deepens," *Peking Review*, No. 12 (March 19, 1976), pp. 9-11.

[49]The April 9, 1976 issue of *Peking Review*, No. 15, contains the actual text of the C.P.C. Central Committee's resolution appointing Hua Kuo-feng First Vice-President of the C.P.C. Central Committee and Premier, as well as the text of the resolution dismissing Teng Hsiao-ping (p. 3). The latter resolution states that Teng would be allowed to retain his Party membership "so as to see how he will behave in the future."

[50]Editorial Departments of *Renmin Ribao*, *Hongqi*, and *Jiefangjun Bao*, "The Great Cultural Revolution Will Shine For Ever," *Peking Review*, No. 21 (May 21, 1976), p. 9.

[51]*The New York Times*, June 16, 1976, p. 1.

7.1 "Transform Educational Position in Schools With Mao Tse-tung's Thought"

Guided by Chairman Mao's series of brilliant directives and inspired by the spirit of the CCP 9th Congress, and while "grasping revolution and stimulating production" and earnestly carrying various work of struggle, criticism and transformation, our Chiahsing Chemical Works have roused the broad worker masses to show active concern for and take part in the educational revolution, taken over the control of Nanhu Middle School of Chiahsing, and supervised the small teams from Hangchow University and Chekiang University who are carrying out practice of educational revolution in our works. We have done some work and produced some results in the proletarian educational revolution. . . .

Through revolutionary mass criticism, we deeply realize that everything will be wrong unless the working class take a part in the educational revolution. Comrade workers said aptly, "A factory that produces inferior products will bring losses to the State; a school that produces inferior products will cause the country to change its political color." . . .

HOLD HIGH THE RED BANNER—THE BRILLIANT BANNER OF CHAIRMAN MAO'S IDEA OF EDUCATIONAL REVOLUTION

The course of our close grasping of educational revolution has been a course of our study of Chairman Mao's idea of educational revolution, severe criticism of arch-renegade Liu Shao-ch'i's counter-revolutionary revisionist line for education, and raising of consciousness of implementation of Chairman Mao's proletarian line for education. We closely combined mass study with mass criticism, and were able to study deeper and criticize more thoroughly than ever. Through mass study, mass criticism and practice of educational revolution, we are able to understand more profoundly than ever Chairman Mao's idea of educational revolution and our enthusiasm in joining in the educational revolution has risen higher. . . .

HANDLE PROPERLY ONE RELATIONSHIP—THE RELATIONSHIP BETWEEN STRUGGLE, CRITICISM AND TRANSFORMATION AND EDUCATIONAL REVOLUTION

When the university's educational revolution teams first arrived in our works, some of our comrades thought that the teams would solve partly the problem of labor shortage and also help technical innovations. Study of chairman Mao's idea of educational revolution enabled us to realize that such way of thinking was wrong. The educational revolution teams came to our works because they wanted to carry out practice of educational revolution while receiving re-education from the working class. . . .

At the beginning, some comrades of the educational revolution team of Chekiang

Revolutionary Committee of Chiahsing Chemical Works, Chekiang Province, "Transform Educational Position in Schools With Mao Tse-tung's Thought," Peking, *Kuang-ming Jih-pao,* April 3, 1970, *Survey of China Mainland Press,* No. 4639 (April 20, 1970), pp. 4-10.

University shut themselves in a room and there wrote textbooks. The master workers pointed out to them: "It won't do to 'Make cars in a closed room.' You cannot produce good textbooks there. You should come to the workshop and write together with us workers."

Later, they came to the workshops, discussed the outline of what they wanted to write with the master workers and wrote and compiled textbooks with them. Whenever they met with problems, they would ask the master workers for advice. The result was good.

Chairman Mao's great directive, "Take the road of Shanghai Machine Tool Works of training technicians from among workers," has pointed out the direction for educational revolution in colleges. While "grasping revolution and stimulating production" in our own works, we have selected workers with practical experience for training and set up a "workers short-term technical training class" together with the college teams, in order to raise the theoretical and technical levels of the workers. This has not only accumulated experience for educational revolution, but also promoted the development in depth of the technical revolution and technical innovation movement in our own works.

Facts show that successful carrying out of struggle, criticism and transformation in a factory will create favorable conditions for educational revolution, and that the development in depth of educational revolution will in turn promote the struggle, criticism and transformation movement in a factory. . . .

ORGANIZE A FORCE—OF ACTIVISTS WITH THE SPARE-TIME WORKERS PROPAGANDA TEAM AND WORKERS LECTURER GROUP AS THE BACKBONE
*

In accordance with the demands of the university educational revolution teams and Nanhu Middle School, we organized a workers lecturer group with members elected by the worker masses themselves and approved by the revolutionary committee of the Works. Comrades of the workers lecturer group are not detached from production. They teach mainly during their spare time, using their production time only when absolutely necessary. Of the 36 worker-lecturers, more than 20 have already given lessons from the teacher's platform. They have given lessons not only to middle school students but also to university students.

Some of the university students who had taken lessons from worker-lecturers said with profound feeling, "The worker-lecturers bring politics to the fore in giving lessons. They deal with abstruse subjects in a practical and easily understandable manner. Our own university lecturers are unable to teach in a better way." . . .

STRICTLY GRASP THE SUCCESSFUL RE-EDUCATION OF INTELLECTUALS
*

We realized that the most important principle of all was the bringing of proletarian politics to the fore and the most important task of all was the re-education of intellectuals with Mao Tse-tung's thought. Educational revolution is first of all an ideological revolution. We have concretely done the following things:

(1) Paying attention to the living study and living application of Chairman Mao's works.

We have armed the heads of the revolutionary teachers and students with Chairman Mao's great doctrine of continuing revolution under the dictatorship of the proletariat and his brilliant ideas of educational revolution, and repeatedly organized the comrades of the teams to study the "Three Constantly Read Articles," "The Orientation of the Youth Movement," and the series of Chairman Mao's directives on educational revolution. We study together with them, carry out criticism with them, and struggle against self and repudiate revisionism with them. . . .

(2) Grasping class education and education on the struggle between the two lines.

We regularly ask old workers, who suffered much in the old society and hated it deeply, to give the teachers and students class education by recollecting past bitterness and thinking of present sweetness, thus increasing their consciousness of the class struggle and the struggle between the two lines. The family histories of the old workers, so full of blood and tears, often move comrades of the teams to tears. We have also given the teams lessons on the history of the struggle between the two lines in the Chiahsing area, in our Works, or in a workshop. The story of the master workers' living study and living application of Mao Tse-tung's thought during the great proletarian cultural revolution and their dauntless spirit of launching attacks on the small handful of class enemies has given comrades of the teams an impressive lesson, greatly deepening their understanding of Chairman Mao's proletarian revolutionary line and their hatred for Liu Shao-ch'i's counter-revolutionary revisionist line, and so strengthening their will to continue to make revolution.

(3) Grasping mass criticism against the counter-revolutionary revisionist line for education.

In relation to the realities of our Works, the old master workers have angrily exposed and condemned the crimes of the counter-revolutionary revisionist line for education. They compared the intellectuals in the Works who were deeply poisoned by the counter-revolutionary revisionist line for education with other intellectuals who successfully integrated themselves with the workers and who were able to create things, giving a living lesson to the teams from the positive and negative angles. The workers also told the teams what sort of intellectuals were welcomed by the workers and what sort of intellectuals were not welcomed, making the revolutionary teachers and students feel that "the direction for advance is clear and their work has a future." . . .

7.2 "Brilliant 'May 7 Directive' Is Guideline for Running Socialist Engineering College Well"

Obeying great leader Chairman Mao's "May 7 Directive" and his teaching, "It is necessary to revolutionize education," and inspired by the spirit of the Party's "9th Congress," the worker-PLA Mao Tse-tung's thought propaganda team stationed in Chengchow Engineering College and the revolutionary committee of this college have dispatched a number of educational revolution teams to carry out revolution of education in factories and in the countryside. The team which has gone to Ch'iliying in Hsinhsiang area is a good one. In the past year, the revolutionary teachers and students of this team have on the one hand received re-education from the workers and poor and lower-middle peasants and, on the other hand, revolutionized education while helping build a chemical fertilizer plant in Ch'iliying. The broad masses of

Investigation Group under Honan Provincial Revolutionary Committee and Worker-PLA Propaganda Team stationed in Chengchow Engineering College, "Brilliant 'May 7 Directive' Is Guideline for Running Socialist Engineering College Well' (Report on an investigation made by Chengchow Engineering College's educational revolution team sent to Ch'iliying), Peking, *Kuang-ming Jih-pao*, May 7, 1970, *Survey of China Mainland Press*, No. 4660 (May 20, 1970), pp. 74-81.

workers and poor and lower-middle peasants say happily: "Our chemical fertilizer plant is an outgrowth of the simultaneous development of large, medium-sized and small enterprises, the integration of indigenous and foreign methods of production, and the integration of intellectuals with the masses of workers, peasants and soldiers. It is a great victory of the directive of walking on two legs and a great victory for Mao Tse-tung's thought."

REVOLUTIONIZING MAN'S THINKING IS A QUESTION OF PRIME IMPORTANCE

*

Most of the teachers and students actively accepted this assignment. But, some others were afraid that "they would not achieve any results" and "they would not learn anything." The propaganda team realized that this state of affairs reflected that the pernicious influence of the revisionist line of education had not been totally eliminated and the basic question of whom we should serve has not yet been solved. . . .

A tremendous change takes place in the thinking and feelings of the teachers and students after they have fought together with the workers and peasants in the past year. They have become as rustic as the workers and poor and lower-middle peasants; they sweat as much as the workers and poor and lower-middle peasants do. The workers and poor and lower-middle peasants say: "They are the intellectuals who walk the same road with us — the road of revolution, and whose hearts are linked with ours — red hearts that are loyal to Chairman Mao."

SCHOOL OF A NEW TYPE WHICH COMBINES TEACHING-LEARNING, DESIGNING AND CONSTRUCTION WORK

Obeying Chairman Mao's brilliant "May 7 Directive," this team combined teaching-learning, designing and construction work, running itself first as a school and, meanwhile, as a designing department and a construction work team. In the past year, they have designed and helped build three projects including Ch'iliying Chemical Fertilizer Plant. Meanwhile, the teachers and students have heightened the levels of their political thinking and their work to a very large extent.

This school of a new type has its superiority in several respects:

(1) *Under the Party's leadership, the working class firmly grasps the power of education.* This team sets up a leading group with workers as its mainstay and with revolutionary teachers and students taking part in it. The workers take charge not only of politics, but also of teaching-learning, designing and construction work. Meanwhile, a contingent of activists in revolution of education has been formed during the practical struggle of educational revolution in the past year. When some teachers and students show wavering and setbacks ideologically, the propaganda team promptly educates them. This insures that revolution of education will constantly progress in triumph in the direction pointed out by Chairman Mao.

(2) *Combination of teaching-learning, designing and construction work benefits remolding of thinking of the intellectuals.* Before drawing a design, the teachers and students learn from the workers. When meeting a problem in designing, they seek advice from the workers. When discovering a question while doing construction work together with the workers, they get together with the workers to study and solve it. The broad masses of workers take an active part in the revolution of education, constantly giving the teachers and students re-education. The workers say: "They can form one with us."

(3) *Education is integrated with productive labor and the quality of teaching is improved.* Students of this team not only have heightened their political thinking

relatively quickly, but also surpassed graduates of the old-type university in actual ability of work. It happened once that when the teachers were away, the students, on the basis of practice of a preceding stage, accomplished the designing of a project which involved very complicated work. The user unit was deeply satisfied with this project. The teachers were greatly surprised when they returned and saw this design. They said: "Chairman Mao's revolutionary line surely brings up useful people."

(4) *Technical innovation in designing and construction work is promoted.* Doing construction work together with the workers on the worksite, the designers can seek advice from the workers at any moment and solve their doubts and difficult problems. Because the teachers and students had integrated themselves better with the workers and peasants, 8 tons of rolled steel was saved by using 3,000 square meters of wooden beams and slabs in the structural design of rebuilding of the posts and telecommunications building of the telegraphic bureau of Hsinhsiang municipality.

A WORKSITE IS TAKEN AS CLASSROOM, TEACHING – LEARNING IS CONDUCTED IN THE COURSE OF PRODUCTION

The purpose of taking the worksite as the classroom is to integrate classroom teaching and on-the-spot teaching with designing and construction work in accordance with the needs of designing and construction work. The course of teaching-learning can be chiefly divided into the three stages of explaining questions by enlightenment, putting the knowledge into practice, and making improvement by exchange of experience and by application.

Before making a design, the workers' opinions are solicited through investigation and study and the teachers explain the basic principles and the methods of calculation and suggest some reference materials for the students to study. Then the students carry out designing under the guidance of the workers and the teachers. When the design is completed, the students of each group take part in the items of construction work they have designed, and examine the theories they have learned and the design they have made. Finally, the teachers and the students sit together at a meeting to sum up and exchange experience and the teachers make commentaries theoretically.

In this way, it is possible to go through a complete course of teaching-learning from individual cases to ordinary cases and from practice to theory. The students not only learn theories, but also learn skills in the course of practice.

This way of teaching-learning is completely agreeable to Chairman Mao's teaching, "Practice—understanding—again practice—again understanding." . . .

"THREE-IN-ONE" RANKS OF TEACHERS WITH WORKERS AS MAINSTAY

Chairman Mao points out: "In the problem of transforming education it is the teachers who are the main problem." The educational revolution team of Chengchow Engineering College which has gone to Ch'iliying takes the worksite as the classroom, carries out teaching-learning in the course of production, and gradually sets up a "three-in-one" contingent of teachers with workers as its mainstay. . . .

The remolding of the teachers' thinking is an important question in the building of the "three-in-one" contingent of teachers. The aim of this remolding is first to solve the basic question of whom we serve and then to solve the question of studying professional work once again. . . .

This educational revolution team holds this point of view: The contingent of teachers of a socialist engineering college should be composed of workers, teachers, and engineers and technicians who have practical experience. The workers have rich practical experience, the teachers have much more book knowledge, and the engineers and technicians are relatively experienced in designing. In the course of teaching, they show their skills to the full, make up for their shortcomings by learning from each other's strong points. The three of them together will form a very powerful force.

> Investigation Group under Honan Provincial
> Revolutionary Committee and Worker-PLA
> Propaganda Team stationed in Chengchow
> Engineering College

7.3 "Operation of Factories by Schools Helps To Push Forward Educational Revolution"

On September 12, 1958, our great leader Chairman Mao came to Wuhan University to inspect the chemical factory operated by the teachers and students of Wuhan University on the basis of self-reliance under the guidance of Chairman Mao's proletarian line of education. At that time he gave an important instruction: "The students' voluntary request for half-work and half-study is a good thing. This is a natural tendency in the operation of factory by schools in a big way. We should approve such requests and should support and encourage them," and "In the reform of the method of teaching attention should be paid to the development of the activeness of the broad masses of teachers and students and the concentration of the wisdom of the masses by all means."

Chairman Mao's great instructions greatly encouraged the teachers and students of Wuhan University; however renegade Liu Shao-ch'i, Wang Jen-chung and their agents in Wuhan University were frightened to death by these instructions and hated them deeply. In 1961 they colluded with one another and fanatically denounced the chemical factory as "marring the scenery of Lochia Shan" and "disrupting the order of teaching in the school." They also took advantage of the power they usurped to eliminate the chemical factory.

In April last year during the jubilant days of the convocation of the 9th Party Congress, with a heart boundlessly loyal to Chairman Mao and a profound hatred toward renegade, hidden traitor and scab Liu Shao-ch'i and his followers, the worker-PLA Mao Tse-tung's thought propaganda team led the students to implement conscientiously Chairman Mao's "May 7 Directive" and re-establish the chemical factory. During the past year the chemical factory continued to consolidate and develop itself; thus it effectively promoted the ideological revolution of the teachers and students, successfully trial-manufactured and produced several products urgently needed by the state and gained useful experience in educational revolution in universities of natural sciences.

OPERATION OF FACTORY BY SCHOOLS IS A REVOLUTION

The implementation of Chairman Mao's instructions about "Schools operating factories" is a revolution. Facts demonstrate that schools must first do a good job in

Hupeh Jih-pao Correspondent, *Ch'angchiang Jih-pao* Correspondent and the Reporting Group of Wuhan University, "Operation of Factories by Schools Helps To Push Forward Educational Revolution" (An investigation report on the September 12 Chemical Factory of Wuhan University), Peking, *Kuang-ming Jih-pao* June 21, 1970, *Survey of China Mainland Press*, No. 4697 (July 15, 1970), pp. 69-74.

the ideological revolution of man before they can do a good job in operating factories. . . .

The firm and correct political orientation greatly stimulated the revolutionary enthusiasm of the teachers and students. They used the spirit of "fearing neither hardship nor death" to accomplish missions of scientific research and production. Working in a chemical factory the teachers and students had to face poisonous gas and strongly corrosive, inflammable and explosive raw materials everyday, but they insisted on working in places where there were danger and hardship. They said: "To go to places of hardship is a good way to temper the revolutionary spirit of man.". . . .

PRACTICING THE THREE-IN-ONE COMBINATION OF TEACHING, SCIENTIFIC RESEARCH AND PRODUCTION

Under the guidance of Chairman Mao's proletarian line of education, the chemical factory practiced the three-in-one combination of teaching, scientific research and production to push forward the penetrating development of educational revolution.

The road followed by universities of natural sciences in the past was the road of "teaching has nothing to do with production and scientific research is only for the collection of data"—in other words the road of so-called "pure theory." But after the re-establishment of the chemical factory such "Liu poison" of the counter-revolutionary revisionist line of education was still affecting some of the teachers and students. As a result, those in charge of teaching paid no attention to scientific research or production and those engaged in scientific research and production failed to study the situation of teaching.

During the first attempt on the development of teaching activities the teachers spoke a great deal in the classrooms about various concepts of the "fundamental theories" but the students failed to understand or remember them. But a student who used this practical experience gained during his participation in production and scientific research to do the explaining made everybody understand the theory immediately. Thus a big debate developed around this teaching activity, which made everybody realize that although the operation of factory by schools and the direct participation in manual labor by the teachers and students opened up a broad way for the three-in-one combination of teaching, scientific research and production, it will still be impossible to implement well Chairman Mao's proletarian line of education if the remnant poison of the counter-revolutionary revisionist line of education is not thoroughly eliminated. Through the summing up of experience they overcame the idea of "division of work is tantamount to division of a house," closely combined teaching with scientific research and production, and extensively developed mass teaching and scientific research activities.

In accordance with Chairman Mao's great teaching, "Practice, understand; practice again and understand again," this factory pushed forward the development of production by developing teaching activities around production and scientific research as well as through teaching and scientific research. As they performed manual labor the teachers taught the students on the spot so as to enable the students not only to work but also understand why should things be done the way they were. Whenever there were problems in production which had to be solved urgently the teachers and students discussed them together and then formulate plans for improvement and mobilize the masses to engage in scientific experimentation. In this way results of scientific research were quickly applied to production, the contents of teaching were enriched, and the ability of the teachers and students in analyzing and solving problems was cultivated.

As they engaged in teaching around production and scientific research, they also enhanced the practice of democracy in teaching and "officers teaching soldiers, soldiers teaching officers and soldiers teaching one another;" and students also mounted the teachers' platform in addition to the teachers themselves. Old workers with practical experience were also invited to engage in on-the-spot teaching.

Practice demonstrated that the combination of teaching, scientific research and production and the development of mass teaching and scientific activities not only helped to strengthen the labor viewpoint of the teachers and students but also promoted the ideological revolutionization of the teacher and students and made it possible to concentrate the wisdom of the masses fully to promote and elevate teaching, scientific research and production together.

7.4 "Aomen Road No. 2 Primary School, Shanghai, Puts Extracurricular Activities on the Agenda of Its Revolutionary Committee"

Obeying Chairman Mao's great teaching, "New China must care for her youth and show concern for the growth of the younger generation," Aomen Road No. 2 Primary School, Shanghai municipality, concretely grasps the students' extracurricular activities, enabling the students to develop briskly and in a lively manner.

A FIRM HOLD MUST BE TAKEN OF AFTER-CLASS LIFE

The position of the students' extracurricular activities has always been a place where a violent struggle between the two classes and between the two ideologies takes place.

For some time in the past, some students have read bad books, sung bad songs, played bad games and heard bad stories after school hours, and some of them, being tempted and corrupted by the class enemy, even went astray. This new trend of the class struggle attracted the serious attention of the school leadership and the teachers. Great leader Chairman Mao says: "All departments and organizations should shoulder their responsibilities in ideological and political work. This applies to the Communist Party, the Youth League, government departments in charge of this work, and especially to heads of educational institutions and teachers." They studied this teaching given by Chairman Mao and deeply felt that taking a firm hold of the students' after class life was a major problem which would not allow even a moment's delay.

How should the students' life after school hours be managed and organized well? This involved a course of understanding. At first, some teachers fully occupied the students' time after school with meetings and other collective activities. Some other teachers "confiscated" the bad books the students read and the sling shots they played with, thinking that this would prevent the rise of problems from among the

Revolutionary Committee of P'ut'o *Ch'u*, Shanghai Municipality, and Reporter of Shanghai *Red Young Fighter Bulletin*, "Aomen Road No. 2 Primary School, Shanghai, Puts Extracurricular Activities on the Agenda of Its Revolutionary Committee," Peking, *Jen-min Jih-pao*, July 10, 1970, *Survey of China Mainland Press*, No. 4706 (July 29, 1970), pp. 77-79.

students. Actually, this method did not bring good results.

Primary school students are in a period of physical and intellectual development and are filled with vigor and vitality and demand various kinds of beneficial activities. These activities play an important role in forming their world outlook. Therefore, using Mao Tse-tung's thought to occupy the front of the students' extracurricular activities is a major problem directly concerning the upbringing of successors to the revolution, and the characteristics of the teenagers and the students' extracurricular activities must be seriously grasped in accordance with the characteristics of the teenagers and children.

ORGANIZING AFTER-CLASS LIFE IN ACCORDANCE WITH THE CHARACTERISTICS OF TEENAGERS AND CHILDREN
*

While leading the extracurricular activities, the school revolutionary committee pays particular attention to the following five points:

1. It constantly grasps revolutionary mass criticism and forbids the recurrence of counter-revolutionary revisionist trash in extracurricular activities. For example, when carrying out sports tournaments, it criticizes the ideas of "winning championships" and "seeking the limelight" and clearly explains the meaning of the athletic activities.

2. It conducts ideological education. In the course of winter swimming, some students fear hardship and cold. Grasping their living ideas, the teachers promptly educate them, making them understand that winter swimming can build up the health and foster a firm revolutionary will.

3. It pays attention to the mass character of the extracurricular activities. Returning to their classroom, the students of the extra-curricular activity groups at the school level push forward the extra-curricular activities in the classes. Many classes have organized story telling groups, criticism groups, basketball teams, invigorating the students' life after school.

4. It perseveringly adheres to the principle of hard work and plain living. As a result of the universal development of extracurricular activities, there are insufficient grounds and tools for carrying out these activities. They adopt indigenous methods and solve the problem by their own efforts.

5. Proper arrangements are made for combining labor with rest. The students are deeply interested in extracurricular activities. They must be guided correctly to rationally arrange the school studies, extracurricular activities, household chores and ours.

In the past year, this primary school has actively unfolded and correctly led the students' extracurricular activities, making the students' mental aspects go through a tremendous change.

In the extracurricular activities, the students read revolutionary books, sing revolutionary songs, tell revolutionary stories, make scientific and technical experiments, and play games rich in revolutionary content, thereby effectively resisting the erosion by bourgeois decadent ideas and increasing their abilities to distinguish right from wrong.

The teachers join the students in their extracurricular activities, thereby further cementing their relationship with the students. Some students say happily: "Now the teachers study, make criticism, labor and carry out activities together with us. Their hearts are linked with ours!"

7.5 "A Middle School That Serves the Three Great Revolutionary Movements"

The K'ueits'un Agricultural Middle School in Hsuch'ang *hsien* was one personally founded by Comrade Yang Shui-ts'ai in September 1963. Since its inception, the school, following Chairman Mao's great teaching that "education must serve proletarian politics and be coordinated with productive labor," and under management by poor and lower-middle peasants, has produced a group of new-born forces for the building of socialism, thereby impelling the development of the three great revolutionary movements in the rural areas. Said the poor and lower-middle peasants: This school is one that undertakes creative study and application of Mao Tsetung thought, an experimental station for the popularization of advanced farm experiences, and a good place for the training of farm technicians.

TAKING THE ROAD OF SCHOOL MANAGEMENT POINTED OUT BY CHAIRMAN MAO

This school was founded and developed in the course of an acute struggle waged by the masses of poor and lower-middle peasants against the revisionist educational line of the renegade, hidden traitor and scab Liu Shao-ch'i.

Since the great proletarian cultural revolution was initiated and particularly since the publication in 1968 of Chairman Mao's directive that "in the rural areas, schools should be managed by the poor lower-middle peasants — the most reliable ally of the working class," a powerful impetus has been given the masses of poor and lower-middle peasants and the revolutionary students and teachers in the agricultural middle school in K'ueits'un village. Holding high the banner of revolutionary mass criticism, they sternly criticized Liu Shao-ch'i's counter-revolutionary revisionist educational line, further strengthened the leadership of the poor and lower-middle peasants' management committee over the school, and firmly grasped the power in education.

However, "the defeated class still struggles." Just as they were deeply criticizing the renegade Liu Shao-ch'i's counter-revolutionary revisionist fallacies such as the "theory of going to school in order to become an official" and just as the prospective graduates were actively preparing to return to their production teams to engage in farm production, a gust of evil wind was stirred up in society. A small pack of class enemies took the opportunity to incite the students, saying: "Students of the agricultural middle school know nothing but how to labor. This time they are going to face the test with maize threshers and grafting knives!"

Under the influence of this foul wind, some who were more infected with the revisionist educational line complained that the agricultural middle school was "not regular" and that the things one learned were "not systematic," and therfore they demanded the establishment of what they called a regular school.

The *hsien* and commune revolutionary committees immediately grasped this problem and organized the poor and lower-middle peasants and revolutionary teachers and students to make a creative study and application of Mao Tsetung thought, to

Investigation Team of Hsuch'ang District Revolutionary Committee and Hsuch'ang *Hsien* Revolutionary Committee, "A Middle School That Serves the Three Great Revolutionary Movements" (Report of an Investigation on K'ueits'un Agricultural Middle School, Hsuch'ang *hsien*, Honan), *Hung-ch'i [Red Flag]*, No. 8 (July 21, 1970), *Extracts from China Mainland Magazines*, No. 687-688 (August 10 & 17, 1970), pp. 58-64.

strongly criticize the counter-revolutionary revisionist educational line of the renegade, hidden traitor and scab Liu Shao-ch'i, and to look back to the course taken by Comrade Yang Shui-ts'ai in leading the poor and lower-middle peasants to set up the agricultural middle school. This considerably raised the class consciousness and the consciousness of struggle between the two lines on the part of the masses of poor and lower-middle peasants and revolutionary teachers and students. They said: It is an excellent thing that our agricultural middle school was founded on Chairman Mao's educational line and persists in serving the poor and lower-middle peasants and the three great revolutionary movements! . . .

SETTING UP A NEW TEACHING SYSTEM

This school has reformed the old educational system and set up a new one in accordance with Chairman Mao's great teaching that "the period of schooling must be shortened and a revolution in education must be carried out" and "with the main emphasis on study, other things should also be learned."

1. Enrollment. Students are enrolled without regard for their cultural level, all year-round (no seasonal enrollment) and irrespective of whether they are cadres or commune members. They are sent to the school by the poor and lower-middle peasants on the latter's request, in accordance with the needs of the three great revolutions and with the approval of the poor and peasants' management committee. They come from and return to the production teams.

Among the students are ones in their early teens who make study their principal occupation and at the same time learn other things, and also old poor peasants in their fifties who aim at acquiring specialized technical knowledge (for instance, grafting of fruit trees, farm machinery techniques, and scientific experiments in farming). After their admission, they will first study the "three constantly read articles" ["Serve the People," "The Foolish Old Man Who Removed the Mountains" and "In Memory of Norman Bethune], hold meetings to discuss the results of their study and application of these works, fight self and criticize revisionism, and adjust their thinking on study for the sake of serving the three great revolutionary movements. Moreover, they participate in collective productive labor at regular periods. Then, on the basis of their different conditions, they are put in different classes. The key subjects will be determined and teaching begins.

2. Academic system. It is extremely flexible. There are two-year long-term classes as well as short-term classes that last several months or even a few days. In the main, the length of a class is dictated by the needs of the three great revolutionary movements. A class may be long or short as the needs determine, and long-term classes are coordinated with short-term ones.

For the long-term classes, the emphasis is placed on study while other things are also to be learned. While studying well the socialist cultural lessons, the students will study the technical lessons required by local farm and forestry production. Upon graduation, they will return to their production teams to take part in productive labor and the work of their teams.

Short-term classes are not restricted by the schooling system. Students are sent to the school or taken back to their production teams whenever this is dictated by the needs of the revolution and production. Take an example. K'ueihsi No. 7 production team required the services of a bookkeeper, and the school let a student graduate in advance and return to the production team to be a bookkeeper. His diligence and ability to keep proper accounts has endeared himself to the poor and lower-middle peasants.

For the past several years, in compliance with the requests of the poor and lower-middle peasants, a total of 37 students were graduated in advance in order to return to their production teams to be team leaders, bookkeepers, storekeepers, or militia cadres. This strengthened the building of basic-level leading groups.

In the case of short-term classes, various types of training classes are held by separate groups for purposes of training propaganda forces and technical personnel for the production teams. Every time a training class is held, proletarian politics is put to the fore. As the first lesson, the "three constantly read articles" are studied, and the first meeting held is one to fight self and criticize revisionism. Hence, although the class is short in duration, the students are able to acquire the idea of a serving the people and relatively efficient techniques.

In winter last year, an upsurge of electrification swept the countryside, entailing the need for large numbers of electricians. Thereupon, the agricultural middle school set up a training class for electricians. In all, 38 electricians were trained for 15 production brigades. The difficulties created by the shortage of electricians were thus solved initially.

When the masses demanded to be taught to sing revolutionary songs, the school immediately set up short-term training to teach revolutionary songs, producing more than 400 singers for the 28 production brigades of the commune.

3. Examination. The school has eliminated classroom examinations. Instead, it attaches importance to the performance of the students in their daily creative study and applicaiton of Mao Tsetung thought, in their fight against self and criticism of revisionism and in their productive labor. Putting into practice the principle of integrating theory with practice, it tests the students in the course of practice and let practice determine the results of study.

For example, electrical study-workers with practical experience were invited to be teachers. Beginning with the planning, installation and overhaul of circuits and ending with switching of lights and starting motors, field teaching was closely integrated with practice. The students learned and applied what they had learned simultaneously.

Thus practice is an examination. When the grafting of fruit trees is studied, the entire process of the selection of ears, the care of shoots, and the sprouting of shoots is taken as a period of examination. Those who are serious about the care of shoots and bring about a high rate of survival of strong shoots are considered as passing the examination; otherwise, they will be required to continue practice in the second year of grafting.

Such a kind of examination not only makes it possible to have theory better guide practice and for practice to enrich theory, but also makes it possible more effectively to cultivate in the students the revolutionary spirit of thoroughly and completely serving the people.

4. Vacation. The vacation system here is not determined by the winter and summer seasons. It is determined by the needs of the three great revolutionary movements in the rural areas. The principle of vacation is this: "There are no fixed vacations, they are determined by the busy and slack seasons. During slack seasons there will be concentrated studies, while in busy farm seasons more time will be devoted to practice."

During the slack winter season, the students often study up to the 28th or 29th of December of the lunar calendar before they have holiday, and go back to school on the 3rd or 4th of January. When a busy farm season sets in, they go on holiday in advance, so that they may during labor directly be educated and tested by the poor and lower-middle peasants. They see their vacation as the continuation of their classroom learning in the agricultural middle school. Whether they are good in thinking, active in labor, or are capable of integrating study with practice is left to the judgment of the poor and lower-middle peasants.

The school takes the opinions of the poor and lower-middle peasants on the students as opinions for the school itself. It does persistently what satisfies the poor and lower-middle peasants and immediately corrects the errors pointed out by them. It resolutely does all things at the request of the poor and lower-middle peasants for the three great revolutionary movements.

After the publication of the Communique of the 9th Party Congress, the school organized the students to make a serious study of it and let them return to their teams to carry out propaganda activities. During summer vacation last year, the cotton and maize fields were attacked by pests. Some production teams did not see a serious danger in this and did not think of cure. Others wanted a cure but did not know how.

In the light of the harm done by the pests and the requests of the poor and lower-middle peasants, the school twice recalled the students from vacation and took them to the big fields to check the damage done by the pests, explaining to them the methods of prevention and cure before they resumed their vacation. After they returned to their teams, under the guidance of the team cadres, they mobilized the masses to unfold activities of killing pests, which were quickly eliminated. This was greatly appreciated by the poor and lower-middle peasants.

7.6 "Persevere in Letting the Poor and Lower-Middle Peasants Manage the Schools"

"Control of schools by the poor and lower-middle peasants must be carried on persistently." This question brought forth by the revolutionary committee of Chang-tung and Changhsi production brigades, Hai-an *hsien,* Kiangsu, is a very important one.

Chairman Mao pointed out: "In the countryside schools should be controlled by the most reliable allies of the working class — the poor and lower-middle peasants." During the past two years primary schools in the countryside underwent profound changes under the control of the poor and lower-middle peasants. Practice demonstrated that this instruction of Chairman Mao's is the orientation for educational revolution in the countryside and a powerful weapon for thoroughtly destroying the bourgeois educational system.

In a class society education is a tool for class struggle. Control of schools can only be control of the class. The class which controls the schools carries out its line and fosters successors for its class. Chairman Mao's call for the "control of schools by the poor and lower-middle peasants" is for the purpose of putting an end to the phenomenon of bourgeois intellectual elements ruling the schools and practicing dictatorship in the realm of education against the bourgeoisie. Therefore the perseverance of "control of schools by the poor and lower-middle peasants" is the perseverance of the dictatorship of the proletariat and Chairman Mao's proletarian revolutionary line in the realm of education.

At present comrades in some localities think: Now that the poor and lower-middle peasants have already grasped civil power, the work of class purification and Party consolidation and Party building in schools has been completed, the rank and file of

"Persevere in Letting the Poor and Lower-Middle Peasants Manage the Schools," Peking, *Jen-min Jih-pao*, September 20, 1970, *Survey of China Mainland Press*, No. 4749 (October 1, 1970), pp. 122-123.

teachers has been consolidated, children of the poor and lower-middle peasants have entered schools and educational revolution in the countryside has been "generally settled" there is nothing more to be done in the poor and lower-middle peasants' control of schools. Dominated by this kind of idea, the poor and lower-middle peasants in some localities slackened or even gave up their control of schools. Such ways of thinking and acting are wrong.

Chairman Mao taught us: "In the political and ideological realm the struggle which decides whether socialism or capitalism wins can be settled only after a long period of time." Comrades who think educational revolution has been "generally settled" fail to see the protractedness of the class struggle in the realm of education, fail to recognize the difficulty of the struggle to consolidate civil power in the countryside, and fail to understand that when things go bad it is still possible to lose the civil power which the poor and lower-middle peasants have seized. We must never slacken the control of schools by poor and lower-middle peasants. We must persevere in it till the end!

As educational revolution continues to penetrate in depth new problem arises incessantly. We must promptly solve these problems correctly before we can implement Chairman Mao's proletarian line for educational revolution. Naturally there are difficulties in solving these problems, but we cannot give up our perseverance in the control of schools by poor and lower-middle peasants because there are difficulties. In reality we can overcome the difficulties as long as we study and apply Mao Tse-tung's thought in a living way, give prominence to proletarian politics, mobilize all the poor and lower-middle peasants, and rely upon the revolutionary teachers and students. In the course of solving these problems we shall incessantly acquire new experience which will incessantly heighten the standards of the poor and lower-middle peasants' control of schools.

Control of schools by poor and lower-middle peasants is not a matter which concerns only those poor and lower-middle peasants responsible for controlling the schools, it is a matter which concerns also all the poor and lower-middle peasants as well as the leaderhsips at various levels. Party organizations and revolutionary committees at various levels, especially party organizations and revolutionary committees of the *hsien*, commune and production brigade level, must further overcome the tendency of belittling the cultural and educational front, realistically strengthen the leadership, help those poor and lower-middle peasants who are responsible for the control of schools to overcome difficulties, sum up experience, realize their own ideological revolutionization and carry out educational revolution in the countryside through to the end.

7.7. "Apply Mao Tse-tung's Thought to the Training of a Force of Teachers"

Our Yunchiang Commune originally had 15 middle and primary school teachers. They are mostly not from families of poor and lower-middle peasants but the majority of them are good or relatively good. Yet their world outlook remains a bourgeois one. To establish a force of proletarian teachers, we, apart from helping the original teachers to strive to transform their world outlook in the course of actual struggle, selected a total of 15 poor and lower-middle peasants and demobilized servicemen with a high level of political consciousness and with the necessary qualifications for teaching work and young intellectuals with two years of tempering in labor to go to the school to serve as full-time teachers.

To enable the worker-peasant-soldier teachers to resist the invasion of bourgeois ideas and persist in applying a proletarian world outlook to the transformation of schools, we must arm them with Mao Tse-tung's thought and continuously heighten their political consciousness. Meanwhile, we should help them to improve their vocational level.

We grasped mainly the following several tasks:

To help teachers forster the idea of teaching for the sake of revolution. Under the influence of the reactionary "theory of the life of a teacher being one of suffering," some comrades were still inclined to look down on teaching work. Therefore, in selecting and cultivating teachers, we first helped them solve the fundamental question, "For whom we teach," kept arming them with Chairman Mao's doctrine of continuing the revolution under the dictatorship of the proletariat, and organized them in studying Chairman Mao's works every day and in continuously fighting "self" and criticizing revisionism. By running Mao Tse-tung's thought study classes and holding individual heart-to-heart talks, we constantly gave them class education and education in the struggle between the two lines. This enabled them to understand the relationship between the grasping of power in the cultural field and the consolidation of the proletarian dictatorship, to strengthen their sense of honor and sense of responsibility in taking up educational work and to temper themselves to acquire a red heart "devoted to teaching for the sake of revolution."

To educate teachers in the need of maintaining forever the true features of laboring people. Chairman Mao teaches us, "Through participation in collective productive labor, the cadres maintain the most extensive, constant and close ties with the working people." That new teachers are treasured is just because they come from families of poor and lower-middle peasants with the smell of the earth about them. To maintain forever the true features of working people, we made it a rule that apart from participating in shock labor during the busy farming season, they should in ordinary times regularly participate in the collective productive labor of production brigades and in some important meetings of commune and brigades to maintain close ties with the poor and lower-middle peasants. . . .

To handle well the relations between new and old teachers. With the consolidation of the contingent of worker-peasant-soldier teachers, there appeared the problem of the relations between new and old teachers. The proper handling of the relations between new and old teachers is of very great significance in the proper handling of the educational revolution.

The Revolutionary Committee of Yunchiang Commune, Juien *hsien*, Chekiang, "Apply Mao Tse-tung's Thought to the Training of a Force of Teachers," Peking, *Jen-min Jih-pao*, October 15, 1970, *Survey of China Mainland Press,* No. 4765 (October 26, 1970), pp. 10-12.

In handling the realtions between new and old teachers, we gave the new teachers such education as to enable them to call into full play their intitiative. Politically and ideologically, the new teachers helped the old ones in the living study and application of Mao Tse-tung's works and receiving re-education from workers, peasants and soldiers to transform their world outlook. Vocationally, the former joined the latter in studying how to achieve in teaching the aim of putting proletarian politics first, and at the same time, emulated the strong points of the old teachers. In livelihood, the demand was for mutual concern, mutual love and mutual help between the new and the old teachers. . . .

To foster an attitude of modesty in learning. Whether in the political and ideological field or in the vocational field, new teachers need an elevation of their standards. Therefore, we constantly organized them to study Chairman Mao's great teachings, "To be good teachers, we must first be good pupils," and "learning in a humble and respectful manner and learning in a down-to-earth manner." We first demanded that they adopt a humble attitude politically and learn from the workers, peasants and soldiers and from the right party capable of giving education.

Once on their way back to school from an outing the students of Kanch'iao Primary School passed by clumps of peach trees. As they walked they kept reciting in a resonant voice the "Three Main Rules of Discipline" and the "Eight Points for Attention," none of them yielding to the lure of ripe juicy peaches dangling from trees.

This had the old teachers deeply moved. They felt that the students excelled them in the study of Chairman Mao's works and in the living application of such works, as far as many problems are concerned. As teachers, they must learn humbly from their students.

7.8 "Extracts From Chinese Middle School Level Science Textbook"

[The following translations are excerpts from a science textbook—one in a series of such texts—designed for use by Chinese middle school students.]

Excerpt No. 1: "Quotations of Chairman Mao" (opening page)

In the productive struggle and scientific experiment, human beings continuously develop; so does the nature. They never stop at the horizontal line. Therefore, human beings must continue to synthesize their experience to discover, to invent, to create and to advance.

In order to gain freedom from the nature, it is necessary for human beings to employ natural sciences to understand, to control, and to change the nature; then he will obtain freedom from the nature.

Chinese people have will power as well as ability; they must catch up with, and surpass the standard of the advanced nations in the world in the near future.

Prepare for war, prepare for famine, and work for the people.

Excerpt No. 2: "What is a particle? What is an atom?" (p.1)

Chinese Middle School Level Science Texts, Vol. 4, *Chemistry* (Shanghai: People's Publishing House, 1970-71), pp. 1-4, S.M. Hu (trans.).

The great leader Chairman Mao taught us: "While observing any matter, we must examine its substance, and take its phenomenon as the guide to the gate; as soon as we enter the gate, we must grasp firmly its substance. This is the reliable method of scientific analysis."

There are many many kinds of matter with different colors and forms in this world. However, all of them are composed of material. For instance, water, carbon dioxide, food, sugar, salt, alcohol, copper, iron, aluminum, lime, glass, etc. are matter. So far we have known thousands and thousands of them; all of them are composed of particles. The particle is the smallest unit of a certain kind of matter with its unique chemical characteristics, that can exist all by itself.

Excerpt No. 3: "Half-Life" (p. 7)

Chairman Mao taught us; "In the productive struggle and scientific experiment, human beings continuously develop; so does the nature. They never stop at the horizontal line. Therefore, human beings must continue to synthesize their experience to discover, to invent, to create, and to advance. Along with the advancement of scientific techniques, people will discover more elements of shorter "half-life.""

Excerpt No. 4: "Why do we have to refine matter in its 'highly-pure' and 'super-pure' form?" (p. 10)

Water and salt are common matter we see every day; but if someone asks you, "Is this 100 per cent pure water, or is this 100 per cent pure salt," how will you answer?

Chairman Mao taught us, "Through practice, we discover truth, again through practice, we prove truth and develop it." Human beings prove, through practice, that there is no 100 per cent pure water, nor 100 per cent pure salt; this is to say that there is no 100 per cent pure matter.

7.9 "Bring Up New Men Who Develop Morally, Intellectually and Physically"

Chairman Mao teaches us: "Our educational policy must enable everyone who receives an education to develop morally, intellectually and physically and become a worker with both socialist consciousness and culture." The primary school is a place for conducting elementary education. In order to train the younger generation into new men who develop morally, intellectually and physically, it is necessary, beginning from the primary school, to carry out conscientiously Chairman Mao's proletarian policy of education.

Party Branch and Revolution Committee of No. 3 Primary School of Tali *Chen*, Ta-an *Hsien*, Kirin, "Bring Up New Men Who Develop Morally, Intellectually and Physically," Peking, *Jen-min Jih-pao*, January 13, 1972, *Survey of China Mainland Press*, No. 5064 (January 28, 1972), pp. 174-177.

EARNESTLY TEACH LESSONS OF CLASS STRUGGLE IN CLOSE CONJUNCTION WITH THE STUDENTS' THINKING

Class struggle is a main subject the young people must learn. Since the campaign of re-opening schools to make revolution began, we have been paying closer attention to educating the teenagers and children in class struggle and teaching this main subject by various means. For instance, teachers and students are organized and sent deep into factories and the countryside to investigate "three histories," and the various grades have invited old workers and old poor peasants many times to report on their past sufferings and present happiness. We have learned from practice that, in conducting education as mentioned above, it is necessary to link the recollection of the history of class struggle with the current class struggle and with the students' thinking, so as to educate the students to the point.

The teachers and students once went to Hait'o commune to investigate the "three histories." Many students gave comparatively concrete and graphic accounts of the exploitation of peasants by landlords in the old society. But when coming to the current class struggle and struggle between the two lines, they became muddle-headed and could not give clear accounts. In our opinion, in investigating the "three histories" and conducting class struggle, it is necessary to let them know the class struggles of the past as well as the present. We again organized the teachers and students to investigate into the village history of Huchiawopu and the new trend and new characteristics of the current class struggle there. The old poor peasants were asked to give accounts of the conditions of the class struggle and the struggle between the two lines ever since the agrarian reform in this village. Their accounts were recorded and brought back to the schools for hearing by all teachers and students, so that the broad masses of teachers and students might understand more deeply the protractedness and complexity of class struggle and the struggle between the two lines.

Student Kuo Ch'ang-ch'ing knew that his father suffered bitterly in the past. He gnashed his teeth in anger whenever the old society was mentioned in a lesson of class education. But he did not see clearly the class enemies who were corrupting him and so he did not hate them. His behavior was representative of that of some students. Accordingly, we asked his father to come to our school to make a report on his past sufferings and present happiness and, citing the hidden class enemies' sinister scheme of winning over successors from us and frenziedly restoring capitalism, to tell the students clearly that if capitalism was restored, we would suffer again and millions of heads would roll. After the meeting, Kuo Ch'ang-ch'ing wrote two articles, one of them entitled, "Comparing My Boyhood with Papa's," not only expressing his hatred against the landlord and capitalist classes, but also uncovering the class enemies. Many students also strengthened their idea of class struggle and consciously resisted corruption by the ideology of the exploiting classes.

CORRECTLY HANDLE THE RELATIONSHIP BETWEEN INTELLECTUAL EDUCATION AND MORAL EDUCATION, PROMPTLY OVERCOME THE PHENOMENON OF BELITTLING TEACHING AND LEARNING OF CULTURE

Correct handling of the relationship between intellectual education and moral education is an important problem in the all-round implementation of Chairman Mao's policy of education. During the initial period of the campaign of re-opening schools to make revolution, we criticized "intellectual education first" and there emerged the phenomenon of belittling the teaching and learning of culture; when emphasis was laid on teaching and learning lessons of socialist culture well, the phenomenon of "intellectual education first" recurred. Why was this possible? The basic cause was that we did not have high consciousness of the line struggle and failed to distinguish between the two lines on education. With reference to realitites, we re-studied Chairman Mao's teachings on the revolution in education and came to understand that: If we exclusively grasp intellectual education and not moral education, we shall lead the students down a wrong track politically and shall again commit the mistake of taking the revisionist line in education; if we exclusively grasp moral education and not intellectual education, the students will be unable to acquire practical skills for serving the people. For this reason, we must grasp moral education and intellectual education together. . . .

PROCEED FROM THE STUDENTS' REALITIES TO CARRY OUT REALLY WELL THE ACTIVITIES OF LEARNING INDUSTRIAL WORK AND LEARNING FARMING

In organizing students to learn industrial work and farming, attention should be paid to changing the students ideologically and helping the students cultivate the viewpoint toward labor and ideological feelings toward the laboring people. But the students are still young and are in the period of physical growth. For this reason, in arranging time for labor and choosing jobs of labor, we stress the need to proceed from realities and promptly examine and correct the phenomenon of devoting too much time to manual labor which was prevalent for some time in the past. We rule that students of the third grade (9 years old) and above spend only 20 per cent of their time on participating in labor which they are capable of doing. For instance, in the carpenter workshop in the school, they take part in the labor of making teaching aids and repairing desks and benches; in the factories outside the school, they participate in the activities of packing products and sorting rubber; in the fields managed by the school and in the production teams, they participate in the labor of applying manure, thinning out seedlings, weeding the fields and picking grain. . . . .

Learning of industrial work and farming must be combined with the learning of lessons of socialist culture. This problem must also be handled in relation to the realities of the primary school students. The reason is that while in school the primary school students should devote most of their time to learning to read and writing essays and acquire some fundamental cultural and scientific knowledge, and it is unsuitable and infeasible to arrange too many jobs of industrial work and farming for them and to impose unreasonably high demands on them. Our method of work is to take the contents of various subjects into consideration and to teach lessons in realtion to realities where possible. For instance: A drought occurred in the spring of last year. Vegetable seedlings were lacking in the school's agricultural farm. A certain class went to the fields to learn the lessons on *Plant Life* in the subject of general knowledge for primary school while carrying out supplemental planting of seedlings, so that the students could understand better the contents of the lesson.

ACTIVELY CARRY OUT MASS CULTURAL AND SPORTS ACTIVITIES WHICH NOT ONLY ADHERE TO THE MAIN ORIENTATION BUT ALSO HAVE FRESH AND LIVELY CONTENT

Moral education, intellectual education and physical education are closely related to one another. If effort is made to grasp moral education and intellectual education exclusively and not physical education, it will not only be impossible to meet with the needs of the teenagers and children but will do them harm physically and impede them from developing morally and intellectually. But some comrades dare not grasp spare-time activities for students, or they conduct these activities in a very monotonous way. This also is detrimental to the physical growth of the teenagers and children. We have criticized this wrong method of work. . . .

The school has set up a red library and organized a cultural and art propaganda team; meanwhile, it extensively unfolds sports activities of more than 20 events including basketball, table tennis, horizontal bar, rope skipping, kicking of shuttle-cock, etc. The school has also set up a literary and art propaganda team and a sports representative team. With the members of these teams as backbones, various grades and classes have set up small cultural and sports activities. . . . Under the guidance of and with the help of the teachers, they have composed and staged short literary and art performances of various kinds, learned to stage the revolutionary model plays and sing revolutionary songs, and to tell stories about the revolution.

The extensive unfolding of cultural and sports activities benefits the students physically and mentally. In the past, poisoned by "intellectual education first," many students engaged themselves in reading and buried themselves in books, thereby injuring their physical health. Now, the students take part in cultural and sport activities of various kinds, which suit their ages and liking and have rich political content. Their mental outlook and physical condition have become much better. The whole school is full of joy and vigor.

7.10 "Firmly Insist on Selecting Students From Among Workers and Peasants Who Have Practical Experience"

The selection of students from among workers and peasants who have practical experience is a socialist newborn thing. Party committees at all levels must intensively propagandize Chairman Mao's ideas of educational revolution and his proletarian line for education as well as the great significance of student recruitment by universities and other institutions of higher learning. They must earnestly launch revolutionary mass criticism and criticize the old system of student enrollment and such fallacies as "cultural work is dangerous," "it is unfortunate to be a teacher," "going to school in order to be an official" and its revised version, "going to school is useless." They must resolutely oppose departmentalism, perfunctoriness, and such bad practices.

Student recruitment is a serious political task. Party committees at all levels must, in accordance with Chairman Mao's teaching, "Proletarian politics must be put in command," personally take action to strengthen leadership and grasp student recruitment for universities and institutions of higher learning as an important task concerning the fostering of successors to the revolutionary cause of the proletariat and consolidation and strengthening of the proletarian dictatorship. (*Shansi Jih-pao*, February 12, 1972)

*

"The line is the key link. Everything falls into place when it is upheld." The

---

"Firmly Insist on Selecting Students From Among Workers and Peasants Who Have Practical Experience" (Extracts from the press in various parts of the country), Peking, *Kuang-ming Jih-pao*, March 16, 1972, *Survey of China Mainland Press*, No. 5102 (March 28, 1972), pp. 46-49.

admission of workers, peasants and soldiers into universities is an important act of implementation of Chairman Mao's educational line, an act that concerns the fostering of successors to the revolutionary cause of the proletariat and the consolidation of the proletarian dictatorship.

In carrying out student recruitment, it is necessary to persevere firmly from beginning to end in Chairman Mao's class line and mass line, adopt the method of voluntary application, recommendation by the masses, approval by the leadership, and re-examination by the universities concerned, and select outstanding workers, peasants and soldiers for admission into universities.

The work of student recruitment can certainly not be fulfilled by the educational agencies and student enrollment groups alone. Party committees at all levels must pay serious attention to it and all agencies concerned must closely coordinate student recruitment with various other work. The broad revolutionary masses must study, propagandize, and implement Chairman Mao's proletarian educational line with practical action. Subject to the conditions for student enrollment, they must impartially and selflessly send in applications and actively recommend candidates, so that all may truly attach importance to and feel concern for student recruitment work, and together fulfill the task of student recruitment for the universities. (*Kueichou Jih-pao*, February 21, 1972)

*

The recruitment of students must be conscientiously discussed by the masses and they must make the recommendations. The process of student recruitment should be made a process of study, propagation, and implementation of Chairman Mao's proletarian line for education and policy. It is necessary to uphold firmly the centralized leadership of the Party and seriously implement the Party's class line which attaches importance to family backgrounds but not exclusive importance, and which places more emphasis on political performance. Outstanding workers, peasants and soldiers should be selected for the universities who study assiduously Marxism-Leninism and Mao Tse-tung's thought, who are conscious to a certain degree of class struggle, line struggle, and the continuing revolution, who have close ties with the masses, whose performance in revolution and production is remarkable, and who have two or three years of practical experience. All units which take part in the selection and nomination must overcome departmentalism and correctly handle the relations between the part and the whole, making the interests of the part serve those of the whole. Unwillingness to select and recommend backbone cadres of one's own unit is not in conformity with the interests of the proletariat.

In student recruitment work, it is also necessary to sum up in earnest experience in last year's pilot schemes. In particular, it is necessary to sum up and popularize the typical experience of mobilization of the masses and handing of the Party's policy to the masses, to which the Party committees attach such importance. Meanwhile, it is also necessary to work strictly in accordance with the Party's policies and principles and resolutely oppose and resist perfunctoriness and other improper styles of work. (*T'ien-chin Jih-pao*, March 4, 1972)

*

The recruitment of worker-peasant-soldier students for the universities from the forefront of the three major revolutionary movements is a task of the greatest significance. The selection of outstanding workers, peasants and soldiers with practical experience for enrollment in the universities and the fostering and training of a force of intellectuals of the proletariat in accordance with Chairman Mao's instruction, "Select students from among workers and peasants who have practical experience," is an important measure for implementing Chairman Mao's proletarian line for education, an important task that bears on the fostering of successors to the revolutionary cause of the proletariat and the consolidation of the dictatorship of the proletariat, and a criticism of Liu Shao-ch'i's counter-revolutionary revisionist line for education.

With the institutions of higher learning recruiting new students, putting into practice a new system of student enrollment, and selecting outstanding workers, peasants and soldiers with practical experience for enrollment today in accordance with Chairman Mao's directive, the phenomenon of domination of schools by bourgeois intellectuals will of course be changed further and the schools will become truly socialist new-type universities.

It should also be seen that practice of the new system of student enrollment will help to form a massive force of intellectuals of the working class for our country to meet the needs of our rapidly developing socialist revolution and socialist construction. (*Hsin-hua Jih-pao*, March 5, 1972)

*

Socialist universities must implement in its entirety Chairman Mao's guideline for education: "Those who receive education should be able to develop morally, intellectually, and physically, and become cultured laborers with socialist consciousness." To insure the total implementation of this guideline, the first thing to be done in recruiting students in overall consideration of the moral, intellectual, and physical conditions of the student-candidates.

Student enrollment today brings the "moral" condition to the fore and firmly puts moral development in the first position. Students to be enrolled must first be subjected to political scrutiny. Outstanding workers, peasants and soldiers are selected for enrollment in universities who are conscious of class struggle and line struggle, who study assiduously Marxism-Leninism and Chairman Mao's works and earnestly remold their thought in the three major revolutionary movements, and who maintain close ties with the masses. This is a basic condition that insures the good quality of the students enrolled.

However, insistence on "moral development first" dies not mean abandonment of intellectual development. What we oppose is not intellectual development, but the placing of intellectual development in the first position. It is wrong to fail to pay attention to either political character or the cultural level. (*Chi-lin Jih-pao*, March 7, 1972)

7.11 "Some Experiences in Teaching English to Primary One Students"

Under the leadership of the Party committee of the commune and supported by departments concerned, Chennan School, Chinhsing School and Chennan Primary School in Chiangwan commune, Paoshan *hsien*, Shanghai municipality, began teaching English to first grade students of primary schools from May 1971. Certain results have been scored up to the present and the workers, peasants and soldiers as well as foreigners highly praise the instruction. At present, the students have grasped the pronunciation of more than 60 commonly used words and learned to sing more than ten revolutionary songs in English, including "The East Is Red" and the "Internationale." Recently, some of the classes have already started teaching the alphabet. Comrades in these schools realize profoundly that to grasp the teaching of foreign languages in primary schools well and to let primary school students begin the study of foreign languages at the age of seven or eight will help to lay a good foundation for them to learn foreign languages well.

At the beginning, leadership squads of the schools and teachers had different opinions about the feasiblity of primary one students learning a foreign language. Some of the comrades thought:

(1) As primary one students do not have any foundation in Chinese, they cannot grasp the rules governing the foreign language.

(2) As the children are still young and some of them are in the process of changing teeth, they cannot pronounce correctly and therefore it is impossible to lay a good foundation for pronunciation.

(3) Imposing an extra burden on the students will affect their health.

However, many comrades disagreed with these viewpoints but thought instead that although the foreign language did have its own unique rules, yet they could be grasped through practice. Although primary one students did not have much foundation in Chinese to speak of, yet they could imitate and learn well. Although teeth changing could indeed produce difficulties in pronunciation (such as the pronunciation of sibilants), yet foreign primary school students also had the same problem; therefore this difficulty could be overcome as long as teachers assumed their responsbility seriously, gave the children correct guidance and corrected their methods of pronunciation as the situation required.

After an analysis on the students' workload, they admitted that the addition of two sessions of foreign language a week was indeed an increase of burden on the students. But this workload could not be considered heavy when compared with that in higher grades. Furthermore, since there is still neither writing nor dictation nor extracurricular work, the burden on the students should not be considered too heavy.

After several discussions and investigations, everybody's view began to become unified. Thus they came to the conclusion that as long as the leadership and teachers paid attention to this subject ideologically, adopted a correct method of teaching and fully mobilized the students' initiative to learn the foreign language for the sake of the

---

Foreign Language Instruction Investigation Group of the Education Bureau of Shanghai Municipality, "Some Experiences in Teaching English to Primary One Students," Peking, *Kuang-ming Jih-pao*, March 25, 1972, *Survey of China Mainland Press*, No. 5111 (April 12, 1972), pp. 104-106.

revolution, it was possible for primary school students of seven or eight to learn the foreign language successfully.

The following is the method the schools adopted in the practice of teaching the foreign language:

(1) Emphasis is laid on acquiring the ability to listen and speak without teaching the alphabet and spelling during the first year. In view of the possiblity of confusion and interference of the two languages since primary one students have to learn Chinese romanization in addition to English, they are not taught the English alphabet and phonetics for the time being; instead, conversation is taught first.

In the course of teaching conversation, the students' correct pronunciation is to be grasped so that they may understand, speak, and sing in the language as well as see the form of the written words and the shape of the mouth for different sounds. If the English alphabet and spelling are taught after the students have basically mastered Chinese romanization (toward the end of the first grade), there would be no fear of confusion between the two languages.

Primary school students are enthusiastic about learning the foreign language and are quick to learn, but they are also quick to forget; therefore it is difficult to consolidate what they have learned. In view of this, we must let them practice repeatedly to deepen their impression.

(2) Methods of teaching should be simple and include reading, singing and acting. Primary school students of seven or eight would lose interest if the teacher only explains the pronunciation of words or recites sentences. Consequently, in the classroom, the teacher should not only use objects in daily use as aids for teaching, but also use teaching materials which contain slogans, short sentences, passages of poems or songs, etc. In the meantime, the teachers should use gestures while teaching so as to make the learning process more vivid. For example, when teaching the lessons of "We Love Chairman Mao Arduously" and "Study Well and Improve Ourselves Everyday," the teacher may join together words which have already been learned to make them into sentences for the students to recite and act out in the form of poems or songs. When teaching "People of the World Unite To Overthrow Imperialism!" the teacher hangs a map of the world on the wall and explains the international situation to the students. This will deepen the students' impression as well as liven up the atmosphere of the classroom.

To enable the students to grasp pronunciation correctly, the teacher must explain according to the students' ability to understand and try to use as few linguistic terms as possible. During examination, the teacher hangs pictures of rifles, pencils, hammers and sickles on the wall and lets the students compose short sentences with English words already learned according to ideas suggested by the pictures. Then after discussions or preparations by groups, the students may come up to the rostrum and speak to one another in English. This method is active and vivid. It helps to consolidate the students' memory of sentence patterns and cultivates the students' ability to think and express themselves.

(3) Students of the classes organize foreign language detachments which regularly conduct such cultural activities as recitals, singing, dancing, etc., in English. These students learn their lessons before others outside class and take the lead in speaking and singing in the class. Thus they successfully play the role of the backbone.

(4) Other subjects of study are coordinated with the results of foreign language teaching: Teachers of other subjects choose the proper moment to repeat or mention English words already learned to deepen the students' impression.

In the practice of foreign language teaching, the schools realize that requirements on the part of the teachers and teaching materials are higher when it comes to teaching a foreign language well to primary school students of seven or eight years of age. The teachers must not only be able to pronounce the words correctly, but also know how to teach in a way suitable to the children. Teaching materials must be consistent with the rules governing the foreign language as well as suitable for children of our country to learn. At present, our teachers and teaching materials still cannot totally meet these requirements. They must continue to work hard to attain this aim.

7.12 "Mass Physical Training"

In last February's round-the-city race, a traditional mass sports activity in the capital during the Spring Festival, the Peking No. 26 Middle School had the most participants. Many gave a good account of themselves, and its girls' relay team placed fifth. Prior to this, more than 100 boys and girls in the school formed some 20 teams to take part in a middle school cross-country run held by the city's Chungwent District. One of the girls' teams won the championship while three others came fourth, sixth and eighth, and the boys' teams came second, third, eighth and tenth. Curious over these successes, which had won widespread acclaim, we paid the school a visit.

Upon our arrival at 6:30 in the morning, we saw some 500 students training on the sports grounds — some practicing throwing the javelin, discus, hand-grenade and other objects, some running or practicing the high jump and long jump, and some playing ball games. At 7:30, the students gathered on the large field or in the courtyards, doing setting-up exericses to music broadcast over the radio. Classes began at 8. From 8 through 4 p.m., we saw over a dozen classes taking physical training lessons on the grounds. During the interval after lunch and after 4 o'clock in the afternoon, the students played ball games and engaged in various other activities. So keen are the youngsters on the ball games that they throng the sports grounds even on Sundays.

The No. 26 Middle School has 3,070 boy and girl students in 54 classes, with five full-time and three part-time physical training teachers. The school has adequate sports facilities, including nine basketball courts, one volleyball court, one football field and ten table tennis tables. Apart from school teams for football, boys' and girls' basketball, volleyball, table tennis and track and field, many grades and classes have their own teams.

How to organize such large contingents in regular training? What ideology should be used to guide their activities? What results have been obtained from mass physical training? And what is the relationship between moral, intellectual and physical development? Answers to these questions were given by a physical training teacher whom we interviewed.

Through the Great Cultural Revolution, the teacher began by way of introduction, we have come to understand that in physical training there is also the question of "For whom?" Since the purpose is to build up the people's health, we should stress the mass character of such training. It is wrong to train just a few "stars"; our duty is to help the majority of students take an interest in physical training and actively participate in sports activities.

"Mass Physical Training," *Peking Review*, No. 14 (April 7, 1972), pp. 11-13.

Having made this clear, we have bent our efforts in this direction.

First of all, we do our best to popularize those sports which give a comparatively large amount of exercise but require no particular skill, such as running, tug of war, skipping and throwing the handgrenade. We have introduced a kind of relay race with the participants running back and forth on a 60-meter-long track. With 20-30 on a team, as many as 40-60 can take part in each race. Everyone can run, so if we make proper arrangements, the students will all be willing to join. Tug of war also gives the body quite a lot of exercise. With 20 on each side, 40 can join in each contest.

Secondly, we pay proper attention to combining athletic meets with everyday sports activities, using competition to stimulate training. It is natural that an upsurge in mass activity precedes every such meet. However, we used to only stress getting good results and did not combine competition with everyday training. The result was students started training only a few days before a competition and laid off when it was over. The accent now is on popularization. Before an athletic meet starts, every grade and class is required to hold trial competitions to select its representatives. To do this, it has perforce to start training two or three months in advance, and the net result is there will be many small-scale athletic meets before the actual school meet is held, with over 90 per cent of the students having taken part.

To induce more students to take an interest in track and field, which lays a good foundation for other sports, we have made due arrangements in the rules of competition. Since placings are determined by the total number of points won by a team which can field only a definite number of contestants, we have stipulated that points be given to everyone who has competed according to the rules, with only one point difference for each placing. In this way, all the contestants are encouraged to do their best for the team. Both in making preparations and in holding the school athletic meet, we have done away with the past practice that only a few are kept busy while the majority look on unconcerned. Now we mobilize the non-contestants to do various work, such as serving as umpires, judges and timekeepers, and we ask the teachers to explain the rules to them beforehand. All this makes them doubly enthusiastic about learning the rules. Thus an increasing number of working personnel are trained, and more and more students take a great interest in athletics.

Matches in various ball games are quite common between classes or grades and between teachers and staff members and students. In addition to athletic meets every spring and autumn, the school teams often compete in inter-school tournaments.

Increased interest after sports have become popular among the students spurs them on to raise their standard. Drawing on their initiative, we give them lectures on various sports during physical training classes and morning and afternoon training sessons, and put them through a rigorous basic training course. Those grades or classes which have not done well in the previous athletic meet are all the more anxious to show improvement and, after hard training, they often do better in the next meet. The other grades and classes are not complacent about past successes either, but continue to forge ahead. When such friendly emulation is the order of the day, steady improvement is assured for one and all.

Students showing promise are sent in groups to the spare-time physical culture and sports school attached to the Peking Gymnasium for short or long-term specialized training. With their standard raised, they constitute a major force in helping promote sports in our school.

No effort has been spared to foster good sportsmanship among the students. Fine examples of this during competitions are frequently propagandized throughout the school. Equal attention is paid to using sports activities to educate the students ideologically and properly handle the relationship between physical training and study and between physical and moral development. Recently, to help the students take examination seriously, we held a forum in which several students holding responsible posts in their grades or classes and sports activists discussed how they correctly handled this relationship. Their views, broadcast over the loudspeaker or made public in the wall newspapers, received the close attention of all the students.

We always encourage the students to repair and make the sports equipment themselves. When table tennis became increasingly popular and tables weren't enough, we called upon the students to build eight brick and cement tables in the open air. And whenever the wooden tables have to be repaired, they always do it themselves. This helps them cultivate the habit of caring for public property and of taking part in physical labor.

Practice over the past year or so has given us tangible results. As more and more students take part in sports, they have in general grown taller and put on weight, with much better health and stamina acquired through a period of training. In particular, girl students' physiques have greatly improved. More energetic, the students have shown better discipline and are keener on their studies.

Winding up his discourse, the teacher said: We are now aware as never before of the benefits of promoting mass physical culture and sports. Chairman Mao's teaching "With us, therefore, the raising of standards is based on popularization, while popularization is guided by the raising of standards" has given us the correct orientation. There are many shortcomings in our work and we have to make still greater efforts in order to do a good job of promoting physical culture and sports among the masses.

7.13 "Nursery Classes Universally Set Up in Hsihsinchuang Brigade, Ku-an *Hsien*, Hopei Province"

(NCNA Shihchiachuang, May 5, 1972) Under the leadership of its Party branch and its revolutionary committee, Hsihsinchuang brigade, Ku-an *hsien*, Hopei Province, has set up "nursery classes" universally in its various production teams and actively conducts education for young children. Now over 85 percent of the children between the age of four and six in the whole brigade have entered the "nursery classes." In this way, it is possible not only to free a large group of women laborers in the countryside, but also to lay a good foundation for elementary education. This wins the praise of the poor and lower-middle peasants.

Women of Hsihsinchuang brigade greatly raised their political consciousness during the great proletarian cultural revolution. They actively asked permission to participate in the three major revolutionary struggles. After its establishment, the revolutionary committee of the brigade adopted some measures to free some of the women from household labor, but a group of women still could not participate in productive labor because they were busy with taking care of their children. . . .

The brigade revolutionary committee decided to charge a woman committee member to take special care of this work and set up a "three-in-one" young children's education leading group comprising cadres, young children's teachers and

"Nursery Classes Universally Set Up in Hsihsinchuang Brigade, Ku-an *Hsien*, Hopei Province" (NCNA, Shihchianchuang, May 5, 1972), Peking, *Kuang-ming Jih-pao*, May 6, 1972, *Survey of China Mainland Press*, No. 5137 (May 19, 1972), pp. 203-205.

representatives of parents of the young children. Each production team transferred a woman commune member who was good in doing political and ideological work and belonged to a relatively high cultural level to serve as teachers of the young children. A "nursery class" was set up in each production team. The young children lived and ate at home and were sent to the nursery class by their parents every day.

Many of the women who had young children were overwhelmed with joy when they heard this news. They expressed their will to work more vigorously in grasping revolution and promoting production.

The poor and lower-middle peasants unanimously sent their children to the "nursery class." They regarded this as a joyful occasion. But, some people were worried that the children might not be taken good care of in the "nursery class."

Commune member Ku Su-fen had a child son. She and her mother-in-law looked after the child every day, carrying him on their backs when walking and holding him in their arms when sitting, and they were reluctant to send him to the "nursery class." The comrade of the young children's education leading group came to their home and patiently did ideological work on them, making them understand that it was incorrect to lavish their love upon and pamper the child and that they should bring the child up as a successor to the revolution. They happily sent the child to the "nursery class." In collective life, the child acquired a great deal of knowledge, learned to sing revolutionary songs and became more lively and lovely. The mother and the grandmother were very happy. They were relieved of the burden of taking care of the child. They went together to participate in collective productive labor.

Whether or not the young children's education could be consolidated after it got started was chiefly determined by the teachers of the nursery class. When this brigade initially set up the "nursery classes," some teachers feared that they would be blamed if they did not take good care of the young children, so that they were ill at ease when they met with difficulties in their work. In view of this thinking, the brigade revolutionary committee held a Mao Tse-tung's thought study class and organized the teachers of nursery classes to study Chairman Mao's "Serve the People" and his other works, making them raise their consciousness of serving the people whole-heartedly. The teachers of the nursery classes actively took good care of the young children and taught them well. They formerly waited for the children's parents to send their children to the nursery class and to take them away after the class. Later, they went on their own initiative to take the children to the class and to bring them home when class was over. In the past, they only organized the children to play games, sing songs and read. Later, they helped the children wash their hands and face, cut hair for them and mended their clothes. What they did won the praise of the poor and lower-middle peasants.

When this brigade started to prepare the conduct of education for young children, there were no rooms, teaching aids, or toys. What should be done? Some people suggested that the brigade give money and material for building classrooms and allot a sum of money for buying teaching aids and toys. The poor and lower-middle peasants disagreed with this suggestion.

They said that it was more suitable to run "native nursery classes" in the spirit of hard work and plain living. They eagerly volunteered to spare some rooms. Eventually, the nursery class teachers said: "The nursery class should be run in the home of its teacher." Thus, the problem of room was solved. By way of telling the young children stories of the revolution, the nursery class teachers wrote stories of the good personalities and good deeds of the village or composed songs of these personalities and deeds and taught the children to sing these songs, thereby solving the problem of teaching material. When teaching aids were lacking, they made some by their own effort. When there were no toys, they taught the children to gather clay and made many toys with clay. To cultivate the children's good thinking of loving to do labor, they led the children to pick leaves of the caster oil plant and feed caster oil silkworms in summer and to pick rice ears and beans during the autumn harvest.

The Party branch and the revolutionary committee of the brigade perseveringly and conscientiously grasped the study and ideological work of the nursery class teachers. They organized the teachers to do intensive study once a month so as to exchange experience and study and solve the problems cropping up in their work.

In the past few years, in Hsihsinchuang brigade, thanks to the persistent efforts to conduct education for young children, the women maintained their labor attendance rate at 95 percent and higher, contributing their share toward securing a bumper harvest in agriculture. Because their household work was reduced, the women could spare more time to take part in study. They continuously raised their ideological consciousness. In the "nursery class," the children cultivated the idea of loving to do labor and to study and loving the collective.

7.14 "The 'May 7' Cadre School"

A new thing born in the Great Cultural Revolution, "May 7" cadre schools are all over China. Every province, municipality and autonomous region as well as many special administrative regions, counties and cities, all have this type of school. More than a hundred belong to the departments under the Central Committee of the Chinese Communist Party and the State Council.

Those who have been sent to the school include veteran cadres who went through the Long March, the War of Resistance Against Japan or the War of Liberation; cadres who joined the revolution after liberation; those who went from their homes to schools and from there to government offices and who were lacking in practical experience; and young cadres who had been Red Guards. While at cadre school, they get their regular wages and the same welfare facilities as when they are on the job. The term generally is for a year or so, the least six months, the most two to three years.

VERSATILE ACTIVITIES

Regardless of seniority or how high a post held, everyone is an ordinary student, a "May 7" fighter. At the Chingkou "May 7" Cadre School in Kirin Province, the former director of the agriculture bureau becomes a pig-breeder, the former secretary of the city Party committee a carpenter, a department head a cart driver and a county head a cook.

Students' lives are many-sided. They do productive manual labor as well as study. They criticize the bourgeoisie and do mass work. The school also organizes militia training and cultural and sports activities. Some schools set aside time for students to study their vocations or raise their general educational level.

The "May 7" cadre school is a school for training cadres at their posts in rotation.

How does the school accomplish its tasks? How do students study? It can be generalized as follows:

Studying Marxist-Leninist Works. In the light of the revolutionary struggle and their ideology, the students study the works of Marx, Engels, Lenin and Stalin and

"The 'May 7' Cadre School," *Peking Review*, No. 19 (May 12, 1972), pp. 5-7.

Chairman Mao's works to raise their level of Marxism and their consciousness of the struggle between the two lines, thereby raising their ability to distinguish between genuine and sham Marxists.

The students at the Huangho "May 7" Cadre School in Honan spend half a day studying and the other half doing manual labor. In the busy farming season, they work during the day, studying in the morning or evening. Last year they studied the *Manifesto of the Communist Party, Critique of the Gotha Programme* and *The State and Revolution* as well as *On Practice* and *On Contradiction*. They pay special attention to linking theory with practice and often organize group discussions and criticism meetings.

Participating in Class Struggle. Students at cadre schools take part in class struggle and in criticizing the bourgeoisie to temper themselves. They often link their work and ideological problems with their mass criticism of swindlers like Liu Shao-chi, of the theory of the dying out of class struggle, the bourgeois theory of human nature, the theory of productive forces, idealist apriorism, the theory that doing manual labor is a punishment and the theory of going to school in order to get an official post. Some cadre schools carry out various political movements in step with the movements in the units they belong to. Some have sent students to rural people's communes to take part in or help local people carry out a political campaign like attacking active counter-revolutionaries, campaigns against embezzlement and theft, extravagance and waste and specualtion.

Taking Part in Productive Labor. Cadre schools devote themselves mainly to agricultural production. Where conditions allow, they branch out into forestry, animal husbandry, side-occupations and fisheries. At the same time they go in for small industries, such as machine-repairing, manufacturing of chemical fertilizers, insecticides, paper-and brick-making, and sugar-refining.

Every cadre school has cultivated land — much was once wasteland — ranging from hundreds to thousands of *mu,* parts of which are reclaimed tracts along sea coasts or lakeshores and on barren hillsides and alkaline slopes. Inner Mongolia's Ikh Chao League cadre school converted much sandy land into fertile fields by covering the sand with layers of mud.

"Plain living and hard struggle" and *"self-reliance"* is the motto of all the cadre schools.

The object of students taking part in industrial or agricultural productive labor is not only to create material wealth for the country but mainly to better their ideology and to transform their subjective world as they transform the objective world.

Cadres of the General Office of the Chinese Communist Party's Central Committee turned the building of their school into a process of edifying their thought. Instead of choosing a ready-made site, they preferred to build it from scratch. They turned 5,000 *mu* of lakeshore and other wasteland into fields, and built dormitories and factories on their own. They dug canals, wading knee-deep in mud. They went into icy streams to get sand and braved eye-stinging smoke to burn limestone in the kilns. They fought floods to save people's lives and property. They met all these trials head-on to gain the revolutionary spirit of "fearing neither hardship nor death."

Going Among Workers and Peasatns. Students often leave their schools for short stays in nearby people's communes or factories. Living, eating and working alongside workers or peasants, they learn from them and carry out social investigations among them at the same time. They also do mass work, such as organizing workers and peasants to study philosophy, helping them get some general education and aiding local Party organizations carry out Party rectification and Party building. All these activities aim at raising their ideological level and reforming their world outlook.

TRANSFORMING MAN

Cadres come to the schools in turns. They go back to their original posts after "graduation," or are transferred to new work. Practice has shown that their stay at cadre schools, brief as it is, is excellent training. The great majority of students come out of the schools changed in outlook in more ways than one.

One artist at the Kuantang Cadre School in Hunan Province who had joined revolutionary work straight from school had not liked to draw peasants because he considered their weatherbeaten faces no objects for art. After entering the cadre school, he had a chance to live and eat with peasants, and made some social investigations into their lives. He found out the tragic histories of many peasant families in the old society under the exploitation of the landlord class. His sentiments changed, and he began to have a great compassion for the once-downtrodden peasants. He said: "Before, I looked at things according to bourgeois aesthetic standards; the more I drew, the farther from the laboring people I got. Now, the more I draw peasants, the closer I feel to them."

Lin Hsiang-wei, vice-director and chief engineer at the designing institute in Hunan, had designed a highway bridge which wasted tons of bricks because he wanted it fancy. The workers criticized him, without convincing him he was wrong. After going to the Kuantang Cadre School, he happened to be working at a brick-kiln. A rush assignment in summer had him drenched in sweat and covered with dirt in the sweltering heat day after day. Only then did he fully realize what it meant to make one brick. He said with genuine feeling: "It's only after you've taken part in labor that you get to feel akin to the workers and peasants." During a fierce rainstorm, Lin ran to the kiln and covered up the clay molds, though he got soaking wet. He often expresses his determination to continue to make revolution and thoroughly transform his old ideas, to become an intellectual welcomed by the workers, peasants and soldiers.

Veteran cadres with much revolutionary experience also gain a great deal from going to cadre school. It puts them back in the war years and helps them get rid of bureaucratic airs and the inactivity that crept up on them in peace time. It rejuvenates them.

Fang Fu-chin, a veteran of the 25,000-*li* Long March of the Chinese Red Army in 1934-35, was one of the first to enroll at the Meitsun Cadre School under the Kwangchow Railway Bureau. Once there, he was reminded of the militant life he used to lead in the Chingkang Mountains, Yenan and Nanniwan in the early days of the revolution. Invigorated, he joined the rank and file in climbing mountains to fell trees, and went wherever the difficulties were greatest. Out of consideration for his years, comrades often told him to take a rest. He refused, saying: "You may replace me in labor, but that'll never transform my ideology."

Yang Li-feng is a new cadre from a poor peasant family. She entered college in 1960 wearing a pair of simple cloth shoes her mother had made for her. Under the influence of the revisionist line in education, she developed the bourgeois idea of wanting to get up in the world. So she put the cloth shoes at the bottom of a chest. When schoolmates asked her to tell them her family history, she refused, ashamed of past poverty.

At the Hsiushuihotzu People's Commune in Faku County, Liaoning Province, Yang took part in peasant activities to recall past bitterness and praise the new life. She told commune members how her feelings had changed after going to college. The peasants helped her, saying: "You must understand that you've not only forgotten your family's bitter past, but that of your class. You've not only put away the cloth shoes, but the true qualities of the laboring people." Enlightened, Yang plunged into productive labor with renewed zeal and wore her cloth shoes again.

After coming out of cadre schools, most cadres are full of life, keep in close touch with the masses and have a good style in their work and way of living. The masses of

2

86   TOWARD A NEW WORLD OUTLOOK

workers, peasants and soldiers welcome their progress made in this period of "studying once again." They say: "We have full confidence in cadres who can work both at
the top and down at the grass roots, and who keep close to the people."

ORIGIN OF CADRE SCHOOLS

"May 7" cadre schools were set up in all parts of the country according to
Chairman Mao's May 7, 1966 Directive. This directive pointed out that the "army
should be a great school. . . . In this school, our army should study politics and
military affairs, raise its educational level, and also engage in agriculture and side-
occupations and run small or medium-sized factories. . . . Our army should also do
mass work. . . . Also our army should always be ready to participate in the struggles
to criticize and repudiate the bourgeoisie in the cultural revolution." It also called on
people in other fields to "learn other things" while mainly engaging in their own
work. "They should also learn industrial production, agricultural production and
military affairs. They also should criticize and repudiate the bourgeoisie." They must
study "politics and raise their educational level." "Those working in . . . Party and
government organizations should do the same."

In 1968, when Proletarian Cultural Revolution was developing in depth, the question of how to carry forward the cadres' ideological revolutionization and revolutionize government institutions was discussed on a wide scale. In October that year
Chairman Mao issued the call: "*Going down to do manual labor gives vast numbers
of cadres an excellent opportunity to study once again: this should be done by all
cadres except those who are old, weak, ill or disabled. Cadres at their posts should
also go down in turn to do manual labor.*"

Cadres at every level all over the country enthusiastically responded to this call
and asked to go to the most difficult places to do manual labor and to "*study once
again.*" The "May 7" cadre schools were set up to meet these needs, and in the
single month of October alone new ones appeared almost every day.

The guiding thought of these cadre schools which upholds the system of cadre
participation in collective productive labor was pointed out by Chairman Mao and
the Party Central Committee long before 1968.

Cadres doing productive labor is the fine tradition of the Chinese Workers' and
Peasants' Red Army, the Eighth Route Army and the New Fourth Army, as today it
is the tradition of the People's Liberation Army. In any army of the people, officers
and soldiers help the masses in manual labor wherever they are. After liberation,
cadres in government and Party organizations have learnt to carry forward this
tradition. The system of cadre participation in collective productive labor for fixed
periods has been in effect since 1958, and cadres have been taking turns in going to
the countryside or factories.

In 1964, after summing up the experience of revolutionary struggle in China and
studying the positive and negative experiences in the international communist
movement, Chairman Mao pointed out: "*By taking part in collective productive
labor, the cadres maintain extensive, constant and close ties with the working
people. This is a major measure of fundamental importance for a socialist system; it
helps to overcome bureaucracy and to prevent revisionism and dogmatism.*"

7.15 "Establish A New System of Examination Through Practice"

At the beginning of 1971 when some of the courses of the experimental class of our department were about to conclude, we found it necessary to review and sum up our teaching work. In the meantime, we also needed a system to encourage the advanced students and help the backward ones so as to raise their consciousness continually in studying for the sake of revolution. Under such circumstances, the question of whether we still wanted examinations arose.

Most of the teachers and students held that there should be examination, but some of the teachers failed to draw a clear line of distinction between the two roads. For fear of being accused of "controlling, restraining, and suppression" the students, they wanted to give up examination so as to avoid contradiction. There were also comrades in the leadership squad who feared this and that. They could not make up their mind and were afraid of conducting examination.

Confronted with this situation, leaders of the department repeatedly studied together with the teachers and students Chairman Mao's relevant instructions. This made everybody realize that the most important shortcomings of the old system of examination were: First, the system of examination was used as principal means to punish the students. Secondly, the system made the studens memorize mechanically what they had learned and turned them into ideologically paralyzed bookworms. Such a system of examination which served the purpose of training successors for the bourgoisie, must be abolished. The new system of examination serves the purpose of training successors to the revolutionary cause of the proletariat. Its aim is to help the students consolidate and deepen through examination the theoretical knowledge and skills they have learned. In the meantime, the new system of examination also helps to examine the results of teaching so as to facilitate study and improvement of teaching work to improve the quality of teaching gradually.

After understanding was unified, the teachers and students indicated that they must reform the system of examination according to Chairman Mao's instructions instead of abolishing the system of examination altogether.

CLARIFY THE AIM AND IMPLEMENT THE MEASURES

But how is examination to be administered? Some comrades advocated open-book examination while others advocated closed-book examination. Now we let everybody discuss and see which method of examination was better.

After a discussion, everybody's understanding was unified. They thought the method of examination to be adopted should depend upon the characteristics of the subject and requirements in study and should also serve the purpose of examination.

In open-book examinations the students can concentrate and think individually within a certain time limit as well as analyze and answer the questions by themselves. Therefore this method is good for examining the students' analytical ability. A small number of students who really have difficulty in answering the questions may consult other people so that they can learn something through examination. However, there are some subjects which must be remembered. For such subjects, closed-book examination can consolidate the results of study so that the students can apply them

---

Department of Chemistry, Kirin University, "Establish A New System of Examination Through Practice," Peking, *Jen-min Jih-pao*, June 24, 1972, *Survey of China Mainland Press*, No. 5167 (July 3-7, 1972), pp. 54-57.

to practice. Consequently, here closed-book examination is more suitable.

In January this year we conducted an examination in our department on the subjects of physics and organic chemistry and obtained relatively good results. The students said: Through examination we can have a firmer grasp of certain fundamental theoretical knowledge which we fail to grasp deeply during ordinary times. In the meantime, we can also apply such theoretical knowledge to practice.

Now how should examination questions be prepared? We realized through practice that we should pay attention to the following when we prepare questions:

Inject clear ideological content in the questions whenever possible — For instance, our questions for organic chemistry were prepared in combination with the non-mercury catalyst experiments conducted by the teachers and students at the Kirin Carbide Plant. In the past, the mercury catalyst method of production used by capitalist countries was adopted for the production of acetaldehyde from ethine hydrate; but this method is harmful to the human body and the non-mercury catalyst experiment was aimed at solving this problem. Through a comparison of the advantages and short-comings of the mercury and non-mercury methods, the students were able to grasp the quality and condition of reaction of acetylenes and aldehydes in organic chemistry as well as receive a profound line education.

Questions must be practical—Last year, students of high molecule chemistry section went to No. 4 Chemical Plant of Kirin Municipality to conduct teaching on dacron products and to study theory in combination with practical production in the plant. In the examination at the end of the course, we let the students apply the principles of chemistry which they had already learned to the designing of a process for the recovery and comprehensive utilization of potassium salts from dacron production. In the past, relatively expensive potassium salts were washed away into the drainage during the process of production. Now the teachers and students, working together with the master workers during the examination, solved this problem rationally. In this way they made contribution to the development of comprehensive utilization and the students also learned practical knowledge.

Questions must be comprehensive and flexible—For instance, one of the questions in the organic chemistry examination was: What principle products are produced by vinylite ester acetate under the condition of diluted alkali? Here students who had grasped all-round knowledge and could apply them in a versatile way could give three products, but those whose knowledge was not versatile enough could give only two or even just one. Such question can judge the depth and breadth of the students' grasping of knowledge, help us to understand the students' ability to analyze and solve problems and facilitate the study and improvement of teaching.

SUM UP EXPERIENCE AND ENHANCE THE ACHIEVEMENTS

How are we to grade the examination papers? This was one of the more acute questions in the struggle of reforming the system of examination. The leadership of our department was mainly afraid that grading was liable to lead us to the old road of "marks in command." Some of the teachers were afraid that grading was not easy to do and that after grading ideological work would also be difficult to perform. Meanwhile, some of the students were afraid of getting poor marks.

Thus we mobilized the broad masses of teachers and students to develop a discussion before the examination on the question of whether examination papers should be graded. Everybody thought: Grading in examination is like quality specifications for products manufactured in a factory where quality must be inspected. Consequently we must also have a quality standard for students in socialist universities, who must be red as well as expert. This is fundamentally different from "marks in command" under the revisionist line of education.

We adopted a democratic way of grading and combined it with the appraisal of teaching and appraisal of learning. Our ways are:

First, combination of democratic grading with the ceaseless strengthening of the students' consciousness in learning for the sake of revolution. At the beginning, some of the students of a relatively higher cultural level thought they were doing fairly well and therefore failed to review and sum up seriously what they learned. In the examination they made mistakes which they should not have made. During the process of democratic grading, fellow students and teachers helped them to correct their attitude toward learning.

Second, combination of democratic grading with the summing up and exchange of study experience. During the grading of the papers, we demanded every student to show how he thought the questions out and how he solved them so as to achieve mutual discussion, mutual elevation and exchange of study experience. This enabled the students to learn knowledge and methods which they could not learn in classrooms. The result of this practice proved to be very good.

Third, combination of democratic grading with examination of teaching. Generally speaking, we can find out during the examination at the end of a course whether the teachers content of a teacher's teaching, teaching attitude and teaching method could meet the requirements for the penetrating development of educational revolution. Consequently, democratic grading was beneficial to the improvement of teaching and improvement of teaching quality.

7.16 "Big Schools Where Education in Ideology and Political Line Is Carried Out—Criticizing Swindlers Like Liu Shao-chi for Slandering the '7 May' Cadre Schools"

Seven years have elapsed since the publication of Chairman Mao's brilliant "7 May" directive. This directive is an important component of Chairman Mao's theory of continuing the revolution under the dictatorship of the proletariat; is an important guarantee for implementing the party's basic line for the historical period of socialism; and is a great guiding principle in consolidating the dictatorship of the proletariat, preventing capitalist restoration and building socialism.

Over the past few years, the "7 May" cadre schools, which were set up in accordance with Chairman Mao's "7 May" directive and with his instruction on sending cadres to do manual work, have provided the broad masses of cadres throughout the country with an excellent opportunity to study once again. In the "7 May" cadre schools, cadres have studied Marxism-Leninsism-Mao Tsetung Thought, learned industrial work, farming and military affairs, taken part in the three great revolutionary movements, criticized revisionism, carried out mass work, and have received re-education by the poor and lower-middle peasants. As a result, they

---

'7 May' Cadre School Under the All-China Federation of Trade Unions, "Big Schools Where Education in Ideology and Political Line Is Carried Out—Criticizing Swindlers Like Liu Shao-chi for Slandering the '7 May' Cadre Schools" (Peking Domestic Service in Mandarin, 1400 GMT, 9 May 73, B), *Foreign Broadcast Information Service: People's Republic of China*, No. 73-92 (May 11, 1973), pp. B1-B4.

have raised their consciousness of class struggle and the struggle between the two lines and of continuing the revolution and have fostered the style of hard struggle. Practice has proven that "7 May" cadres schools are revolutionary melting pots for re-educating cadres during the socialist revolution, are an important way of revolutionizing cadres ideologically, and are big schools in which education in ideology and political line is carried out.

Proceeding from their reactionary class stand and taking a hostile attitude toward all new socialist things, swindlers like Liu Shao-chi maliciously attacked the "7 May" cadre schools by alleging that sending cadres to such schools is another form of unemployment. This is out-and-out counter-revolutionary slander, which constitutes a big exposure of their reactionary features.

Is it good or bad for cadres to go to "7 May" cadre schools? Different answers to this question reflect the basic opposition between the two classes, two lines and two world outlooks. Chairman Mao has pointed out: "In order to guarantee that our party and country do not change their color, we must not only have a correct line and correct policies but must train and bring up millions of successors who will carry on the cause of proletarian revolution." "It is an extremely important question, a matter of life and death for our party and country. It is a question of fundamental importance to the proletarian revolutionary cause for a hundred, a thousand, nay ten thousand years." . . .

The "7 May" schools are great new creations resulting from the proletarian line in educating cadres, and occupy an important position for training and bringing up a contingent of proletarian cadres . . . To correctly implement Chairman Mao's revolutionary line, it is necessary to establish the proletarian world outlook. By receiving education in the "7 May" cadre schools, the broad masses of cadres have remolded their world outlook and have raised their consciousness of implementing Chairman Mao's revolutionary line, thus making contributions to consolidating the dictatorship of the proletariat.

With a counter-revolutionary political "sense of smell," swindlers like Liu Shao-chi felt that the dictatorship of the proletariat would certainly be strengthened by sending the broad masses of cadres to the "7 May" cadre schools. Therefore, they were most fearful of and had the bitterest hatred for such schools. This is why they maliciously slandered the "7 May" cadre schools and those cadres who had been sent to the schools. By preaching the theory "another form of unemployment," swindlers like Liu Shao-chi actually opposed Chairman Mao's proletarian line in educating cadres in an attempt to change the party's basic line and policies for the historical period of socialism, subvert the dictatorship of the proletariat and restore capitalism. . . .

Proceeding from the stand, viewpoint and counter-revolutionary aims of the exploiting classes, swindlers like Liu Shao-chi blurred the basic distinction between proletarian cadres and bourgeois bureaucrats, holding that cadres are overlords who cannot help but hold themselves aloof, call the tune, tyrannically abuse their power and ride roughshod over the people. In the eyes of swindlers like Liu Shao-chi, the cadres who have been sent to the "7 May" cadre schools and have become "7 May" fighters have been dismissed as officials and are unemployed. The theory of "another form of unemployment" is one of their schemes aimed at disintegrating the ranks of proletarian cadres and subverting the dictatorship of the proletariat. By attacking the "7 May" schools, swindlers like Liu Shao-chi were vainly attempting to stir up the discontent of cadres with being sent to do manual work, to lead cadres on to the evil revisionist road, to turn the proletarian cadres serving the people into revisionist overlords drawing high salaries and living a comfortable existence and to make sure cadres act as their reactionary tools and social basis for restoring capitalism. But this is nothing but a daydream by this handful of conspirators and careerists.

The difference between ourselves and swindlers like Liu Shao-chi over the question of educating cadres in the final analysis involves the struggle between the two ideological lines, namely, the struggle between the materialist theory of reflection and idealist apriorism and between the materialist conception of history and the idealist conception of history.

The struggle centers on the quesiton of whether the world should be transformed in accordance with the proletarian world outlook or with the bourgeois world outlook.

7.17 "On Reforming Written Chinese"

The written language of our country, said Chairman Mao in 1951, must be reformed and oreinted to the use of a phonetic alphabet as is common with the world's other written languages. He added that alphabetization of the Chinese characters requires much preparatory work and before realizing this it is necessary to simplify the characters in order to facilitate their present-day use. In 1958, Chairman Mao called on all cadres to learn *putung hua*, the "common speech" which is the standard spoken Chinese.

Chairman Mao's instructions are the guiding principles for reforming the Chinese written language.

NECESSITY

Chinese characters currently used constitute one of the time-honoured written languages with far-reaching influence in the present-day world. Historically, they have made indelible contributions over the past several thousand years. These characters sitll serve as a media which we must use today and for a considerable period of time to come, and they will continue to play their due role. However, we have to admit that the Chinese characters — ideograms — have their serious drawbacks mainly because they must be learnt and memorized one by one since each has its own special form. Most characters require numerous strokes and are complex in structure, not to speak of the total number of characters. The commonly used ones number around 5,000 and thse together with those used in specialized fields of work, the names of people and places and classical writing amount to somewhere between 8,000 to 10,000. Since the Chinese characters are difficult to pronounce, recognize, memorize, write and use, the Chinese people have long wanted a language reform. But in the old society their hope was no more than castles in the air. It was only after the masses of the people were liberated politically and economically under the leadership of the Chinese Communist Party and demanded raising their cultural level that reform of the written language has become realistic.

While engaging in the cause of socialist revolution and construction, the masses are eager to master the written language as quickly as possible so as to study Marxism-Lininism-MaoTsetungThought and obtain cultural and scientific knowledge. But the complicated and difficult characters are an obstacle to their efforts. Hence the necessity to reform the written language.

Wen Hua, "On Reforming Written Chinese," *Peking Review*, No. 32 (August 10, 1973), pp. 11-13.

The advantages of reforming the characters are manifold. It helps lessen the students' burdens, improve teaching quality and shorten the time for study, all favorable to implementation of Chairman Mao's proletarian line on education. It creates favorable conditions for typing, printing, telecommunications and other work to become highly mechanized and automated as well as computerized. It also helps strengthen the unity of our country's various nationalities and facilitates the study of the Chinese language, both spoken and written, by foreign friends, thereby promoting mutual study, friendship and unity between the Chinese people and other peoples of the world.

1st row: Evolution of the character *ma* (horse). 1. pictograph. 2. characters in complex form. 3. simplified character. *2nd row:* Evolution of the character *dou* (struggle). 4. pictograph. 5. characters in complex form. 6. simplified character.

A written language never remains unchanged. Its development is governed by its own objective law. The history of both Chinese and foreign written languages proves that they generally have gone through a process of gradual development from pictographic to ideogrammic languages. Judged by its historical development, each letter of the Latin alphabet which is a phonetic one stands for the shape of a specific object and is a "pictograph." After a prolonged process of development, the letters finally became purely phonogrammic ones and at the same time their forms were simplified. This is also true of the Chinese characters. Following the development of Chinese society and the evolution of writing tools down through the centuries, not only have the forms of these characters undergone many evolutions and become more and more simplified, but their phonogrammic components have gradually increased with the appearance of more and more picto-phonogrammic characters. At present, the many new simplified characters created by the masses are a reflection of the tendency of the development of these characters. This notwithstanding, the characters still have not been freed from the ideogrammic system and many problems which are hard to solve still exist in studying and using them. Therefore, to develop the Chinese written language into one using a phonetic alphabet is the pressing demand of the masses and conforms with the objective law governing the development of the Chinese characters.

THREEFOLD TASKS

The change from characters to a written language using a phonetic alphabet means a fundamental reform of the system of written Chinese. This calls for a greater amount of arduous and complicated work and takes a longer transition period compared with written language reforms in some countries (in most cases they only switch from one phonetic alphabet to another.) On behalf of the Party and the People's Government, Premier Chou En-lai put forward in 1958 three tasks for the reform of written Chinese, namely, simplification of the characters, popularization of the common speech and implementation of the Scheme for the Chinese Phonetic Alphabet. These are important taks which should be actively and persistently carried out before alphabetization becomes a reality.

The first task involves simplification of the forms and reduction of the number of Chinese characters. Although this is only a reform within the framework of the present character system and not a fundamental reform of the written Chinese, it suits the urgent needs of the masses and, in particular, makes it easier for school-age children and old people who were deprived of any school in the old society to learn to read and write. The simplified characters recommended for use since 1956 have been widely used in the nation's newspapers, magazines, books and textbooks and have gained popular approval. Through practice in the past decade and more, the masses have more and more keenly felt the need to continue the work of simplifying the characters. They have taken the initiative to simplify them of their own accord and this has become an irresistible tide of the times. The simplified characters originate from the masses and in turn serve them. In simplifying the characters, therefore, it is necessary to follow the mass line and carry out the principle of *"from the masses, to the masses."* This requires the department in charge of language reform to go deep among the masses, collect, sift and classify the simplified characters and work out a second Scheme for Simplifying the Chinese Characters, so as to do a good job of this work step by step on the basis of soliciting the opinions of the masses and the experts concerned.

The second task, poularizing the common speech which uses the Peking pronunciation as its standard, the dialect spoken in north China as its basic form and the modern vernacular style of writing as its grammatical structure, is an important preparation for alphabetizing written Chinese. With a vast expanse of territory, China has a great diversity of local dialects. Such a state of affairs adversely affects the political, economic and cultural life of our people and makes for difficulties in alphabetizing our written language. It is therefore necessary to make big efforts to popularize the common speech so as to meet the needs of the present development of our socialist revolution and construction and the need to orient our written language to alphabetization as is common with other languages in the world.

Since the directive on the popularization of the common speech was issued by the State Council in 1956, there has emerged a nationwide upsurge in spreading and learning it and more and more people are able to understand and speak it. The popularization work has achieved some success and stress is now laid on popularizing the common speech in commercial, communications, post and telecommunications departments and the service trades as well as in schools in areas using local dialects. Meanwhile, special attention is paid to handling the relations between the common speech and dialects well. That is to say, popularizing the common speech does not mean prohibiting and abolishing the dialects.

Carring out the Scheme for the Chinese Phonetic Alphabet and popularizing the phonetic alphabet — the third task — is another important preparation for achieving alphabetization. The Scheme for the Chinese Phonetic Alphabet approved by the National People's Congress in 1958 has been warmly welcomed by the masses and widely used in various fields of work. Teachers in most primary schools throughout the country have used the phonetic alphabet to teach their pupils to learn the Chinese characters and the common speech.

STRUGGLE BETWEEN THE TWO LINES

Written language is a system of symbols recording speech. It does not bear any class nature itself, but the work of reforming it has a clear-cut class nature. Subordinated to the political line of a particular class, reform of written language serves the interests of that class. The language reform which we are now carrying out is part and parcel of our socialist revolution and construction and serves to consolidate the dictatorship of the proletariat. Precisely because of this, the fierce struggle between the proletariat and the bourgeoisie and between the proletarian revolutionary line and the bourgeois reactionary line at home inevitably finds expression in the reform work. The bourgeois Rightists widely attacked this work in 1957. A handful of class enemies who had usurped the leadership in the cultural and educational departments even more rabidly opposed Chairman Mao's many directives on reforming the written language. They slandered alphabetization as "slavish imitation" and spread the fallacy that "simplified characters are helpful for immediate needs, but will cause losses in the long run." While advocating preserving the dialects, they mouthed such nonsense as "everything will be all right even if the common speech is not popularized for a hundred years." Even more, they abused that part of power in their hands to abolish the study of the Chinese phonetic alphabet in primary schools, and restricted and obstructed its use in various fields of work.

They opposed reforming the Chinese written language simply because this is favorable to the laboring people in their effort to study revolutionary culture and master revolutionary theory. They advertised the landlord and capitalist classes' culture and deprived the working people of their right to learn to read and write for the purpose of fooling and deceiving the people and pushing their counter-revolutionary revisionist line, subverting the dictatorship of the proletariat and restoring capitalism. All this serves only to expose them as vassals of the reactionaries at home and abroad.

Since the Great Proletarian Cultural Revolution began, we have smashed the counter-revolutionary revisionist line of Liu Shao-chi and other political swindlers. As in other work, language reform is now being brought to a new phase of vigorous development. While making energetic efforts to study Chairman Mao's directives on reforming the written language, the department concerned is now conscientiously summing up experience, relying on the masses to carry out deep-going investigations and study and soliciting opinions from all quarters, so as to actively and steadily reform written Chinese.

7.18 "Why the University Enrolling System Should Be Reformed"

The course for pushing the revolution in higher education was charted by Chairman Mao's important directive of July 21, 1968 which, among other things, pointed out: *"Put proletarian politics in command and take the road of the Shanghai Machine Tools Plant in training technicians from among the workers. Students should be selected from among workers and peasants with practical experience, and they should return to production after a few years' study."*

Under the impact of the Great Proletarian Cultural Revolution and the movement to criticize revisionism and rectify style of work, the revolution in education, with the July 21 directive as its guideline, has made much headway in the past five years, setting in motion profound changes on the university campus. Institutes of higher learning began enrolling students again in 1970. Thousands of worker, peasant and soldier students have entered the university portals. Together with the revolutionary teachers, they applied Marxism-Leninism-Mao Tsetung Thought to the transformation of universities and pursued their studies along the road of being red and expert (politically and professionally qualified.) The first group of students selected from among workers, peasants and soldiers have already graduated or will soon complete their courses this year. Meanwhile, a greater number of them are expected to be enrolled.

AN IMPORTANT PART OF EDUCATIONAL REVOLUTION

Reforming the enrolling system is an important part of the revolution in education. To select university students from among workers, peasants and soldiers and send them back to their midst after graduation has opened the way for the implementation of the principle that *"education must serve proletarian politics and be combined with productive labor."* This is of far-reaching significance to the building up of a new and mighty contingent of working-class intellectuals and the realization and consolidation of the all-round dictatorship of the proletariat over the bourgeoisie in the superstructure.

What sort of people the universities enroll and train directly mirrors the political orientation of education. Enrollment is a matter which exerts influence on a whole generation and has a bearing on which road should the young people be guided to take. Before the Great Cultural Revolution, when the revisionist line held sway in education, the old university entrance examination system served as an important check-post for bourgeois intellectuals to dominate the campus. Ostensibly paraded as "equality before marks," actually it was cultural autocracy of the bourgeoisie. The aim was to keep the university gates closed to workers, peasants and soliders and their children. Working like a baton, this system herded the young people along the wrong road of "studying in order to become an official" and "giving first place to intellectual development" and encouraged them to climb the ladder of intellectual aristocracy. This entrance examination system and educational line ran counter to the needs of the socialist cause.

So when the Great Proletarian Cultural Revolution personally initiated and led by Chairman Mao began, action was first taken in the cultural and educational fields.

Chu Yen, "Why the University Enrolling System Should Be Reformed," *Peking Review,* No. 38 (September 21, 1973), pp. 19-21 [This is an abridged translation, prepared by the editors of *Peking Review*, of an article originally published in *Hongqi*, No. 8, 1973].

And when this great revolution was on the rise, it was not by chance that the Red Guards, with the support of the workers, peasants and soldiers, lost no time in toppling the old entrance examination system. After Chairman Mao's July 21 directive had been made public, the universities initiated reforms in the enrolling system, and the long-cherished desire of millions upon millions of workers, peasants and soldiers was realized. Choosing university students from among workers, peasants and soldiers is a revolution in the history of education and an important achievement of the Great Proletarian Cultural Revolution.

Adherence to the reforms in the enrolling system is bound to meet with repeated struggles. One must take note of the fact that "*what is antiquated tries to re-establish itself and maintain its position within the newly acquired form.*" To select students according to the July 21 directive, it is necessary to firmly put proletarian politics in command, give first place to political quality and attach due importance to practical experience. These are the premises, and it is necessary to supplement them with an appropriate test of the entrants' cultural level. Nevertheless, the way this test is conducted involves not only methods but the political line. It is imperative to make a sharp distinction between such a test of cultural level and the defunct university entrance examinations. Students are selected primarily on their political merits and practical experience. The cultural test is aimed merely to verify the practical experience of the entrants and their ability in using basic knowledge to analyse and solve practical problems. In so doing we can do a better job in choosing students on the basis of their moral, intellectual and physical qualities instead of testing how much of the middle school textbooks they can repeat by rote.

In this way, the educated youth will be encouraged to take a more active part in the three great revolutionary movements of class struggle, the struggle for production and scientific experiment and earnestly accept re-education by the workers, peasants and soldiers. This has been fully borne out by practice in the last few years. If the selection of students is decided solely on their cultural level which in turn is judged only by examinations of book knowledge alone, there is a great likelihood of misleading the young people on to the capitalist road of "studying behind closed doors" and divorcing themselves from workers and peasants. We must investigate and study by various means to find out the entrants' ideology and cultural level. We must never again take them by surprise at examinations nor judge by examination papers alone the wisdom, ability and political level of workers and peasants who are well-grounded in practical experience. Hasn't the old university entrance examination system from liberation up to 1966 given us enough lessons? What reason is there for not discarding this system which the bourgeoisie valued as a magic weapon? Did the imperial examinations of ancient times produce men of real learning and ability? Rather, it was quite often the case that those who did not make the grade at the preliminary examinations had some real knowledge and talent. Therefore, only by following Chairman Mao's directive and reforming the old examination system can we push the revolution in education forward and create favorable conditions for the healthy growth of the young people.

RELYING ON WORKERS, PEASANTS AND SOLDIERS

Since the new system of enrollment entails selection of students from among workers, peasants and soldiers, we must firmly rely on the worker, peasant and soldier masses. In the days of feudalism the imperial examinations were in the sole charge of the "examiners." So were the university entrance examinations when education was under the domination of the revisionist line. The power of these "examiners" symbolized the dictatorship of the exploiting classes in the sphere of education. To invest the masses with the power of enrolling university students as is done today embodies working-class leadership and supervision by the worker and peasant masses in education. Here recommendation by the masses is basic, not something to be trifled with as mere formality. The masses know best who are up to the requirements to go to the university and who are not, and they are the best qualified to give recommendations. It is wrong for decisions to be taken by a few people behind the backs of the masses.

By doing a conscientious, good job in appraisal and recommendation out of a revolutionary sense of responsibility, the worker and peasant masses not only can pick outstanding youth for the universities according to the Party's policies, but can also give the young people an important ideological and political education. For this will enable all, the recommended and not recommended alike, to gain a clearer understanding of orientation, bring forth their vigour and vitality and advance along the road of integrating themselves with workers and peasants.

A GOOD BEGINNING

Practice in the past few years has borne out most conspicuously the superiority of selecting university students from among workers, peasants and soldiers. The new enrollment system has given impetus to the revolution in higher education and changed the face of the universities. This finds expression above all in political orientation. The new-type university students have all done several years' productive labor in factories or the rural areas and gained some practical experience. This is all to the good. But what is of primary importance is not that they have picked up some practical experience preparatory to taking up specialized studies but that learning from society and from workers and peasants they have raised their political consciousness, filled their minds with sound ideas and come to realize gradually the correct orientation of their growth. For those at the age of twenty or so, it is a matter of importance to the remoulding of their world outlook that their thinking, guided by the workers and poor and lower-middle peasants, is stamped with the brand of the workers and peasants. Thus they will see clearly they owe it to the working class and the poor and lower-middle peasants that they are given a university training. In this way, a more solid ideological foundation is laid for further solving the problem of for whom they study. Bearing in mind that "the workers, peasants and soldiers need us," the overwhelming majority of the graduates will return to the front line of the three great revolutionary movements full of vigor and vitality, and be one with the masses as before. The workers, peasants and soldiers say in their praise: "They look our way and do not turn their backs on us."

In sharp contrast to this, the old-type universities induced the young to keep aloof from workers and peasants. Some university students from worker or peasant families were so corrupted by bourgeois ideas that they were completely alienated from workers, peasants and soldiers. So goes one saying: "Bumpkins the first year and urbanized dandies the second, they cut ma and pa dead the third." Doesn't the comparison give us much food for thought?

Chairman Mao has always stressed: *"In the final analysis, the dividing line between revolutionary intellectuals and non-revolutionary or counter-revolutionary intellectuals is whether or not they are willing to integrate themselves with the workers and peasants and actually do so."* That the workers, peasants and soldiers welcome university graduates of the new type testifies to the complete correctness of Chairman Mao's orientation for the educational revolution.

Since worker, peasant and soldier students come from and return to the practice of the three great revolutionary movements, the object of higher education and the aim of training both differ from the past. This calls for a fundamental reform in the university syllabus. Once they set foot on the university campus, the worker, peasant and soldier students propel continuously the development of the educational revolution and effect changes, in an increasingly profound way, in the principles, contents and methods of teaching and even in the ranks of teachers.

A major problem in the reform is to employ the dialectical-materialist theory of knowledge and carry out the principle of *"uniting theory and practice"* so as to do away with the evil practice of divorcing theory from practice. Many teachers have come to understand that more often than not the way the worker, peasant and soldier students go about their studies differs from what is required by the old methods of teaching. This is because these students, having been in contact with practice, demand teaching to proceed from practice and by the method of enlightenment. Such being the case, the outmoded standards of teaching can no longer remain intact. In the past two or three years, the teachers and students, putting their heads together, have introduced bold reforms and begun to accumulate some valuable experience. This consists in energetically guiding the students to learn theory from practical experience, to apply the theory learnt and to concentrate efforts on cultivating the ability to analyse and solve problems. It requires teachers to help students give full play to their initiative and creativeness and organize and guide them to study by themselves. The purpose is to enable the students to make lively progress. Facts have proved that so long as the reform is carried out satisfactorily in this direction, the period of schooling can be shortened, courses made fewer and better and the quality of teaching improved, all adding up to better results.

TEACHING QUALITY IMPROVED

Some people are skeptical of workers, peasants and soldiers entering the university. Their doubts are focused on the quality of teaching and study, the quality of knowledge in particular. Basing themselves on mistaken viewpoints and wrong methods, these people judge new reforms by old concepts and evaluate new things with an old yardstick. Hence they cannot draw a correct conclusion.

We cannot talk about the quality of teaching apart from the political line. Political orientation is the first criterion of the quality of teaching. No matter how much one learns, it is useless if the orientation is wrong. What after all is knowledge in terms of cultural level? How do we judge whether one's knowledge is great or little, profound or shallow? These questions can only be answered correctly by the application of the dialectical-materialist theory of knowledge which puts practice in the first place and declares: *"The one and only purpose of the proletariat in knowing the world is to change it."*

Under the old educational system, however, students were confined within the school walls. For years many of them did not see how the workers worked and the peasants farmed, but recited and memorized rules and formulas year in and year out. The more they studied, the more foolish they became. When practical problems of class struggle for production came up, their smattering of knowledge and great ignorance were there for all to see. Was there any "theoretical depth" to speak of?

We do not want to train bookworms but people who can play a useful part in socialist revolution and construction. As the students will leave the university after a few years' study, they are not expected to master all the knowledge which they can use all their lives. What is important is that they acquire a correct world outlook and methodology, master basic theoretical knowledge, learn how to use theoretical knowledge to analyse and solve problems and continue to increase this ability in the course of future practice. The worker, peasant and soldier students now pay greater attention to taking part in practical struggles from which they can draw new strength. Wherever they are they identify themselves with workers, peasants and soldiers, learn from the masses and put the knowledge they have learnt from books to good use. Many of them have already made grafitying achievements after taking up jobs again.

Our revolution in education is advancing, the ranks of teachers are being reformed and their level raised along with the deep-going development of this great revolution. Our teaching methods and materials are being steadily improved and perfected. In the course of practice, we have deepened our understanding of the laws of proletarian education. All this will surely serve to raise the quality of teaching constantly.

Profound changes have been brought about on the university campus since the admission of worker, peasant and soldier students in pursuance of Chairman Mao's July 21 directive. There have been wide repercussions in society, too. This is a very good thing. Fundamentally speaking, these repercussions mean dealing the bourgeoisie and the old forces of habit a big shock. This shows that, instead of taking over the educational system and ideology of the exploiting classes intact, we are carrying out a reform and making a revolution. The cause we have undertaken is *"the most radical rupture with traditional ideas."*

In China, the exploiting classes ran education for several thousand years and the revisionist for 17 years. By dint of the Great Proletarian Cultural Revolution, a fundamental revolution in education has just begun. Bourgeois influence is stubborn and the trial of strength between the two classes remains intense and long-drawn-out. If we fail to do our work well, a capitalist restoration is possible at any time. We must not take a casual attitude towards the struggle in this sphere, but must foster the revolutionary steadfastness of the proletariat, adhere to the philosophy of struggle, continue to make war on the old system and ideas and enthusiastically nurture and develop revolutionary newborn things.

7.19 "Interviews With Middle School Graduates Recently Arrived in Hong Kong (October, 1973)"

While on Sabbatical leave from the State University of New York at Stony Brook during the 1973-74 academic year, studying social, cultural and educational developments in Southeast Asia, the author took the opportunity to conduct an extensive series of interviews with Chinese youths from the People's Republic of China who had recently arrived in Hong Kong. These interviews included both individuals who had obtained official permission from the government of the People's Republic of China to leave the country, and individuals who had left China illegally and had crossed the border into Hong Kong.

The editors have selected two interviews (the transcripts of which were prepared from translations made by S. M. Hu) which offer the reader an opportunity to note certain points of agreement and consistency, as well as points of difference and disagreement in the responses (perhaps reflecting the differences in the interviewees' "world outlooks") to the interviewer's questions.

The editors have chosen not to use the actual names of the two interviewees, but rather to simply identify them as an 18 year old male and a 20 year old male, recently arrived in Hong Kong from the People's Republic of China.

INTERVIEW NO. 1

Interviewee: 20 year old male

S. M. Hu and E. Seifman, "Interviews With Middle School Graduates Recently Arrived in Hong Kong (October, 1973)," S. M. Hu (trans.).

Interviewer: S. M. Hu

Time/Place: October 14, 1973, Kowloon, Hong Kong

[Note: Q = Question, R = Response.]

Q: Which part of China did you come from?

R: Kwangchow, not very far from here.

Q: How long have you been in Hong Kong?

R: I have been here for almost one month.

Q: And have you already got a job?

R: Yes, through some relative's help.

Q: That's very nice. Did you come by train?

R: Heavens no! I secretly crossed the border together with three other young guys; we swam for three hours in order to get to Hong Kong, because we could not stand the condition in Kwangchow.

Q: What do you mean by "condition?"

R: Well, I mean the living and education there.

Q: Can you give me an example?

R: Yes, for instance, you can't really buy what you want; food and material are rationed. When we were sent down for labor work we had to do exactly what we were told; no freedom at all.

Q: What kind of labor work did you do?

R: I was sent to Sunwai Brigade, in Shendei, working with some other 3,000 people to raise silk worms for silk production. In that unit, there were many jobs such as gathering berry leaves for the silkworms, cleaning the trays, feeding the silkworms, etc.; but we had to do what they told us to do.

Q: How many years were you there?

R: Three whole years; it was terribly hard and the living was even worse than in Kwangchow.

Q: Are all school graduates "sent down" for labor work?

R: Yes, they certainly are! Labor work begins at primary school.

Q: Did you learn anything from the labor work?

R: No, nothing.

Q: Could you go back to school, after the labor work?

R: Yes, but who wants to. I did not learn anything during my junior middle school; how could I go on?

Q: Why didn't you learn?

R: Because of poor teachers. Some of them don't even know as much as the students do.

Q: What kind of school did you attend?

R: Middle School #24 in Kwangchow, a government supported school; still we had to pay a few "dollars" for tuition—five "dollars" each semester.

Q: Do you happen to remember how many schools there are in Kwangchow?

R: I don't know how many primary schools, but there are 109 middle schools. All the schools there are numbered instead of being given a name.

Q: Did you like your school? . . . Why?

R: No. . . . Because I did not learn anything, as I said; I was a Red Guard during the Cultural Revolution.

Q: Why did you want to join the Red Guards? And how?

R: I was in my early teens then and did not think much. All my classmates were Red

Guards, so I wanted to be one too. There were no specific requirements for joining Red Guards. All you had to do was give them your name.

Q: Can you tell me more about the Red Guards, such as the organization and tasks?

R: Well, the organization was very loose; it was formed almost overnight and impossible to have any kind of organization. During the Cultural Revolution we did not do much except for making free trips to Peking and attacking bourgeoisie with any accusations that we could find.

Q: What happened to the Red Guards after the Cultural Revolution?

R: Most of the Red Guards are now working in the factory or in the village; but those who had committed severe crimes were punished.

Q: So you did not actually have any classes during the Cultural Revolution?

R: Correct. We had no classes, no examinations, no nothing.

Q: When did you get back to school after the Cultural Revolution?

R: I did not get back to school; that was why I was sent down in the village so long.

Q: Are all the schools back in session now?

R: Yes, all schools are open now and I saw some changes.

Q: What kind of change?

R: Well, the major ones are: they don't have to do labor work as long as we did; there are examinations now and you have to pass in order to be promoted to the next grade, otherwise you stay behind; English begins at the primary grades, etc.

Q: Do you know what are the subjects they study now in primary and middle schools?

R: Yes, there are political language arts, arithmetic, applied language (such as letter writing and business recording), military and physical training, and labor work for primary school; Mao Tse-tung thought education, agricultural bases (mathematics and sciences), revolutionary literature, military and physical training, and labor work for middle schools.

Q: Where did you obtain your texts?

R: We bought our own from the appointed bookstore.

Q: Is it true that the peasants, the workers, and the soldiers are teaching and editing texts?

R: No, they don't really know anything—how can they teach? They only do some practical demonstrations; for instance, to show us how to make bamboo chairs; things like that.

Q: Did you have political instructions such as Chairman Mao's quotations?

R: Yes, we surely did; we learned it in class and after class as well.

Q: What kind of schedule did you have in school?

R: We began at eight in the morning. There were four classes before noon and three in the afternoon, plus extra-curricular activities. By the time we were dismissed it was about five p.m.

Q: Do you recall what sort of extra-curricular activities you had?

R: Yes, we learned how to attack bourgeoisie and do labor work.

Q: Do all the schools have summer and winter vacations?

R: Yes, summer vacation is about one and one-half months, and winter vacation is about three weeks. However, most of the students are sent to do labor work during these vacations.

Q: Do you know the organization called Revolutionary Committee?

R: Yes, certainly! It is a Communist Party organization that stays in each school.

Q: What do they do?

R: I don't know exactly; but the way they acted, they seemed to control and make decisions on everything in school.

Q: As you see it, which has more power, a principal or the Revolutionary Committee?

R: Of course, the Revolutionary Committee!

Q: Suppose that you did not come to Hong Kong, would you continue to work or go to college?

R: I had to work because I could not go to college.

Q: Why not?

R: I only officially finished junior middle school; besides, the government is now tightening up college admissions.

Q: How does the government tighten up college admissions?

R: The process now includes: recommendation by the masses, excellent record on political performance, and re-examination by the college—which was not previously included.

Q: From your point of view, why does the government want to tighten up college admissions?

R: Because they want to raise standards. You see, this is the first time after the Cultural Revolution that there are graduates from middle school and college—and they know what kind of academic standard the students have. I have some classmates who were recommended but afraid to go.

Q: Why were they afraid?

R: Well, they learned so little in middle school and did not think they could pass the examination; nor could they handle the college work, even if they passed the examination.

Q: So where are they now?

R: They are sent by the government to the factory to work.

Q: Do you think it is a good system to have the government find a job for you?

R: No, because you have no choice. Sometimes they send you to faraway places where you don't know anybody.

INTERVIEW NO. 2

Interviewee: 18 year old male

Interviewer: S. M. Hu

Time/Place: October 30, 1973, Kowloon, Hong Kong

Q: I am glad to have this opportunity to talk with you. Where were you in China?

R: I was in Foochow, Fukien.

Q: Ah, I was from Fukien too, and had been in Foochow for about one month during the Japanese invasion. How is the place now?

R: Very nice, clean and quiet; people are busy in work.

Q: You speak very good Mandarin, without a typical Foochow accent. Did you learn it in school?

R: Yes, we all speak Mandarin in school; we learned "pinyin" [a phonetic romanization] at the early grades in primary school.

Q: When did you come to Hong Kong?

R: I came last July after my graduation from middle school.

Q: Why did you want to leave China?

R: I did not really want to leave but have to go to Indonesia to take care of my uncle's business there; he is over 70 years old and has no son.

Q: It is said that the government does not let young people leave; how were you able to obtain the permission to leave?

R: It is not true! As long as you have a proper reason you will get the permission. There have been more than 5,000 permissions granted in my province alone this year.

Q: Are there many young people who apply for permission to leave the country?

R: I am not sure, but I don't think so.

Q: Where did you go to school in Fukien?

R: Middle School #11 in Foochow—a big school.

Q: Did you have to pay?

R: Yes, we paid about eight "dollars" each semester.

Q: Did you stay through until you were graduated?

R: Yes, I did.

Q: Was your schooling interrupted by the Cultural Revolution?

R: Yes, but I did not join the Red Guards.

Q: Why not?

R: I was only eleven years old at the time and didn't know anything.

Q: What happened to you during the Cultural Revolution?

R: We had very few classes going on; all the little kids wandered around doing nothing.

Q: Do you recall any specific incidents during that time?

R: No, except for having no classes.

Q: When did you get back to school?

R: In the fall of 1969, I think.

Q: How did you continue the courses which were interrupted for so long?

R: We either went through very quickly or skipped it. In other words, we finished all the courses but not all the content materials.

Q: What were the courses you studied? Do you remember?

R: Yes, they were: political literature, agricultureal bases (physics, chemistry, mathematics, and economics), military and physical training, and labor work.

Q: Do you happen to know what are the subjects for primary school?

R: I think they have political language arts, arithmetic, military and physical training, and labor work.

Q: Did you have English class?

R: Yes, but now English teaching begins at the primary level.

Q: Did you have political instructions such as Mao Tse-tung thought?

R: Yes, we did in class—and in some extra-curricular activities in the afternoon.

Q: Specifically, what kind of extra-curricular activities did you have?

R: We had sports, labor work, and meetings to learn political concepts.

Q: How about the primary school students, do they have political learning too?

R: Yes, they do; but they only learn some revolutionary terms.

Q: Do you know about the Revolutionary Committee?

R: Yes. There is usually one Revolutionary Committee in each school.

Q: What do they do?

R: Their function, I suppose, is to supervise the principal. They don't have anything to do with the students directly—they are rather nice.

Q: How about the labor work? Were you sent to the village?

R: All the students have long-term (during summer and winter vacations) and short-term (during the school year) labor work in the village and/or in the factory—depending upon the location of the school and the time available. Yes, I was working in a factory where I did various chores for the workers.

Q: Is this the kind of work that most of the students do?

R: No, it depends upon the age; some of them join the workers in production.

Q: How is the labor work arranged?

R: Usually the classes rotate to take turns in the factory or in the village.

Q: Do the teachers participate too?

R: Yes, the teachers also work; since they have to take the students to the factory or the village, they join the workers or the peasants in production. However, the labor work is reduced a great deal now.

Q: How do the students take the hard manual work?

R: It is O.K.—I suppose that as a kid we didn't think much about it, but followed the crowd so-to-speak because the entire class went.

Q: How many years of study are there for primary and middle schools?

R: There are five years for primary schools and the same for middle schools.

Q: What kind of schedule do you have each day?

R: We begin at eight in the morning and have seven class all day, with a break for lunch and a period of extra-curricular activities at the end.

Q: How many students are there in an average class?

R: About forty; usually the lower grades are more crowded.

Q: Did you have good teachers?

R: Yes, they were all right; but some were not too good.

Q: Other than the regular teachers, did you have peasants, workers, and soldiers teach in your school?

R: Yes, they showed us some practical work, but did not really conduct a class.

Q: Are there many young people who want to be a teacher?

R: I don't think so.

Q: If you did not come to Hong Kong, would you go to college?

R: Yes, but I am not sure that I would be recommended. Besides, I do not know if I could pass the entrance examination. I did not learn much in middle school.

Q: What do you mean by "recommended?"

R: I mean not all students are able to take the entrance examination. They have to be recommended first by the masses, together with an outstanding record in political learning and activities; they then go to the college to take the entrance examination.

Q: Then not everybody can go to college?

R: That is correct. However, not many students want to go either.

Q: Why not?

R: Because the students are more anxious to go to work.

Q: Do students have to look for a job after graduation?

R: No, the government will send all the graduates who do not continue schooling to different places to work.

Q: Do you think it is a good idea for the government to have such a plan?

R: Yes, I think so, because you don't have to worry about getting jobs.

7.20 "Socialist 'New Things' In Education"

During the fall of 1974, a twenty-person delegation of the U.S.-China Peoples Friendship Association (East Coast Region) visited the People's Republic of China. As a member of this delegation, Shi Ming Hu toured five cities and their surrounding countryside, visited communes, hospitals, factories, schools, etc., and had the opportunity to interview many of the individuals whom they met during the visits.

Site visits were made to schools at all levels—primary and middle schools, universities, and May 7 Cadre Schools. The school visitations generally began with an introduction by a representative of the Revolutionary Committee of the school who provided an overview of the history of the particular school, after which there was a tour of the school itself followed by a question and answer session and an opportunity to talk informally (in English and Chinese) with students and teachers.

Several English speaking translator-guides accompanied the delegetion, made the appropriate arrangements for visitations, and provided the necessary introductions and translations. Extensive tape recordings made by Shi Ming Hu during the three week sojourn were later transcribed by the editors and provide the basis for the following "documents" in which spokespersons of the Revolutionary Committees of the several schools explain how there has been a conscious effort in Chinese education to develop and strengthen the "socialist new things" which have emerged or further developed since the Cultural Revolution in the continuing struggle between the two-lines, between the capitalist line as manifested in a bourgeois world-outlook and the socialist line epitomized by the development of a proletarian world-outlook. The continuing struggle between the two-lines, with its emphasis on the dialectical process of remolding one's world-outlook, is at the heart of the movement to criticize the policies and philosophy of Lin Piao and Confucius, and the campaign to emphasize the "dictatorship of the proletariat."

We have chosen the short paragraph structure in order to retain the authenticity of the interviews and to convey some sense of the dynamics of the actual translations provided by the English speaking translator-guides. Sentence construction, grammatical usage, and syntax will vary sonewhat from translator-guide to translator-guide.

PRIMARY SCHOOL

School: Lu Wan District (Shanghai) Second Central Primary School
Date: November 14, 1974
Spokesperson: Mr. Shen, Deputy Chairman of the Revolutionary Committee
  [After introducing the members of the school staff.]

This afternoon we are very pleased to meet our American friends coming for a visit. On behalf of the personnel, of the teachers and pupils here, I express warm welcome.

The name of our primary school is called Lu Wan District Second Central Primary School.

This school was set up in 1956 in order to meet the development in the educational field. We have a total number of 1,300 students divided into 29 different classes; a total number of teachers and staff of 69—out of 69, 60 are teachers.

Since the start of the Great Proletarian Cultural Revolution, educational reform has been going on in our school, with relying on the broad masses of the workers, peasants, and the soldiers, and the broad masses of teachers and the pupils here.

S. M. Hu and Eli Seifman, "Socialist New Things In Education."

The curriculum in our primary school includes: politics, Chinese language, mathematics, music, physical culture, fine arts, and physical labor.

For the students above the fourth grade there are extra subjects which include: foreign language, history and geography, and a basic knowledge of science and technology.

English is taught in some classes on the second grade, but this is still on an experimental stage in our primary school.

So we have English teaching on order to know if the children of the age of 7 or 8 can master the English language.

On the first grade this year we have "tri-mathematics", that is oral mathematics, written mathematics, and the Chinese abacus. This tri-mathematics is characterized by the increasing of the teaching quality.

Since the beginning of the Cultural Revolution, the education to the youngster has become the most important part of the society.

The integration of education, of school, neighborhood, and of family has come into being. Now we are giving education to the children on the basis of class education, education on internationalism, and education on communist morality.

In order to raise the political consciousness of, and the professional knowledge of, the students, the teachers are linking their theory with practice.

Some children very often go to the factories of the people's communes with the guidance of the teachers.

So they go to the factories of the people's communes to know something about industry and agriculture, and in turn, the students get a re-education from the broad masses of workers, peasants and soldiers.

So in order to raise physiques of the pupils, different kinds of recreational as well as athletic activities have been going on.

We have a lot of kinds of extra curricular activities for the children; they include basketball playing, fine arts playing [drawing], choral singing, and paper cutting; and in order to raise the physique and the sight of the eyes we have taken special measures to protect them [i.e. the eyes].

In line with Chairman Mao's teaching on education, the teachers are making a strenuous effort to rear the children in order to help them to become "workers with socialist consciousness and a culture," and to let them "develop" morally, physically, and intellectually."

That was my brief introduction to our primary school. My brief introduction will be followed by tour visit to some classes and some extra curricular activities. Then we will come back to this meeting room again for questions and answers.

MIDDLE SCHOOL

School: Kueilin Middle School
Date: November 9, 1975
Spokesperson: Mr. Chang, Chairman of the Revolutionary Committee

We have a pleasure to have our friends from the China-American Friendship Association here. On behalf of the teachers and students and working staff of this school I express warm welcome to our American friends.

This school is called Kueilin Middle School; it was set up in 1905 and has a history of seventy years.

This is a full-time middle school including junior and senior school.

We now have 32 classes; 18 senior classes and 14 junior classes. The enrollment of our school is 1,424 students.

There are 790 students studying in senior classes and 634 studying in junior classes.

We have 748 boy students and 676 girl students, and a teaching and working staff of

140—among them 88 male comrades and 54 women.

Under the wise leadership of the Party and Chairman Mao, during these twenty years tremendous changes have taken place in our school.

The number of students has increased two-fold.

In the old times just the rich people's children studied in the schools, but now all laboring children are studying in the school.

The construction area increased five-fold as against that before Liberation [1949]. Most of the buildings were built up after Liberation. It reaches 30,000 square meters.

For instance, the books in our library; before Liberation we just had 3,000 books but now we have 15,000 books in our library.

And we have a big increase in teaching equipment [i.e. especially science teaching equipment].

For example, the teaching equipment in the Physics Department; in the past we just had 578 teaching equipment, but now [we have] 3,528.

Especially after the Great Proletarian Cultural Revolution and the movement to criticize Lin Piao and Confucius, the political consciousness of teachers and students greatly heightened.

We transformed our teaching system—teaching content and teaching method. As for the teaching system, in the past the length of schooling was six years, but now it has been shortened to five years.

As for the teaching content, we do in line with Chairman Mao's teaching on education.

Our educational principle is to enable the children to receive an education to "develop morally, intellectually and physically, and become a worker with both socialist consciousness and culture."

We take the ideological education into first place.

We often give the students education on ideology and political life to train the students to have the spirit to study for the revolution and take the road of integrating themselves with workers and peasants.

As for the teaching curriculum, we have both political classes and classes on [socialist] culture.

As for the subjects, we have Chinese language and literature, mathematics, English, physics, chemistry, history and geography, the science of medical [physiology] and health, physical training, and music.

As for the teaching method, we aim at integrating theory with practice; that is to say, theory and practice go together.

Apart from vocational studies we also take the students to go to the communes and factories to do practical work there.

Our school runs a little factory and a farm. In our factory we have chemistry workers, high pressure workers, and mechanical workers.

Later on you will see the products of the factory. [Plastic bottle caps].

As for the farm of our school, we have 100 mu [1 mu = $^1/_6$ acre] of farmland and two fishing pools. We mainly produce rice and peanuts.

We carry out teaching by combining industry and agricultural production, and in this way we heighten our teaching level.

For example, in the past when we had the mathematics test, we just had the test in class, but now we combine the test we let students measure the features [irrigation systems] by themselves and we think this is a kind of test which combines theory and practice.

As for the contingent of our teachers, apart from vocational teachers, we also invite the workers, peasants and soldiers to do teaching in our school—and also the technicians in the other factories; they are taken as part-time teachers in our school.

We think this will do good to heighten our teaching level.

As for the teaching method, we pay attention to the practical method of elicitation.

We pay attention to let students think for themselves on their own and to raise their ability to analyze and solve problems independently.

In order to let students develop "morally, intellectually and physically" we also pay attention to their physical training.

We practice "three exercises." Let me explain what these "three exercises" mean; it means do morning exercises in the morning, and do exercises after an interval of two classes and then continue classes. And then to train the eyes we have traditional Chinese eye exercises to avoid shortsightedness.

We also have many kinds of sports. We also have [an] art propaganda team in this school, which gives performances.

Under the guidance of Chairman Mao's revolutionary lines the students are brought up healthy.

As for some students who are left behind, they are catching up during the movement to criticize Lin Piao and Confucius.

We feel it is a great encouragement that we have so many American guests here, and we feel very happy. We think your visit will pave the way and make a contribution to improve the friendship relationship between China and American.

UNIVERSITY

School: Peking University
Date: November 21, 1974
Spokesperson: Mr. Yeh, Vice-Chairman of the Revolutionary Committee

Today we are delighted to have our American Friends from the East Coast branch of the U.S.-China Peoples Friendship Association. I would like to extend our warm welcome on behalf of the members of the Revolutionary Committee of Peking University.

At the moment, in this university we are carrying out the proletarian revolution in education. There is a movement to criticize against Lin Piao and Confucius going on vigorously on a nationwide scale in China. This nationwide movement against Lin Piao and Confucius has further promoted the proletarian revolution in education.

Today we would like to tell you something about the proletarian revolution in education carried out in our University and also the movement to criticize against Lin Piao and Confucius.

[Following an exchange of greetings and introductions.]

Perhaps we should first tell you something about the history of this University and also the educational activities going on in our University. After that we shall conduct a further discussion.

[Here begins a presentation of the historical development of Peking University from its founding in 1898.]

Before the Cultural Revolution, due to the interference and sabotage of Liu Shao-chi's counter revolutionary revisionalist educational line, Chairman Mao's revolutionary education line was unable to be carried through in this University.

After the Cultural Revolution, particularly with the leadership of the working class leading the whole University, to carry out a criticism and repudiation against counter revolutionary revisionist educational line [was carried out]. Through that, there has been a fundamental change in our University.

We have started out proletarian revolution in education since the end of 1969, following Chairman Mao's teaching that education should "serve proletarian politics and combine with productive labor."

We have improved our system of enrollment. After the Cultural Revolution we have criticized the wrong idea that appeared in this University before the Cultural Revolution that intellectual knowledge comes first, and also just to test what the students study by giving them examinations of what they know about the book knowledge.

Now we select students from among the workers, peasants and soldiers that have practical experiences, and we judge whether they are qualified to come to this University according to their political attitude, their practical experiences, their knowledge, their level of schooling, and their physical condition.

In the method of enrollment, we also criticize the old way that they used to choose students from those who could get higher marks in their entrance examinations.

The new way is that those who want to come to this University will make their application and they will be commented on and recommended by the workers who are the lower-middle peasants around them, and approved by the authorities where they are working and re-examined by the University authorities.

We chiefly enroll those young workers or peasants who have had over two years of practical experience in the factories or the communes.

We also enroll the workers, peasants, technicians or cadres who are rich in their practical experiences. These people are not restricted to the requirements of age or educational qualifications.

Since 1970, so far we have enrolled over 8,000 students from the workers and peasants and soldiers under the new enrollment system. All these students are boarding in the University.

Those workers who have the seniority of over five years will be paid with their original wages or salary during their stay in the University. The others, while they are studying in this University, their living expenses will be paid by the government.

The tuition fee and medical care and the expenses for the sheets and papers are all paid for by the University.

We feel that the students coming from among the workers, peasants, and soldiers they are provided with the following characteristics:

First, they have a clear understanding of what they are studying.

The old university students [were] influenced by the revisionist educational line; often they would seek their personal interest or their personal gain.

Their chief goal to study was to get a higher mark so that they could get a better job after they graduated.

The students coming from among the workers, peasants, and soldiers, they have increased their feelings of [for] the working people through their practice. So, they consider to go to the university is a commitment given to them by the working class.

They don't just come to the university to study book knowledge; they have what they call "three tasks."

They come to the university to study, to run the university, and to transform the university with the ideology of Marxism, Leninism, and Mao Tsetung Thought.

We have student representatives attending [participating in] the administration at the departmental level as well as the university level.

The representatives from the students will attend the working out of the teaching plans, as well as the compiling of the teaching materials and how to give lessons in class and then the summary.

So if they discover that which teacher's actions do not correspond to Chairman Mao's teaching, then they can give criticism or put up big character posters.

Of course, on the other hand, if they find any teacher does very well they can also put up big character posters to praise him.

This is their political right.

The next characteristic is that because all the workers and peasant students they have certain practical experiences, so they are able to integrate theory with practice while learning theory.

In studying theory, not only that they should be able to understand that theory, but what is more important is how to put them [theories] into actions, how to apply them [theories] in practical situations.

That's about the change in enrollment.

We have also changed our teaching system.

Under the old educational system, the students were limited in [to] the University campus.

All the teaching activities were carried out centered around classrooms, books, and teachers.

Under that kind of educational system, that [education] was severly divorced from proletarian politics, divorced from the masses of the workers and peasants, and divorced from productive labor.

That was a tradition from the Confucist philosophy passed down over 2,000 years.

All the Confucist [Confucian] schools were advocating reading books behind the door [i.e. closed off from the outside society].

They advocated that only those who read a lot would be the nobles and those who read better could become high officials.

The revisionist educational line was also trying to run our University—trying to induce the student to look down upon the working people, the workers and peasants, and to have blind faith on book knowledge and on the expert.

But eventually they would turn out to be spiritual aristocrats.

Now, in our teaching we carry out the principle of having theory integrated with practice.

In our faculty of science, we have gradually established a new educational system with the integration of teaching, scientific research, and production.

We have set up seven factories and workshops in our University. We are able to manufacture, within our University, big size and middle size electronic computers, and other electronic instruments and chemical products.

We have also established contact with sixteen other factories outside the University regularly.

As for the faculty of liberal arts, of course we cannot run a factory of literature, or a factory of economy or philosophy.

Our principle is to "take the whole society as a big factory" for the faculty of liberal arts.

That is to say, the students studying in the faculty of liberal arts would often go outside of the university to study, to make investigations.

For the students in the faculty of liberal arts and the faculty of sciences, in the departments of foreign languages, in addition to the fact that they should study revolutionary theory and the vocational knowledge related to their subjects; they also have to go outside of the University to society to learn class struggle, struggle in production and scientific experiences, to learn from the workers, peasants, and soldiers, and to learn through practice.

For instance, students studying in the Department of Economics, not only study the theory of economics by [according to] Marx, Lenin and Chairman Mao, but at the same time they also have to go to the factories and the countryside and communes to make practical investigations.

To study how the products are made, up to the circulation of the commodity—the whole thing.

Students in the Department of Language and Literature should also go to the factories and countryside to learn how to write their articles through practice.

We call this new educational system to run our University in an "open-door way."

Since this year this movement to criticize against Lin Piao and Confucius helped us to promote our principle of running our University in an "open-door way."

For the upper part [earlier] of this year, we have [had] over thousands of teachers and students who went to over hundreds of factories, communes, shops, and army units to make investigations or to criticize Lin Piao and Confucius.

In this way, the students in our University have actually engaged in the movement to criticize against Lin Piao and Confucius carried out in society — not only within this University.

For instance, for the students in the faculty of liberal arts, they were formed into small groups to go to the factories, communes, and army units to study together with the workers, peasants and soldiers, Marxism, Leninism, and Chairman Mao's works; and to criticize together with them the works written by Confucius and the Legalists. They study the class struggle between Confucius and the Legalists, and the class struggle throughout history.

In the upper part of this year, the teachers and students together with the broad masses of workers and peasants, they have written over 2,000 articles, and 300 of these articles were published in newspapers—and they have also written a few scores of books.

In the meantime, by achieving all this they have also carried out their teaching activity through all these activities.

As the teaching is formed in the way that it is integrated with the task given to them, so they have undergone a series of change [s] in the content of teaching, in the method of teaching, in the examination [s], and also in the changing relation between the teachers and students.

Take the contents of teaching for instance. In the past, in the faculty of liberal arts they used to teach the students in the Department of Philosophy, Department of History and Department of Literature, usually they always taught the student to have respect for Confucist [Confucian] ideas and [to] oppose Legalist ideas.

In the movement of criticizing against Lin Piao and Confucius we have had to make a transformation of the old teaching materials with the view point of Marxism, Leninism, and historical materialism.

About the teaching courses, the students used to be required to study a few scores of courses.

Usually they should [would] start with fundamental knowledge, basic knowledge, and then professional basic knowledge, and then professional knowledge.

It would take a long time to finish all that.

After they had completed all that, usually there would a a lot of theory and regulations [principles] in the mind of the student and yet they did not know how to use them [i.e. these theories and principles].

Now we arrange the teaching program according to the tasks given to us; so we have all improved our courses set up for the students.

For instance, the students in the Department of Chinese Language and Literature in the old times they had to study modern Chinese language, ancient Chinese language, history of the Chinese language, etc.

Now the teaching program is arranged through criticizing against Confucist books or the Mencius books, and also through studying the books written by the Legalists.

In the method of teaching, nowadays the teacher would study and discuss and analyze together with the students about the relevant problem.

All the teaching activity is carried out under the instruction of the teacher, but if any student would have some new ideas or profound understanding about the theory he can also take [give] a lecture.

For students in the faculty of science, apart from arranging their teaching program according to the tasks given, they also arrange their teaching program according to some of the products needed to be produced from [by] the factory.

Our aim is that the students should be provided with the following abilities after they have studied in this University:

The ability to solve problems, to analyze problems, and to study on their own.

To adopt this new educational system does not mean thoroughly to solve the problems of theory integrated with practice; but also in order to help the students to "develop morally, intellectually, and physically" in their initiative and vigorous ways in order to become "a worker with a socialist mind and culture."

Students are required to study 3 or 4 years for a regular department where there are courses. The majority of them will study 3 years; only the students in the Department of Theoretical Physics will study 4 years.

So we have shortened the length of schooling 2 or 3 years compared with the pre-Culture Revolution days.

In addition to that we have also run short term courses and refresher courses according to the needs of the society.

These short term courses or refresher courses are set up for the workers, peasants, and cadres to give them some short term training in certain fields.

The shortest period for these short term courses will be two weeks, and the longest will be around one year.

These short term courses are not only run inside the University, but the short term courses are also set up in the factories and communes.

For instance, short term courses on the radio technology and math concepts offered in the factory.

This form of running the short-term courses is very much welcomed by the workers and peasants. They say that the door of [the] university has really been opened to the workers and peasants.

Since 1970 up to now, we have had 3,000 graduates from this university and there are 5,000 students studying in the regular courses of this University.

Judging from the situation of the gradutes, we feel that although the length of the schooling has been shortened, the ability of the student to analyze problems has exceeded that before the Great Cultural Proletarian Revolution because of the educational revolution and the students' political consciousness.

For instance, for our first batch of graduates, in order to examine their level of education, we asked them to do three months of graduate field-work.

In that three months the students, either from the faculty of liberal arts or science, they were all engaged in some sort of scientific research activity.

The students in the faculty of science, they completed 389 items of scientific research products. . . .

For instance, they made use of the residue from oil refining to use them for raw materials to make Dacron.

And so far there are already 100 items of scientific research already used in our industrial and agricultural production.

For the students in the faculty of liberal arts, they have written over 1,700 articles of different styles and different themes; over 700 articles were published in our newspapers and they have also written 25 books—some already published.

For the students studying in the Department of Foreign Languages, they have translated 1,600,000 words using over a dozen different languages.

This was not able to be imagined—to be able to score such a great achievement in such a short period—before the Cultural Revolution.

As a whole, we should say that our revolution in education is still on a tentative stage.

Chairman Mao has made many detailed instructions on the revolution in education.

We need more practice and experience to carry out and aim at all the instructions worked out by Chairman Mao.

We believe that as long as we can summarize our experiences in an earnest way, then we can achieve greater gains in our educational revolution.

That's all for the general introduction.

MAY 7 CADRE SCHOOL

School: Western District May 7 Cadre School (Peking)

Date: November 21, 1974

Spokesperson: Mr. Lee, Vice-Chairman of the Revolutionary Committee

On behalf of all the Revolutionary Committee members and the students who are studying in our school I express my warmest welcome to you.

Today I will give you a brief information on the school. After that we shall go and have a visit in the school and come back for discussion after our visit. Does that sound agreeable to everybody?

[The visitors confirm this arrangement.]

The students in our school were very happy to hear that our American friends have come to visit the school; they have prepared some small items for us today [i.e. singing, dancing, performances, etc.].

Now I shall give you a brief account of our school.

The Western District May 7 Cadre School was set up October, 1968 according to Chairman Mao's May the 7th Directive.

Chairman Mao's May the 7th Directive was put forward in 1966.

In this May 7th Directive Chairman Mao called on the people that "the workers should engage in industry, that the peasants should engage themselves in agriculture, and students should engage themselves in education."

The PLA [People's Liberation Army] commanders and soldiers, staff workers and government workers, commercial workers, should learn politics and military affairs and also criticize and repudiate the government.

They should involve themselves in mass work and carry out investigations.

This is the context of the May 7th Directive.

Our school has taken the May 7 Directive as our guiding factor and we have named our school in rememberance of this May 7th Directive.

Chairman Mao issued another instruction on October 4, 1968 that cadres should take part in manual labor. This instruction was issued during the Great Proletarian Cultural Revolution.

When this instruction was put forward all cadres and staff members in all parts of the country responded to this call, and so May 7 Cadre Schools were established in every part of the country.

The May 7 Western District Cadre School was also established in this period.

Our school now has a history of more than 6 years.

In these years we have trained 7,800 cadres and teachers in our school.

In these 6 years our school has produced more than 1.6 million kilos [1 kilo = 2.2 lbs.] of different kind of grain for the state.

In this way we have trained cadres and teachers, and at the same time we have also added some material to the state and reduced the burden of the state.

The cadres and teachers—we call them students now—who are studying having a short course in our school at present, account about 350.

We have cultivated 750 mu of land [1 mu = $^1/_6$ acre].

Through their study and after tempering themselves in this school, there has been a tremendous change in the ideology of these students.

The students take part in studying while engaged in productive labor.

This course will last for 6 months. In these 6 months, 40% of the time will be used for studying Marxism-Leninism-Mao Tsetung Thought.

The rest, 60% of the time, the students will be engaged in production in manual labor.

As Chairman Mao has told us, all our work is to change the ideology of the teachers. We have taken this principle as our guiding factor and have studied Marxism-Leninism and Mao Tsetung Thought.

We have combined theory with productive labor and have trained out cadres to become proletarians, workers who will serve the people wholeheartedly.

This is the aim and task of our May 7 Cadre School.

After their 6 months of studying and manual labor, these students have achieved advantages in three aspects.

The first aspect is that they have raised their ideology and they have come to know the great significance of cadres taking part in productive labor.

Party cadres are ordinary workers [here] and they should not lord over the people. So cadres must engage themselves in production.

In this way, the cadres can maintain a close link with the masses, and they will know the mind, suggestions, and desires of the people.

Through these channels they will know the actual conditions which exist among the people.

This provides a very good opportunity to learn from the masses.

In this way they can prevent themselves from subjectivism and at the same time prevent revisionism.

After this training they will be able to serve the people better.

Some old cadres who have been studying in our school said that, "If you don't sharpen a knife it will become rusty," and if cadres don't take part in productive labor revisionism will emerge.

Only by taking part in productive labor can a heart be truly linked with the masses and we can implement and carry forward the Party policy in a better way.

The second aspect in which the students have made some advantages is that they have combined theory with practice.

It is a very important point for the students to learn Marxism-Leninism and Mao Tsetung Thought in our school.

After taking part in the criticism of Confucius and Lin Piao, and combining production with theory by studying Marxism-Leninism and Mao Tsetung Thought.

Especially for the cadres who have entered school right from their houses [homes] and went to their office [work] right after graduation, for these kinds of cadres there has been a special significance of this.

This kind of cadres who have come to work right after their graduation and who have not taken part in production before for a certain years of time, these cadres have a certain amount of book knowledge but the book knowledge is divorced from practice.

By taking part in study and manual labor, these cadres will complete their knowledge by combining theory with practice in our school.

So, some of the cadres have said that these feelings, that "true knowledge comes out of practice and only through practical ways can we examine one's knowledge."

The third point is that they have promoted the feelings of the working people.

In their period of schooling here the cadres also have the opportunity to go to the nearby people's commune.

By going to the people's commune, they eat, live, work and study together with the peasants there.

When these students go to the people's commune, they would invite the poor and lower-middle peasants to tell them the history of their family, the history of the village, and give them [i.e. the "students" of the May 7 Cadre School] class education.

After coming back from work, they would use the time for carrying out social investigation and to involve themselves on a mass way to benefit the people.

Through such courses, these students have come to learn that grain is not very easy to come [obtain].

They come to know that all our materials are all created by the working class.

The broad masses of people are the molding force in creating world history and they are the masters of history.

Some students said that before [before their experience at the May 7 Cadre School] they only knew that rice was a good thing to eat, but "now we know it is very difficult to grow."

So they know that they should not waste grain, they should not waste the food, and at the same time they have promoted a deep love for the working class.

They are determined to serve the people better.

These are the advantages of the students who have been trained in our school.

The May 7 Cadre School is a new thing which emerged during the Proletarian Cultural Revolution.

Through our experiences we have made a conclusion that the May 7 Cadre School is a very good type of form in which we can train revolutionary cadres.

It is an effective measure for preventing and opposing revisionism.

We have [are] still lacking experiences because the history of the May 7 Cadre School is not long. The May 7 Cadre School itself is a new thing.

For instance, how do we promote the ideology of the cadres in a better and quicker way? This has to be discussed and carried forward in the future.

We are also trying to combine productive labor with theory in a better way.

So this has to be studied and probed in the future in our practical work.

So this is my brief introduction of our school. I think the main thing is to invite our friends to have a look. If you still have further questions you may ask them while we are visiting.

We hope these selected documents, covering a wide range of different levels of Chinese formal "schooling"—primary, secondary, university, and May 7 Cadre School—will provide an overview of contemporary policies as well as convey some sense of the attitude of the Chinese people toward what they call the "socialist new things in education."

We are currently in the process of transcribing and editing extensive tape recordings made during the actual tours of the various schools and the question-and-answer sessions following these tours. We hope to be able to report on the analysis of these transcriptions at a later date.

7.21 "The Constitution of the People's Republic of China"

PROCLAMATION OF NATIONAL PEOPLE'S CONGRESS
OF PEOPLE'S REPUBLIC OF CHINA

The Draft Revised Text of the Constitution of the People's Republic of China, which the Central Committee of the Communist Party of China submitted to the First Session of the Fourth National People's Congress for its deliberation, was unanimously adopted by the Congress on January 17, 1975. The new "Constitution of the People's Republic of China" is hereby promulgated.

> Presidium of the First Session of the
> Fourth National People's Congress
> of the People's Republic of China

January 17, 1975
Peking

CONTENTS

PREAMBLE
CHAPTER ONE: GENERAL PRINCIPLES
CHAPTER TWO: THE STRUCTURE OF THE STATE
 Section I. The National People's Congress
 Section II. The State Council
 Section III. The Local People's Congresses and the Local Revolutionary Committees at Various Levels
 Section IV. The Organs of Self-Government of National Autonomous Areas
 Section V. The Judicial Organs and the Procuratorial Organs
CHAPTER THREE: THE FUNDAMENTAL RIGHTS AND DUTIES OF CITIZENS
CHAPTER FOUR: THE NATIONAL FLAG, THE NATIONAL EMBLEM AND THE CAPITAL

PREAMBLE

The founding of the People's Republic of China marked the great victory of the new-democratic revolution and the beginning of the new historical period of socialist revolution and the dictatorship of the proletariat, a victory gained only after the Chinese people had waged a heroic struggle for over a century and, finally, under the leadership of the Communist Party of China, overthrown the reactionary rule of imperialism, feudalism and bureaucrat-capitalism by a people's revolutionary war.

For the last twenty years and more, the people of all nationalities in our country, continuing their triumphant advance under the leadership of the Communist Party of China, have achieved great victories both in socialist revolution and socialist construction and in the Great Proletarian Cultural Revolution, and have consolidated and strengthened the dictatorship of the proletariat.

Socialist society covers a considerably long historical period. Throughout this

---

"The Constitution of the People's Republic of China" (Adopted on January 17, 1975, by the Fourth National People's Congress of the People's Republic of China at its First Session), *Peking Review,* No. 4 (January 24, 1975), pp. 12-17.

historical period, there are classes, class contradictions and class struggle, there is the struggle between the socialist road and the capitalist road, there is the danger of capitalist restoration and there is the threat of subversion and aggression by imperialism and social-imperialism. These contradictions can be resolved only by depending on the theory of continued revolution under the dictatorship of the proletariat and on practice under its guidance.

We must adhere to the basic line and policies of the Communist Party of China for the entire historical period of socialism and persist in continued revolution under the dictatorship of the proletariat, so that our great motherland will always advance along the road indicated by Marxism-Leninism-Mao Tsetung Thought.

We should consolidate the great unity of the people of all nationalities led by the working class and based on the alliance of workers and peasants, and develop the revolutionary united front. We should correctly distinguish contradicitions among the people from those between ourselves and the enemy and correctly handle them. We should carry on the three great revolutionary movements of class struggle, the struggle for production and scientific experiment; we should build socialism independently and with the initiative in our own hands, through self-reliance, hard struggle, diligence and thrift and by going all out, aiming high and achieving greater, faster, better and more economical results; and we should be prepared against war and natural disasters and do everything for the people.

In international affairs, we should uphold proletarian internationalism. China will never be a superpower. We should strengthen our unity with the socialist countries and all oppressed people and oppressed nations, with each supporting the other; strive for peaceful coexistence with countries having different social systems on the basis of the Five Principles of mutual respect for sovereignty and territorial integrity, mutual non-aggression, non-interference in each other's internal affairs, equality and mutual benefit, and peaceful coexistence, and oppose the imperialist and social-imperialist policies of aggression and war and oppose the hegemonism of the superpowers.

The Chinese people are fully confident that, led by the Communist Party of China, they will vanquish enemies at home and abroad and surmount all difficulties to build China into a powerful socialist state of the dictatorship of the proletariat so as to make a greater contribution to humanity.

People of all nationalities in our country, unite to win still greater victories!

CHAPTER ONE
GENERAL PRINCIPLES

Article 1   The People's Republic of China is a socialist state of the dictatorship of the proletariat led by the working class and based on the alliance of workers and peasants.

Article 2   The Communist Party of China is the core of leadership of the whole Chinese people. The working class exercises leadership over the state through its vanguard, the Communist Party of China.

Marxism-Leninism-Mao Tsetung Thought is the theoretical basis guiding the thinking of our nation.

Article 3   All power in the People's Republic of China belongs to the people. The organs through which the people exercise power are the people's congresses at all levels, with deputies of workers, peasants and soldiers as their main body.

The people's congresses at all levels and all other organs of state practice democratic centralism.

Deputies to the people's congresses at all levels are elected through democratic consultation. The electoral units and electors have the power to supervise the deputies they elect and to replace them at any time according to provisions of law.

Article 4   The People's Republic of China is a unitary multi-national state. The areas where regional national autonomy is exercised are all inalienable parts of the People's Republic of China.

All the nationalities are equal. Big-nationality chauvinism and local-nationality chauvinism must be opposed.

All the nationalities have the freedom to use their own spoken and written languages.

Article 5   In the People's Republic of China, there are mainly two kinds of ownership of the means of production at the present stage: Socialist ownership by the whole people and socialist collective ownership by working people.

The state may allow non-agricultural individual laborers to engage in individual labor involving no exploitation of others, within the limits permitted by law and under unified arrangement by neighborhood organizations in cities and towns or by production teams in rural people's communes. At the same time, these individual laborers should be guided on to the road of socialist collectivization step by step.

Article 6   The state sector of the economy is the leading force in the national economy.

All mineral resources and waters as well as the forests, undeveloped land and other resources owned by the state are the property of the whole people.

The state may requisition by purchase, take over for use, or nationalize urban and rural land as well as other means of production under conditions prescribed by law.

Article 7   The rural people's commune is an organization which integrates government administration and economic management.

The economic system of collective ownerhsip in the rural people's communes at the present stage generally takes the form of three-level ownership with the production team at the basic level, that is, ownership by the commune, the production brigade and the production team, with the last as the basic accounting unit.

Provided that the development and absolute predominance of the collective economy of the people's commune are ensured, people's commune members may farm small plots for their personal needs, engage in limited household side-line production, and in pastoral areas keep a small number of livestock for their personal needs.

Article 8   Socialist public property shall be inviolable. The state shall ensure the consolidation and development of the socialist economy and prohibit any person from undermining the socialist economy and the public interest in any way whatsoever.

Article 9   The state applies the socialist principle: "He who does not work, neither shall he eat" and "from each according to his ability, to each according to his work."

The state protects the citizens' right of ownership to their income from work, their savings, their houses, and other means of livelihood.

Article 10   The state applies the principle of grasping revolution, promoting production and other work and preparedness against war; promotes the planned and proportionate development of the socialist economy, taking agriculture as the foundation and industry as the leading factor and bringing the initiative of both the central and the local authorities into full play; and improves the people's material and cultural life step by step on the basis of the constant growth of social production and consolidates the independence and security of the country.

Article 11   State organizations and state personnel must earnestly study Marxism-Leninism-Mao Tsetung Thought, firmly put proletarian politics in command, combat bureaucracy, maintain close ties with the masses and wholeheartedly serve the people. Cadres at all levels must participate in collective productive labor.

Every organ of state must apply the principle of efficient and simple administration. Its leading body must be a three-in-one combination of the old, the middle-aged and the young.

Article 12   The proletariat must exercise all-round dictatorship over the bourgeoisie in the superstructure, including all spheres of culture. Culture and education, literature and art, physical education, health work and scientific research work must all serve proletarian politics, serve the workers, peasants and soldiers, and be combined with productive labor.

Article 13   Speaking out freely, airing views fully, holding great debates and writing big-character posters are new forms of carrying on socialist revolution created by the masses of the people. The state shall ensure to the masses the right to use these forms to create a political situation in which there are both centralism and democracy, both discipline and freedom, both unity of will and personal ease of mind and liveliness, and so help consolidate the leadership of the Communist Party of China over the state and consolidate the dictatorship of the proletariat.

Article 14   The state safeguards the socialist system, suppresses all treasonable and counter-revolutionary activities and punishes all traitors and counter-revolutionaries.

The state deprives the landlords, rich peasants, reactionary capitalists and other bad elements of political rights for specified periods of time according to law, and at the same time provides them with the opportunity to earn a living so that they may be reformed through labor and become law-abiding citizens supporting themselves by their own labor.

Article 15   The Chinese People's Liberation Army and the people's militia are the workers' and peasants' own armed forces led by the Communist Party of China; they are the armed forces of the people of all nationalities.

The Chairman of the Central Committee of the Communist Party of China commands the country's armed forces.

The Chinese People's Liberation Army is at all times a fighting force, and simultaneously a working force and a production force.

The task of the armed forces of the People's Republic of China is to safeguard the achievements of the socialist revolution and socialist construction, to defend the sovereignty, territorial integrity and security of the state, and to guard against subversion and aggression by imperialism, social-imperialism and their lackeys.

CHAPTER TWO
THE STRUCTURE OF THE STATE

Section I. The National People's Congress

Article 16   The National People's Congress is the highest organ of state power under the leadership of the Communist Party of China.

The National People's Congress is composed of deputies elected by the provinces, autonomous regions, municipalities directly under the central government, and the People's Liberation Army. When necessary, a certain number of patriotic personages may be specially invited to take part as deputies.

The National People's Congress is elected for a term of five years. Its terms of office may be extended under special circumstances.

The National People's Congress holds one session each year. When necessary, the session may be advanced or postponed.

Article 17   The functions and powers of the National People's Congress are: to amend the Constitution, make laws, appoint and remove the Premier of the State Council and the members of the State Council on the proposal of the Central Committee of the Communist Party of China, approve the national economic plan, the state budget and the final state accounts, and exercise such other functions and powers as the National People's Congress deems necessary.

Article 18   The Standing Committee of the National People's Congress is the permanent organ of the National People's Congress. Its functions and powers are: to convene the sessions of the National People's Congress, interpret laws, enact decrees, dispatch and recall plenipotentiary representatives abroad, receive foreign diplomatic envoys, ratify and denounce treaties concluded with foreign states, and exercise such other functions and powers as are vested in it by the National People's Congress.

The Standing Committee of the National People's Congress is composed of the Chairman, the Vice-Chairmen and other members, all of whom are elected and subject to recall by the National People's Congress.

Section II. The State Council

Article 19   The State Council is the Central People's Government. The State Council is responsible and accountable to the National People's Congress and its Standing Committee.

The State Council is composed of the Premier, the Vice-Premiers, the ministers, and the ministers heading commissions.

Article 20   The functions and powers of the State Council are: to formulate administrative measures and issue decisions and orders in accordance with the Constitution, laws and decrees; exercise unified leadership over the work of ministries and commissions and local organs of state at various levels throughout the country; draft and implement the national economic plan and the state budget; direct state administrative affairs; and exercise such other functions and powers as are vested in it by the National People's Congress or its Standing Committee.

Section III. The Local People's Congresses
And the Local Revolutionary Committees
At Various Levels

Article 21   The local people's congresses at various levels are the local organs of state power.

The people's congresses of provinces and municipalities directly under the central government are elected for a term of five years. The people's congresses of prefectures, cities and counties are elected for a term of three years. The people's congresses of rural people's communes and towns are elected for a term of two years.

Article 22   The local revolutionary committees at various levels are the permanent organs of the local people's congresses and at the same time the local people's governments at various levels.

Local revolutionary committees are composed of a chairman, vice-chairmen and other members, who are elected and subject to recall by the people's congress at the corresponding level. Their election or recall shall be submitted for examination and approval to the organ of state at the next higher level.

Local revolutionary committees are responsible and accountable to the people's congress at the corresponding level and to the organ of state at the next higher level.

Article 23 The local people's congresses at various levels and the local revolutionary committees elected by them ensure the execution of laws and decrees in their respective areas; lead the socialist revolution and socialist construction in their respective areas; examine and approve local economic plans, budgets and final accounts; maintain revolutionary order; and safeguard the rights of citizens.

Section IV. The Organs of Self-Government
Of National Autonomous Areas

Article 24 The autonomous regions, autonomous prefectures and autonomous counties are all national autonomous areas; their organs of self-government are people's congresses and revolutionary committees.

The organs of self-government of national autonomous areas, apart from exercising the functions and powers of local organs of state as specified in Chapter Two, Section III of the Constitution, may exercise autonomy within the limits of their authority as prescribed by law.

The higher organs of state fully safeguard the exercise of autonomy by the organs of self-government of national autonomous areas and actively support the minority nationalities in carrying out the socialist revolution and socialist construction.

Section V. The Judicial Organs and the
Procuratorial Organs

Article 25 The Supreme People's Court, local people's courts at various levels and special people's courts exercise judicial authority. The people's courts are responsible and accountable to the people's congresses and their permanent organs at the corresponding levels. The presidents of the people's courts are appointed and subject to removal by the permanent organs of the people's congresses at the corresponding levels.

The functions and powers of procuratorial organs are exercised by the organs of public security at various levels.

The mass line must be applied in procuratorial work and in trying cases. In major counter-revolutionary criminal cases the masses should be mobilized for discussion and criticism.

CHAPTER THREE
THE FUNDAMENTAL RIGHTS AND
DUTIES OF CITIZENS

Article 26 The fundamental rights and duties of citizens are to support the leadership of the Communist Party of China, support the socialist system and abide by the Constitution and the laws of the People's Republic of China.

It is the lofty duty of every citizen to defend the motherland and resist aggression. It is the honorable obligation of citizens to perform military service according to law.

Article 27 All citizens who have reached the age of eighteen have the right to vote and stand for election, with the exception of persons deprived of these rights by law.

Citizens have the right to work and the right to education. Working people have the right to rest and the right to material assistance in old age and in case of illness or disability.

Citizens have the right to lodge to organs of state at any level written or oral complaints of transgression of law or neglect of duty on the part of any person working in an organ of state. No one shall attempt to hinder or obstruct the making of such complaints or retaliate.

Women enjoy equal rights with men in all respects.

The state protects marriage, the family, and the mother and child.

The state protects the just rights and interests of overseas Chinese.

Article 28   Citizens enjoy freedom of speech, correspondence, the press, assembly, association, procession, demonstration and the freedom to strike, and enjoy freedom to believe in religion and freedom not to believe in religion and to propagate atheism.

The citizens' freedom of person and their homes shall be inviolable. No citizen may be arrested except by decision of a people's court or with the sanction of a public security organ.

Article 29   The People's Republic of China grants the right of residence to any foreign national persecuted for supporting a just cause, for taking part in revolutionary movements or for engaging in scientific activities.

CHAPTER FOUR
THE NATIONAL FLAG, THE NATIONAL
EMBLEM AND THE CAPITAL

Article 30   The national flag has five stars on a field of red.

The national emblem: Tien An Men in the centre, illuminated by five stars and encircled by ears of grain and a cogwheel.

The capital is Peking.

7.22 "Program (Draft) of Educational Revolution for Experimental Primary Schools in Shanghai"

GENERAL PRINCIPLES

Both the great proletarian cultural revolution and the movement to criticize Lin Piao and Confucius have caused profound changes in the features of experimental primary schools. However, the struggle between the two classes and the two lines has not come to an end. With a view to operating experimental primary schools genuinely as instruments for the dictatorship of the proletariat in accordance with Chairman Mao's proletarian line on education, it will be necessary to deepen the educational revolution in a planned and systematic manner.

The basic task of primary education, according to the Party's basic line, is to educate children with Marxism-Leninism-Mao Tsetung Thought, to organize students to take an active part in the three major revolutionary movements — class

"Program (Draft) of Educational Revolution for Experimental Primary Schools in Shanghai," *Hsueh-hsi yu P'i-p'an* [*Study and Criticism*], No: 4 (April 16, 1975), *Selections from People's Republic of China Magazines*, No. 822 (May 19, 1975), pp. 2-6.

struggle, the struggle for production and scientific experiment, in order that students can acquire from childhood a rough understanding of the basic views of Marxism, criticize the reactionary doctrines of Confucius and Mencius, set up the idea of becoming an ordinary laborer, and "become a laborer with socialist consciousness and culture."

"Education must serve proletarian politics and be integrated with productive labor." We must persist in running schools with open doors, linking theory with reality and conducting teaching and learning in the manner of self-enlightenment. We must implement to the letter Chairman Mao's "May 7" Directive, so that while in school, students will study not only literature but also industry, agriculture and military affairs as well as criticizing the bourgeoisie.

The Party's centralized leadership must be upheld. Under the Party's leadership, we must closely rely on the working class and the poor and lower-middle peasants, give full scope to the political role of workers propaganda teams, strengthen and consolidate the worker-peasant-soldier lecturers groups, persevere in combining social, family and school education, intensify the work of uniting, educating and transforming existing teachers ranks so as to make the educational revolution a social revolution in the true sense of the word.

Primary schools are important positions in which the proletariat and the bourgeoisie engage each other in a bitter fight to win over the youngsters; indeed, they constitute an extremely vital aspect of the proletarian dictatorship in the superstructure. All cadres, teachers and students must determinedly be loyal to the Party's educational undertaking in the struggle between the two classes and two lines and contribute their all to the training of successors to the revolutionary cause.

IDEO-POLITICAL EDUCATION

Article I   All work of schools is geared to changing students' thinking in order to enable them to establish gradually and from childhood the proletarian world outlook.

While in school, students should, in conjunction with various political movements and the Party's central work, seriously study Marxist-Leninist and Chairman Mao's works. In this regard, the different characteristics of various classes should be taken into consideration: for lower classes the main emphasis is to be placed on study of selected quotations, while for higher classes selected original works may be appropriately studied and selected quotations may be studied too. At the same time, revolutionary mass criticism should be launched in depth. Reactionary views of the revisionist educational line — such as "one who excels in learning will become an official" and "intellectual education first" — should be subject to constant and repeated criticism in conjunction with practical struggle.

Students should be organized on a regular basis to participate in class struggle activities in society.

Article II   Ideo-political education should be conducted in a way that takes the actual conditions of the children into account; it should be concrete and lively. For instance: Compare their childhood with that of their parents, write revolutionary children's songs, hold story-telling meetings, organize them for visits, etc. Students of higher classes may also be organized purposefully to conduct social investigations so as to learn from society.

We should uphold the principle of letting students educate themselves and encourage them to make use of such forms as big-character posters and big debates, to set up the class concept in practical struggle, acquire the ability to distinguish between right and wrong, and bravely promote the revolutionary spirit of going against the tide.

TEACHING WORK

Article III   Teaching work of schools must be guided by the Marxist theory of knowledge; it is necessary to persist in running schools with open doors, in the teaching method of self-enlightenment, and in following the mass line.

Various subjects should be taught systematically, purposefully and in an open-door manner. Not only must the practice of teaching in a closed classroom be opposed, but that of letting things run their natural course and formalism must be opposed.

In preparing lessons teachers should seriously study their subject material, understand the actual conditions of the students, and conduct research and prepare lessons with them.

In accordance with Chairman Mao's "ten major teaching methods," in giving lessons in the classrooms full advantage should be taken of the perceptual knowledge acquired by students in the course of learning in an open-door manner, so that from the typical to the general and from the concrete to the abstract, they may be enlightened to ponder over and analyze the problems before them. They should be allowed and encouraged to raise questions, express their views and hold discussions. The practice of having "officers teach men, men teach officers, and men teach men" should be promoted in order to create a lively situation in the classroom.

Article IV   An examination is aimed at testing students' ability to analyze and solve problems, at reviewing and consolidating the fruit of teaching. Examination subjects should be linked to reality and should be published in advance. During an examination students may refer to books and hold discussions. Forms of examination should be flexible and varied and an examination may be held on the spot. Evaluation of examination results should give prominence to democracy and the three-way combination of the leadership, teachers and students should be insisted upon. Students who have creative ideas about learning should be encouraged to put forward their ideas. An examination is to be held once every term.

Article V   Utmost importance should be attached to students' extracurricular reading, scientific and technical activities. Existing extracurricular activity groups on meteorology, making airplane models, fine arts, acupuncture, semi-conductor, electrical and mechanical work, and literature should be elevated on the basis of popularization so as to serve the three great revolutionary struggles.

LEARNING INDUSTRY, AGRICULTURE AND MILITARY AFFAIRS

Article VI   Learning industry, agriculture and military affairs aims at allowing students to get in touch with workers, peasants and soldiers in the early days of their childhood, to learn from the latter, to set up the idea of becoming an ordinary laborer, and to be promoters for restriction of bourgeois right.

Learning industry, agriculture and military affairs should be conducted in a manner suited to local conditions and on the principle of carrying out the activities in the vicinity of the school.

Time arrangement: Students of middle and lower classes should participate mainly in labor in workshops inside the school for two hours per week; students of higher classes should gather together twice every term to learn industry, carrying out their activities mainly in workshops inside the school for a week each time. Students should learn farming before and after spring plowing, three kinds of crash work and autumn harvesting, with the main stress on understanding the rural conditions and taking part in some farm labor of which they are capable. In learning military affairs students may make study visits to armed forces units and combine this with training.

In the course of "learning these three things," it will be necessary to step up education on ideology and safety and to oppose the practice of using students as normal laborers.

LITERARY, SPORTS AND HYGIENIC ACTIVITIES

Article VII Since primary school students are in the period of physical and intellectual growth, it will be necessary to give full consideration to their work, study, recreation, sports and rest.

Subjects taught in school should be arranged in a way beneficial to the physical and mental health of students and no excessive burden should be placed on them.

Daily broadcasting physical exercises and other physical exercises should continue. Noon break should not be less than one hour.

Extracurricular literary and sports activities of a mass nature should be broadly developed. Sports teams and physical training units of schools and classes should be organized well, and a success should be made of seasonal single-event contests and annual sports meets. It is necessary to organize students to sing and write revolutionary songs and tell revolutionary stories in a big way, to make a success of revolutionary literary and art detachments and choruses and to hold regular literary and art festivals.

Article VIII Education on common hygienic knowledge should be intensified among students, who should be helped to cultivate hygienic habits. Serious attention should be paid to protecting their eyesight and to improving the lighting equipment in the classroom. Guidance should be given them in taking an active part in popular patriotic health campaigns.

RED LITTLE SOLDIERS ORGANIZATION

Article IX Red little soldiers are a mass organization of children. Under the leadership of the Party branch, we should give attention to fully developing their political role.

Red little soldiers should make demands on themselves according to the five criteria of successors, display the spirit of daring to think, to speak, to break through, to act and to make revolution, and unfold political activities with themselves as masters. Such activities should be held once a week.

The work of recruiting Red little soldiers should be discussed and decided upon mainly by the Red little soldiers themselves.

Instructors of Red little soldiers should follow the principle of placing the main emphasis on guidance and oppose the practice of doing the work for them. Red little soldiers should be helped to continuously raise their political level and work ability and to create conditions for activities.

TEACHERS AND LEADERSHIP

Article X "The problem of teaching reform is mainly the problem of teachers." Teachers should conscientiously study Marxist-Leininist and Chairman Mao's works and, while participating in the three great revolutionary struggles and getting in touch with the worker and peasant masses, strive to transform their world outlook and contribute to the educational undertaking of the Party.

Teachers must place proletarian policies in command, delve into professional research, and strive to be both Red and expert, specializing in one thing and capable of doing many things.

Apart from joining students in learning industry, agriculture and military affairs, teachers should during summer vacation organize about two weeks of industrial and farm labor (with the exception of the old, the weak, the sick and the crippled.)

Worker-peasant-soldier lecturers groups should continue to be consolidated and developed on the present basis.

Article XI   The Party branch should serve as fighting citadel of the school. Under its leadership, the political roles of the school's revolutionary committee, workers propaganda team, worker-peasant-soldier lecturers groups, the CYL and Red little soldiers should be brought into full play.

THREE-WAY COMBINATION OF SCHOOL, FAMILY AND NEIGHBORHOOD ORGANIZATION

Article XII   Leading groups of three-way combinations should be set up and strengthened. Joint meetings of neighborhood cadres, parents and teachers should be held regularly to study and analyze the educational problems relevant to children. Schools should take the initiative to rally the revolutionary comrades of nearby factories and shops and in other trades to take an interest in the students' ideo-political education so as to turn the proletarian educational revolution into a great social revolution in every sense of the word.

7.23 "Considerations on the Concept of Culture"

As a member of the U.S.-China Peoples Friendship Association (USCPFA) Delegation, Eli Seifman visited the People's Republic of China during the summer of 1975 to study educational policies and practices, and surveyed a wide range of different types of schools and educational institutions. One of these was Peking's Central Institute for National Minorities, established in 1951 for the training of members of China's national minorities. The curriculum is organized around the offerings of several departments: politics, minority languages, Chinese language, art, history, cadre training, and preparatory school.

The students in the Politics Department study theory and politics of Marxism-Leninism and Mao Tse-tung Thought. The Language Department trains interpreters for the national minority languages — providing advanced instruction in both the spoken and written languages. The Art Department trains cultural workers for national minorities in the fields of music, fine arts and dance. At the time of the visit no students were studying in the Chinese Language Department or the History Department — the plan was to enroll students in these two departments in the autumn of 1975. The Cadre Training School trains students who will then return to the national minority areas to serve as cadres. Students in the Preparatory School study for varying periods, according to their educational background or previous training, before taking the regular courses at the Institute or going on to more advanced studies in higher education at other universities.

During the question and answer session following a tour of the Institute, a member

---

Shi Ming Hu and Eli Seifman, "Considerations on the Concept of Culture," Transcript of question and answer session at the Central Institute for National Minorities, Peking, July 22, 1975.

of the USCPFA Delegation asked a question about the language reform policy which initiated a dialogue and led to an extensive discussion of the very nature and conception of "culture." The following transcript was prepared by the editors from tape recordings made during the visit to Peking's Central Institute for National Minorities on July 22, 1975. The major spokespersons were Chin Ke-jun and Fei Xiao-tong. Chin Ke-jun, the Responsible Person for the Entertaining Group, a member of the Zhuang nationality, was formerly a student at the Institute and is currently an Institute cadre member. His comments were translated into English by Comrade Xie, the guide-interpreter of the China Administration for Travel and Tourism (CATT). Professor Fei Xiao-tong spoke in English and from time to time also helped with the translations.

*

USCPFA Delegate: Concerning the five written languaes, what is the policy of the Institute in training minority groups to read in these languages. In other words, are they trained to read their minority language *and* to read Chinese at the Institute—and institutes like this throughout China?

Comrade Chin Ke-jun: The students of that Department all come from the area where their minority people live and they study the Han language at this Institute and also learn their own language as well. After graduation they will become interpreters, translators.[1]

Professor Fei Xiao-tong: The object of our Department is to train interpreters. We take students from their own nationality, who know their own language, and we improve their knowledge, their art—how you say, their literacy, their handling of their own language on the one hand and besides (the handling of) the Han language in order to enable them to become interpreters.

USCPFA Delegate: My question is the *written* language, not the spoken language—I understand that, I'm talking about the written language. Is there any movement to standardize the writing of these minority languages; that's what I'm trying to say—to ask?

Professor Fei Xiao-tong: I['ll] explain that to you. Since Liberation we try to help those nationalities who are without written system—first. Then those who are with written system, like the Xinjiang people. And we adopted a unified plan for Latinization, including Han. You know that, if you take bank notes [i.e. paper currency] you can see there the Latinized Han language. And my granddaughter now is starting to learn the Han, learn[ing] the primary school textbook beginning from these Latinized letters.

USCPFA Delegate: If you Romanize the language you destroy the culture.

Professor Fei Xiao-tong: You think so?

USCPFA Delegate: The argument has been that if you Romanize Chinese, you destroy the whole history of Chinese culture. So if you Romanize Korean, Uighur, and all of those you—

Professor Fei Xiao-tong:—You explain[ed] your view, which is different from mine.

USCPFA Delegate: Yes sir. [Laughter from the group.]

Professor Fei Xiao-tong: Language is a means of communication, if you go a little deep, and characters [are] used to express oral language into written form.

USCPFA Delegate: I understand.

Professor Fei Xiao-tong: Language is an expression of culture—if I'm right. The *content* of language is what matters, that's [the written Chinese characters] the *form* of language—we're not changing *language*, we're changing the form of expression of oral language into written system. Is this all right [i.e. clear]?

USCPFA Delegate: I understand, but if that is true then why don't you Romanize Chinese?

Professor Fei Xiao-tong: What's the relation of language and culture? That's the question we are addressing, see, and I can understand your point of view and mine is different from this [i.e. from yours].

USCPFA Delegate: Is it the policy of the present Chinese government to do away with characters [Chinese characters]? Is it the policy of the present Chinese government to do away with the written Chinese characters and Romanize the Chinese [written language]? Is that a government policy?

Professor Fei Xiao-tong: [Professor Fei translates the question into Chinese.]

Comrade Chin Ke-jun: We hope that Romanizing the letters will not destroy the culture, because the written language is some marks [Professor Fei interjects, "symbols"] of the language and to make the symbols more scientific will help the development of the written language. Some minority national languages used to have Arabic letters. It is not very exact to express the language. The Arabic letters were made according to the feature of Arabic language.

Professor Fei Xiao-tong: Arabic letters used to express Uighur language has historical origin. They originally not used Arabic letters. They [i.e. the Arabic letters] are also introduced from others. Is that clear?

USCPFA Delegate: Yes, that's clear.

Professor Fei Xiao-tong: No vowlels.

Comrade Chin Ke-jun: It lacks vowels.

Professor Fei Xiao-tong: They omit vowels in the written system. The Arabic writing omit[s] vowels in writing system. Unless you know the oral language, then can read from the text—if they omit vowels.

Comrade Chin Ke-jun: [Professor Fei Xiao-tong translates] Even the consonants use the Arabic system cannot exactly explain the sound of the Uighur language. Is that clear? So this is adapted foreign system to the Uighur language rather unscientifically. So that means we adopt Latinized[ation] to improve—it's more scientific—more directly, correctly express their oral language through written system. Is that clear?

[CATT Guide-Interpreter translates] Arabic letters are complicated and have more difficulties to study these kinds of letters.

Professor Fei Xiao-tong: And hold back our task to surmount literacy, universal literacy. Is that right — "surmount"? That hindered the work of universal education for the mass of the Uighur people.

Comrade Chin Ke-jun: In 1961 we began to use new Roman letters. The practice proves that Latin letters give more convenience in writing language and it makes [it] easy for the people to study Uighur language.

Professor Fei Xiao-tong: Take one instance to show how more convenient. To introduce new terms to the minority languages we use Latinized forms. It's much easier to adopt new terms. That means *help* to develop culture instead of *destoy* culture. What we destroy is those which is useless culture in the past. So in our difference [of opinion] actually is the question of the relation between culture and the language, and what means "culture." Is that clear?

[The question and answer session moved on to other topics (current research on national minorities, staff organization of the Institute, governance of the national minority autonomous regions, etc.) but a question by another USCPFA delegate, dealing with the policy of teaching ballet and the national minority dances, brought the discussion back to the issue of the nature of "culture."]

USCPFA Delegate: I was most impressed with the dance class we saw. . . . Where are the teachers trained?

Comrade Chin Ke-jun: Some of the teachers are graduates of that Department of this Institute [i.e. the Art Department, which has three specialities: music, fine arts, and dance], and some are assigned by the State from other music schools. Some are graduates of Shanghai Dancing School and Peking Dancing School, and came to this Institute.

To teach the dances of minority nationalities better, the teachers will go to [the] minority area to learn the features of dance of minority nationalities before they give teaching [instruction] to the students.

So they have both experiences of teaching ballet and minority nationality dance.

USCPFA Delegate: I guess what I really wondered was whether there was still some of the Russian influence in the ballet training.

Professor Fei Xiao-tong: We take anything which is good.

USCPFA Delegate: I was wondering whether some of them had been trained by the Russians?

Comrade Chin Ke-jun: The policy of studying ballet is in accordance with Chairman Mao's instructions, "make the past serve the present and make foreign things serve China."

Ballet is something created by the various people of Western countries. We learn from these dances and we combine with our folk dance. The ballet, "Children of the Grassland" is an example. [CATT Guide-Interpreter interjects, "You saw it."]

Professor Fei Xiao-tong: This is come again to your question of "culture." See, we develop culture as a concept. To us it's a developing process. It should not stop in the museum.

NOTE:
    [1]The People's Republic of China is a unitary multi-national state, consisting of a Han (ethnic Chinese) "majority" comprising approximately 96 per cent of the population, and 54 other "minority" nationalities — Zhuang, Hai, Uighur, Yi, Tibetan, etc. "Rapid Growth in China's Minority Population," *Peking Review* (October 4, 1974), pp. 30-31, 38. In English, the term "Chinese" does not distinguish between someone who is a citizen of the People's Republic of China (Zhong guo ren). and someone who is a member of the Han majority nationality (Han zu ren). The term "Han language" therefore refers specifically to the written and spoken language of the Han majority. The Constitution of the PRC stipulates that "All the nationalities have the freedom to use their own spoken and written languages." "Constitution of the People's Republic of China," Adopted January 17, 1965, Article 4, *Peking Review* (January 24, 1975), p. 4.

7.24 "The Great Cultural Revolution Will Shine For Ever"

THE GREAT CULTURAL REVOLUTION WILL SHINE FOR EVER

In commemoration of the 10th anniversary of the May 16, 1966 "Circular" of the Central Committee of the Communist Party of China

Ten years ago, the May 16 *Circular* of the Central Committee of the Communist Party of China was drawn up under the personal guidance of our great leader Chairman Mao. This brilliant Marxist document sounded the clarion call for the Great Proletarian Cultural Revolution and illuminated the course of its triumphant advance. Today, having won great victories in the struggle to criticize Teng Hsiao-ping and repulse the Right deviationist wind to reverse correct verdicts, we warmly celebrate the 10th anniversary of the Great Cultural Revolution and restudy the *Circular*, which gives us a deeper understanding of the necessity and far-reaching significance of the revolution and greater confidence to persevere in continuing the revolution under the dictatorship of the proletariat.

The *Circular* was drawn up in the fierce struggle between the proletarian headquarters headed by Chairman Mao and the bourgeois headquarters with Liu Shao-chi as its chieftain. It incisively criticized Liu Shao-chi's counter-revolutionary revisionist line, exposed the reactionary essence of the "February Outline Report,"[1] refuted the fallacies against the Great Cultural Revolution spread by those Party persons in power taking the capitalist road, armed the whole Party with the Marxist-Leninist theory of class struggle and proletarian dictatorship, and called on us to expose and criticize the bourgeois representatives in the Party and seize that portion of leadership they had usurped. The formulation of the *Circular* proclaimed the bankruptcy of the "February Outline Report." Since then the Great Proletarian Cultural Revolution has been forging ahead vigorously.

Chairman Mao has pointed out: "*We couldn't do without the Great Proletarian Cultural Revolution.*" This great revolution, which had been brewing for a long time, was the inevitable outcome of the acute struggle between the two classes, the two roads and the two lines. For years the renegade, hidden traitor and scab Liu Shao-chi and company had made frenzied efforts to push the counter-revolutionary revisionist line and stubbornly stuck to the capitalist road. They did their utmost to oppose Chairman Mao's revolutionary line on all fronts: clamouring about capitalists "having merits in carrying out exploitation" and about "consolidating the new-democratic order;" drastically slashing the number of co-operatives and practicing *san zi yi bao*[2] lauding to the skies the reactionary films *Inside Story of the Ching Court* and *The Life of Wu Hsun*; and resisting the criticism of the play *Hai Jui Dismissed From Office*. For a period of time Liu Shao-chi's bourgeois headquarters was in control of Party power and the power in the cultural and propaganda fields and in many localities. Capitalism and revisionism were rampant in the ideological and cultural departments under its control. Hordes of ghosts and monsters came out into the open and filled our press, radio, books and works of literature and art. A grave situation in which the bourgeoisie exercised dictatorship over the proletariat de-

The Editorial Departments of *Renmin Ribao, Hongqi,* and *Jiefangjun Bao, Peking Review,* No. 21 (May 21, 1976), pp. 6-10.

veloped in certain spheres in the super-structure. Material incentives and "bonuses in command" were widely practiced to lure people to the capitalist road. In a fairly large majority of factories and enterprises, leadership was not in the hands of real Marxists and the masses of workers. Our socialist economic base was not solid. If the Great Cultural Revolution had not taken place, it would not have taken long before a counter-revolutionary restoration on a national scale would inevitably occur, our Party would turn into a revisionist party, and the whole of China would change its political color.

With great Marxist-Leninist insight, Chairman Mao perceived in good time the grave danger that the capitalist-roaders in the Party were subverting the dictatorship of the proletariat. Chairman Mao pointed out in the *Circular: "Those representatives of the bourgeoisie who have sneaked into the Party, the government, the army and various spheres of culture are a bunch of counter-revolutionary revisionists. Once conditions are ripe, they will seize political power and turn the dictatorship of the proletariat into a dictatorship of the bourgeoisie."* In the course of the present struggle to beat back the Right deviationist attempt to reverse correct verdicts, Chairman Mao has again pointed out: *"You are making the socialist revolution, and yet don't know where the bourgeoisie is. It is right in the Communist Party – Those in power taking the capitalist road. The capitalist-roaders are still on the capitalist road."* In these important instructions, Chairman Mao has profoundly analysed the changes in the class relations and the characteristics of class struggle during the period of socialism, advanced the scientific thesis that the bourgeoisie is in the Communist Party, developed Marxism-Leninism and further clarified for us the orientation for continuing the revolution under the dictatorship of the proletariat.

In the past decade we have waged struggles against Liu Shao-chi, Lin Piao and Teng Hsiao-ping. All these struggles have proved that the bourgeoisie is indeed inside the Communist Party. The capitalist-roaders in the Party are the bourgeoisie's main force in its trial of strength with the proletariat and in its efforts to restore capitalism. The crux of the matter here lies in the fact that these capitalist-roaders are persons in power who have sneaked into the very structure of the dictatorship of the proletariat. Chieftains of the revisionist line, like Liu Shao-chi, Lin Piao and Teng Hsiao-ping, hold a very large proportion of the Party and state power. They are thus in a position to turn instruments of the dictatorship of the proletariat into instruments for exercising dictatorship over the proletariat, and they are therefore even more ruthless in their efforts to restore capitalism than the bourgeoisie outside the Party. They could use the power in their hands to recruit deserters and renegades, form cliques to pursue their own selfish interests, rig up a bourgeois headquarters, work out a revisionist line and push it from top to bottom. They could consolidate and extend bourgeois right, protect their own interests, namely, the interests of the "high officials" who practice revisionism, embezzle and squander huge amounts of social wealth, energetically engage in capitalist activities, undermine and disrupt the socialist relations of production. Donning the cloak of Marxism-Leninism and flaunting all sorts of ensigns, they are able to mislead for a time a number of people who lack an understanding of the real situation and do not have a high level of consciousness, deceiving them into following their revisionist line. In short, they are political representatives of the bourgeoisie and, in their trial of strength with the proletariat, they are commanders of all social forces and cliques that resist the socialist revolution and oppose and undermine socialist construction.

Teng Hsiao-ping, the arch unrepentant capitalist-roader in the Party, played the commander's role in vehemently stirring up the Right deviationist wind which culminated in the counter-revolutionary political incident at Tien An Men Square. Before the Great Cultural Revolution he was the No. 2 chieftain of Liu Shao-chi's bourgeois headquarters. The two bourgeois headquarters of Liu Shao-chi and Lin

Piao were smashed during the Great Cultural Revolution and, when Teng Hsiao-ping was criticized by the masses, his words flowed in a spate of vows, such as "I'll mend my ways" and "I'll never reverse the verdict." But, once he resumed work and was in power, he threw off his disguise and, with hatred grown tenfold and frenzy increased a hundredfold, brought all his experience in counter-revolutionary political struggle into play, cooking up a program, preparing public opinion and mounting an organized and planned attack on the Party, with the spearhead directed at our great leader Chairman Mao.

"Take the three directives as the key link" — this was Teng Hsiao-ping's political program for reversing correct verdicts and restoring capitalism. Preaching the theory of the dying out of class struggle and the theory of productive forces, this revisionist program opposes taking class struggle as the key link and denies the Party's basic line and the necessity for the Great Cultural Revolution. Teng Hsiao-ping attempted to make it the "general program for all work" for a long time to come and to impose it on the whole Party and the people throughout the country in order to pave the way for an all-round restoration of capitalism.

"Seize ideological positions" — this was a move Teng Hsiao-ping took to prepare public opinion for his scheme to reverse correct verdicts and restore capitalism. After he came to power, especially during last July, August and September and afterwards, political rumors were afloat and strange tales passed around here, there and everywhere in society. All these rumors and strange tales originated with Teng Hsiao-ping and were fabricated by Teng's rumor-mongering company. Teng Hsiao-ping and his followers feverishly created counter-revolutionary public opinions by various base means to hoodwink the people and create splits. In doing this, they spearheaded their attack at the Party Central Committee headed by Chairman Mao and raised a hue and cry to clear the way for Teng Hsiao-ping to usurp the Party leadership and seize state power.

"The first and foremost thing is to grasp leading bodies" — this was the organizational measure Teng Hsiao-ping adopted in his attempt to reverse correct verdicts and restore capitalism. He opposed the setting up of "three-in-one" revolutionary leading bodies, attacked and pushed aside the old, middle-aged and young cadres who upheld Chairman Mao's revolutionary line, mustered unrepentant capitalist-roaders and put them in important positions, and knocked together "restorationist legions" in his attempt to reverse correct verdicts and restore capitalism. He did his utmost to keep in the Party renegades and special agents, who had been identified as such during the Great Cultural Revolution, so that they could stage a comeback sometime in the future.

"Carry out all-round rectification" — this was the plan of action Teng Hsiao-ping mapped out for his scheme to reverse correct verdicts and restore capitalism. The moment he issued the order for "rectification," the sinister wind to reverse correct verdicts sprang up. Through "rectification" he aimed at making a clean sweep of Chairman Mao's revolutionary line and policies, the achievements of the Great Cultural Revolution and the superiority of the socialist system. The so-called rectification was in essence an attack on the proletariat by the bourgeoisie and an attempt at capitalist restoration.

All these acts by Teng Hsiao-ping were a continuation and development of the reactionary "February Outline Report," which Chairman Mao had already criticized in the *Circular*. Teng Hsiao-ping's "taking the three directives as the key link" is a carbon copy of the revisionist line which the *Circular* describes as *"completely denying that the several thousand years of human history are a history of class struggle,"* *"completely denying the class struggle of the proletariat against the bourgeoisie, the proletarian revolution against the bourgeoisie and the dictatorship of the proletariat over the bourgeoisie."* The *Circular* exposes Peng Cehn for deliberately spreading rumors to divert people from the target of the struggle and scathingly denounces his "rectification campaign" as one aimed at attacking the proletarian Left and shielding the bourgeois Rightists. Teng Hsiao-ping went still further. His line is a continuation of the counter-revolutionary revisionist line pushed by Liu Shao-chi and Lin Piao. If this line were followed, not only would the achievements of the Great Cultural Revolution be nullified but those of the Chinese revolution as a whole would also go by the board. The capitalist road taken by Teng Hsiao-ping would lead back to the semi-colonial and semi-feudal old China and reduce China to an appendage of imperialism and social-imperialism. As Chairman Mao pointed out in the *Circular* when he criticized the representatives of the bourgeoisie: *"They are faithful lackeys of the bourgeoisie and the imperialists. Together with the bourgeoisie and the imperialists, they cling to the bourgeois ideology of oppression and exploitation of the proletariat and to the capitalist system, and they oppose Marxist-Leninist ideology and the socialist system;" "their struggle against us is one of life and death, and there is no question of equality. Therefore, our struggle against them, too, can be nothing but a life-and-death struggle."*

The tremendous historic merits of the Great Proletarian Cultural Revolution personally initiated and led by Chairman Mao lie in the fact that the scheme of the bourgeoisie inside the Party to restore capitalism was smashed resolutely and in good time, its counter-revolutionary revisionist line was criticized and that portion of the Party and state leadership it had usurped was seized back, thereby ensuring that our country continues to advance along Chairman Mao's revolutionary line. The Great Cultural Revolution's merits also lie in solving, in both theory and practice, the cardinal question in the contemporary international communist movement, namely, how to consolidate the dictatorship of the proletariat and prevent the restoration of capitalism. Hundreds of millions of workers, peasants and soldiers, revolutionary cadres and revolutionary intellectuals have come to realize every more deeply that the Great Cultural Revolution *"is absolutely necessary and most timely."* They warmly hail: "The Great Cultural Revolution is excellent!" Only unrepentant capitalist-roaders like Teng Hsiao-ping harbor bitter hatred for it. Bent on settling old scores and reversing the correct appraisal of the Great Cultural Revolution, he offended the great majority of people. They do not agree with him nor will they allow him to carry on. *"Reversing correct verdicts goes against the will of the people."* The will of the people, the Party and the Party members is for continuing the revolution and against restoration and retrogression. It is precisely for this reason that the great struggle personally initiated and led by Chairman Mao to repulse the Right deviationist attempt to reverse correct verdicts has won the wholehearted support of the entire Party, the whole army and the people throughtout the country. The struggle has the full approval of the people and is to their great satisfaction. Those who attempted to reverse correct verdicts and settle old scores were extremely isolated and were soon brought to defeat.

We have won great victories, but the struggle has not come to an end. The struggle to criticize Teng Hsiao-ping's counter-revolutionary revisionist line must be carried on in depth. We must never slacken our fighting will. The handful of class enemies will not be reconciled to their defeat. Drawing lessons from their failure, they are studying tactics and methods of how to deal with us. The revolutionary people must be soberly aware of this.

Chairman Mao has pointed out: *"Lenin spoke of building a bourgeois state without capitalists to safeguard bourgeois right. We ourselves have built just such a state, not much different from the old society: there are ranks and grades, eight grades of wages, distribution according to work, and exchange of equal values."* As long as these conditions still exist, as long as classes, class contradictions and class struggle exist and as long as the influences of the bourgeoisie and international imperialism and revisionism exist, the historical phenomenon that *"The capitalist-roaders are still on the capitalist road"* will remain for a long time to come. On the first anniversary of the *Circular,* Chairman Mao gave us this admonition: *"The present Great Cultural Revolution is only the first; there will inevitably be many more in the future."* During the current struggle to repulse the Right deviationist attempt to reverse correct verdicts, Chairman Mao has again pointed out: *"After the democratic revolution the workers and the poor and lower-middle peasants did not stand still, they want revolution. On the other hand, a number of Party members do not want to go forward; some have moved backward and opposed the revolution. Why? Because they have become high officials and want to protect the interests of the high officials." "Will there be need for revolution a hundred years from now? Will there still be need for revolution a thousand years from now? There is always need for revolution. There are always sections of the people who feel themselves oppressed; junior officials, students, workers, peasants and soldiers don't like bigshots oppressing them. That's why they want revolution. Will contradictions no longer be seen ten thousand years from now? Why not? They will still be seen."* Therefore, we must prepare ourselves ideologically for a protracted struggle against the capitalist-roaders and for continuing the revolution under the dictatorship of the proletariat.

Chairman Mao said at the beginning of this year: *"Without struggle, there is no progress." "Can 800 million people manage without struggle?!"* The ten years of the Great Proletarian Cultural Revolution was a decade in which we advanced through struggle and brought tremendous changes to our country. Studying Marxism-Leninism-Mao Tsetung Thought in the course of struggle, hundreds of millions of people have greatly raised their consciousness in combating and preventing revisionism and continuing the revolution. Chairman Mao's proletarian revolutionary line has found its way even deeper into the hearts of the people. By getting rid of the stale and taking in the fresh, our Party has grown in strength and become more vigorous than ever. Our army has grown strong, after going through new tests and making fresh contributions to the people in "supporting industry, supporting agriculture, supporting the broad masses of the Left, exercising military control, and giving political and military training." The militia has contributed to the consolidation of proletarian dictatorship through participation in the struggle to defend the motherland and in class struggle in society. The "three-in-one" combination of the old, middle-aged and young has been adopted in the leading bodies at all levels, and millions upon millions of successors to the proletarian revolutionary cause are steeling themselves and maturing in the course of struggle in accordance with the five requirements put forward by Chairman Mao. The socialist revolution in education, literature and art, medical and health work, science and technology has advanced in giant strides in the course of the acute struggle between the two lines. Vast numbers of educated youth have gone eagerly to settle in the countryside, and cadres at all levels have perservered in taking the May 7 road. The mass movements to learn from Tachai in agriculture and to learn from Taching in industry have surged ahead. Agriculture, industry and the entire national economy are thriving. Our great motherland is a flourishing scene of prosperity. The Great Proletarian Cultural Revolution has further released the energies of the people in their hundreds of millions. The tremendous impact of this revolution, which is just beginning to show itself, will make itself felt with greater force with the deepening of the revolution.

We must continue our triumphant advance and carry forward the excellent situation. The broad masses of Party members, cadres and other people must conscientiously study Chairman Mao's important instructions concerning the Great Cultural Revolution and the struggle to repulse the Right deviationist attempt, study the theory of continuing the revolution under the dictatorship of the proletariat, get a clear understanding of the questions of where the bourgeoisie is to be found and enforcing all-round dictatorship over the bourgeoisie, and persist in combating and preventing revisionism and continuing the revolution. We must acquire a profound understanding of the brilliant victories and tremendous significance of the Great Cultural Revolution, whole-heartedly support the socialist new things, and consolidate and develop the achievements of the Great Cultural Revolution. We must deepen the criticism of Teng Hsiao-ping, beat back the Right deviationist attempt to reverse correct verdicts and deal resolute blows at all counter-revolutionary disruptive activities. We must unite over 95 per cent of the cadres and of the masses under the general objective of criticizing Teng Hsiao-ping, and continue to do a good job in the revolution in the superstructure and the economic base. We must *"grasp revolution, promote production and other work and preparedness against war"* and continuously advance socialist construction in all fields.

The proletariat is full of revolutionary optimism. We have faith in dialectics. We firmly believe that *"the supersession of the old by the new is a general, eternal and inviolable law of the universe."* (Mao Tsetung: *On Contradiction.*) However many twists and turns there are on the road of revolution and however many ups and downs it encounters, the truth of Marxism-Leninism-Mao Tsetung Thought is irresistible and the masses of the people who account for over 95 per cent of the population invariably want revolution. Revolution will inevitably triumph over reaction and the newborn over the decadent — this is a law of history. It is just over a century since the founding of Marxism, and the old world has been shattered to pieces. Today capitalism and revisionism are declining like "a setting sun the the west wind." The clowns who go against the tide of history may have their own way for a time but will eventually be swept on to the garbage heap of history by the people. As Marx and Engels stated, *"Its* [the bourgeoisie's] *fall and the victory of the proletariat are equally inevitable."* (*Manifesto of the Communist Party.*) While commemorating the 10th anniversary of the *Circular,* we are full of revolutionary pride as we look back on the course of struggle of the Great Cultural Revolution, view the excellent situation in which "orioles sing, swallows dart," and look forward to the bright future when "the world is being turned upside down." Under the leadership of the Party Central Committee headed by Chairman Mao, we are determined to persevere in taking class struggle as the key link and carry the continued revolution under the dictatorship of the proletariat through to the end.

Chairman Mao's proletarian revolutionary line is invincible, and our advance cannot be stopped!

The Great Proletarian Cultural Revolution will shine for ever!

(May 16, 1976)

NOTES:

[1]The "February Outline Report" refers to the "Outline Report on the Current Academic Discussion Made by the Group of Five in Charge of the Cultural Revolution" which was approved for distribution on February 12, 1966 to the whole Party by the counter-revolutionary revisionist Peng Chen who employed the most dishonest methods, acted arbitrarily, abused his powers and usurped the name of the Party Central Committee. This outline report opposed carrying the socialist revolution through to the end, opposed the line formulated by the Central Committee of the Party headed by Comrade Mao Tsetung for carrying out the Cultural Revolution, attacked the proletarian Left and shielded the bourgeois Rightists, and its aim was to prepare public opinion for the restoration of capitalism. It was a reflection of bourgeois ideology in the Party and was out-and-out revisionism.—*Tr.*

[2]This refers to the extension of plots for private use and of free markets, the increase of small enterprises with sole responsibility for their own profits or losses, and the fixing of farm output quotas for individual households with each on its own.—*Tr.*